P9-DDY-561

Acclaim for Kirstin Downey's

THE WOMAN BEHIND THE NEW DEAL

"The New Deal was a big deal for America—and, as Kirstin Downey shows in this illuminating and sparkling book, Frances Perkins, my predecessor as labor secretary, was the moving force behind much of it. Her legacy included Social Security, unemployment insurance, and other initiatives that have improved the lives of generations of Americans. With wit and insight, Downey recounts this singular woman and invites us to celebrate her life."

—Robert B. Reich, professor of Public Policy at the
University of California at Berkeley,
former U.S. secretary of labor

"Kirstin Downey gives Frances Perkins the biography she deserves, the story of a fierce advocate who put people first, a public servant who was actually worthy of the name, and a bracing reminder of what inspired government can do. Perkins ignored the glass ceiling and changed America. This book is a joy!"

—Nick Taylor, author of *American-Made:
The Enduring Legacy of the WPA:
When FDR Put the Nation to Work*

"In Downey's skilled hands, Frances Perkins at last emerges as a pivotal figure in the most transformative twelve years of twentieth-century American history." —Christopher N. Breiseth, president and CEO of
The Franklin and Eleanor Roosevelt Institute

"For his presidency to succeed, FDR needed a strong labor secretary to restore jobs and confidence. Perkins was that loyal lieutenant, as well as his unrelenting prod and social conscience."

—Mary Leonard, *Pittsburgh Post-Gazette*

"The story of Ms. Perkins turns out to be, in the sympathetic hands of Ms. Downey, a remarkably good read, surprisingly full of dramatic twists despite that motherly hat and low-profile manner."

—Priscilla Taylor, *The Washington Times*

"The current economic woes have, among other things, focused attention once again on the New Deal. Books about the economics, the politics, and the personalities of the time have surfaced. Still, as a new book by award-winning business journalist Kirstin Downey suggests, one of the most influential figures in shaping the New Deal turns out to be a name few know today—and turns out to be a woman. Eight years of research, new documents and interviews with family members were among the many sources Downey drew on for her new and compelling portrait of 'The Woman Behind the New Deal.'" —Sarah Bagby, NPR

"It's a provocative title, but Downey convinced me that Fannie Perkins, of Beacon Hill, Worcester, and Mount Holyoke College, was the woman behind the New Deal. Her book could not be more timely."

—Alex Beam, *The Boston Globe*

"Reading the biography of FDR's labor secretary Frances Perkins brings to mind the old saying about how Ginger Rogers had to do everything Fred Astaire did, except backward and in high heels. Perkins, the first female Cabinet member, not only had to do more than her male counterparts to prove herself . . . [she] notched a place in history simply by taking the job. But she earned it through a jaw-dropping number of accomplishments. Perkins took a major role in shepherding through Social Security, unemployment insurance, child labor laws and the minimum wage."

—Michael Hill, Associated Press

KIRSTIN DOWNEY

THE WOMAN BEHIND THE NEW DEAL

Kirstin Downey is a frequent contributor to *The Washington Post*, where she was a staff writer from 1988 to 2008, winning press association awards for her business and economic reporting. She shared in the 2008 Pulitzer Prize awarded to the *Post* staff for its coverage of the Virginia Tech shootings. In 2000, she was awarded a Nieman fellowship at Harvard University. She lives in Washington, D.C.

www.kirstindowney.com

The

WOMAN

BEHIND

—— *the* ——

NEW DEAL

The WOMAN BEHIND the NEW DEAL

The Life and Legacy of Frances Perkins—
Social Security, Unemployment
Insurance, and the Minimum Wage

KIRSTIN DOWNEY

ANCHOR BOOKS
A Division of Random House, Inc.
New York

FIRST ANCHOR BOOKS EDITION, FEBRUARY 2010

Copyright © 2009 by Kirstin Downey

All rights reserved. Published in the United States by Anchor Books, a division of
Random House, Inc., New York, and in Canada by Random House of Canada Limited,
Toronto. Originally published in hardcover in the United States by Nan A. Talese,
a division of Random House, Inc., New York, in 2009.

Anchor Books and colophon are registered trademarks of Random House, Inc.

Grateful acknowledgment to Furthermore: a program of the J. M. Kaplan Fund,
for their support.

Frontispiece photograph of Frances Perkins courtesy of
Mount Holyoke College Archives and Special Collections.

The Library of Congress has cataloged the Nan A. Talese edition as follows:
Downey, Kirstin.
The woman behind the New Deal : the life of Frances Perkins, FDR's Secretary of
Labor and his moral conscience / Kirstin Downey.
        p.   cm.
Includes bibliographical references and index.
1. Perkins, Frances, 1880–1965.   2. United States. Dept. of Labor—Biography.
3. Women cabinet officers—United States—Biography.   4. Women social
reformers—United States—Biography.   I. Title.
HD8073.P38D69 2009
331.092—dc22 [B] 2008023208

Anchor ISBN: 978-1-4000-7856-1

Author photograph © Evan Giordanella

www.anchorbooks.com

Printed in the United States of America
10   9   8   7   6

. . . be ye stedfast . . .

I CORINTHIANS 15:58

Contents

Acknowledgments

I came to Washington as a young business reporter to work for the *Washington Post* in 1988. I remember the first time I heard Frances Perkins's name. I was taking a bus tour of the city to familiarize myself with its political landmarks. Frances Perkins had a cameo role in the tour leader's comic shtick. "Which woman in American history had the worst childbirth experience?" he asked. Pause. No one answered. "Frances Perkins," he said. "She spent twelve years in Labor." It drew a big laugh from a crowd that seemed to know as little about her as I did.

Over the next two decades, as big stories developed and I probed the history of the government's responses to the situations, I was referred to Frances Perkins again and again, but only by much older people, almost in a kind of distant whisper. Age discrimination? Frances Perkins had talked of the problem. Long work hours? Frances Perkins. Workplace injuries, and what rights did employees have to be compensated for the loss of their health? It was a refrain in Frances Perkins's life.

I began to hear her name more often when I started writing a newspaper column called On the Job, which allowed workers to raise important workplace questions. One day I received a plaintive letter from a man who wrote that he was being locked in the office at the end of each workday as the boss counted the money in the till. He asked if I thought it was unsafe: "Even a rat has an escape hole," he wrote. I began to investigate the fire safety code and its origins, and then I called Judson MacLaury, staff historian at the Labor Department, to ask him about famous workplace fires. He arranged to send me information on the Triangle Shirtwaist fire, and then casually asked whether I knew that a young social worker, Frances Perkins, had actually witnessed that 1911 disaster. Eureka.

A decade-long detective project began. Digging this woman's legacy out of the ruins has required an effort as archaeological as historical, of long years spent, nights and weekends, sifting through hundreds of thousands of documents and interviewing dozens of Frances's friends and relatives, many of them very old. Frances's papers had been deposited willy-nilly in more than a dozen archives across the northeastern United States, with revealing documents housed, often poorly organized and unrecognized, in obscure corners of other collections. The story of how former president Theodore Roosevelt selected her to head the Committee on Safety after the Triangle Shirtwaist fire was written up in pencil on a pad of yellow paper, jotted down by an obscure New Yorker, and stored almost forgotten in a warehouse in the Maryland suburbs. A fascinating correspondence about efforts to save leaders of the International Labor Organization from the Nazis was lost at Harvard University amid a large volume of papers on suffrage leaders. Of course, historians putting the records together closer to the era in which Frances Perkins lived would have known that Frances was both a suffrage leader and a labor advocate, but scholars born later did not easily make that connection.

Two extremely important sources of information were Frances's 1946 biography of FDR, called *The Roosevelt I Knew*, which became a key source for New Deal scholars for many years, and an extensive oral history, running to five thousand pages, compiled by the Columbia University Oral History Research Office. They are invaluable, partially because of the wealth of details they offer, but also because Perkins recalled, almost verbatim, conversations she had had over a lifetime, and events at which she was a participant and eyewitness. The interviews were conducted in the 1950s, when Perkins was in her seventies.

Many items of potential importance have disappeared. Letters that might have shed light on the nature of Frances's close relationships with several women friends are gone. Mary Harriman's papers were destroyed in a warehouse fire in New York. The children of Caroline O'Day, one of the first U.S. congresswomen, allowed their mother's papers to be thrown into a rubbish heap.

A few dramatic turns of events allowed some documents to survive. For example, some condolence letters sent by close friends to Frances when Mary died suggest an intimate friendship between the two women. Historian Winifred Wandersee had planned to write a biography of Frances Perkins and was given access by Frances Perkins's only child, Susanna Wilson Coggeshall, to some personal correspondence. She asked Susanna questions about what the letters suggested about her mother's life, and Susanna cut off further access to the letters, something she did to other aspiring biographers as well. Winifred had taken notes on the letters, however. She died of cancer before she could complete her biography, but she arranged for her research to be archived at Cornell University. Some of the letters that she cited in those files are now mysteriously missing from Frances Perkins's papers at Columbia, but survive in handwritten form, in Winifred's hand, at Cornell, thanks to her brother Richard's devotion to his sister's memory.

Professor Maurice Neufeld, a colleague of Frances's at Cornell, found a cache of notes and letters in her desk after her death. Frances had left the papers there while she took a trip, but she fell ill and died in New York City. Fearing that Susanna might destroy the documents, Neufeld secretly copied these papers before handing the originals to Susanna. He stored the documents at the Library of Congress, with instructions not to release them publicly until his death. Neufeld died in 2004, and the documents were made available without restriction for the first time. It was within those notes that Frances poured out her sorrow at her inability to give wholehearted love to her difficult daughter. She wrote these kinds of thoughts down for herself to better prepare for discussing them in confession and in prayer, and they give us insight into her most private musings.

Historian O. L. Harvey spent more than a decade laboriously handwriting index cards chronicling the correspondence that crossed the desk of the secretary of labor for the first few decades of the agency's existence. He is an unsung hero. He made the link between Frances Perkins and Donald Hiss, as correspondence that connected the two was removed from Labor Department files but rediscovered in the 1950s. He flagged it for future scholars by printing out the information in the letters on pink index cards rather than the traditional white ones.

Frances's friends and family also provided access to letters in their own private collections. Several boxes of letters between *New York Times* reporter Louis Stark and his wife had been stashed away in a closet in Ellicott City, Maryland; some fascinating letters were found in the attic of the family home of Judge Charles Wyzanski in Cambridge, Massachusetts.

Susanna's death in 2003 opened up one small box of personal documents, which had never before been seen, even by archivists at Columbia.

They described the mental health problems and physicians' reports on Susanna and Frances's husband Paul Wilson, who both suffered from bipolar disorder. During her lifetime, Susanna had denied that her father had ever been ill, and did not disclose these facts to prospective biographers, allowing it to appear that Frances had been an overly controlling mother, or that she had pretended that her husband was mentally ill to get rid of him. Concealing that information allowed a generation of people to believe that Frances had been a failure as a wife and mother. It was unfortunate that Susanna did not have the personal bravery to allow the facts to come out during her own life, but it is commendable that she did not destroy these documents and made it possible for them to be reviewed after her death.

Many, many people helped to make this book possible. Librarians, historians and labor leaders gave generously of their time. Professors John Kenneth Galbraith, John Dunlop, and Christopher Breiseth shared penetrating insights about the woman they knew as a friend and colleague. Judson MacLaury provided access to unique documents. The Gilder Lehrman Institute, Furthermore, the Robert M. MacNamara Foundation, the Franklin & Eleanor Roosevelt Institute, and the Nieman Foundation at Harvard University gave this project support and funding without which it could not have gone forward. My editors at the *Washington Post* generously granted me leave to pursue the research; my colleagues at work gamely filled in for me while I was gone. Tomlin Coggeshall, Frances Perkins's beloved grandson, and his partner, Christopher Rice, spent hours sharing their memories and gave me access to family photographs never before published. They live together at the Brick House, the Perkinses' family home in Newcastle, Maine, surrounded by the beautiful gardens and sweeping lawns Frances loved.

My mother, Melinda Young, my sister Elizabeth Gately, my brother Eric Hoppe, and my children, Rachel and Alex, have been endlessly supportive. My dear husband, Neil, read every word of this manuscript and offered good counsel and thoughtful insights. My agent, Gail Ross, believed in this project; her colleague Howard Yoon prepared a wonderful book proposal. Lorna Owen, my editor at Nan Talese/Doubleday, was enormously encouraging and skillfully reshaped the text, and Nan Talese championed the book from its inception. Marilyn Thompson artfully shrinkwrapped the manuscript when it had grown too unwieldy and Mimi Kusch provided invaluable editing assistance. All these people have listened endlessly to me as this book developed, and each helped shape the final product. I love you and I salute you all. Please forgive me for the occasions when I seemed to be living more in the 1930s than in the present day, for the times I was late to dinner, missed the movie, forgot the birthday card.

Any errors in this book are my own. I have done my best to work as carefully as possible. I pray any errors I may have made are minor and easily correctable by future scholars.

I am deeply grateful for having been given the chance to get to know Frances Perkins.

Kirstin Downey
May 2008

The

WOMAN

BEHIND

—— *the* ——

NEW DEAL

PROLOGUE

On a chilly February night in 1933, a middle-aged woman waited expectantly to meet with her employer at his residence on East 65th Street in New York City. She clutched a scrap of paper with hastily written notes. Finally ushered into his study, the woman brushed aside her nervousness and spoke confidently. They bantered casually for a while, as was their style, then she turned serious, her dark, luminous eyes holding his gaze.

He wanted her to take an assignment but she had decided she wouldn't accept it unless he allowed her to do it her own way. She held up the piece of paper in her hand, and he motioned for her to continue.

She ticked off the items: a forty-hour workweek, a minimum wage, worker's compensation, unemployment compensation, a federal law banning child labor, direct federal aid for unemployment relief, Social Security, a revitalized public employment service, and health insurance. She watched his eyes to make sure he was paying attention and understood the implications of each demand. She braced for his response, knowing that he often chose political expediency over idealism and was capable of callousness, even cruelty.

The scope of her list was breathtaking. She was proposing a fundamental and radical restructuring of American society, with enactment of historic social welfare and labor laws. To succeed, she would have to overcome opposition from the courts, business, labor unions, conservatives.

"Nothing like this has ever been done in the United States before," she said. "You know that, don't you?"[1]

The man sat across from her in his wheelchair amid the clutter of boxes and rumpled rugs. Soon, he would head to Washington, D.C., to be sworn in as the thirty-second president of the United States. He would inherit the worst economic crisis in the nation's history. An era of rampant speculation had come to an end. The stock market had collapsed, rendering investments valueless. Banks were shutting down, stripping people of their lifetime savings. About a third of workers were unemployed; wages were falling; hundreds of thousands were homeless. Real estate prices had plummeted, and millions of homeowners faced foreclosure.

His choice of labor secretary would be one of his most important early decisions. His nominee must understand economic and employment issues, but be equally effective as a coalition builder.

He was a handsome man, with aquiline features, and he studied the plain, matronly woman sitting before him. No one was more qualified for the job. She knew as much about labor law and administration as anyone in the country. He'd known her for more than twenty years, the last four in Albany, where she had worked at his side. He trusted her and knew she would never betray him.

But placing a woman in the labor secretary's job would expose him to criticism and ridicule. Her list of proposals would stir heated opposition, even among his loyal supporters. The eight-hour day was a standard plank of the Socialist Party; unemployment insurance seemed laughably improbable; direct aid to the unemployed would threaten his campaign pledge of a balanced budget.

He said he would back her.

It was a job she had prepared for all her life. She had changed her name, her appearance, even her age to make herself a more effective labor advocate. She had studied how men think so she could better succeed in a man's world. She had spent decades building crucial alliances. Still, she told the president-elect that she needed time to make her decision.

The next day she visited her husband, a patient in a sanitarium. He was having a good day, and he understood when she told him about the job offer. His first impulse was to fret for himself, asking her how this new job might affect him. When she assured him that he could remain where he was and that her weekend visits would continue, he gave his permission.

That night in bed, the woman cried in deep, wailing sobs that frightened her teenage daughter. She knew the job would change her life forever. She would open herself to constant media scrutiny, harsh judgment from her peers, and public criticism for doing a job a woman had never done before. Yet she knew she must accept the offer. As her grandmother had told her, whenever a door opened to you, you had no choice but to walk through it.

The next day she called Franklin Roosevelt and accepted the offer. Frances Perkins would become the nation's first female secretary of labor.

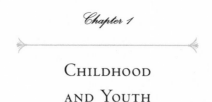

Chapter 1

Childhood
and Youth

 *F*annie Coralie Perkins knew by the age of ten that she would never be a conventional beauty, that unlike many women of her day she could not rely on physical attractiveness to open doors to her future. Her mother, Susan Bean Perkins, delivered the message when she took her daughter shopping for a hat. It was 1890, and the day's fashionable hats were slim and narrow, festooned with colorful ribbons and topped with flowers and feathers that added inches to a woman's height.

Susan Perkins passed by the pretty hats and pointed instead to a simple three-cornered tricorn style, similar to the ones worn by Revolutionary War soldiers.

"There, my dear, that is your hat," she told the girl in a matter-of-fact way. "You should always wear a hat something like this. You have a very broad face. It's broader between the two cheekbones than it is up at the top. Your head is narrower above the temples than it is at the cheek bones. Also, it lops off very suddenly into your chin. The result is you always need to have as much width in your hat as you have width in your cheek bones. Never let yourself get a hat that is narrower than your cheekbones, because it makes you look ridiculous."[1]

The hat would come to symbolize the plain, sturdy, and dependable woman who became Frances Perkins, and the mother's blunt advice to an awkward young girl left a lasting impression. From her earliest days, Fannie felt strangely out of step with the women of her time, her mother and sister included. She realized that rather than beauty, she must find other qualities and skills to set her apart, to help her achieve her idealistic goals. The dour-looking figure in the tricornered hat—the image seen throughout the years in filmstrips and photographs—disguised a woman whose intelligence, compassion, creative genius, and fierce loyalty made her an exceptional figure in modern American history.

Her mother's verdict on her looks, seared in memory for life, almost certainly overstated the case, for pictures from the time depict a child romantic in appearance, with long curls and a thoughtful look. Still it became fact that when people spoke of Frances Perkins, they almost always spoke of her character, not her outward appearance.

⁂

Fannie Perkins was born on April 10, 1880, on Beacon Hill, a few blocks from Boston Common, but her birthplace was almost a technicality. The place she considered home was where she spent her childhood summers, with her beloved grandmother at a homestead pioneered in the early 1700s by her great-great grandfather.

It was perched on a sweeping bend of the Damariscotta River in Newcastle, Maine, at a site filled with historic debris grown over into green meadows, sprawling over hundreds of acres to a place known as Perkins Point. Frances played amid the rubble pile left from the old stockade, erected in the years when families defended themselves against Indian attacks, and among the remains of discarded, half-baked bricks, reminders of the family's riverfront brick-making factory, which had made the family wealthy for a short time.

Perkins bricks had built many of the buildings in downtown Newcastle and as far away as Boston. The boom came in the 1840s. But the business failed a decade later after Boston financiers bought out the brick production of a number of local companies, including the Perkins operation, and merged them into a single corporation. The new business owners arranged for a large order from the Newcastle area to Halifax, Nova Scotia; the bricks were shipped, only to have the financiers disappear with the money. Every area brickyard went bankrupt. Afterward, all that remained of the once-prosperous Perkins business was the family home, built by their own hands, known as the Brick House.[2]

The family looked back at its glorious past while its present went to seed. By the 1870s, the decade before Fannie's birth, the family had turned to dairy farming for its sustenance. Her father, Frederick, blue-eyed, fine-boned, and refined, educated as a member of the upper class, had married Susan Bean, plump and down-to-earth, a woman from another old Maine family who was admired locally for her skills at animal husbandry. Soon Frederick was pining for a better life for himself and his family. He and Susan moved to Boston, where his brother Augustus had established a law practice. Frederick took a job as a retail clerk at a Boston department store. That was where Fannie was born, at a house on Joy Street.

But Frederick found his prospects in Boston unpromising. In 1882, he moved his family, this time to a fast-growing and gritty industrial city, Worcester, Massachusetts, some forty miles west of Boston. It was a place where a newcomer could afford to launch a business of his own. With a partner, George S. Butler, he opened a stationery and office supply store, prospering as the city's business base developed. In 1884, when Fannie was four years old, Frederick and Susan had a second child, Ethel.

Fannie grew up middle-class in Worcester, a shopkeeper's daughter. While her father built his business, they lived in boardinghouses before finally settling into a comfortable frame house in an upper-middle-class neighborhood. Staunch Congregationalists, they were faithful church-goers.[3]

The family nonetheless thought of their ancestry as storied and heroic, and with some reason. The most dramatic family tales came from a paternal grandmother, Cynthia, who was born in 1809 and lived to be 101. Fannie's tightest family bond was to this woman, who had endless aphorisms about how people should behave when they faced adversity. In her adult life, Fannie frequently referred to her grandmother's witticisms, particularly when facing difficult decisions. She came to pride herself on the "Yankee" values they shared—self-reliance, democratic beliefs, tenacity, physical endurance, contempt for complainers, and a tendency to be close-mouthed, particularly about people and things she held most dear.

Their ancestors were Scotch and English Protestants who arrived in the colonies before 1680, landing first in the Pilgrim settlement of Scituate, Massachusetts, before making their way to Maine. Even Fannie's voice, with its rich and rather British-sounding New England accent, with long A's and dropped R's, carried faint echoes of that original Anglo-American heritage.

Wending their way through the Perkinses' family tree were strains of brilliance, traces of manic depression, and a propensity for acts of public altruism that cost the doers dearly—all key characteristics in Frances's personality as well. The family was particularly proud of one glorious and tragic ancestor, attorney James Otis, the incendiary Revolutionary War patriot who famously railed against "Taxation Without Representation" when he denounced that system as tyranny. Otis was clubbed in the head by a British officer—an injury from which he never fully recovered. Future president John Adams described Otis's disintegration with sadness, observing in his diary that Otis became "liable to great inequities of temper, sometimes in despondency, sometimes in rage."[4]

The Civil War was also more than a chapter in a textbook to young Fannie—and provided even more proof of the risks of public participation in political life. Cynthia's cousin General Oliver Otis Howard visited the summer Fannie was fifteen. Howard had lost his right arm at the battle of Fair Oaks in Virginia, and Fannie was drafted into service as his scribe, a chore she found tedious at the time but that she would later vividly remember. Howard had founded Howard University in Washington and became chief of the Freedmen's Bureau, where his efforts on behalf of blacks led to criticism and censure by southern sympathizers. He was pilloried in Washington, falsely accused of misusing funds, and hounded from office, but the family admired him.[5]

Fannie was an exceptional child, unusually verbal and articulate, and she discovered that she had more in common with her father than with the other members of her immediate family. As a teenager, Fannie had little to say to her mother and sister. Her sister, Ethel, was a moody girl who was uninterested in academic pursuits. She took ill as a teenager, and completed high school only with the help of a tutor. She soon turned her attention to her marriage prospects. Her mother, basically kindly but plain-spoken and peppery to the point of abrasiveness, didn't grasp what a remarkable child she had in Fannie. She was stultifyingly conventional. Fannie's affection for both these women was dutiful rather than heartfelt.

Fannie's father must have been lonely in his marriage. Frederick, handsome and elegant, and Susan, portly and stolid, were ill suited to each other. Susan must have seemed a good choice of wife at the time of their marriage, when he was trying to make a living at dairy farming, but when he opted for another life in Massachusetts, the two seemed to have grown irrevocably apart. He clearly preferred spending time with Cynthia, his mother, who shared his interest in U.S. history, rather than with his wife, who occupied her free time with handicrafts, including painting pottery.

He focused particular attention on his precocious daughter, Fannie.

He taught the child to read Greek when she was eight and he began to prepare her for college. At the time, only 3 percent of women went on to higher education. Fannie attended Worcester Classical High School, along with other affluent children, most of them boys. Students learned the traditional curriculum, including Latin and Greek.[6]

Fannie therefore had an unusual childhood for the time. It was a conservative era, with a string of Republican presidents predominating in politics and straightlaced Queen Victoria on the throne in England. Women were expected to be highly circumspect, protected, and closeted. Even Fannie's parents were conflicted about the way they were raising the girl. They were proud of her intelligence but ambivalent about what the future might hold for an educated woman.

Yet new ideas about giving women a broader social role were creeping into public consciousness, and Fannie's father was a fair-minded man. While on a business trip, he attended an evening lecture on women's suffrage delivered by Anna Howard Shaw, the militant physician and orator. He called it "magnificent" and came back home a convert to the idea that women should have the right to vote.[7]

Even as a girl Fannie showed qualities that would propel her forward in her adult life. When she was very young, she tended to be bashful in public, at times too timid to exchange a few words while returning a library book. She preferred to allow others to take center stage, but as she grew, she learned she could force herself to speak out and take the lead when it was needed. In an emergency she didn't hesitate to take control, showing her quick wit and calm, such as the time she staunched the blood flow from another child's wound by adeptly twisting a handkerchief into a tourniquet.

Sometimes she felt the urge to shock people and flout authority, and did it with some glee. In staid and middle-class Worcester, where people liked to think of themselves as upwardly mobile, Fannie proclaimed herself a Democrat, a party allied with the urban poor. Worcester, of course, was proudly Republican, as were Fannie's parents, and professing an allegiance with the lower classes drew a satisfyingly startled reaction from adults.[8]

From her earliest years, Fannie felt other people's pain acutely and lamented their suffering. Her mother, active in the church, frequently tended to the needs of poor neighbors and encouraged her daughter to befriend them as well. Fannie was also greatly affected by the tales brought back by foreign missionaries seeking to win converts to Christianity. Their descriptions of the plight of hungry children touched Fannie and inspired what she called a kind of "vicarious physical agony."[9]

But while Fannie's parents were quick to provide a food basket for a hungry family, they also felt themselves superior to the poor. Fannie's parents weren't apt to blame misfortune on social injustice; they were more inclined to see drunkenness as causing poverty than poverty as causing drunkenness.

Fannie found herself pondering more deeply the reasons why some people were poor while others were not. Sometime during her teen or early adult years, she read a book that opened a "new world" to her. Written by Jacob Riis, a friend of progressive Republican president Theodore Roosevelt, it was called *How the Other Half Lives*. Riis, a police reporter for the *New York Tribune* and the Associated Press, wrote about life on New York's Lower East Side, where more than one hundred thousand people lived in homes not fit for human habitation and where thousands of abandoned children had no homes at all, surviving on scraps and by street theft. In one account, Riis described a child starving to death after his father grew too ill to work because of lead poisoning he contracted on the job.[11]

Riis's stories seemed almost unimaginable in quiet and smug Worcester. Writer Frederick Lewis Allen called the era a "time of complacency," once the depression of 1893 passed and populism died. Muckrakers had yet to begin disturbing the peace with their pungent observations. But changes were afoot, and among sensitive people like Frances, Riis's book found fertile ground.

While some recognized it and some did not, large fissures were developing in the nation's social fabric. The gap between rich and poor, urban and rural, grew wider every year of Fannie's childhood. America itself changed dramatically, shifting from an agricultural to an industrial nation, with millions of immigrants flooding into the country. The rapid influx began in 1880, the year Fannie was born. In 1900 about 449,000 immigrants arrived; by 1907, the number rose to 1.3 million. The influx stirred resentment in the native-born population. Fannie saw newcomers being abused by the native born, and it struck her as unjust that people who benefited from their labor would despise them. Fannie was developing an acute sense of social justice, and the treatment of immigrants drew her attention in the same way she had noticed the travails of the poor.[12]

⚘

*U*pon graduation from high school, Fannie enrolled in Mount Holyoke, the women's college near her Worcester home. Fannie could easily travel to and from the school by train. The eighteen-year-old soon fell in love with the college. Compared with workaday Worcester, the campus was idyllic. A small village green faced the school, with a fountain and a statue of a Civil War soldier. Across the street, the college's Gothic and Romanesque buildings rose amid broad and rolling lawns.

Mary Lyon, the school's founder, had had a spiritual mission, not just an educational one. She sought to prepare girls for lives of high purpose as missionaries and teachers; almost all her students were Protestants and were expected to attend religious services faithfully. Her motto: "Go forward, attempt great things, accomplish great things."

When Fannie entered Mount Holyoke, it had just begun calling itself a college after having been self-consciously labeled a seminary in its first years. Tuition and board cost $250 a year, a relatively modest sum, and the school required about fifty minutes of housework daily from each girl to defray expenses.[13]

Fannie settled into campus life, sharing a room with a Worcester friend in Rockefeller Hall, an impressive four-story brick building funded by oil millionaire John D. Rockefeller. Enormous parlors on the dormitory's bottom floor, furnished with rocking chairs, Brussels carpets, and mahogany woodwork, offered spacious mingling areas.[14]

Although she majored in chemistry and physics, partly because a persuasive chemistry teacher pushed her to take more rigorous subjects, she was most impressed by her American economic history course, in which students visited factories and other workplaces to interview workers and take notes on their wages, hours, and working conditions. It was Fannie's first look at modern industrial life, and it was not pleasant. She learned that losing a hand at work meant losing your livelihood, and that factory work usually paid so little and so irregularly that it left families with no savings for future periods of unemployment.

Fannie was not an outstanding student, but her excellent social skills set her apart. She had overcome the extreme shyness of her childhood and was known as something of a jokester and even a master kite-flyer. Her popularity made her a natural leader. She chaired the school's YWCA committee and performed in student dramas, including a role as Brutus in *The Lamentable Tragedy of Julius Caesar.* When the junior class ran into financial problems, Fannie devised a plan for what came to be called the "junior lunch," a midmorning sandwich sale that soon refilled the coffers and became a university institution. But while she fit in as part of the pack, she was also more inclined than the other girls to think independently and to raise questions about society and its workings.[15]

A turning point in Fannie's college life came in 1901, when the university's new president, Mary E. Woolley, arrived. One of the first women to graduate from Brown University, as well as a biblical history scholar and an administrator from Wellesley College, Woolley wanted to turn Mount Holyoke into a top-flight institution. As a junior and the class vice president, Fannie was on the welcoming committee that greeted Woolley. The friendship they formed lasted throughout Woolley's life.

Woolley was not a traditional woman. She was not married and did not seem to feel that she had suffered for the lack of it. Instead she sought friendship and companionship from female friends, particularly her colleague Jeannette Marks, with whom she maintained a close and affectionate relationship. Woolley's life presented to the girls at Mount Holyoke the novel idea that marriage was a possibility for the future, but not a requirement for a satisfying life.[16]

Woolley wasn't the only woman who would leave an indelible mark on Fannie. As she neared graduation, in February 1902, Fannie met a woman who would have an even greater influence on her life. Florence Kelley, executive secretary of the National Consumers League, came to the college on a national lecture tour to speak about the organization she was building: a group dedicated to abolishing child labor and eliminating tenement work and sweatshops. Her goal was not to get better prices for consumers, but to help consumers understand the implications of their purchases—that goods bought cheaply often came with a steep price for workers, who made them under poor circumstances, bad wages, and hazardous conditions. She sought to mobilize middle-class support for promoting what she called "enlightened standards for workers and honest products for everybody."

Kelley, middle-aged, divorced, and raising three children on her own, was remarkably different from any of the other women Fannie had known. She was fiery, energetic, and infused with idealism, but she was also pragmatic. The daughter of a famous progressive Republican congressman from Pennsylvania and the niece of Philadelphia abolitionist Sarah Pugh, an early women's suffrage advocate, she came from a long line of people with a sense of civic responsibility, the same as Fannie. Kelley was a Quaker who accepted defeat with equanimity, confident that her efforts would eventually succeed because of their essential morality. She had already had notable career success, having served as chief inspector of factories in Illinois, the first time any woman had been appointed to such a position in the country.

Kelley was also one of the most politically radical people that Fannie had ever met. She had translated a book by Friedrich Engels, *The Condition of the Working Classes in England in 1844,* from German into English, and she was a Marxist, a position that she later softened into socialism. In 1901 the Socialist Party platform included many ideas deemed dangerous by conservatives: an eight-hour workday, the right to organize labor unions, establishment of free employment offices, and the creation of public parks and children's playgrounds.

Kelley brought new social science methods to her work—some of the same research techniques that Fannie studied in her economic history/ course. Kelley's motto at the National Consumers League was "Investigate, record, agitate," and she required her workers to prove their cases, not just assert them.[17]

In Kelley, Fannie would discover the perfect mentor, friend, and guide.

Graduation came in 1902, and with it the end of contact with new ideas and the taste of intellectual freedom that Fannie had enjoyed. The graduating girls prepared to return home, as was customary for young women. The prospect of returning to Worcester, however, weighed on Fannie's mind. As she finished senior year, serving as class president, she seemed like a different girl to her parents, much more distant than she had been when she left for college four years earlier.

She had grown more strong-willed, more embued with a sense of mission. When she spoke as class president at the last prayer meeting of her senior year, she chose as the text St. Paul's message to the early Christians: "Therefore my beloved brethren, be ye stedfast, unmoveable, always abounding in the work of the Lord. . . ." And the class she led, Mount Holyoke 1902, chose the words "Be Ye Stedfast" as its motto.[18]

Burning with a desire to help the poor, Fannie decided she didn't want to go home. She traveled to New York City—against her parents' wishes—to seek some kind of social work. Her parents pleaded with her to abandon the plan. To her father, New York City was a "den of iniquity and a strange place."[19]

Fannie marched into the New York office of the Charity Organization Society, a fifteen-year-old consortium of philanthropic organizations that later became the United Way. Social work was still a new field, and the Charity Organization Society had the reputation of attracting the best in the profession. Undeterred by her youth and inexperience, she demanded a meeting with Edward T. Devine, the group's director, and declined to be interviewed by other office staffers. Devine finally agreed to speak with her. He asked what she wanted to do, and she said she wanted to see the poor, give them help, and untangle their problems.

"Well, that's very interesting," Devine said. "What would you do if you were sent out to a family who had applied for help, and you came into their tenement, and you found the father drunk on the bed, the children done up with sore throats and sick, no food in the house. The mother was bustling around pretty disheveled and disorderly looking. The dishes were piled high in the sink. The father was drunk and obviously had just beaten his wife. What would you do?"

"Well, I'd send for the police at once and have the man arrested, of course," the twenty-one-year-old girl said. The smile on Devine's face broadened.

"That isn't exactly what we would recommend," he said, explaining to her that the best way to rehabilitate the family was to get the parents back to work, sober them up, and teach them to help themselves. [20]

In simple but gentle words, he told Fannie that she was too young, unworldly, and inexperienced for the work, and she lacked the judgment and life experience to effectively assist those in need. Devine suggested books to read and sent her on her way with an armload of social work newsletters.

Rebuffed in her first foray into social work, chastened and heeding her parents' admonishments, Fannie dutifully returned home. Her parents didn't want her to pursue graduate studies and preferred that she begin looking for a suitor and get married.

She shared her disappointment with her Mount Holyoke classmates in a class letter in December 1902. "Well, nothing seemed to turn up for me, and I made up my mind that it was my mission to stay at home and make my family miserable," she said, trying to spin away her mournful outlook.[21]

She took several teaching jobs, including brief stints at Bacon Academy in Colchester, Connecticut, and Monson Academy in Massachusetts. A job at Leicester Academy in Worcester had brought her back home. Fannie and her sister, Ethel, volunteered at the Union Gospel Mission, a small-scale settlement house in Worcester, which provided recreational activities to women workers.[22]

She missed college life and revisited several times. "Take my advice and go back when you can," she told her classmates. "It's grand and if you use your imagination, you'll believe that 1902 girls are under every cap and gown and you won't be lonely."[23]

In 1904, two years out of college, Fannie heard about an opening to teach science at a women's college in Chicago. She corresponded with the school by mail and took the job sight unseen. Nearly desperate to escape Worcester, Fannie prepared to head west away from her family, which she was finding anything but inspiring: boring, smug, and content with their lot.

Fannie also gave another reason for her departure, spoken in jest, but which conveyed her sense of being unappreciated at home: "A prophet has no honor in his own country."[24]

Chapter 2

BECOMING
FRANCES PERKINS

*F*or a young woman seeking to launch a new life in the early 1900s, no place offered better possibilities than Chicago. Fast-growing and diverse, the metropolis had first captured the nation's imagination when it hosted the 1893 World's Columbian Exposition. As the home base of civic reformer Jane Addams's Hull House, Chicago also became the focal point for the nation's social activism and a new center for intellectual thought. It was only natural that Fannie, who was drawn to social work and looking for adventure, left Worcester and moved there in 1904.

Fannie landed first in Lake Forest, Illinois, a sylvan Chicago suburb that was becoming one of the nation's wealthiest communities. She took up her duties as a science teacher at Ferry Hall, a women's college for affluent young ladies. At Lake Forest and in Chicago, Fannie began what would become a lifetime pattern of moving simultaneously in two worlds—mixing with the elite while advocating reforms to benefit the poor.

Immediately upon arriving, she reinvented herself. She changed her name, her faith, and her political persuasion.

The name change came first. Sometime before the printing of the 1904–1905 Ferry Hall catalogue, which listed her among the faculty, Fannie Coralie Perkins became Frances Perkins. She may have felt that her given name lacked dignity and carried an unfortunate association with a woman's posterior. It was an easy name to ridicule, and indeed, people used the name when they wanted to belittle or patronize her. It's unclear why she chose the name Frances, and she didn't explain, even to her family. Frances, however, was an old family name, and taking it allowed her to keep her initials, a practical concern for a woman who liked monogrammed linens. Like other feminists of her day, she may also have recognized that having a gender-neutral name would give her employment advantages.

But there was little place for ardent feminism at Ferry Hall. The all-girls school played the role of genteel younger sister to nearby Lake Forest College, which was more academically rigorous. Its campus sprawled over green lawns on a bluff overlooking Lake Michigan. The Victorian era still reigned, and Frances's life was strictly circumscribed. As a female teacher, she was required to live on campus, sharing a student dormitory. Teachers observed strict curfews and obeyed house rules, including mandatory attendance at prayer services. Everyone rose to a chorus of alarm clocks at 6:20 a.m., heard the morning bell ring at 7:00, ate meals together, and observed a 10 p.m. lights-out policy.

School administrators sought to reassure parents in countless ways that they need not worry about their daughters becoming intellectuals. Catalogues from Frances's years on staff described the course work. "Four daily periods of 45 minutes each are required," the 1906–1907 catalogue said. "No less amount of work will be permitted except for special reasons, and no greater amount should be attempted."

At Ferry Hall, scholastic expectations were low, even by the day's standards, with an emphasis on music, art, French, German, and cooking. Frances taught science, the curriculum's most challenging course. Students were not required to take it, but some chose to do so with Frances's encouragement. She presided over a sparsely equipped laboratory and a large, spartan room. Frances was known there as imaginative, witty, fashionable, and popular with the students.[1]

In June 1905, near the end of her first year, Frances rejected her family's faith and left the Congregationalist Church. She was confirmed at a fledgling Episcopalian church just up the hill from campus. Instead of the simple Protestant churches she knew in her childhood, the Episcopalians built grand religious edifices. Her new house of worship, the Gothic-inspired Church of the Holy Spirit, was consecrated on the day she joined.[2]

She did not make the change lightly. She sought a more structured religion with a more formal ceremony. Indeed, the Episcopalian faith she embraced came very close to Catholicism. She reveled in its elaborate and archaic rituals. They helped her remain serene and centered at times of stress. The church's teaching also gave her substantive guidance about the right path to take when confronted with decisions, and the hopeful message of Christianity helped her retain her optimism. Her devotion waxed and waned over the years, but nonetheless served as a bedrock and a way to seek meaning in life when so much seemed inexplicable. These religious leanings became progressively more pronounced over time. When friends once questioned why it was important to help the poor, Frances responded that it was what Jesus would want them to do.

Joining this church, however, also placed Frances in the most upscale milieu in tiny Lake Forest. Her religious convictions were real, but her switch to the Episcopalians also gave her a ready social stepladder.

The Church of the Holy Spirit's rapid construction was financed through donations and fund-raising events. At a church-benefit horse show, held the week after Frances joined the church, affluent socialites, including debutantes Lolita Armour and Helen and Jane Morton, salt-company heiresses whose grandfather had served as Grover Cleveland's secretary of agriculture, showed off their ponies. Members of the Swift family, driving their four-in-hand carriage, were the show's stars.

Later that summer, Frances vacationed in Europe with two friends and their mother from New York. In England, she visited Blenheim Palace, the palatial home of the duke of Marlborough and his American wife, Consuelo Vanderbilt. While there, Frances met for the first time a short, bug-eyed man with a piercing mind and an equally sharp wit, Winston Churchill. He was the son of the duke's younger brother, and English protocol ranked him low. However, his recent reporting exploits for the *London Morning Post,* escaping from the Boers during the South African campaign, attracted much attention. He was also half-American, since his own mother, Jennie Randolph Churchill, was a New Yorker by birth and a descendent of Revolutionary War soldiers. Frances found young Churchill memorable and, as she often did, stored his name and face away in her encyclopedic memory.[3]

In spite of the trappings of her elevated social circles in Chicago, she also became acquainted with the city's hardscrabble side. She befriended a young woman teacher whose aunt served on Hull House's board of directors and the aunt, in return, helped Frances get involved in social work projects there on weekends and during vacations.

Hull House, the nation's leading settlement house, was located in a ghetto, an overpopulated Chicago neighborhood strewn with garbage.

Its founder, Jane Addams, a Republican progressive, modeled her establishment on London's Toynbee Hall, a place where British liberals introduced education and social reform to the lower classes. At Toynbee Hall, located in a bleak working-class district where Jack the Ripper had left one of his victims, wealthy young people lived among the poor, and, despite the potential for mere posturing, actually did much good. Addams visited Toynbee Hall in 1888, and upon returning to Chicago, she and a friend looked for a building to set up a similar enterprise.

The goal was to rekindle the sense of community that had frayed in America as the Industrial Revolution divided the nation into haves and have-nots. Settlement houses were actually boardinghouses where people lived and ate communally as a large extended family dedicated to civic improvement. Many had a religious motivation. Social workers and community activists lived there in exchange for working with needy families. But poor people also partook of settlement house hospitality. There they might attend a class or learn a skill, but they could also hear musical performances or listen to lectures and political debates. In that way, rich and poor intermingled, sometimes for the first time.

Addams's Hull House offered job training, health services, child care, a library, and a savings bank. It operated a kindergarten, day care center, English-language and U.S. citizenship classes, and clubs for new mothers, camera enthusiasts, and aspiring artists and musicians. Addams cultivated like-minded young people, and the reputation of Hull House quickly grew. The success of the establishment spawned a national movement, and soon hundreds of affiliated settlement houses were operating across the country.

In short order, Frances went from being a drop-in guest worker to a regular visitor and an occasional resident, although her Ferry Hall obligations prevented her from moving there full-time. She saw the settlement house workers as her true family, and they felt the same. Frances is "one of us," Addams said.[4]

An incredible array of people passed through the portals of Hull House. Among its early residents were Walter S. Gifford, who became board chairman of AT&T; Sidney Hillman, an aspiring trade unionist; Gerard Swope, the future president of General Electric; W. MacKenzie King, who became Canada's prime minister; jazz musician Benny Goodman; and Ramsay MacDonald, the British statesman. Regular visitors included attorney Clarence Darrow and architect Frank Lloyd Wright.

Her association with such famous men further expanded Frances's social network. She was only twenty-five years old, but already she was developing a calculated strategy of cultivating influential friends. These casual introductions would allow her to seek counsel and get assistance at key moments, even years later.

One particularly noteworthy contact Frances made was Upton Sinclair, who had recently completed his muckraking novel about the meatpacking industry, *The Jungle*, which was released in 1906. In Chicago, Frances met the same people he had—the factory workers, entrepreneurs, and shady politicians. Walking in Sinclair's shoes, Frances had her own personal introduction to the urban poverty she had first read about in Riis's book. Between 1870 and 1900, Chicago had mushroomed from a town of 300,000 to a booming metropolis of about 1.7 million, including some 1.3 million first-generation immigrants drawn there by fast-growing businesses. Many new residents lived without basic sanitation services, overcrowded in shoddily built houses, in neighborhoods swept regularly by contagious diseases. Affluent families escaped to suburbs like Lake Forest and commuted by horse car or rail lines. The poor were left trapped in decaying city tenements, frequently with only social workers to provide them with assistance. These social workers had been eager to help Sinclair with his research and he spent much time with them.[5]

Working at Hull House, Frances, now in her late twenties, finally found the place to do the kind of work she had sought from Edward Devine. She helped distribute food baskets and fresh milk to starving children. Often the parents earned far too little money—sometimes only pennies after their employers deducted fees and charged them for using equipment—to support their families. Little could be done about the underlying imbalance of power, but witnessing cases in which employers hired workers, especially immigrants, and then refused to pay them, Frances devised a technique for getting recalcitrant employers to pay up by warning them she would tell their landlords they were not fulfilling their obligations.

Frances considered her Hull House sojourn life-changing. She saw situations firsthand that she had only read about in books, and came to realize how difficult it was to unravel these social problems. She admired and was inspired by Jane Addams and the other Hull House women, and learned much from them. She also came to see the magnitude of the opposition they faced, not just from business executives and officials but also from newspaper publishers, many of whom were equally conservative and suspicious of social change.

It was undoubtedly at Hull House that Frances first began to feel animosity toward reporters. Hull House had opened just three years after the Haymarket Riot in 1886. Unionists had rallied in support of an eight-hour day. As the police marched in to disperse the crowd, someone threw a bomb, killing one policeman and wounding many bystanders. The events made Chicago residents wary of radicals, and Hull House was viewed as a magnet for such malcontents. Its residents noticed that many reporters who visited Hull House came with an agenda of discovering a dangerous "nest of anarchism" and they learned to avoid or evade them—a lesson Frances took to heart.[6]

During her time in Chicago, Frances heard her first fiery labor speeches as union activists took to the stump to describe bad pay and working conditions. She stood in a hallway with Graham Taylor, son of the founder of another Chicago settlement house, discussing the problems of the working poor. "The only answer to this is the organization of all the working people into trade unions," he told her heatedly. It would allow sufficient wages without the need to rely on charity or public assistance.[7]

Frances was startled but intrigued. She always liked new ideas, and Taylor's view was sharply at odds with the opinions held dear by Frances's family, who considered trade unions "an evil to be avoided." Her fledgling interest in the labor movement marked one more way she was drifting away from her parents' world.[8]

Her letters home underscored the growing gulf between Frances and her family. She was seeing and hearing many things in the Chicago tenements that appalled her, but she didn't try to tell her parents about the incidents she witnessed. Instead her letters were light in tone and filled with inconsequential items. She had come to realize her family neither knew nor especially cared about what she was doing at Hull House. Yet one thing was clear in Frances's mind: Social work was her calling. Since she was not independently wealthy, like some of the Hull House women, she began looking for paid positions doing social work.

In 1907, Frances heard about a job in Philadelphia. The work entailed investigating another issue described by Upton Sinclair—that of immigrant women pushed into sexual slavery. Bogus employment agencies offered women good jobs but instead lured them into boarding-houses that turned out to be bordellos. There they were drugged and offered to paying customers. Many women who fell into this trap developed infectious diseases or committed suicide. Frances's job was to find ways to put pimps and drug dealers out of business, to detect, confront, and bring to law enforcement's attention the establishments preying on women: work considered daunting for even the most experienced social workers. Of all the work available to Frances, this was the type her parents would have found most appalling. Without hesitation, she accepted the position and moved to Pennsylvania.

Frances's title was general secretary of a new group called the Philadelphia Research and Protective Association, founded by Hull House alumna Frances Kellor. Paid $50 a month, Frances barely made enough money to live. She was expected to raise funds to pay both her salary and research costs. On a tight budget, she wore years-old clothes and used introductions from family and friends to dine out at other people's homes. She regularly pawned her watch when she needed cash, retrieving it again when she got a paycheck. To support the fledgling organization, she solicited donations from public-spirited Philadelphians, many of them Quakers and descendants of the old abolitionists, by speaking on her investigations into bordellos, a topic many found titillating.

Frances tackled the challenges with gusto. She visited back-alley lodging houses and questioned girls about how they came to Philadelphia and how they were supporting themselves. She found widespread evidence that not only European immigrants but young black women from the rural South were being transported to the city for prostitution. She hired an African-American Cornell University graduate to work with her, and together they built a list of reputable boardinghouses to steer young women away from the worst places.

Frances examined 111 employment agencies to determine their legitimacy. She applied for jobs and tried them out. At one point, she posed as a housemaid looking for a job to see what the agencies would offer. She also visited 165 fleabag lodging houses in which young women were housed. In some she met the lowest-paid prostitutes. She discovered widespread overcrowding and poor sanitation, and went on to help shut down four houses of ill repute by testifying before city public safety officials about what she had seen inside their walls.[9] Sometimes Frances laughed when imagining how her family, ignorant of this seamy side of life, would react if they knew what she was doing.

There were real risks in disrupting the livelihoods of pimps and other criminals. One night a pair of "really evil" men whose business she had been disturbing with her investigations accosted her on a deserted street.[10] Frances rounded a corner and unexpectedly turned on them, thrusting at them with her umbrella, shouting out their names. Startled, they turned and ran. Putting up a bold front could vanquish even a determined adversary, Frances realized. Undeterred by the threat, she soon succeeded in prodding officials into shutting down the men's illicit establishment.

Struggling to survive on her own salary, Frances interviewed girls who earned half as much, or $6 a week, doing factory work. They lived in basements and survived on bread and bananas. Many relied on cash gifts from or dinners with men to make ends meet. And as she and other social investigators observed, such reliance could be only a short step from prostitution.

She learned that women were almost always paid less than men, were given less desirable jobs, and were barred by their gender from union participation. It became clear to Frances that she needed to continue her education in order to debate these economic and labor issues more effectively.

The Wharton School of Finance and Commerce at the University of Pennsylvania in Philadelphia was her obvious choice. Although most Ivy League schools prohibited female attendance at the time, Penn had recently begun accepting women.

Frances recalled the school being "very conservative . . . and founded to teach people about the protective tariff." [11] Still, she found many other points of view. Studying alongside men for the first time, she realized the depth of her own intelligence.

During these years Frances appears to have had her first serious romance. Amid the pool of eligible young men she met at Penn, aspiring businessmen who could have given her the conventional life her parents sought for her, Frances instead found Joseph E. Cohen, an intelligent and witty printer who was an official in the typographical workers union. Cohen was a very different type from the other men she had known. He was Jewish and a radical—anathema to Frances's conservative Republican parents. Thin and bespectacled, Cohen lived a monkish life, devoted to his union work and the Socialist Party. Cohen was a pupil and friend of socialist leader Eugene Debs, by then a candidate for president on the socialist ticket.

Along with Cohen, and his brother, George Caylor, Frances became a committed socialist during that period. The three of them would stroll together down Philadelphia's Walnut Street, with George on one side of Frances and Joe on the other, intensely engaged in conversation about how the Socialist Party could save America's soul. Their friends thought Frances was in love with Joe Cohen and might have married him if he had asked her. But Cohen showed no desire to marry, and frustratingly enough, he showed physical affection only toward women who were somehow unavailable.[12]

Hoping to have children but with no relationship forthcoming with Joe, Frances no doubt felt it was time to move on. Simon Patten, a professor at Wharton under whom she had studied, had been impressed by Frances's aptitude and suggested that she continue her studies. In 1908 he helped her arrange a fellowship at Columbia University. So seven years after her first foray into New York, Frances returned to make the city her home. This time, however, she headed there with a job in hand, and with recommendations to the people who had previously rejected her.

In the years that followed, she never mentioned Cohen, though she continued to correspond with him. She also concealed her onetime Socialist Party membership, insisting that she had been apolitical and didn't even know what party she belonged to until she joined the Democrats several years later. She was already erasing her tracks.

Chapter 3

THE YOUNG ACTIVIST
HITS NEW YORK

*F*rances felt sweet vindication when she reached New York in 1909. She had never taken no for an answer, and with her move she showed naysayer Edward Devine the strength of her resolve. She moved into a settlement house associated with Hull House and studied at Columbia, focusing on the problems of the poor. Her course work examined social and economic conditions, and she earned a master's degree in political science in June 1910. In her free time, Frances again made connections that would serve her for decades, cultivating influential friends and benefactors who would include the Astors, Vanderbilts, Cuttings, and Livingstons. She moved to Greenwich Village, a center of intellectual ferment, living amid radicals and writers, lesbians and libertines, painters and partygoers, sensualists and suffragists, immigrants and ideologues—all whose ideals turned the neighborhood "into a beacon of American possibility in the new age."[1]

Frances was euphoric. In the stimulating atmosphere of the Village, the small-town girl from Worcester found that her work among the poor gave her a certain social cachet. She circulated smoothly, saying the right things while storing up witty observations that she would share with her closest friends. She went dancing with an admirer, Will Irwin, a reporter and editor at *Collier's* magazine. She frequented avant-garde art shows, concerts, lectures, and political rallies; she walked on the beach. She shocked her friends from Mount Holyoke by trumpeting her support for the family-limitation movement, which was illegal because birth-control information was deemed obscene.

Although Frances had come to New York to study social work, she was still unsure what shape her career should take. Articulate and adept at disguising her emotions, Frances considered becoming an actress, then retreated when she was told she wasn't pretty enough to play the ingenues. And in a neighborhood awash in talented writers, Frances, too, thought about becoming one herself, a way to bring in some extra money. She published several short stories—true-love tales with happy endings, set in the American West, a place she had never been—stories that have been impossible to trace because she wrote under assumed names. But her confidence was shaken when she was turned down for publication by no less a person than novelist Theodore Dreiser, who was editing *Delineator* magazine, a women's publication that targeted Midwest farm wives. Dreiser, still recovering from the unenthusiastic reception of his novel *Sister Carrie*, pronounced Frances's piece "too sophisticated" for the magazine's market. She admired Dreiser and never wrote fiction again.

At parties, she listened to Jack Reed, soon to be seduced by Russian Communism, wax rhapsodic about the inner purity of Mexican peasant revolutionaries led by bandit Pancho Villa. Frances saw Reed as passionately irrational. Yet she commented later, "In those days, nothing upset us. We didn't get upset about anybody's ideology . . . You didn't get upset because people had funny ideas. That was America."[2]

Meanwhile Frances developed a talent for gaining the confidence of others and then serving as a sounding board for their dreams and aspirations. She had the deep mystical streak common in many very religious people, and she once noted that she saw people's auras, allowing her to target those worthy of cultivation. Frances described the auras as "sparks" radiating from certain people, and her visual memory kept these individuals plainly in her mind.[3] This sixth sense would guide her in bringing together particular people to accomplish particular tasks. She also recognized other people with finely honed instincts, who were guided by their intuitions as much as by actual information. It gave her an uncanny ability to spot people of unusual promise before they were widely recognized by others.

One man she singled out as especially interesting was Robert Moses, a young investigator at the Bureau of Municipal Research who traveled in the same government-reform circles as many of her social worker friends. On a sunny summer day, Frances and Robert Moses traveled with a group of friends on a picnic outing, taking a ferry across the Hudson River to New Jersey. Standing next to Frances on the deck, Moses confided in her his grand vision for remaking New York City. He leaned against the rail and looked across the waterfront below Riverside Drive to the barren, muddy, debris-strewn wasteland that was traversed by the New York Central railroad. Gesturing enthusiastically, Moses painted a picture to Frances of a beautiful park, running the river's length, where strollers could enjoy the views, families could bicycle together, and sailors could dock their boats at a public marina. He saw Riverside Park as though it were already a reality. He was willing to share these thoughts with others, but he was arrogant and abrasive and few people took the time to listen, as Frances did.

Three decades after Moses described an imaginary Riverside Park to Frances, he oversaw its construction and would later emerge as the mastermind of New York's urban transformation, changing the shorelines, building state highways and public buildings, and creating sprawling waterfront parks along the Hudson River and Long Island Sound.[4]

Similarly, the gangly, red-haired journalist Sinclair Lewis turned to Frances for help editing an early manuscript, a book that became *Our Mr. Wrenn*. Lewis's career as a newsman was foundering, but the book's success set him on course to win the Nobel and Pulitzer prizes, which he received for books including *Babbitt, Arrowsmith*, and *Elmer Gantry*. A country boy from Minnesota who lacked certain social graces, Lewis fell in love with Frances, or at least told about a dozen friends that he had. One summer night he yelled a marriage proposal up to her bedroom window from the street below, attracting attention throughout the neighborhood.

Lewis often behaved wildly, in part because of his heavy drinking. His behavior irritated the more polished members in their circle, which included Howard Brubaker, a well-known columnist; Arthur Bullard, a writer and diplomat; and a new man who had entered their midst, a good-government reformer named Paul Caldwell Wilson. They poked fun at Lewis, considered him a pest, and looked for ways to shed him.

Frenetic and uncontrolled, with a clumsy manner and a taste for ill-fitting clothing, Lewis somehow aroused Frances's protective maternal instinct. She did not reciprocate his romantic feelings and deflected them by pretending he was joking. They shared a fondness for playacting, imitating the voices and speech patterns of others. Lewis put these skills to use in his novels about middle-class hypocrisy in small-town America, and Frances incorporated them into her storytelling, used to good effect in social settings and in defusing tensions. She confided to him details of her life and childhood, and he listened and remembered it, as only a man in love will do. Passionate admiration is always appealing, especially for a young woman who has never thought of herself as beautiful, and Frances spent more time with him than she acknowledged, even as she fended off his proposals.

Undeterred, Lewis continued to strive to appeal to Frances. He wasn't particularly interested in the women's-right-to-vote movement and later ridiculed it, but with Frances intensely committed, Lewis joined her in a parade, even holding a banner at one point. Will Irwin, her friend from *Collier's,* had gone on a similar march and reported that male participants needed courage because male hecklers, often fortified by alcohol, would taunt them unmercifully. But the movement was no laughing matter to Frances.[5]

🔺

*F*rances Perkins built her closest female friendships around the suffrage movement. She spoke regularly on street corners, advocating constitutional change to permit women to vote. She traveled with a female friend or acquaintance who would literally carry the soapbox and provide moral support when the crowd turned sour. She developed a knack for turning foes into friends through the use of gentle humor. The women experimented with new feminist protests. One afternoon, for example, Frances and a group of women friends ostentatiously smoked in public in a hotel lobby, just to assert a woman's right to do so.

Frances eventually emerged as a leader in the movement, with a visible place on the podium. At a feminist meeting at Cooper Union, Frances advocated dramatic change in the relationships between men and women. "Feminism means revolution, and I am a revolutionist. I believe in revolution as a principle. It does good to everybody."[6]

In a class letter to her considerably more conservative Mount Holyoke classmates, Frances described the suffrage campaign as one of her "serious pastimes." Suffrage, she told them, "is either execrated so heartily or championed so ardently by all of you that it needs only the bare statement of the fact that I'm one of the 'real ones' to explain the situation perfectly. I fear that only a somewhat antiquated reverence for plateglass windows keeps me from being one of the stone-throwing kind."[7]

🔺

*B*ut as her graduate studies neared an end, she began to look for a job. So in April, when the National Consumers League in New York City approached Frances about heading their office in the city, the opportunity seemed heaven-sent. The league advocated workers' rights and protections, and Frances had begun to believe that overwork and low pay were the root causes of many of the nation's social problems. The job would permit her to work closely with the inspirational Florence Kelley, whom she had first heard speak at Mount Holyoke a decade earlier and later lauded at Hull House, where she had been a legendary early resident.

Kelley's reputation had grown in the intervening years. Kelley's and other social workers' research into Pittsburgh's housing, schools, court system, sanitation, and workplace standards had resulted in substantial municipal reforms, and became a model for social investigators examining other cities.[8]

But Frances was older and savvier than she had been when she took the job in Philadelphia. This time she asked for a full-time secretary and boldly requested $1,200 a year. The league countered at $1,000 a year, a barely livable salary but still $400 more than she earned in Philadelphia, and it agreed to hire a stenographer for her. Frances accepted and soon found herself running the league's New York City office.[9]

Her early work for the league focused on four areas: poor conditions in cellar bakeries, long hours and poor wages for women, child labor, and workplace fire hazards.

The grassroots league relied heavily on consumer education to help promote better working conditions for workers. Low prices usually came at a human cost. The league lobbied against sweatshops, long hours, and unsanitary conditions. It sought corrective legislation at the state level because the U.S. Supreme Court had repeatedly ruled that federal laws on these subjects were illegal because they violated contract law or restricted interstate commerce.

The league granted manufacturers the right to use a special white label in their clothing if they could guarantee that they paid workers good wages and offered sanitary conditions. Employers were urged to limit workdays to twelve hours and to pay $8 to $10 a week. The league asked members and consumers to buy only white-labeled items.

But many employers refused to comply. At Bloomingdale's and Macy's, for example, many salesgirls earned $3 a week, and even experienced workers received $6 a week for their fourteen- to sixteen-hour workdays. The worst conditions, Frances later recalled, were at Altman's, a favorite of lady club members who had to wrestle with their consciences after learning of Frances's findings. One after another, the women notified Mr. B. Altman that they were canceling their accounts and would resume shopping only if the store raised wages to $5 a week, offered clerks paid holidays and overtime, provided adequate toilets, and allowed workers to sit rather than stand.

Many of the goods bearing the league-approved white label were less attractive than those made without regard for worker conditions. Members had to forgo pretty silk underwear, for example, because the only white-labeled goods available at the time were coarse cotton nightgowns trimmed with machine-made embroidery. Women had to literally wear their liberalism on their sleeves if they chose to support better working conditions. Frances called it a "training of the conscience."[10]

The once-shy girl was growing in confidence. She held conferences to raise issue awareness and scouted for speaking engagements to tout the league's efforts. Frances's goal was to recruit three hundred new members a year. She also used those months to inspect twenty-six laundries, hire and train an investigator, and monitor personnel policies at New York's City Hall.

"No stone left unturned," she noted in an October 1911 league report.

Eliminating child labor, however, was her principal aim. Children in these years were employed in factories, offices, and coal mines. Their small, nimble hands could handle tasks that older people could not master, but the children frequently suffered serious injuries as a result of doing work too heavy for their undeveloped frames, particularly when they were fatigued near the end of a typical twelve-hour day. Frances had seen the consequences firsthand: A teenage girl she knew from her settlement house work had gotten her hand tangled in candy-dipping machinery and it was cut off.

Frances had visited the child at home and arranged for a doctor to tend to the wound because the employer had simply sent the girl home from work. But the factory owner wasn't solely to blame for these incidents: Parents who were impoverished pulled their children out of school and instead put them to work, either at workplaces or in the tenements where they lived, and the poorly educated youngsters then grew into desperately poor adults themselves.

Frances frequently ended her speeches by quoting a poem by Sara M. Claghorn called "Little Toilers":

The golf links lie so near the mills,
That nearly every day,
The laboring children can look out,
And see the men at play.[11]

As she had hoped, Frances came under the direct tutelage of Florence Kelley, who saw the league's work as the Lord's calling and instilled this belief in others.

Kelley insisted on rigorous research before proposing reforms. Once she settled on a course of action, she brought employers and workers together to mediate solutions.

Frances admired this strategy, the same she had seen Addams use at Hull House. "This was a real work of genius . . . bring all parties to the situation into conference to try to devise a remedy for the ill you have found, and then, having devised a remedy, tell people about it and push and push and press and talk and be not afraid, no matter how much you are abused, until the right idea has established itself and the risks have been taken."

Kelley's focus on social issues and her pacifism led some to call her un-American. But to Frances, Kelley's position represented a "patriotism based upon the love of the men and women who were fellow citizens."[12]

They debated among themselves how best to improve bad working conditions. After a few years grappling with the issues, Frances came to believe that part of the answer was unionization. Her first prominent appearance in the *New York Times,* in November 1910, came in a letter to the editor supporting wagon drivers seeking a reduction in their work hours. "That any group of men should be obliged to strike for an eleven-hour work day in this enlightened age, when the eight-hour day is already established as the attainable standard, seems to us to indicate that in the cause of social progress the fair-minded members of the community should see to it that the demand of the striking expressmen for a shorter working day is granted," Frances wrote on behalf of the league.

But unions were only part of the answer. Frances was coming to view unions as naturally self-protective and eager to preserve their own advantages. She also believed that employers inevitably had the upper hand—making it essential that another strong independent body, such as government, level the playing field.

"I'd much rather get a law, than organize a union, and I think it's more important," she said.[13]

Yet passing laws was more difficult than she expected. For four years the league in New York had been pushing a state bill to limit women's work hours to fifty-four a week, arguing that female workers needed legislative protection because of their additional home and family obligations. Though the league supported shorter hours for all workers, it had concluded that a universal reduced workday would never pass and that women needed shorter hours more urgently than men. While many legislators expressed sympathy about women's long hours, industry opposition had killed the bills.

A novice at lobbying, Frances had to figure out how to turn around the effort. She started with introductions. She leaned on her friends to introduce her to influential people in Albany, then prevailed on them to introduce her to others. Republican judge Marcus T. Hun helped her because of his daughters' friendship with Frances.

She built up her ties with other progressive Republicans. In January 1911, former president Theodore Roosevelt, who was becoming increasingly liberal, addressed her in a letter as "My dear Miss Perkins." She had asked him to attend a league meeting in New York, and although he couldn't attend, he gave her a letter she could circulate that underscored his support for laws prescribing work-hour limitations for women and toughened enforcement by the courts. He also endorsed the Consumers League's efforts to restrict child labor.[14]

Even though the reformers had friends in high places, some legislators remained elusive, mainly because the women lobbying for the bill did not even have the right to vote. At a state senate hearing on the bill, members of the Committee on Labor and Industry listened carefully when business leaders testified in opposition. After the businessmen left, the senators all filed out, except for the committee chairman. The women advocates testified to a nearly empty room.

Some men thought that giving women more free time might cause them to behave immorally. "You'd better keep women fully occupied," Governor John A. Dix, a Democrat, told Frances privately.[15]

The Democrats blamed their inaction on the work-hour bill on the Republicans, an argument that became harder for them to make the next year, when they controlled both the State Assembly and the Senate.

Chapter 4

THE TRIANGLE
SHIRTWAIST FIRE

On March 25, 1911, Frances left her small apartment on Waverly Place to have Saturday afternoon tea at a splendid townhouse a few blocks away at 26 North Washington Square. It was owned by her close friend Margaret Morgan Norrie, a New York aristocrat descended from two different signers of the Declaration of Independence. The windows looked out on Washington Square's dramatic white arch, designed by society architect Stanford White.

Long before Greenwich Village became the progressive hub of intellectuals and artists, the neighborhood had been an upper-class bastion, the genteel neighborhood of the old New York barons, including families like the Norries. But now many of the city's richest families, and certainly the most newly rich, had moved uptown, building grand manors along Fifth Avenue. Part of their motivation was to escape the Village's most recent residents, immigrant poor crowding into nearby tenement houses.

Lured to America by advertising brochures and the hope of a better future, the newcomers, many of them Italians or East European Jews, were drawn to jobs in the factories that also sprang up in the neighborhood. Rich and poor lived uncomfortably together, and their children occupied Washington Square Park in an uneasy truce—the wealthy children accompanied by nannies and playing with bicycles and dolls, and the children of the poor running wild, in packs, mostly unsupervised. Their older brothers and sisters, some as young as ten, already worked in the factories alongside the adults.[1]

Frances and the other guests were just sitting down to tea when they were startled by shouts and the piercing sound of fire whistles. They rushed to the door to investigate. The butler told them a big fire had erupted on the other side of the square. Looking across the park, Frances saw flames shooting out of the windows of a ten-story building diagonally across from the Norrie home. It housed the Triangle Shirtwaist manufacturing company, a firm they all knew, which employed hundreds of workers, mostly young and impoverished immigrant women. It was a crowded firetrap. The workers were crammed elbow to elbow, their sewing machines packed in tightly, with threads and fabric scraps strewn across the floors and pushed into bins. The girls worked long hours, often six days a week, as they had been doing on this particular Saturday, sewing blouses in the Gibson Girl style, with puffed sleeves and tight bodices, that were worn by fashionable young women like Frances and her friends.

Holding her long skirt as she ran, Frances raced along the edge of park, past the arch, maneuvering around the wrought-iron fence, rushing toward the scene.

Frances could see people gathered at the upper windows of the high-rise, trying to escape the smoke and flames, locked into the building and unable to get to an exit. Some workers hung out of the windows, dangling by their hands, clinging desperately. She could hear the helpless firemen below, lacking ladders that could reach them, yelling to the workers not to jump and desperately setting up emergency nets.

As she approached, Frances saw people beginning to plummet to the ground. "One by one, the people would fall off," she said. "They couldn't hold on any longer—the grip gives way."[2]

Then, just as she arrived at the base of the building, Frances saw a worker deliberately jump to her death. Then another. And another.

"There began to be panic jumping," she said. "People who had their clothes afire would jump. It was a most horrid spectacle. Even when they got the nets up, the nets didn't hold in a jump from that height. There was no place to go. The fire was between them and any means of exit. There they were. They had gone to the window for air and they jumped. It's that awful choice people talk of—what kind of choice to make?"

One woman walked deliberately to the ledge, removed her wide-brimmed hat, and threw it into the air. Then she opened her handbag, extracted the few bills and coins that made up her pay, and flung them to the ground. The coins rang on the cobblestones as she jumped. Three windows away, one girl struggled to restrain another from jumping, but the second girl twisted loose and fell. The other clung to the ledge for a moment, then let herself fall forward into space.

One young man assisted three women, one by one, to the ledge and handed them over to their deaths, almost as though he were helping ladies into a carriage. As he brought a fourth girl to the window, she put her arms around him and kissed him. He dropped her into the void. Then he jumped himself, his coat fluttering upward as he fell.[3]

Frances stood there, stunned, clutching her throat, as thousands of spectators crowded around, staring, standing in silence or crying or screaming. Swirling clouds of smoke rose into the air.

In all, 146 workers, mostly young Jewish and Italian women, died that day. Frances was deeply shaken. Even more troubling to Frances and other onlookers was the fact that almost two years previously the workers had pleaded for help and had been rebuffed, even persecuted, for complaining about their work conditions.

In 1909, soon after Frances had arrived in New York City, about twenty thousand women who worked at Triangle and other clothing factories had streamed out into the streets in a mass protest, demanding that government officials intervene with employers to improve pay, give them reliable work schedules, and eliminate unsanitary and unsafe workplace conditions. It "was a true example of an angry, emotional outburst such as fiction writers often depict as the beginning of a revolution," Frances said later.[4]

The strikers were led by a tiny, fiery redhead named Rose Schneiderman, a Russian immigrant. The factory owners fought back. The picketers were harassed and intimidated by hired Pinkerton guards; the police beat many of them and carted them off to jail. Some were lodged in a courthouse known for housing prostitutes, another tactic meant to discourage them. "You are on strike against God," one magistrate told a woman picketer as he sentenced her to jail.[5]

Unlike most strikes, however, this one caught people's attention. Many progressives had already visited settlement houses and had heard of workplace abuses, particularly those inflicted on young immigrant women. The strikers won the support of a phalanx of wealthy, liberal New York women, including friends of Frances such as Margaret Norrie; Alva Belmont, whose daughter Consuelo had married the Duke of Marlborough; and Anne Morgan, the daughter of all-powerful financier J. P. Morgan. Dubbed the Mink Brigade, these unlikely allies carried picket signs along with the female strikers and bailed them out of jail, pledging property they owned as security. Heiress Mary Dreier took things one step farther when she went to jail alongside the striking workers, causing city officials to trip over themselves securing her release. Many of the companies reached settlements with their workers. The management at Triangle was a notable exception. There, the owners refused to make many concessions, and the employees returned to work.

With that dispute fresh in people's memories, many New York City residents reacted to the fire with shock, outrage, and grief, and a group of leading citizens called a public meeting a week later at the Metropolitan Opera House to discuss the event. Frances sat attentively in the audience. Schneiderman rose to speak.

"This is not the first time girls have been burned alive in this city," Schneiderman said. "Every week I must learn of the untimely death of one of my sister workers. Every year thousands of us are maimed. The life of men and women is so cheap and property is so sacred! There are so many of us for one job, it matters little if 140-odd are burned to death. . . . We have tried you, citizens! We are trying you now and you have a couple of dollars for the sorrow of mothers and brothers and sisters by way of a charity gift. But every time the workers come out in the only way they know to protest against conditions which are unbearable, the strong hand of the law is allowed to press down heavily upon us."[6]

Many listeners were moved by her words, but Frances, with her keen sense of civic responsibility, took it as a personal call to action. Until that time, Frances had imagined her life taking a direction similar to Margaret Morgan Norrie: married, doing volunteer social work while living comfortably and well. Now she began to suspect that much more might be needed of her. Workplaces needed to be made safer and more humane, but she had already lost her innocence about the ease with which those changes might occur, and she realized a lifelong commitment was needed.

The moment also marked the first time that she recognized that tragedies could be turned into positive events. She realized it might be possible to capitalize on the outrage the city felt to get substantive reforms made.

It is without doubt that the Triangle fire was a turning point. It reoriented her life. Journalist Will Irwin, a close friend, summed it up: "What Frances Perkins saw that day started her on her career."[7]

Chapter 5

Finding Allies
in Tammany Hall

*W*itnessing the Triangle fire had galvanized the thirty-one-year-old social worker, and it came at a time when her early idealism had begun fading away. Surveying the political scene in New York, she realized it was naive to expect people to recognize the errors of their ways and hasten to correct social problems. To achieve major change she needed allies, politicians who actually had the power to make things happen. In New York, that meant cultivating Tammany Hall, the shady and corrupt political machine that most upstanding citizens viewed with distaste.

Tammany Hall politicians used favors to win popular support. They passed out shoes to poor children, took impoverished families on boating jaunts, gave food to the hungry, and paid for the funerals of the penniless. They offered help to illiterates who got in trouble with the law. For waves of immigrants arriving indigent and friendless on American shores, Tammany Hall stretched out the only welcoming hand they saw. Recipients of the ring's largesse were glad to reciprocate with their votes.

Tammany Hall operatives who won public office used it to enrich themselves. Many became immensely wealthy. They took bribes from companies seeking public contracts for city services, sought payback from saloon-keepers trying to retain their liquor licenses, demanded services in kind from brothel-owners, took a cut from the paychecks of civil servants for whom they had gotten jobs. This system meant that the contractors who got the government projects often did substandard work and that many government employees were incompetent or unscrupulous. People who voted for Tammany Hall candidates might get a food basket at Thanksgiving, but they paid for it with bad roads and second-rate schools.

The organization's tentacles reached everywhere, even into the courts, affecting who got arrested, convicted, or acquitted, because the machine controlled police and judicial appointments.

Frances had first encountered Tammany Hall upon her arrival in New York, when she lived in the settlement house. A social worker who also was living there asked Frances to help a family in distress. A teenage boy, the sole support of his mother and two younger sisters, had been arrested and faced a prison term. His family was running out of food and rent money and risked disintegrating if he went to jail.

She turned first to Devine's Charity Organization Society, whose officials undertook a lengthy investigation. While the study was under way, Frances and a few friends donated their own meager resources to help the family. After a long while, an agency official told Frances that the inquiry found the woman unworthy of help because one of her children appeared to be illegitimate.

Frances was incensed. Something needed to be done. Putting her reservations aside she turned to Thomas J. McManus, a man known simply as The McManus, the Tammany Hall leader who ruled Hell's Kitchen with an iron hand and served as ward boss for the Hartley House neighborhood.

She went to his headquarters. She passed through the portals and found roughnecks, thugs, and hoodlums milling ominously about, smoking and spitting tobacco juice. She asked to be directed to Mr. McManus, and a clerk waved her inside.

Squaring her shoulders, Frances entered his smoke-filled offices. In his Irish brogue, The McManus asked why she had come, and she told him it was because of a boy in trouble. McManus asked if she lived in his district, and Frances gave the street number, without adding that it was Hartley House. She feared that mention of a settlement house would throw him off; she knew Tammany Hall officers disliked the upper-crust reformers active in the settlement houses because they were also usually advocates of good-government reforms.

The McManus asked a few more questions about the boy's situation, and then promised he would try to "fix it up." He asked her to come back the next day. By the next afternoon, the boy had been released from jail.[1]

Frances never knew exactly how The McManus had done it. He likely called in a favor at the courthouse, perhaps from an unqualified court official who got his job in exchange for a kickback. Still, the experience taught her the valuable lesson that venal politicians can sometimes be more useful than upstanding reformers.

Her encounter with The McManus marked the beginning of Frances's long alliance with Tammany Hall. Frances's perceptions of right and wrong were changing. She began to find key supporters in unlikely corners. Big Tim Sullivan and his brother Christy, state legislators who made their money shaking down contractors, for example, were converted into important allies in her fight to improve workplace conditions. Some of these men had been troubled by the Triangle fire, as girls who had died in the blaze had been their constituents, and now they were willing to help.

Tammany Hall was at the height of its power. The previous November, voters threw Republicans out of office after numerous bribery and embezzlement scandals. The Democrats took power. In 1911, Tammany Hall, the single largest Democratic political block, controlled both legislative chambers and the governorship. The next year the Republicans took the assembly but the Democrats still held the Senate and the governorship. Tammany Hall effectively controlled not just the city of New York but the entire state, including the state capital, Albany.

Again Frances had to march bravely into a place where other women of her class were reluctant to go. Her lobbying for the National Consumers League took her to Albany at least once a week. The Dutch-founded city had deteriorated into a maze of booze joints, gambling halls, and sleazy rooming houses. Its riverfront was a polluted industrial wasteland. Traveling there took courage, especially since Frances typically stayed in cheap lodging houses to save money for the league. Even stepping inside the palatial capitol building took a certain resolve. Its red carpets were soiled by ash from cigar-smoking legislators, and brown stains marked the spots where tobacco chewers had missed the spittoons. There was hardly a woman in sight, and Frances avoided the lunchroom so she would not be seen as "too bold" by the male diners. Instead she prowled the halls, trying to collar any legislator she could reach.[2]

As Frances began her work there, trying to find ways to advance her agenda, a man named Charles Murphy, a New York City saloon owner, was just taking over the helm of Tammany Hall. Hard-bitten and rough, he nevertheless sensed that the political winds were changing. He installed new leadership in Albany, choosing two promising young men, good friends who became known as the Tammany Twins. Frances made it her business to get to know them, too.

Robert F. Wagner, a German immigrant who had put himself through law school, became president of the Senate. He was Northern European and Protestant, as were most of the social reformers, and they viewed him as the one of the pair most likely to enact government reforms and boost workforce protections.

But Frances was more impressed with the less physically imposing of the duo, the industrious young assemblyman Al Smith, who served briefly as speaker of the house before becoming minority leader. A Catholic of Irish and Italian descent, Smith had grown up in the New York City slums. At fourteen, he had gone to work at the Fulton Fish Market to support his widowed mother, brothers, and sister. An early convert to Tammany Hall, he was being groomed by Murphy to be the next party leader.

Largely self-educated, with a gravelly accent and bad table manners, Smith pored over the state budget and developed a minute knowledge of individual legislative bills. He was homely, with a big nose and a scrawny neck, but he was diligent and had a quick mind. As she had with Sinclair Lewis and Robert Moses, Frances quickly saw qualities in him that other people might have missed.

"Al Smith had turned out to be a fine orator with a command of language, a pungent, racy talk in the language of the people, a gift for the figure of speech that would make people remember things and would also make them laugh at the same time," she said. "He really was quite extraordinary and if you ever saw him perform on the floor, you'd never forget it."[3]

In the summer of 1911, a few months after the Triangle fire, Frances met with Smith to update him on the status of the fifty-four-hour workweek bill. She thought she had enough votes to win passage, and was about to take a much-needed vacation. Smith told her to go, but not for the reasons she hoped. It had been decided, he said, that the issue would never come to a vote. He told her that an important Democratic Party campaign donor, the Huyler Candy Company, opposed the legislation and would ensure its defeat. The Bloomingdale retail family also opposed it.

Frances didn't believe him. Many people had assured her that action was imminent. She canceled her trip and spent the next weeks in Albany waiting for the bill to come up for a vote. It never did. She went back to the drawing board.

Now Frances targeted the Huyler family for what she called a "campaign of education." She enlisted help from wealthy and influential supporters of the National Consumers League, and before long members of the Huyler family found themselves greeted and entertained by the likes of industrialist and philanthropist R. Fulton Cutting, the great-nephew of steamship inventor Robert Fulton, and Virginia Potter, daughter of prominent New York cleric Henry Codman Potter. On a separate front, she arranged for the Bloomingdale family, who were Jewish, to be personally contacted on the issue by influential rabbi Stephen Wise.

In the spring of 1912, Tammany Hall leader Murphy gave the nod for the bill to be considered again. It passed easily in the Senate but hit a roadblock in the Assembly, after lobbyists for the canning industry sought an exemption. Eventually the measure passed—but the women who worked some of the longest hours in the state had been purposely excluded. The exception made the bill unpalatable to the National Consumers League and other social organizations. In short, the Assembly had passed the reform measure in a way that its main backers considered unacceptable. If the House and Senate could not find an acceptable compromise version, the bill would die.

Frances agonized for twenty-four hours. She discussed the problem with league lawyers and supporters. Board member Pauline Goldmark visited her in Albany to strengthen Frances's resolve to reject the unacceptable bill.

Frances discussed it with Smith and The McManus, who both said little. Finally Tim Sullivan leveled with her. He said that Tammany leader Murphy had issued orders to pass the legislation in that particular form, so that the reformers would reject it.

"They don't mean to put it through," Sullivan told her bluntly.[4]

Boiling with anger and frustration, Frances realized she'd been tricked. Then Joe Hammitt, another advocacy group lobbyist, helped her to reach a decision.

"How many women are there working in canneries?" he asked.[5]

"About fifty thousand," Frances said.

"How many women are there working in manufacturing in New York State?" he asked.

"About four hundred thousand," she replied.

"If I were you, I'd do what I could for the four hundred thousand," he said.

Frances walked into the corridor, taking refuge behind a curtain to consider her options. She decided she would accept the amendment and do some good for the four hundred thousand women who would otherwise not get the benefit of the bill. But while she pondered, the Senate rejected the Assembly's version of the bill, with even ardent supporters saying they had done so at the reformers' own request.

Frances again turned to Sullivan. With only hours remaining in the session, she told him she would accept half a loaf. Again he tipped her off: The legislators had set up the procedure to make it impossible for another vote to be called. And Wagner, the reformers' ostensible friend, had given orders as Senate presiding officer to block anyone seeking reconsideration.

"Oh, Mr. Sullivan!" Frances cried.

Sullivan paused, and then decided to help her.

"Me sister was a poor girl and she went out to work when she was young," Sullivan confided. "I feel kinda sorry for them poor girls that work the way you say they work. I'd like to do them a good turn. I'd like to do you a good turn."[6]

Sullivan and a group of Republican progressives who supported the bill rushed into the chamber, demanding reconsideration. Pandemonium erupted. Wagner turned pale and then stammered that it was too late to change the rule.

But Sullivan, acting chairman of the rules committee, was able to demand a vote. Supporters of the fifty-four-hour bill, who had been told to reject the amended version with the exception, ran to Frances, who was standing behind a brass rail at the chamber's edge. They asked her if she really wanted them to support it. Nervous but holding her ground, she told them she had decided it was preferable to win a better life for some than to deny it to all.

Standing next to Frances, Pauline Goldmark, a coworker at the National Consumers League, pulled at her coat and objected vehemently, reminding Frances she had been instructed not to allow the cannery workers to be excluded.

"Pauline," Frances said, "this is my responsibility. I'll do it and hang for it if necessary."[7]

While Sullivan and Frances blocked Wagner's maneuvers, Frances noticed that some key supporters had already left to catch the boat back to New York City. She called the boat's captain and asked him to hold the ship.

The legislators straggled back into the chamber to cast their votes. McManus and others killed time with long-winded speeches, allowing more supporters time to return. Finally the bill passed, 27 to 16. The galleries burst into applause.

Wagner sulked; Al Smith laughed and praised Frances's pluck.

Victory in hand, Frances headed back to New York City. Goldmark was still angry. But when Florence Kelley heard the news, she grabbed Frances and hugged her, jubilant at her success.

Still the carping continued. Josephine Goldmark, Pauline's sister, pointedly noted the law's shortcomings in a 1912 league report. Goldmark hailed the passage of a fifty-four-hour workweek for women but chided Frances for striking a deal. "Unfortunately, in the effort to secure this great benefit for tens of thousands of factory workers, the luckless women employed in the canneries were sacrificed," she wrote.[8]

Outside this narrow circle of impractical perfectionists, however, the legislation was viewed as a triumph for Frances. The next year, the law was broadened to include the canneries.[9]

Frances had achieved what a decade of reform efforts had failed to accomplish. Tammany Hall leader Charles Murphy later conceded to Frances that though he had opposed the measure, he knew it was politically popular. He was reconsidering what Tammany's stance on workplace issues should be, and he had decided to stop blocking progressive legislation. Smith and Wagner also began to change their tack. For the first time, Tammany Hall began aligning itself with social reformers.

Around that time, Frances, born into a rock-ribbed Republican family that despised Tammany Hall Democrats, decided that if women ever got the vote, hers would be Democratic. Her childhood jibe had become true conviction. She announced her change in allegiance at a party at her apartment—drawing jeers from her friends, who said she would be aligning herself with "the scum of the earth."

"All I know is this," Frances told them. "When the Republicans are in power in this state, we don't get any social legislation at all. The bills and things I'm interested in make no progress at all. When the Democrats are in power, we make some progress."

"You'd vote for Tammany?" they asked in horror.

"They vote for our legislation," Frances said.[10]

Nonetheless, Frances remained wary of Tammany Hall, knowing the machine could also be vicious. In 1912, William Sulzer, a Tammany Hall man with a checkered record, was elected New York's governor and, once in office, struck out on his own, seeking to pursue an agenda of good-government reforms. Murphy, feeling betrayed by his own creature, responded with fury and initiated an inquiry into Sulzer's past, which turned up numerous instances of ethical lapses and missing money. Under orders from Murphy, the Tammany-controlled state legislature impeached Sulzer, in one of the few cases of full impeachment in U.S. history. Ten months after his election, Sulzer was driven from office. Al Smith and Robert Wagner helped manage the impeachment campaign. A purist might have viewed Smith's political attack on Sulzer as hypocritical, unprincipled, and evidence of a profound lack of independence from the dictates of Tammany Hall. Frances, however, was becoming increasingly practical. She took Smith's actions as a cautionary example, not as grounds for ending the friendship.

Her ability to accept human foibles, to see both failings and strengths, was becoming a core personality trait, bolstering her effectiveness. She found that making deals with imperfect people and focusing on their strengths provided a pathway to actually achieving social change.

Watching the impeachment spectacle, another revelation ended up shaping her in an even more important way. The impeachment debate took place in the hottest part of the summer, near the session's end, and Frances had stayed in the capital to fight for her fifty-four-hour bill. The impeachment decision had made legislators agitated; the mood in the building was edgy; everyone knew the skirmish had more to do with politics than ethics.

As Frances stood outside a capitol elevator one day, the doors opened and a group of worried men came out in a cluster and dispersed into the hallways. Frances greeted state senator Hugh Frawley, a crude little man in a checkerboard-print suit. She knew him only slightly, so she was shocked when he grabbed her hand and told her how badly he felt about what was taking place. Frawley poured out confidential details of the legislators' negotiations with Sulzer, how he and others had begged him to "just drop all this business." Sulzer had refused, sticking, belatedly in life, to his principles.

Frances unsuccessfully tried to comfort Frawley. He let out a long sigh.

"Every man's got a mother, you know," he moaned.[11]

At first, Frances found the exchange amusing and repeated it to her friends. As Frances thought more about it, however, she realized he had trusted her with secrets because she was a woman. He had granted her insider status. She learned from the brief exchange that the way men were able to accept women in politics was to associate them with motherhood.

"They know and respect their mothers—ninety-nine percent of them do," she explained.

She began to see that her gender, a liability in many ways, could actually be an asset. To accentuate this opportunity to gain influence, she began to dress and comport herself in a way that reminded men of their mothers, rather than doing what women usually like to do, which is making themselves more physically attractive to men. She even kept notes on her exchanges with men, including revealing letters that she found humorous, and placed them in a red envelope that she kept with her. She called these observations "Notes on the Male Mind."

The transition to the somber black dress, the pearls, the matronly demeanor were subtly picked up in the press reports. Before that summer, the media had characterized her as perky, pretty, or even dimpled. Her friends had called her fun-loving and praised her kite-flying; her students at Ferry Hall had thought she was fashionable. Now she looked and dressed like a sedate middle-aged mother. Thanks to the new look, some reporters called her Mother Perkins, a nickname she hated, or even worse, Ma Perkins, which she despised. But it was indeed the persona she had chosen to adopt—at least in public.

She was thirty-three years old.

⫸ ———————— ⫷

Teddy Roosevelt
and Frances Perkins

At the same time, another chain of events originating in Albany would have equally profound effects on Frances Perkins's life.

It started on a day in June 1911, during the summer when Frances was working on the fifty-four-hour bill. A plump, bespectacled man had traveled to Albany and stood on the platform of the city's marble-clad Union Station. He was progressive Republican John Adams Kingsbury, and he was waiting expectantly for the event he would later call his life's "greatest moment."

Kingsbury had been a leader in galvanizing community activists after the Triangle fire. As the embers from the fire grew cold and the dead were being transported to a makeshift morgue, Frances and other social workers had gathered at the United Charities Building, where Kingsbury was managing director of the Association for Improving the Condition of the Poor. It was a mournful moment, but Kingsbury shared some good news: His organization's patron, real estate magnate R. Fulton Cutting, had pledged $10,000 to launch an effort to eradicate industrial fires. Kingsbury and the others enthusiastically created a new organization called the Committee on Safety to guide the effort.

The reformers believed the memory of the dreadful fire would inspire a groundswell of support for workplace safety measures. But the human mind often causes horrible sights to be quickly forgotten, and within three months the committee feared its momentum was disappearing. They decided they needed a leader who could command attention: former president Theodore Roosevelt. Kingsbury, a great Roosevelt admirer, was selected to woo him.

Roosevelt was an elusive quarry. The exuberant former Rough Rider, builder of the Panama Canal, and winner of the Nobel Peace Prize for ending the Russo-Japanese War, was a larger-than-life national figure.

He had been elected vice president but then served eight years as president, taking over in 1901 after President William McKinley's assassination and winning election on his own in 1904. He voluntarily stepped down in 1909, passing the reins to his friend and fellow Republican William Howard Taft. The gesture added greatly to Roosevelt's prestige and influence.

But by 1911, Taft had grown more conservative as Roosevelt became more liberal. Roosevelt was concerned about economic disparities in a country in which, by this time, 2 percent of the population controlled 60 percent of the wealth. He worried about the future of egalitarian democracy and began supporting progressive causes and settlement houses as a way to bridge the gap between the social classes. Kingsbury, along with Jane Addams and Florence Kelley, saw Roosevelt as a recruit who could make progressivism palatable to both the masses and the elite.

From the train platform, Kingsbury watched for the arrival of the 20th Century Limited, a luxury express that ran from Chicago to New York City. He had learned that Roosevelt would be on board and was determined to intercept the former president before supporters in New York mobbed him. Kingsbury intended to make his pitch in private, and he viewed a train car as the place most likely to provide a captive audience. Helped by a few civic-minded executives at the New York Central Railway, Kingsbury made arrangements for the train to make an unscheduled stop in Albany, where he would clamber aboard. Now, as the train slowed into the station, Kingsbury moved confidently toward the steps.

A barrel-chested and mustachioed man bounded off the train onto the platform, and Kingsbury immediately identified him as Roosevelt. The two men climbed aboard. Kingsbury's initial nervousness dissipated when Roosevelt walked toward him, hand outstretched. Kingsbury was startled that Roosevelt seemed to recognize him, since they had never met, but Roosevelt had been told to be watching for Kingsbury and he was already aware of the man's mission.

"Delighted to see you, Mr. Kingsbury! Delighted!" the former president boomed. ". . . I'm very anxious to learn from you the details of that tragic Triangle Fire, and to learn about the plans of the Committee on Safety!" [1]

Roosevelt grabbed Kingsbury by the hand, escorted him to a seat next to him, and offered his full attention. Thrilled to be in Roosevelt's company, Kingsbury promptly forgot his mission. Basking in the leader's glow, he soon found himself recounting at length his life's history and his thoughts on education. Roosevelt listened with sincere interest.

Nearing Yonkers, Kingsbury suddenly realized that he had wasted much of his time talking about himself instead of selling Roosevelt on the project at hand. Quickly, he sketched in details of the Triangle blaze and asked Roosevelt to improve the effort's success by chairing the Committee on Safety. Kingsbury saw that Roosevelt already knew much about the project—and his hopes soared.

"Mr. Kingsbury," Roosevelt told him, "I am going to help you. You can tell your committee that I am back of them, that I will support them and their program."

But Kingsbury's euphoria faded as Roosevelt continued. Overwhelmed with requests for committee participation, Roosevelt had decided to take none. But he promised to tell his protégé Henry L. Stimson, a New York lawyer and recent unsuccessful Republican candidate for governor, to take the chairmanship and serve in his stead. He recommended real estate investor Henry Morgenthau Sr. to be the group's treasurer and said Kingsbury should be secretary.

And for executive director?

"Frances Perkins," Roosevelt said, slapping Kingsbury on the knee, the man later recalled. With that lineup, he told him, "you can't fail."

By the time the train crossed the Harlem River, it was done. Still in her early thirties, Frances had been selected by Teddy Roosevelt to run one of the nation's most prominent new reform organizations. She would be charged with improving working conditions, cleaning up unsanitary workplaces, and creating new fire safety standards in the face of widespread employer intransigence and courts that routinely sided with businesses.

Roosevelt's selection of Frances for the post represented yet another of the surprising coincidences that marked her life at every turn. How would a former president have been personally acquainted with a young newcomer to New York City? Frances had paved the way by corresponding with Roosevelt, having approached him to ask for help for the National Consumers League. At that time he had said no, but had left the door open for future requests. No doubt he had also heard good things about Frances from Jane Addams, a longtime Republican whose father had been a close friend of Abraham Lincoln, as well as from Florence Kelley, whose father had served for twenty-nine years as a Republican congressman from Pennsylvania. Both women had strongly endorsed Frances for the safety committee's leadership.

Undoubtedly he also felt a certain camaraderie with her. In addition to the recommendations she received from Addams and Kelley, Frances had qualities that Roosevelt would have recognized. She shared the intense vitality that animated the Roosevelt family, the same intrinsic optimism, the same self-confidence bolstered by conviction.

But while Roosevelt considered hiring Frances a "can't lose" proposition, Frances was less certain it was a winning formula for her own life. She consulted her old Wharton friend Scott Nearing, who urged her to take the position but to be careful not to drive herself to exhaustion, as he knew she was wont to do.[2]

Even forewarned, however, Frances accepted the job and plunged into action with her typical boundless energy. She was formally named executive secretary in June 1912, soon after the fifty-four-hour bill was signed into law.

In fact, characteristically, she was already set on the task before she took the job. In the months after the fire, from her league post, she issued reports that highlighted workplace dangers and made sure they were publicized. She orchestrated events that would provide news stories on the issues and wrote frequent letters to the editor to the *New York Times* and the *Sun* and other newspapers, reminding people of fire hazards.

Around this time, H. F. J. Porter came to see her. An elderly man, wearing spectacles and sporting a Vandyke beard, meticulously dressed in striped trousers and morning coat, Porter was a fire engineer. He'd long been an ardent advocate of improving fire-safety standards, but he had been unsuccessful in drawing attention to the problem.

"The Consumers League is the only organization that has said anything but you haven't said much," Porter sniped at her. Frances said she had made statements as strongly as she could, given what she knew about the problem. She had publicly described hundreds of buildings at risk. There are not hundreds, he said, but thousands.[3]

Now Porter joined her team as a volunteer, teaching Frances about fire-safety hazards. He gave her the first of many lessons about building construction, fire escapes, insurance risks, and the need for sufficient exits and occupancy limitations. He insisted on fire drills to educate workers on escape routes. These were the strategies Frances began promoting in speeches she gave all over the city.

Keeping the Triangle horror alive was a challenge for Frances. In one speech, she highlighted the lingering effects of the fire, telling the story of a girl who had been released from the hospital after two years of treatment. Two women whose daughters had died in the fire had suffered mental collapses and became public charges. A man who escaped by climbing down cables had injured his back, and his family lived only on his wife's meager earnings.

Her efforts bore fruit almost immediately. Within a few months, she had scored notable successes, and the city had established a bureau of fire prevention.

The committee's biggest triumph was the creation of a completely new kind of government entity—the New York State Factory Investigating Commission—a legislative panel empowered to investigate questionable working conditions around the state, and to recommend legislative remedies. Frances had become a great believer in using fact-finding commissions to illuminate social problems and offer solutions. Al Smith, her Tammany friend, advised her to let the legislature create the investigating commission so lawmakers would support its findings. Behind the scenes, the non-governmental Committee on Safety, directed by Frances, pulled many of the strings.

Her Albany lobbying experience and well-developed social network proved invaluable. She had shored up her ties with Republican legislators, but more important, she had won the affection and respect of many Tammany Hall legislators. Governor Dix allowed Frances to pick many of the commission members. Smith had become Speaker of the House, and he was named vice-chairman. Some of his constituents had died in the Triangle fire, and he had become a fervent convert to the commission's work. Robert Wagner was now Senate Majority Leader, and he was named to the commission as well. Frances's Democratic support appeared assured, with both the Tammany Twins on board.

Five of the commission's nine members were lawmakers. The first yearly report artfully flattered and heaped praise on the state legislature. Under the heading "Importance of Investigation," the report said the state had "led the way" in the nation by investigating factory conditions. It spelled out a new civic role for state governments:

"The state not only possesses the power and the right, but it is charged with the sacred duty of seeing that the worker is properly safeguarded in case of fire; that he is protected from accidents caused by neglect or indifference; that proper precautions are taken to prevent poisoning by the materials and processes of his industry, and that he works under conditions conducive to good health, and not such as breed disease."

Four others rounded out the panel. Real estate entrepreneur Robert E. Dowling and bookseller Simon Brentano represented the business perspectives on the committee. The primary voice of labor was Samuel Gompers, president of the American Federation of Labor, a Jewish intellectual who had risen to a leadership role through his position with the cigar-maker's union. This union saw itself as the aristocracy of labor. Cigar-makers tended to be well educated and skillful at controlling their working conditions, even to the point of demanding that readers be engaged to recite great works of literature to them as they worked.

The other labor voice on the state commission was beautiful heiress Mary Dreier, the activist who had gone to jail in defense of the striking Shirtwaist workers. Frances thought Dreier was especially effective, opening her blue eyes dramatically wide in surprise when businessmen balked at making workplace changes that would be expensive to implement. They usually backpedaled furiously when they saw her displeasure.

The factory commission's hearings opened on October 14, 1911. In that year, public hearings were held in New York City, Buffalo, Rochester, Syracuse, and Troy. Two hundred twenty-two witnesses testified, including workers and employers, government officials and union leaders. Field inspectors visited some 1,836 businesses and reported on their findings. A grim picture of workplace life emerged.[4]

The first year's work explored the reasons for the Triangle fire—as a prelude to legislative action to remedy the problem.[5]

The fire's causes were simple: the factory had been overcrowded, making it hard for workers to exit, and they were trapped. Bins near the sewing machines were crammed with fabric scraps, and they caught fire because workmen were smoking pipes and cigars near the bins. Oil leaking from the machinery fueled the flames. Some doors were locked, blocking escape. The steep, narrow stairwells were hard to traverse. The building's one rickety fire escape collapsed. The elevators weren't big enough to handle the crowds working inside.[6]

In the first year, the legislature's Factory Investigating Commission submitted fifteen bills to the legislature, and eight became law. Smoking in factories was prohibited; regular fire drills became mandatory; automatic sprinklers were required in buildings taller than seven stories; and factories were required to be registered so inspectors could check them. These were all path-breaking advances.

Legislation requiring fire escapes, improved building exits, and occupancy limitations failed to win passage that year—but passed in the next. In that second year, twenty-six of the twenty-eight bills proposed by the commission were signed into law.[7]

Factories were required to provide washing facilities, including clean drinking water, and sanitary, ventilated restrooms. Child laborers needed a physician's certification that they were at least fourteen years old.

The legislature extended the commission year after year, with more hearings, testimony, and factory inspections. The commission eventually produced thirteen volumes of recommendations, reports, and testimony, running tens of thousands of pages.

Frances's name appears almost nowhere in the record of the proceedings, but her fingerprints are everywhere. Smith later called her the chief investigator, though she had no such title. Opponents called her the primary instigator. The Factory Commission first operated out of offices at 165 Broadway, rent-free quarters provided by the Committee on Safety, where Frances could oversee its daily activities, before it found permanent quarters conveniently across the street from her office. She stage-managed the hearings, orchestrating these events to telling effect.[8]

Most tellingly, the state commission's initial focus during its first year exactly mirrored Frances's set of priorities in her work at the National Consumers League: poor conditions in cellar bakeries, long hours and poor wages for women, child labor, and workplace fire hazards. The Factory Investigating Commission had the same four main focus areas, and Frances's research was the backbone of its investigations.

The commission usually met on weekends to discuss the week's hearings and to decide on legislative proposals. They came to favor simple, general statutory standards in order to permit flexibility in enforcement. When more specificity was needed, Frances and Bernard Shientag, a young lawyer, would often deliberate over the recommendations—for example, the width of a doorway exit. When they could not agree on the best dimension, they would split the difference, setting the standard as a fifty-six-inch doorway, essentially inventing this kind of workplace legislation as they went along.[9]

Meanwhile, the fire code they created made New York City the national model for hazard reduction in office buildings. Frances emerged as a national expert on fire prevention. On May 13, 1913, two years after the safety committee's creation and a year after she took its helm, Frances gave the keynote address at the National Fire Prevention Association's annual meeting in New York City. She described the Triangle fire's lasting impact on the victims and enumerated the laws passed in response: smoking had been banned in factories; flammable rubbish must be removed daily; factory occupancy was limited; regular fire drills were required; builder owners were given incentives to install automatic sprinklers.

She called on conference participants to go home and lead similar efforts. "We must work together with this idea in mind, that it is human life and happiness which we are trying to save, and that this is the most important thing, the most valuable social and spiritual asset in any community."[10]

Frances's stirring and inspirational message received a standing ovation from the crowd, and one month later the association's leaders formulated the life-safety code that was embraced not only nationally but also globally.

But by 1915, reform enthusiasm was definitely fading, and business people had become more adept at blocking the commission. The United Real Estate Owners, the commission's strongest adversaries, leased space in the building occupied by the factory commission and told its members they could use the space free for their own purposes, to make their opposition more visible. One new commissioner, Laurence M. D. McGuire, vehemently opposed the commission's published findings, saying they would hamper business if enacted. He singled Frances out for criticism, calling her a "professional agitator."

The other commissioners defended Frances, but the handwriting was on the wall. After a spectacularly successful four-year stint, the Factory Investigating Commission had run its course. Frances would later credit the informal group of reformers as an example of intelligent people coming together to make the system work. She said just fifty people could make a difference. She would act on this theory again and again, each time planting herself in the middle of the circle of fifty.[11]

Chapter 7

A Good Match

*M*ost women recall in detail how they met their future husbands, a moment endowed with a sense of destiny, even predestination. Oddly, however, Frances never told anyone, not even their daughter, how she met Paul Caldwell Wilson. Sometimes she said she couldn't recall. Later, it seemed she didn't want to remember.[1]

They came together in New York City sometime around 1910, when Frances was thirty. Paul was four years older, urbane, intelligent, and well-educated, his face framed by a shock of thick, dark hair. His father, a Chicago merchant, had left him with a comfortable inheritance. He carried himself proudly, dressed in well-tailored suits, with the ease of someone used to the best. At a government meeting held on a hot summer day in New York City, when the more conservative men sweltered in their dark, somber jackets, he looked debonair in a beige summer suit. He was an athlete who excelled on the tennis court and an intellect who had mastered the game of bridge.

They must have met through mutual acquaintances, as their lives and interests converged in dozens of ways. The friendship developed slowly, through outings with friends—picnics, hikes, and beach excursions—and grew deeper through correspondence with each other when they traveled separately out of town. And as the affection grew into love, it seemed a more and more fitting match for two warm-hearted young people both eager to start a family.

Born on December 15, 1876, Paul was the second of four boys in a family tended by three live-in servants. He spent his childhood at his family's large home at 2922 Prairie Avenue, the most fashionable street in Chicago's wealthiest district, a boulevard often called Palace Avenue. Second Empire–style mansions with mansard roofs and conservatories alternated with Victorian mansions and French chateaus, all surrounded by ample lawns and tended by battalions of servants. The favored people who lived there mimicked the lifestyles of the European upper classes.[2]

The Wilsons' neighbors included railroad car magnate George Pullman and retailer Marshall Field, a business partner of Wilson's father. Newly wealthy, with money to spare, families on Palace Avenue developed an exquisitely formal pattern of relationships and activities. Wilson's father belonged to the prestigious Union Club; his mother entertained at home on Friday afternoons. Polite etiquette was second nature to Paul and his family, even more than it was to Frances, whose family was middle class.

As a young man, Wilson attended a famous progressive school in Chicago, the Armour Institute, funded by meatpacking magnate Philip Danforth Armour, whose family had worshiped with Frances in Lake Forest when she lived there. The school's goal was to meld students of all backgrounds and prepare them to lead in a changing industrial society. The school's 1893 creation had marked a milestone in Chicago's intellectual development, helping to establish the city as an international center of learning. Among the school's many claims to fame: It housed the country's only specialized course in fire protection engineering.[3]

After graduating, Paul enrolled in Dartmouth College and joined the Sigma Chi fraternity, but he transferred later to the University of Chicago, graduating in 1902 at age twenty-six. After studying political science, and sociology, Paul went to work with his friend Henry Bruere at the International Harvester Company, a farm-equipment company founded by Cyrus McCormick, the inventor of the popular reaper.[4]

The McCormick family wanted to promote good working conditions at International Harvester, where employees benefited from an inexpensive on-site restaurant and various welfare programs. The family saw it as a way to improve labor-management relations and boost productivity. In 1905, around the time Frances moved to Chicago, both Paul and Bruere had left the business world to join the political reform movement. Paul followed his friend to New York City and soon worked with him at the Bureau of Municipal Research, a nonprofit organization that used modern investigative techniques to expose how government misspent money. The bureau devised a model government budget and introduced line-item authorization for expenditures, to allow taxpayers to better understand where money was spent. Shining light on Tammany Hall corruption, the bureau became "the spearhead of municipal reform not only in New York City but throughout the United States."[5]

The bureau's work garnered national attention. It expanded to fifty cities. Paul, a financial statistician, played a key role in detecting and exposing fiscal mismanagement.

In surprising ways, Paul's life overlapped with Frances's. Although they hadn't known each other in Chicago, they had friends in common in New York City. A major benefactor of the Bureau of Municipal Research was the Harriman family, whose daughter, Mary, shared other interests with Frances. Another philanthropist backing the municipal research effort was Cutting, who also funded the Committee on Safety, on which Frances served as executive secretary.

Paul was enormously attractive to Frances. Nevertheless it took some time for him to win her heart. He wooed her gently and persistently over several years, and a well-mannered friendship based on shared values evolved into a passionate love affair. In December 1910, he signed his letters to her "Yours with Sincere Regard." By August 1911, he closed with "As Ever Yours," and by May 1913, he addressed her as "darling" and wrote longingly of his desire to "caress your dear face, to kiss your beloved lips."[6]

When they were apart they exchanged loving letters almost daily. Paul's were leavened with his wry wit: In one he joked that Frances's illegible, chicken-scrawl handwriting could some day expose her to "dire consequences" if a recipient were unable to decipher a few essential words. She wrote earnestly of her political deliberations, as she wondered whether to switch from the Socialist Party to the new progressive movement being headed by Teddy Roosevelt. Paul gave her work advice. When he went to Europe with friends in 1912, he made careful note of his nautical position so she could figure out where he was at sea each day.

"Before you came into my life," she wrote to Paul, "it was a lonesome place—cold and raw and trembling except on the outside . . . You stormed into my heart somehow and I could never let you go. . . ."[7]

Paul first appears in Frances's recorded recollections in the summer of 1912. Fresh with the success of the fifty-four-hour bill, she accompanied him by train, along with his friend Henry Bruère, to the Democratic National Convention in Baltimore. Though women couldn't vote, Frances had grown keenly interested in the political process and wanted to observe.

Attending the convention was a fateful decision, only partly because of Paul's presence. It also drew Frances closer to the Democrats at a time when she was captivated by the spell of Teddy Roosevelt, who was running for president as a Bull Moose Republican.

In the summer of 1913, following long family custom, Frances traveled to Maine. While away, she wrote to Paul daily, sometimes twice a day, even sending letters by special delivery. "To think I write you like this! I am a different woman. I am indeed," she wrote in one letter.

He responded with equal ardor: "I feel you and your perfect love have power to make me see things anew. . . . I want, I need to tell you everything. I must."[8]

Paul came to visit Frances at her family's home that summer, and they apparently scandalized her parents and family by kissing good-bye at the train station. Paul was apologetic about any embarrassment that it might have caused her. But her family's puritanical reaction only exacerbated the irritation Frances was already feeling toward them. Frances later wrote Paul that she loved going home to Maine but found aspects of her mother's behavior "horrid and disagreeable," particularly her complaints about the poor quality of the food or bad service from the household help.

"They do get on my nerves," she wrote him.[9]

Frances and Paul were clearly headed for marriage when something happened that propelled things along more quickly. At thirty-seven, although Paul was still working as an investigator at a nonprofit agency, he was closely tied to John Purroy Mitchel, who was running for mayor with a claim that he would clean up Tammany Hall. Mitchel's prospects were uncertain. The popular incumbent mayor, William J. Gaynor, had decided to seek reelection. If Mitchel won in November, Paul would likely join his administration and prosper, but it seemed far more likely that Gaynor would win.

Mayor Gaynor took a vacation to rest up for the campaign. While on a sea voyage, he died, in early September.[10] With Gaynor's death, the path cleared for Mitchel's mayoral drive, and Paul's own future seemed even brighter. He was about to face a busy campaign season, and he and Frances arranged a hurried wedding.

Both of them wrote their parents to say they were getting married, but they did not give either family time to make plans or even ask them to attend. Frances's father, who by now had become accustomed to being held at some distance from her, wrote to her saying he was a "little surprised" by the haste but supported her decision nonetheless.

"I would have liked to have had you married at home and had a wedding but if you thought it better to have it as you did I suppose it is all right and I will give my consent and my warmest blessing. . . ."[11]

Paul wrote an affectionate letter to his mother in Chicago, and Frances added a note of her own: "I'm so glad you don't mind me marrying Paul. I'll be good to him, you know. He is a dear and I thank you for all that you have given me in giving him life and health and character and sweetness. I'll not forget."[12]

Frances Perkins and Paul Wilson were married in the chantry of Grace Church at 10th Street and Broadway. They announced the event with a simple white card: Paul C. Wilson and Frances Perkins announce their marriage, September 26, 1913, New York City.

Frances normally loved ceremony, and over the years she took great pains to plan the major landmarks of her life so they unfolded in proper accordance with custom. But when she married Paul, she seemed like a woman in a rush. They did not invite their friends; there was no luncheon or tea with toasts to the bride and groom. Witnesses were people pulled from the street.

There seemed to be no good reason for their haste, although the lease on Paul's apartment was expiring. They may have needed to give social legitimacy to a more nontraditional relationship, especially if they expected Paul would soon find himself in the political limelight. Frances was also eager to move quickly to create an appropriate home base to help advance her husband's aspirations.

But much more than convenience was at work. They both embarked on the marriage longing for a partnership with true emotional intimacy, seeking a soulmate. Frances predicted a joyful future "as we summon the courage to really know each other and as with spiritual daring we admit each other to the inner places."[13]

Marriage, however, is always uncharted territory, and the roles of men and women were in a particular state of flux at the time. As the Victorian era ended, feminist thought took hold. Instead of relying on the husband as sole breadwinner, women pondered whether they could be both married and free to pursue their own careers and personal development.

Frances shared these conflicted emotions with Paul. One side of her was the romantic who wrote love stories with happy endings, who wanted love and hoped to have children. The other side had been torn over whether to marry at all. At thirty-three, she was no longer a girl. While other girls had fallen passionately in love with someone they had met in their late teens or early twenties, Frances had enjoyed her independence.

Her friends reacted to her marriage with either dismay or hearty congratulations. Pauline Goldmark, an unmarried woman who had worked with her on the fifty-four-hour bill, saw Frances's marriage as a defection from the social work movement. Pauline and her sister, Josephine, had busy activist careers; their equally intelligent sister Alice, married to a Boston lawyer named Louis Brandeis, had largely retreated from public view.

Yet Sinclair Lewis, the disappointed suitor, put on a good face and wrote congratulating her. "Dear Old France . . . I am very happy to hear of your marriage . . . And, darn it again, I wish I were not so broke—I'd send you a silver tea set, I would."[14]

Kingsbury, her sponsor on the Committee on Safety, wrote to them with jubilation.[15] And Florence Kelley, who had herself known love in her youth, offered the young couple the use of her cliff-side cottage in Maine, surrounded by acres of blueberry bushes with a view of the sea, for an impromptu honeymoon.

Frances sought to launch her life with Paul as a modern relationship. In a handwritten note, Frances described how a forward-thinking marriage should begin, writing in the awkward third-person sentence construction she often used when she was talking about herself and her family:

"Two modern young people who became engaged and are very modern about it. Going to try to win a medal from Mrs. [Charlotte Perkins] Gilman as a prize marriage. Frankly want children and plan for it. Deliberately separate for two months so that they may get into splendid physical and nervous condition. Both give up smoking and drinking entirely for the time in order that they may be in the best condition to give next generation a fair start. Both serious and frank about it. They come back, are married by civil marriage and go off to the woods together."[16]

Paul and Frances planned to take a proper post-nuptial holiday, a six-month honeymoon trip to Europe the summer after the mayoral election, starting with a cruise across the Atlantic. But that was not to happen. The Archduke Franz Ferdinand was assassinated in Sarajevo, launching the chain of events that catapulted Europe, and then the United States, toward the Great War.[17]

Chapter 8

MARRIED LIFE

$\mathcal{A}$fter her wedding, Frances enjoyed a prosperous life in New York City quite different from anything she had known before. Just three years earlier, she had survived hand-to-mouth living in settlement houses. With Paul, she moved into a distinguished red brick townhouse at 121 Washington Place near Washington Square, just down the street from the fine home where she had been on the day of the Triangle fire. The couple hired a German husband-and-wife team to tend the household, leaving them free to focus on work and entertaining.

It was just about perfect: Frances's husband was handsome, rich, and deeply in love with her. Frances's job with the Committee on Safety was professionally rewarding as she racked up legislative victories and made progress toward improving working conditions, saving lives in the process.

Paul's career blossomed as well. Mitchel's campaign struck a chord with voters, and he was elected mayor in November 1913 by a large plurality. Youthful and charismatic, Mitchel was widely believed to be on an upward trajectory, perhaps even toward the presidency. He loaded his administration with friends from the Bureau of Municipal Affairs. Bruere, Paul's good friend, took the post of chamberlain, a position similar to chief of staff, while Paul became one of Mitchel's personal secretaries, overseeing budgetary affairs, and won a substantial pay raise.

The work of Frances and Paul converged, as they brought together people from their two worlds and saw friendships and alliances develop. Frances practically crowed as she described this swirl of activity in a Mount Holyoke alumnae newsletter: "Lots of fun! And sometimes gives one quite a sense of being on the switchboard of contemporary history."

The Wilsons also maintained a beach house, which she described as a "shack in the country on the edge of Long Island Sound." She went every weekend, summer and winter, to relax and unwind, walk and swim.[1]

Early on in her marriage, she decided to keep her own name. Although she used Mrs. Paul C. Wilson in private and on her passport, professionally Frances kept her last name for various reasons, citing different motives at different times. On one level, she said, she'd been "touched by feminist ideas" and was interested in preserving her sense of identity. More pragmatically, she also had seen that in the career world, single women were viewed more favorably than married women. She explained once:

"Mrs. is understood to be awfully occupied in the house and children: 'Your husband's interests must come first.' It's one of the reasons why women aren't hired to do very, very important jobs for which they are thoroughly qualified."[2]

Frances was becoming famous in her own right, and giving up her name would have caused her to lose valuable name recognition. Her high-visibility roles in the Triangle fire safety debate and with the Committee on Safety and the Factory Investigating Commission had made her a minor celebrity in labor circles. She felt her name stood as a "great asset" to her.

Paul agreed—perhaps because there were diplomatic reasons for her to play down her married name. Paul wanted to advance his political career, and some of his wife's activities, such as her support for the birth-control movement, might have proven to be a political liability. Frances was also promoting the dance school run by Isadora Duncan, the ethereal, bisexual performer whose work was a precursor to modern dance, combining gymnastics with free-flowing movements inspired by classical Greek art. Duncan scandalized polite society by dancing seminude, with gauzy costumes, her hair loose and feet bare. She also thumbed her nose at convention by bearing illegitimate children to two different men, refusing to marry either of them because she wanted her freedom. This was hardly the type of association that one would expect of a political wife in 1913.[3]

But there was another reason to downplay their marriage that might have had the most impact. With Paul now a key aide to Mitchel, who had campaigned on an anti-Tammany platform, Frances's connections to Tammany politicians might have proved a political embarrassment.

Tammany Hall sachems despised Mitchel, referring to him as

"Young Torquemada," after the Dominican priest who presided over the Spanish Inquisition, torturing and burning at the stake people he accused of being heretics and nonbelievers.[4]

Keeping her name, however, spurred resentment and criticism from social conservatives. Many considered it illegal, and others believed it should be. It was so rare for a married woman to cling to her maiden name that it was newsworthy. Soon after Frances married, a Hearst newspaper reporter and photographer showed up at their front door eager to write the "full story of why" she was keeping her name. From her earlier experiences at the settlement houses, Frances knew that reporters would usually trivialize issues and uphold the conventions of the day. Moreover, the Hearst papers had been hostile to the Mitchel administration and its stories frequently ridiculed city officials. So Frances treated him as she would many other reporters during her career; she told a bald-faced lie. Frances insisted that he had made the trip for nothing, since of course she was taking her husband's name.[5]

⚜

*M*itchel's inauguration as mayor on January 1, 1914, brought huge crowds of spectators to the steps of City Hall. In a portent of things to come, however, Mitchel became ill with a severe headache during the ceremony and had to cut short his reception. Two thousand people waiting to shake his hand were turned away because he was too sick to stand.[6]

During the following months, as Frances and Paul built their lives around Mitchel's administration, Mitchel's performance as New York's highly visible mayor drew national attention. Frances placed herself squarely in the inner circle. She made her home, particularly a little separate detached building across the garden from the house, the informal gathering place for the men running the city. Even before Mitchel took office, Frances participated in their strategy sessions. The former upstart and critic of the social order now found herself learning important lessons about governing. It was her first tutorial in running a political bureaucracy.

Good-government reformers in New York City and across the country followed with excitement. Many cast Mitchel as a warrior fighting the forces of evil. "He was acute, incisive, masterful," wrote one columnist who had observed Mitchel's performance in a New York City corruption hearing.[7]

On a personal level, the early years of the Mitchel administration were good for Frances and Paul as well. They traveled to Europe several times, sometimes with heiress Mary Harriman and her husband, sculptor Charles Cary Rumsey. Frances's friendship with the Astors, both in the United States and England, also placed the couple within the most elite social networks on both continents.

Yet back at home, Frances and Paul began to realize that the administration's foundation was shaky. Mitchel was brilliant, but he was also emotional and "too intense." Some missteps even caused President Woodrow Wilson to view Mitchel as a rival rather than an ally. Instead of guiding the rising young star, the president distanced himself from the mayor and declined to assist him at pivotal moments.[8]

Mitchel's mercurial moods alienated people unnecessarily. In May 1914, for example, when Mitchel spoke to women's suffrage supporters at Carnegie Hall, the women expected a ringing endorsement from the progressive young mayor. Instead, Mitchel issued a prepared statement which left the women, including his own wife, gasping. Mitchel said he believed the women's right to vote would be attained when men decided it was time. "Until then, my experience does not lead me to believe that they will suffer materially for the lack of it," he said.[9]

The suffrage leaders struck back. Militant feminist Harriot Stanton Blatch denounced him: "The Women's Political Union is after him, and any ambition he may cherish of a future job as mayor or governor or the man higher up will be neatly derailed if women have their way."[10] Mitchel denied expressing opposition to women's suffrage and said he thought the women were misinterpreting him.

He tried to make amends. On October 23, 1916, he sat for over three hours in the bitter cold to watch a three-mile parade of suffrage supporters, some twenty-five thousand strong. It had been a foolish time to alienate potential voters. In 1917, when Frances was thirty-seven and Mitchel faced reelection, women in New York first won the right to vote in state elections. In 1920 women won the right to vote in national elections when the nineteenth amendment to the Constitution was ratified.[11]

His female constituents, however, were not the only ones in whom he stirred up resentment. Mitchel also alienated the average folk by hobnobbing with Manhattan socialites and business interests. As Mitchel's support eroded, he turned to jingoism. Vocally supporting the effort to draw the United States into the European war, he donned a uniform and put himself through military training.[12]

Frances learned much from watching the Mitchel administration unravel. She later said its biggest mistake was alienating the Catholic Church by attacking charity orphanages, which for centuries had been a major provider, sometimes the only provider, of care to the destitute. The city's investigations had shown there were real health and safety problems in those establishments, but the failings were pointed out in a heavy-handed way that alienated the faithful and sometimes prevented meaningful reforms.

At some point the disintegration of the Mitchel administration began to cast a pall over Frances and Paul's household. As the mayor's critics became more vocal, his supporters went on the defensive. Insiders like Paul were discouraged. He began complaining of recurring headaches.

And sometime around 1915, Paul appears to have had an extramarital affair. Frances mentioned it only once, in a letter she wrote to Paul several years later. The woman's name was Rose. Though short-lived, the affair was known within their social circle, and Frances worried that knowledge of it would spread. An oblique mention of the infidelity in the letter to Paul suggests that she forgave him but had not forgotten.

Other fissures were developing in the relationship as well. Frances had begun to sense that her self-esteem was eroding in the marriage. Although by 1915 Frances had begun shutting down the Committee on Safety because its effectiveness was ending, her efforts to bolster Paul's career started to overwhelm her daily life. Maintaining a well-appointed home, suitable for entertaining the mayor and his entourage around the clock, turned out to be a full-time occupation and not as satisfying as leading a reform movement.

She had set the same high standards in homemaking that she upheld in her work life. She insisted that her home be meticulously clean and well organized. She gave her German servants detailed instructions in their duties, requiring them to don clean aprons, caps, and collars before starting each day. Each morning, they were to brush off the front door and pillars, shine the brass, brush off the window rails, and water the trees. Then the breakfast table was to be set, the coffee service prepared, and fruit placed on the table. The servants were to knock on the couple's bedroom door at 7:45 a.m., delivering newspapers and the daily mail. The couple would come down to breakfast afterward. The rest of the day was equally scripted and task-filled.[13]

At some point it had all gotten to be too much. In a letter to Paul, sent from a weekend retreat in Cos Cob, Connecticut, Frances poured out her misery and suggested a separation.

It's like this, dear Paul, you and I have been daily companions and close depending friends for more than two years now. Two people don't share all the experiences, the pleasures, the disillusions, the simple little homely activities without making some personal adaptations, without ceding something of individuality for the sake of the compensating, rewarding comradeship. So gladly have I done this and generously for me the reward in quality in exchanges of service in courage about life seemed great. But being something of a fool as well as an easy going tender hearted woman, I've made some wretched blunders. It's been sweet and lovely—this friendship of ours—and I don't regret any of it but the fact remains that something has happened to me in these years, that I've become a different kind of person with a lesser degree of working efficiency and paler kind of spiritual efficiency.

So if you understand at all Paul, just let me go. I don't mean that I withdraw my friendship—the strength of the bond between us is too great to make that possible even if I wished it but I do mean that I can't play with you all the time and exclusively, that I can't have you in my house all the time on the terms of me belonging.

The letter ended with her asking for his forgiveness. It was clear that she did not want to hurt him. But she understood her own needs. "I can't become my own garden unwatered . . . What shall it profit a man if he gain the whole world and lose his own soul?"[14]

Frances clearly intended to leave her husband. Then she found out she was pregnant.

Chapter 9

MOTHERHOOD

With Frances's pregnancy, everything changed. A marriage on the verge of collapse suddenly improved. The couple had badly wanted children, and Frances, inspired by Louisa May Alcott's *Little Men,* ardently wished for a son, or better yet, a brood of sons.[1] With Paul securely employed, Frances had the freedom to consider how best to manage motherhood. Her concerns about disappearing within the marriage evaporated.

Frances, now thirty-five, suffered a miscarriage, but, always robustly healthy, she soon became pregnant again. Working from her bed to protect the baby's health, she finalized the last details of shutting down the Committee on Safety. She now had a more urgent personal reason for wanting to shed any great responsibility.

In May 1915, Frances grew ill. She developed pre-eclampsia, a severe and often fatal pregnancy-induced condition that causes sudden blood pressure spikes. Both mother and baby were at risk. Women who developed eclampsia often bled to death, died of convulsions, or developed toxemia. The infants are often born prematurely. As the baby's birth approached, Frances learned she would have to be hospitalized for a cesarean section.

In an era without antibiotics, giving birth at the hospital was frequently a prelude to death, since hospitals were breeding grounds for bacterial infections.

Before she left for the hospital, Frances braced for a bad outcome, spelling out to Paul her wishes as to how the baby should be raised if she were to die. "Try harder than you have ever tried anything in life to understand our baby as it grows up. You have so much to give a little one dear Paul, so—oh tenderness, and care, and understanding and the baby will need it all. Put Perkins somewhere in the baby's name and in remembrance eternal let there be sweet talk about me sometimes. Let the baby know all the things that are good and strong about me and draw a merciful veil on my weaknesses so I shall still give him something if it's only ideals."[2]

She had the cesarean section and survived toxemia. The baby, a boy, died stillborn. Paul and Frances were consumed with grief, suffering a sadness so deep the incident was never mentioned again.[3]

But the terrifying childbirth experience did not sour her on motherhood. Although the doctor advised her of the risks, Frances soon became pregnant for a third time, and on December 30, 1916, she gave birth to a baby daughter. They named her Susanna Perkins Wilson, after a maternal ancestor of Frances's named Susanna Winslow, wife of the second governor of the Plymouth colony. Little Susanna was perfect and beautiful, and her parents watched her grow and change with rapt attention.[4]

Despite her feminism, Frances viewed motherhood as a full-time occupation. She planned to retreat from the workforce but stay involved in charity work, as suited her schedule. In articles she wrote throughout her career, she described caring for children as all consuming. She urged women to seek work outside the home only if their salaries covered their expenses and if they could afford excellent child care. She noted that paid employees seldom performed child care as lovingly as a mother.

In the summer after Susanna's birth, while Paul stayed behind in New York City to work, Frances took the nine-month-old baby with her to the old homestead in Maine. Susanna could crawl in the meadow grass, and they could wade in the Damariscotta River. Family pictures chronicled each small advance in Susanna's development.

Paul missed them intensely and wrote to Frances: "In my arms, in my eyes, seeing I cannot do anything so well without you . . . I adore you, I admire you and rely upon you greatly. Your lover, Paul."[5]

But though her marriage had mended and she loved her daughter, Frances again struggled to feel content in domestic life. She began looking for meaningful voluntary, part-time pursuits. At the Women's City Club, where she was a director, she took up the club's appeal for her to lead a political education project for newly enfranchised women voters. Although promising in principle, the project taught Frances the hazards of relying on dilettantes. The women were not seriously committed to the effort. Few wanted to attend the dry and tedious committee meetings. The group disbanded.

Frances then adopted a cause much closer to her heart. She had been deeply affected by her brush with death and by the loss of her infant son. In the spring of 1918, the obstetricians Ralph Lobenstein and J. Clifton Edgar approached her to head a new effort that would provide maternal and infant care to poor women. More women and babies died in the United States than in any other developed nation. New York City in particular had become one of the world's most dangerous cities in which to give birth, especially for immigrants with poor obstetrical care, repeated pregnancies, poverty, and malnourishment.

Frances accepted the challenge, launching what she later called her single "most successful piece of social work."[6] She spearheaded a pioneering organization that had the goal of operating a network of free ob-gyn and well-baby centers across the city.

Frances's alliances again provided crucial support for her work. The Women's City Club of New York decided it would help sponsor the project. Its president was Margaret Poole, one of Frances's closest lifelong friends.[7]

In April 1918, Frances became executive secretary of the new group, named the Maternity Center Association. She organized a board of directors, recruiting from among Dr. Lobenstein's elite private patients, many of whom were young mothers themselves. Among the wealthy young matrons backing and supporting the cause were Mrs. Eugene Meyer, Mrs. Winthrop W. Aldrich, Mrs. John Breckinridge, and Mrs. S. R. Guggenheim. With their generous support, the group's first year's budget was $64,000, more than six times the amount initially available to the Committee on Safety.[8]

Two other women with future ties to Frances soon joined the organization's board. Mrs. Meredith Hare, who had a son about Susanna's age, served on the board with her in 1923 and the omnipresent Mary Harriman Rumsey, with whom Frances was growing increasingly close, joined Frances on the board in 1925.[9]

The board's first meeting was held at the palatial townhouse of Mrs. John S. Rogers, the former Catherine Dodge. Sitting amid soaring ceilings, ornate French Regency furniture, walls hung with European tapestries and rich oriental carpets, Frances and nine other people developed an obstetrics outreach plan for the city's poorest women.

Frances quickly made two important hires, nurses Anne Stevens and Hazel Corbin. Together they hired fifteen to twenty additional nurses, mostly young women returning from the war who needed jobs. They set to work. By the end of the year, the Maternity Center Association had provided care for 1,640 patients and made 3,666 home visits to help women care for newborns. Services were free, although the group accepted gifts of food, milk, or clothing to distribute to the indigent.

The association opened a handful of pilot clinics, including one at Hartley House and another at the Henry Street Nursing Association. Other groups joined the effort, including the Council of Jewish Women, the American Red Cross, the Young Women's Christian Association, and the Urban League, offering clinic space that allowed the group to operate from lower Manhattan to Harlem. By 1919, the Maternity Center Association employed twenty-six nurses operating in sixteen clinics. By 1920 they operated twenty-six clinics and employed thirty-four nurses. Frances Perkins guided the group's growth, recalled field nurse Hazel Corbin, one of the Maternity Center Association's first hires. She was a "very smart woman" whose work helped many families, Corbin said.[10]

Many women badly needed assistance. Each week, Corbin saw some three or four women die, usually from complications from cesarean sections. Most were unaware of complications they should watch for—signs that they were at risk for possibly fatal eclampsia, placenta previa, or toxemia. High-risk women needed to be sent to hospitals so their deliveries could be monitored. Others needed help with basics, such as obtaining hygienic delivery outfits for themselves and their newborns to reduce infections.

Maternity Center workers also sought to provide additional help to the new mothers. Settlement house volunteers visited homes of hospitalized mothers to keep things in order until the mothers returned. The association's funds went not only toward medical care but also for housekeeping support, so that mothers could recover from childbirth and care for their babies properly.

The program expanded. In 1921 the association cared for 8,211 pregnant women, five times as many as they had in 1918. And lives were saved. About 29 percent more babies survived than in areas of New York where similar services were not provided. The maternal death rate declined by 60 percent.

The association became a national training ground for public health nurses and medical students; it also taught midwifery skills to the nurses. The association did medical school outreach, educating doctors in birthing techniques and research. They filled a gap, since many medical schools gave students little obstetrics training. Soon the Maternity Center Association began attracting public health workers from around the globe, who went there to be trained.

Frances found the work soul-satisfying because it produced such immediate and visible results. Nurses that Frances had helped to train presented themselves at the homes of pregnant women, bearing gifts of food and friendship. They returned to the office at night with tales of what they had seen and heard while helping shepherd new lives into the world.

She loved it and remained on the group's board for two more decades as the organization continued to grow. Though the work fulfilled her, however, Frances left as manager after only a year. She was an unpaid volunteer in the position, and developments at home were making it clear to her that she could no longer work without pay.

Something had gone seriously wrong with Paul. In the 1910s, when the Brueres and Wilsons worked closely together, Paul was viewed as well-liked, successful, and vital to the Mitchel administration. But Mitchel's popularity had eroded. Catholics and feminists were irate at things he had said and done. His attempts to reduce government corruption had made him many enemies, and his good-government reform supporters turned out to be fair-weather friends. Wilson found himself a key member of a failing mayoral government. As Mitchel's fortunes declined, Wilson's spirits plummeted.

In the fall of 1917, after a bruising campaign, John Mitchel was trounced in the mayoral election. On January 1, 1918, Mitchel had handed over the insignia of office to a Tammany-backed mayor-elect and departed City Hall. Paul had officially resigned a day earlier.[11]

The defeat left the former mayor and many of his allies feeling crushed and betrayed. Mitchel himself enlisted in the military to fight in the European war, and while in training died under suspicious circumstances when he fell out of an airplane. Military officials said he had forgotten to put on his seat belt. Frances and Paul, however, believed he had killed himself because he was so disappointed by his political defeat.[12]

Paul, now in his early forties, seemed to have taken Mitchel's death harder than anyone. He couldn't pull himself together enough to search for new employment. His good friend Henry Breure wrote to Frances on March 28, 1918, asking why Paul wasn't following up on a job offer he had sent along. The prospective employer had told Breure he could take no "action on the payroll" if Paul did not write soon.[13]

When baby Susanna was about one year old, Paul's despondency began to appear more like mental illness. He spent money wildly and drank heavily. Emotionally volatile, he unwisely placed his inheritance in gold investments, which became valueless. Soon the money he had brought into the marriage was gone.[14]

Frances said later, in one of the few times she discussed his condition, "It was always up and down. He was sometimes depressed, sometimes excited."[15]

This was apparently not Paul's first episode of manic depression. According to his school records from Dartmouth College, he had started off on the right foot as a freshman and had faithfully attended classes, earning good marks. As a sophomore, however, his attendance deteriorated, and his grades plunged. He suffered a mysterious illness that was never discussed, although school records suggest that officials and classmates knew his problems were psychological. He later told his former classmates about his fragile state of health, saying that he had recovered from a nervous breakdown.[16] Paul had left Dartmouth, which he loved, because he had become too ill to continue. He graduated from the University of Chicago after returning home to recover.

Did Frances know he had been ill before? It seems unlikely she would have married him if she had. At that time, scientists were studying how genetic traits were manifested in successive generations. Frances's classroom notes indicate that she stressed these concepts in courses she taught on heredity and sociology. In a course she taught as a part-time instructor at Adelphi College in Garden City, New York, in 1911, her notes indicate that she planned to emphasize heredity because "we all know the relative importance of heredity and environment in social affairs."[17]

But Paul had been an ardent suitor of a woman clearly ready for marriage. Her family background may have subconsciously attracted her to a man who showed intense, even erratic, emotions. Her most famous ancestor, James Otis, was described by John Adams as having dramatic ups and downs in his temperament. Frances was also descended from the Winslow family, many of whose members showed similar manic-depressive tendencies. Some Winslows, including the American poet Robert Lowell, struggled with mental illness and had a fascination with insanity. As Paul's health deteriorated, Frances had to figure out how to handle him. He was quarrelsome and argumentative and at times denied his illness. Getting him to accept treatment was difficult, and Frances soon found herself caring for him. Living with mental illness is a heavy burden for a family, but even more difficult for a woman living alone with a man who is bigger and stronger than she is. Frances had to hire male attendants who could restrain him during his physical outbursts. The easy trust she once had in her husband disappeared and, as she did not believe in divorce, the marriage now made her feel doubly trapped.

"She was uneasy with him from then on," Susanna later reflected. "It was a battleground. They were continually shouting at each other. It wasn't a happy household."[18]

As Paul's mental state deteriorated, Frances became more intense and worried, her "hard black eyes" growing darker. Paul could still be charming, preparing a special coffee he brewed with eggshells and sporting a devil-may-care attitude, but he would grow agitated when asked to assume any responsibility. He couldn't abide any pressure, such as the obligation to look for a job. Frances sent him for treatment to exclusive and expensive sanitariums where he received state-of-the-art care, but he returned home sullen and brought chaos with him. He was in and out of hospitals, and his care was costly; Frances had to pay for it from her meager reserves. She "had to hustle to find things to do that would see us through that crisis," she recalled later. They gave up the house on Washington Place and took a smaller apartment, tended by one part-time servant.[19]

Frances was on her own, with no one to turn to for help. Paul's parents were dead and the one brother with whom he maintained regular contact, Harlan Wilson, lived in California and although sympathetic, could do little to help. Frances's family was equally unable to provide assistance. Her father, from whom she was somewhat estranged because of her liberal politics, had recently died, and she was not close to her mother. "While I could always hope that everything would be all right sometime, with every year that passed I realized that I mustn't take any chance on that. I must always be prepared to meet the situation."[20]

Frances's reward for her labors was her daughter Susanna. Frances would do the handwork on Susanna's lovely hand-smocked dresses, she would take pleasure in seeing her the center of attention at birthday parties held in her honor at Central Park, and she watched her daughter's diet carefully to make sure the child ate nothing that she might not like.

The little girl's blond hair cascaded down to her shoulders in curlicue tendrils. Each night Frances dressed her daughter's hair with loving attention, wrapping each lock in cotton strips to make the long curls popular in the era, with a story told about each lock. This one was Wendy, this one was Peter Pan, this was Tinkerbell, and so on. Frances took joy in Susanna's emerging talents. The child was naturally gifted in art and loved to draw, and she was given the best in art supplies.

Frances had thought herself plain, but she had been given a wonderful consolation prize in having been granted such a beautiful daughter. She wanted her daughter to have all the opportunities she had missed. And so Frances, now the head of the household, set out to give Susanna what family friend Alison Bruere Carnahan called a perfect "fairy-tale life."[21]

Chapter 10

THE INDOMITABLE
AL SMITH

*A*nyone else might have been too busy to help a friend campaign for office, or too disheartened by the Mitchel debacle to want to do so, but Frances managed to find the time in 1918 to help Al Smith win the governorship of New York. She deftly avoided association with the failed Mitchel regime and quietly and persuasively campaigned to help build support for Smith among the upper-class reformers in the state, convincing them that Smith was somehow greater than the machine that had spawned him.

Smith had been in office only a few weeks when Frances heard speculation that she might benefit from his election. It was 1919, and Frances was volunteering another unpaid day at the Maternity Center Association when factory inspector Louis Havens burst into the office and confronted her.

"I want to be the first to congratulate you," Havens said.[1]

"For what?" Frances asked.

"Why, you're going to be a member of the Industrial Commission," he told her. Frances laughed at the preposterous notion. Appointed posts on the state Industrial Commission paid $8,000 a year, and there seemed no way that a woman would be named by the governor to one of the coveted jobs overseeing factory conditions. Females still could not vote in national elections, and hiring a woman for any top-flight job was risky.

Moreover, Frances, then thirty-eight, had made no friends on the state commission, criticizing its members in the strongest terms during her tenure at the Committee on Safety. She had likened commission members to murderers for allowing workplace casualties to repeatedly occur.

Over the next few weeks, Frances heard nothing more about the appointment and tried to forget about it. She had an ailing husband and a two-year-old to raise.

It wasn't, of course, out of the question that Smith would give her the job. Frances knew she had impressed Smith with her bravery in pushing for factory reforms. The two had worked well together on the state commission investigating the Triangle fire, and Frances's efforts on Smith's behalf had helped catapult him into the limelight, attracting professionals and social reformers and expanding Smith's base beyond Tammany Hall.

Frances had also introduced Smith to a person who would become a key aide to him, her friend Belle Moskowitz, who threw herself with zeal into Smith's campaign. Moskowitz was an organizational genius who brainstormed, wrote speeches, and coordinated matters big and small. She helped deliver female voters to Smith, a man who had once opposed women's suffrage but who now, with Moskowitz's guidance, recast himself as a powerful ally of women and children. Smith came to be seen as a candidate supported by Tammany Hall but not tarred by association with it.[2]

Frances heard more from Smith's office soon. On a Sunday morning when she was visiting Washington with Paul, the telephone rang. Smith supporters were on the line telling her that Smith wanted to speak to her as soon as possible. Frances traveled north by train and arrived in Albany at noon on Monday. She met Smith in a small office in the governor's chambers. Not exactly certain what Smith wanted, she had prepared some material on a child labor bill she thought he might want to discuss.

"We'll talk about that later," he said in his thick East Side accent. ". . . I was thinkin'. How would you like to be a member of the Industrial Commission of the State of New York?"[3]

Smith wanted her help. The Industrial Commission, he said, was in "terrible condition," and nobody knew better than Frances how to make it more effective. In addition, with women recently gaining the vote, Smith had decided to bring women into the state's political administration. Few had Frances's credentials and track record. Smith felt comfortable with Frances, having known her for a decade.

She hesitated. Smith probed to understand her reticence: Have you got anything on your conscience that would prevent you from being a public official? Frances said no. Did she fear her husband would object? Frances didn't think so. Smith said he believed the civic-minded Paul would permit her to take the position.

Frances told Smith she needed to consult with one person before accepting the post—her mentor Florence Kelley. Perhaps Kelley would consider social work more worthwhile than the grubby world of politics, she mused.

Smith chided her. "If you girls are going to get what you want through legislation, there better not be any separation between social workers and the government."

Frances took the train back to Manhattan and immediately sought out Kelley, catching her at Pennsylvania Station as she embarked on a trip. They had coffee, and Frances confided that Smith had offered the job.

"Glory be to God," said Kelley, bursting into tears. "You don't mean it. I never thought I would live to see the day when someone that we had trained and who knew industrial conditions, cared about women, cared to have things right, would have the chance to be an administrative officer!"[4]

Frances revealed the real reason for her reluctance. "Well, you know, Mrs. Kelley, there are going to be an awful lot of mistakes made. I'm going to make some of them. That's always true. There will be a lot of things that I know and you know ought to be done that I won't be able to do. Will I just get ruined? Will I get hit over the head by the reformers for that?"

"Not if you give it an honest try," she said.

The prospect of the new job bedazzled and terrified her. She would have the chance to enact long-sought reforms, but she would give up the camaraderie she shared with her fellow women-at-arms at the Maternity Center. It would be a lonely world, separated from female companionship, surrounded by the cigar-chomping, tobacco-spitting opportunists in Albany, men she knew would criticize her. She swallowed hard and accepted the position.

Within two days, precedent was made with Frances's appointment. The *New York Times* predicted the "certainty of a bitter fight against confirmation."[5] Members of the State Federation of Labor voiced opposition to her nomination, then publicly denied that they had opposed her. A New York City businessmen's organization, the 34th Street Association, and the state manufacturers' association also protested Frances as "too radical."[6]

Other critics objected to a woman assuming such a highly paid post, which would make her the top-paid woman in government, not just in New York, but probably in the United States.

Frances's friends rallied around her. Kingsbury organized a letter-writing campaign, and enthusiastic letters and telegrams flooded into the governor's office.[7]

Mary Harriman Rumsey also jumped on board the effort and got a number of New Yorkers, including the heads of the settlement houses, to write to Smith praising Frances and thanking him for naming her. It wasn't a hard sell; Frances was well known and respected among them, but Mary was an important financial patron to them and many people were eager to help out with a letter of endorsement.

Smith staunchly stuck by his candidate. On February 18, 1919, after thirteen Republicans joined the Democratic minority to support her, Frances was confirmed in the Senate on a 34 to 16 vote.[8]

Smith did not learn until after her confirmation that Frances was not a registered Democrat. Soon after her appointment, he summoned her to an early-morning meeting at the Biltmore Hotel. Frances told him she considered herself either an independent or a Democrat but had never chosen a party since she did not have the right to vote. He urged her to become a Democrat, telling her that having a party affiliation placed a person within a political family. She registered as a Democrat.

Now, at Smith's urging, Frances assumed a larger role in setting state policies. She proposed a far-reaching agenda for social, educational, and political change, and she was confident these reforms would help Smith politically. Moskowitz, in the meantime, had become Smith's most valued assistant. Frances, Belle, and Bernard Shientag began helping Smith design a government reorganization plan and expand services as New Yorkers recovered from World War I. It was Frances's second participation in running a government.

As women, Moskowitz and Frances stood out in the governor's inner circle. He invited them to a dinner at a Manhattan restaurant with about a dozen key supporters, all of them male. Looking around the table, the women were happy to see that he had included his wife and mother.

"There were to be ladies present at this meeting tonight, so I asked me wife and me mother to come," he told Frances.[9] Ever the Victorian, Frances appreciated his gentlemanly demeanor and care in protecting their reputations. Still, always one to make the most of every opportunity, she seized this chance to ingratiate herself with Smith's mother, who had been left a widow when Smith was thirteen. During dinner, Frances listened to his proud mother's tales about Smith's exploits and character. She told Frances that Smith had always been a remarkable child, reliable even as a young boy. Frances left the dinner with more insight into her new employer, and it solidified her loyalty to him.

Before the dinner was over, Moskowitz was named executive secretary of the Reconstruction Commission. This ambitious program was designed to help provide employment to able-bodied veterans and health care to disabled soldiers. The commission was charged with building hospitals where soldiers could be treated, revising the tax code to make it more equitable, and paying for the expenses by reorganizing state government so it could function less expensively.

The commission was filled with prominent New Yorkers who endorsed the effort, including Robert Moses, who became the commission's research director.[10]

Frances's admiration for Smith grew. She had always liked his directness, his ability to listen, and his willingness to fight for his convictions. Unlike other politicians, he didn't try to satisfy everyone by making glib promises he would not keep. When a bill she proposed had no chance of passing, he told her so—but he also counseled her on how to push ahead and turn around legislators' opinions.

Cocooned in Smith's good graces and surrounded by allies, Frances still was daunted by the challenge of joining the Industrial Commission. In some sense, Frances's role on the commission would be particularly stressful because she would be acting as the governor's mole. She and Smith had discussed naming a fact-finding group to investigate the commission and propose organizational changes. Shientag would serve as the reform group's counsel.

As her first day approached, Frances prepared herself for a difficult set of encounters. To bolster her nerve, she bought a new dress.

She decided to go in boldly. She started by calling on John Mitchell, the head of the commission. No one had informed her when to start work or where to go, so she asked Mitchell how she should go about getting sworn in. He sounded nonplussed. She told him she would be there at 9 a.m., and he agreed.

Ten years older than Frances, Mitchell was ailing but still handsome and articulate. In labor circles, he was a celebrity. At the age of thirteen, he had gone to work in coal mining, braving the long hours and the ever-present threat of death in deep underground passages. He had risen to become president of the United Mine Workers union. Under his leadership, the union expanded from 34,000 members to 300,000, and won higher wages and shorter working hours. In 1902 he had led a famous and successful strike by 147,000 anthracite coal miners in Pennsylvania that had attracted nationwide attention, causing President Theodore Roosevelt to create a special commission to study mining conditions in the state. Mitchell had become so revered in Scranton that each year residents celebrated a holiday in his name. Now, at forty-nine, Mitchell viewed his Industrial Commission post as a reward for his lifetime achievements.

When Frances arrived, she found Mitchell unprepared for her confirmation ceremony and uneasy at the prospect of working with a woman. She wanted a Bible to hold while she pledged allegiance to state government, and Mitchell wasn't sure where to find one. After a scramble, one was located, and Frances took the oath in Mitchell's office. She was promptly escorted to the office of the commissioner she was replacing and sat down at an empty desk with nothing to do. The secretary watched Frances fearfully. None of the other commissioners came to greet her.

Frances decided to take command of the situation. She called staff members whom she knew from her previous work and asked them about their jobs. She learned that the commission did little work, kept no regular calendar, and studiously avoided issues that might produce political heat. Before long, she had interviewed almost everyone on the staff, becoming thoroughly knowledgeable on department functions, procedures, and problems. She had quickly learned who was competent and who was not.

She introduced herself to the other commissioners, and most of them accepted her. But she could tell that Mitchell and one other man still harbored ill feelings about her. They were insulted she had once written a report that accused the commissioners of moral responsibility for the deaths of workers at a Brooklyn candy factory. At the time, Frances had even circulated a petition demanding that sitting commissioners be replaced—signing her name at the top of the list. To make peace, she apologized.[11]

Now working side by side with Mitchell, Frances made a point of visiting his office almost every day for advice and deferring to him before taking action. To her relief, he increasingly warmed to her, listened to her comments, and allowed her to assume more control of the commission's work.

In fact, Mitchell's grip on power was slipping. In many respects he was, in Frances's words, a "romantic type of figure," a beautiful speechmaker who swayed listeners to his views.[12] But repeated illnesses made him unpredictable. He sometimes failed to appear for long-scheduled events, disappointing his supporters. His credibility in the labor movement also suffered because he had developed close financial ties to business interests. Some questioned how he could have afforded his expensive home in New Rochelle.

The task force investigation began soon after Frances's arrival and lasted more than three months. "All the dirt was hauled right up in front," she said, allowing administrative reforms to be enacted quickly.[13]

As the changes went into effect, Frances virtually ran the commission and reinvented it. Instead of infrequent and lackadaisical meetings, department heads reported monthly about their projects. The commission began rotating factory inspectors from district to district to thwart the development of cozy relationships with businesses. The commissioners also standardized inspection procedures to prevent bias. They pressed workers' compensation officials, who had frequently favored the insurance companies, to improve payments for injuries.

When strikes broke out, Frances and other commissioners traveled to the sites by train and mediated grievances. One incident in particular resonated with Frances as the best example of the twentieth-century face of labor issues.

It occurred in Rome, a town in upstate New York that was undergoing economic and social transformation. Many of its longtime residents worked in factories that manufactured copper products. But as demand rose and production expanded, business owners turned to immigrant laborers, mostly southern Italians, who worked for lower pay. The town's population base changed, creating social tensions in a once-peaceful community. Some of the local factory owners built mansions, drank stronger spirits, and divorced their homegrown wives for women Frances described as a "little more blonde and a little more stylish."[14]

In June 1919, Rome's disaffected copper workers went out on strike, seeking an eight-hour workday and better pay. Their toughest opponent was James A. Spargo, a manufacturer of copper wire and bedsprings. Spargo was a muscular, rough, and aggressive man who drank heavily and lived, as Frances said, with "very loose habits." When striking workers confronted him with complaints, he refused to allow them into his office. When three insisted on entering, he kicked them down the stairs—literally.

Mayhem erupted. Angry workers milled ominously in the streets. Spargo's car was overturned. A man was shot. The local chamber of commerce president was pelted with stones. Some employers wanted the state militia called to quash what they viewed as an incipient rebellion.[15]

Frances took a train to Rome to investigate, then took a taxi to the center of the melee. Twenty men armed with rocks approached the car. Frances introduced herself as an industrial commissioner for New York who had come to investigate. She calmed them down but learned they had stockpiled dynamite and were planning to use it.

Next she met with the attorney for the employers. He had contacted Governor Smith to demand that the state police be dispatched, then had called the state police commander to tell him to expect a call to action. By the time Frances arrived, the state police were en route. A nightmare scenario was emerging: Pistol-packing state police faced off against enraged Sicilians armed with explosives.

She placed her own call to the governor, begging Smith to call off the police. Frances told him she believed she could quell the disturbance by holding hearings, as Teddy Roosevelt had done in the anthracite strike. She would bring the entire Industrial Commission to Rome to participate. Smith agreed to her plan and called back the police.

Frances met once again with the workers and promised to hold hearings into their allegations. Speaking in imperfect Italian, Frances asked them to get rid of the dynamite immediately. They agreed and delivered loads of explosives in suitcases, bags, even a baby carriage. The dynamite was dumped into a canal. Frances sighed with relief.

She needed to show immediate action, so she convinced a reluctant Mitchell and another commissioner to join her in Rome for a preliminary hearing. Full hearings were to begin a few days later, as soon as the other commissioners arrived.

"My plan of action was the usual trick," Frances said. "You meet the workers and you find out what their complaints are. You know what they are. You've been told. But you meet them so they will know you know what they are . . . This is a standard technique. Every mediator does this. It's the ABC. You listen to the employers and you listen to them equally sympathetically. They have their problems, too."[16]

The next step, she said, was to look for common ground and solutions. But the employers were not inclined to negotiate with workers who basically had no rights under the law. The mill owners jointly opposed settlement talks. The negotiations collapsed.

Then Frances found the leverage she needed. Spargo, the truculent man who had booted his workers down the stairs, had written an obscene letter to his employees, addressing them in scatological terms. Other employers knew about the letter, and though they disapproved of both its language and tone, said nothing.

Frances obtained a copy of the letter, hiding it in her handbag, and shared it with Mitchell. At a dramatic point in the hearings, with all of the employers in the room, Mitchell rose to read the vulgar letter aloud, saying it illustrated why feelings had become so inflamed in Rome. Appalled, one of the other employers quickly rose to condemn Spargo and drew applause from the crowd. The favorable response proved to be a breakthrough in convincing employers to resume talks.

Frances's instincts had saved the day. She realized that some employers were ashamed to be identified with Spargo. They also wanted peace with their workers. Soon the strike was settled, and workers returned to their jobs.

Governor Smith had been sweating over the events in Rome as well. The labor unions and the employers were both balking at the prospect of dealing with a woman and Smith's reliance on Frances put him under a good deal of pressure. But afterward, one of the leading officials of the Rome Brass and Copper Company said, "Do us a favor and ask the Governor where he found that woman."[17]

Pleased with her performance, Smith's confidence in her grew.

Frances got to know Mitchell better during the Rome hearings, and her affection for him deepened. During their days together in Rome, Mitchell told Frances about his childhood in the Protestant home of a skilled and responsible miner. His mother had prepared good, hot dinners and helped them bathe each night with water heated on the stove.

He explained to her how a miner learns the craft at his father's knee, developing the knack of safely extracting rock. His story touched her deeply.

Frances's relationship with a handsome man who lavished her with attention filled a void in her life. She was locked into marriage with a mentally ill man for whom she had lost respect; Mitchell and his wife were estranged. Later Frances referred to Mitchell as an "intimate friend"—one of the few times she ever used that term to describe another human being.[18] The relationship might have been a romantic one as well, particularly because of the time they had spent on the road together, staying in hotels in distant cities. They spent hours in close conversation, tête-à-tête, on train trips around the state. It is impossible to know what may have happened, but in later years, Frances grew expansive when she talked about Mitchell, in ways that were uncharacteristic to her, and it was apparent that she had been greatly influenced by him. He had been one of the most successful labor leaders in U.S. history, and his thoughts on labor-management relations made a big impression on Frances.

But events conspired to squelch the incipient relationship early. In September 1919, just a few months after the strike, Mitchell took ill and died of pneumonia.[19] His sudden death shocked Frances. The next surprise came when he was laid in state with a rosary in his hand at an ornate Roman Catholic Church on upper Broadway in Manhattan, which suggested he was Catholic, not Protestant as he had indicated to her. A third surprise was learning that Mitchell's estate was worth $347,000, a surprisingly high sum, including a large quantity of "valuable coal stocks," an unusual and scandalous holding for a man who had represented workers in their negotiations with coal-mine owners.

Whatever his shortcomings or deceptions may have been, Frances saw firsthand the reverence in which Mitchell was held when she attended a memorial service for him in Scranton. The city declared a day of mourning, with all businesses closed, and thousands of mine workers lining the streets to honor him. The "tragic grief" Frances saw in their faces was sincere. Mitchell was buried in a massive stone tomb erected by the United Mine Workers.[20]

Frances's time in power came to an abrupt end in 1920. Amid the Coolidge-Harding presidential landslide, Smith was defeated for re-election as governor, and within a few months Frances lost her post. She soon accepted a job with the Council on Immigrant Education, an immigrant-aid society in New York City backed by the Merchants Association.

It was a low period in her life. She didn't much care for the job and missed the excitement of political life. Her family obligations were taxing and wearisome. Once again, she hoped that Paul could help out by finding a job. But he was unable or unwilling to exert himself. In 1922, when Susanna was five years old, Frances took the humiliating step of begging John Kingsbury for a job for Paul.

Now that Frances had lost her prestigious post, Kingsbury wrote back in a chilly tone. In a brisk, one-page letter he brushed her off.

Frances wrote nothing more to him, but she didn't forget that he had ignored her pleas. Of course, Paul was ill, and it is likely that Kingsbury was worried about associating himself with a job candidate who had mental health problems, but Frances never forgot the embarrassment and slight. Years later, when Kingsbury found himself unemployed and turned to Frances for help, she pointedly declined to find him a government post. She held the grudge for the rest of their lives.

Frances's luck changed when Smith was reelected in 1922, then again in 1924 and 1926. She rejoined Smith in state government, reinvigorating labor policies that had been watered down by the Republican governor who had replaced Smith. Frances was named again to the state agency that oversaw workplace conditions, and again began playing a very large role running the agency.

She had fought for workers' compensation and now found herself administering the state's program, quickly learning how difficult it was to handle cases fairly. Some doctors made their money helping workers bring bogus claims; other doctors helped insurance companies find ways to deny the claims of workers who were legitimately injured.

It was hard to find attorneys skilled enough to handle this emerging new area of law. In one maritime worker's compensation case, Frances believed the injured man deserved payment, but his case was being handled by an incompetent state attorney. Once again Frances turned to a longtime friend for help. She arranged for Henry Stimson, her friend from the Committee on Safety, to argue the case before the U.S. Supreme Court. The case was a hard-fought legal battle against the employer, but Frances's position ultimately prevailed.

Meanwhile new chemicals that had come into use in manufacturing processes made Frances's work even more challenging. Lead poisoning surfaced among workers who made batteries or who worked with lead plumbing fixtures. It could damage the kidneys and nervous system and lead to seizures, aggressive behavior, and mental deterioration. Workers who handled radium suffered bone deterioration.

In Buffalo, workers making rayon thread were exposed to high levels of carbon monoxide, and they began complaining of headaches, vertigo, and indigestion. And silicosis, a lung condition similar to pneumonia or emphysema, developed from exposure to airborne rock dust that came from grinding tools or drills. Grit lodged in a worker's lungs, gradually suffocating him. It was hard to determine, however, whether a health condition was caused by workplace exposure or by some other hazard.

Eventually workplace safety improved under her watch, as she created new standards and encouraged employers to improve safety measures on their own. Compulsory workmen's compensation had monumental effects because employers who had better safety records paid less in workmen's insurance than those who were careless with their workers' lives.

During these years Frances worked mainly in New York City but visited Albany frequently on state business. The city was still rough and seedy, unwelcoming to a woman who was traveling alone, and so the Smiths frequently invited Frances to stay with them in the governor's mansion. After a long workday, Frances would accompany Smith home for dinner. They would be cordially greeted by his wife Katie, who would serve a light meal—generally ginger ale, beer, and sandwiches. Then they often adjourned to the "pink parlor" for music. Katie would play the piano, and Al would serenade them in his deep baritone. In that relaxed environment, Al would unwind, brightening everyone's spirits, and Frances became almost a member of the family.

Increasingly, Smith included Frances in sensitive conversations—the true test of political trust. One evening in November 1925, Frances was trading notes with Belle Moskowitz at Smith's office in Manhattan's Biltmore Hotel. Moskowitz told her they were deliberating over whom to place in the office of mayor. Smith and others thought the dapper Jimmy Walker was the best Tammany candidate, but Walker had humiliated his wife by publicly squiring other women around town, offending many voters.

As Belle and Frances sat nearby and listened, Smith picked up the phone and called Walker. "Jimmy, this is Al Smith. I've got something to tell you, Jimmy. We've decided, after talking everything over, that probably under some conditions we can run you for mayor. . . . But there are some things we've got to correct," Frances recalled him saying. There was a pause.[21]

"You see, it's like this, Jimmy," Smith went on. "We can never elect anybody in this town who's living like you're living. You're not living with your wife. You haven't treated her right. You're running around. The minute you're nominated for mayor, everybody will know that. You know what this town is like, and you know what Tammany Hall is like. Strict Catholic boys they are. You can't get away with that."

"You got to go back to Janet," Smith told him. Smith paused briefly as Walker responded. Frances surmised that Walker was telling Smith his wife wouldn't take him back.

"Jimmy, that's all right," Smith said. "I've had a talk with Janet. Janet will take you back. She believes in the party. She's a good Tammany girl."[22]

Smith advised him to make a public show next Sunday morning leaving St. Joseph's Church with his wife after eleven o'clock mass. "We'll have photographers there," Smith said.

Walker protested, but Smith insisted. "You do your duty," Smith told him.[23]

It was Frances's first experience with a phenomenon she called the "mothball wife," the woman who would be brought out for airing during a political campaign. On Monday morning, newspaper photos showed Walker with Janet, happily exiting St. Joseph's Church as directed. Reconnecting with his wife helped carry Walker into the mayor's office and strengthened Smith's hold on the urban vote.

As his influence grew, Smith developed a national following and decided to seek the Democratic nomination for president. Knowing that his Catholicism and immigrant roots would trouble some voters, Smith knew he needed someone from an impeccable family line and deep roots in America to campaign with him and take his place as New York governor.

He decided that the man for the job was one Franklin Delano Roosevelt.

Chapter 11

FDR AND AL SMITH

*A*s it turned out, Frances already knew Franklin Delano Roosevelt. She had first met him almost two decades earlier. In 1910, when still a newcomer to New York City, she'd been invited to a tea dance at the home of Mrs. Walston Brown, the wife of a New York City banker who threw soirees where proper young people could meet and mingle. There she met a tall, thin man in his late twenties, distinctive in his high collar and pince-nez. Frances noticed him, but didn't catch his name.

During a pause between dances, the young man came alive when someone criticized the progressive ideas of former Republican president Theodore Roosevelt, who had recently left office. Frances watched as FDR made a "spirited defense" of Teddy Roosevelt, noting that he was related to him through his wife, Eleanor. Frances, also an ardent admirer of Teddy Roosevelt, filed this exchange away in her mind.

A few years later, she saw FDR again in Albany on the steps of the ornate state capitol. Frances was there lobbying for the National Consumers League. FDR was a New York state senator then. Dressed in a morning coat, striped trousers, and a derby hat, he stood talking to another man, looking imperiously down at him through his glasses. He struck Frances as a wealthy young man with his nose in the air.

FDR's legislative colleagues didn't particularly like him either. He didn't seem to click with the savvy Tammany Hall politicians. Jimmy Walker thought Roosevelt acted as though he were on a "slumming expedition," and found even FDR's friendliness merely "patronizing."[1] Frances thought Roosevelt was missing an opportunity, that if he had observed and learned from these more experienced politicians, he would have been much more effective.

FDR didn't seem particularly interested in Frances's wage and hour legislation. She was "considerably disappointed" at his lukewarm support for the fifty-four-hour bill, privately making note of his lack of commitment.[2]

Instead of backing her campaign, FDR was pushing an issue with more political payoff. He launched a fight against the Tammany-endorsed candidate for the U.S. Senate, "Blue-eyed" Billy Sheehan, and helped push the successful candidacy of James A. O'Gorman. A wise strategic move for Roosevelt, it attracted the attention of President Woodrow Wilson, who soon named FDR assistant secretary of the navy. That post allowed Roosevelt to catapult himself into the shoes of his famous relative, Teddy, who had served in the same job during the McKinley administration.

In 1920, Frances got a good look at FDR again when she attended the Democratic Convention in San Francisco. Franklin became the party's nominee for vice president as the running mate of James Cox.

Physically, FDR had filled out and become even more striking. He also seemed more amiable, chatting comfortably with people. At one point, with a vote pending, Roosevelt rose for recognition to make a comment, and the convention speakers pretended not to notice. So Roosevelt put his hand on the back of the chair in front of him and simply vaulted toward the front of the auditorium. To Frances, he appeared to be sailing over four or five rows of chairs, landing gracefully, the "most wonderful athletic feat." Then he authoritatively made his point, making an indelible impression on anyone who saw him that day.

"I do remember—nobody who saw it will ever forget—how handsome Franklin Roosevelt was," Frances said.[3]

But Cox and Roosevelt lost the election to Republicans Warren G. Harding and Calvin Coolidge. And less than a year later, at age thirty-nine, FDR was struck by polio while vacationing with his family at Campobello, New Brunswick, leaving him virtually paralyzed from the waist down. He tried to mask the severity of his condition, but Democratic insiders who saw him quickly sensed the truth. People told Frances that his political career was over.

Roosevelt's first public appearance since his illness came in 1924. He was tapped to nominate Smith for president at the Democratic National Convention in New York City, mostly to ensure that a respected Protestant would endorse the Catholic governor. The audience watched as Roosevelt struggled to his feet to speak. They held their breath, Frances said, "weeping inwardly," for the change they saw in him. He crept forward on crutches and awkwardly pulled himself to the platform. But when FDR spoke, his voice was "strong and true and vigorous," Frances said, and his words captivated the crowd.

He had determined that he would return to public life. Guided by Louis Howe, a gnarled newsman, and with the assistance of his wife, Eleanor, Franklin sought to once again widen his sphere of influence. A steady stream of people came to visit him, including Al Smith.

Frances and others began to sense a more fundamental change in his temperament and personality. His illness made him seem more approachable, kinder, more introspective, and Frances found herself warming to him: "I would like to think he would have done the things he did even without his paralysis, but knowing the streak of vanity and insincerity that there was in him, I don't think he would have unless somebody had dealt him a blow between the eyes," she later said.[4]

By 1928, as Smith pressed forward in his campaign for the presidency, Roosevelt was a viable alternative for New York State governor, someone who could replace Smith and continue his work. Smith decided to ask him to run for the office.

Frances thought a race for governor would put Franklin back in action and aid in his recovery. Roosevelt himself wasn't so sure. At a hotel in Rochester, Smith and Frances watched as Eleanor called her husband, who was on a rest cure in Warm Springs, Georgia. They listened as Eleanor gently urged him to run. He said no, but they pushed Eleanor to ask again and again. Roosevelt worried that too much exertion would undermine his fragile health. After much prodding, he agreed, and the campaign was put into motion.[5]

As Democrats gathered in Houston in 1928, family problems distracted Frances from politics. Her aging mother, Susan, had been living with Frances's sister Ethel, a homemaker married to a dentist in Holden, Massachusetts. Susan had often been difficult when she was younger, and she grew suspicious and paranoid as her health deteriorated. She quarreled with Ethel, who had always been volatile herself, and amid anger and recriminations, Susan moved in with Frances. Frances now found herself not only struggling to balance the needs of a mentally unstable husband and a school-age child, but also the concerns of a critical and argumentative old woman. After Susan suffered a stroke, she became demented as well. Frances was left with no choice but to take care of her mother until she died a few months later.[6]

Although Frances and her mother were never particularly close, she was nevertheless badly shaken by her mother's death. Characteristically, she said little about her grief, obliquely describing it in letters. "I have never known anyone to feel quite the same about the death of his mother as he does about the death of other relatives. It has something to do with the beginning of our lives which is so interwoven with one's mother that one never entirely outgrows one's inward sense of dependence."[7]

Frances forced herself to focus. Her livelihood was at stake, with both Smith's and Roosevelt's candidacies hanging in the balance. She knew that Smith faced formidable obstacles in his presidential race. As early as the 1924 convention, for example, at a breakfast gathering of women delegates at the Waldorf-Astoria Hotel, several participants expressed disgust with what they called the "rough, East Side New York" aspect of Smith. They thought even less of his wife, who one female delegate called "common as mud." Frances tried to assuage some of their worries, stressing Smith's love for his homebody wife and kindly mother and his religious convictions.[8]

Frances saw that while Smith was warmly welcomed in New York City, he was viewed quite differently elsewhere. Smith's immigrant childhood in the tenements and his thick New York accent were unfamiliar to residents in some corners of the country. His devout Catholicism stirred ancient hatreds among Protestants, mobilizing the Ku Klux Klan to a counterattack. Smith needed the Southern Democratic bloc to win the presidency, but Southerners were suspicious of him.

Moreover, Smith faced formidable opposition from Republican Herbert Hoover. Frances had been impressed with Hoover since he was secretary of commerce under presidents Harding and Coolidge. He had won appreciation from the nation's homeowners by promoting a system of standardized mechanical parts so that components like faucets could be easily replaced. "When the Republicans picked him for their candidate in 1928, I was guilty of the heresy of saying that one great thing that Al Smith had done for his country was to have forced the Republicans to nominate a good man," Perkins said.[9]

Frances's future prospects were tied to Smith's. Everyone in Albany was aware of his high regard for her. Most New York political reporters viewed her in 1928 as Smith's "likely nominee" for secretary of labor if he defeated Herbert Hoover.[10]

Soon the Democrats called for Frances to hit the campaign trail. To neutralize animosity and convert the skeptical, the Democratic Party dispatched emissaries who would comfortably fit in with voters. Frances, a New Englander with a strong Protestant background, was asked to campaign through the South on Smith's behalf, visiting church groups and social clubs. She was usually accompanied by Irene Langhorne Gibson, one of the famous Langhorne sisters, debutantes from Virginia.

Langhorne's family was well-known in the South, and the politicking went extraordinarily well, particularly after the women stopped focusing on Smith and began emphasizing the Democratic legacy of Robert E. Lee. "The problem was to keep Virginia and all the Southern states voting the Democratic ticket; it was hard," Frances said.[11]

The more Southern they acted, the more effective they were. Gibson's accent took on a Virginia drawl. The two women did little to correct the misimpression that Frances was Irene's older sister, Lizzie Langhorne, who had married a Southerner named Moncure Perkins, and Frances was able to use the opportunity to mention a few of Al Smith's good points—his religious convictions, warm family life, efforts to reduce poverty. Then she would turn to what the crowds considered the most salient issue—the beautiful and glorious memory of Robert E. Lee.

Frances realized that the strongest single base of the Democrats, the South, was only tenuously connected to the party. Al Smith, the son of an immigrant, was a tough sell to these mostly rural voters. Their ties were to the old Democratic Party, not to the new one, which was stressing higher wages for the working poor, new tenement regulation, and better working conditions. The horrors of factory life didn't seem so bad to people who hoped those jobs would migrate their way. Increasingly uncomfortable with the direction of the northern Democratic Party, Southerners needed to be handled carefully, she realized.

Other schisms were evident as well. The women traveled to Maryland's Eastern Shore, making speeches along the way with little guidance from campaign headquarters. Gibson had mistakenly believed that Smith's Catholicism would be more palatable in Maryland because of the state's historical roots in the Roman faith. In fact, the fear of his Catholicism was so great that locals believed the pope planned to relocate to the United States if Smith were elected. Marylanders pointed out an estate that they believed the church had purchased for the pope.

The women found it impossible to convince people in Maryland that the stories were baseless. "It was perfectly clear to them that the whole idea of having Smith for president was for the Roman Catholic Church to get control of the government, military forces and everything else of the United States," Frances said. "The illogic of it hadn't occurred to them and was unarguable with them. It was the most deep-seated prejudice I've ever met."[12]

On another campaign trip, this time through Missouri, Frances traveled with another Democratic party stalwart, Aileen Webb. Usually they met with upper-class ladies at elegant luncheons, but one night they were told they had been asked to give a night lecture in Independence. Senator Harry Hawes worried that the crowd might be rough, and he broke another engagement so he could attend with them. The two women laughed at his overprotectiveness.

But soon they realized that something was amiss. The streets were so mobbed that the driver had trouble edging the vehicle through the town. As the women arrived at the meeting hall, they noticed that banners announcing the speech had been ripped down.

A nervous Democratic Party official met them at the door. He said local residents—Frances was later told they were members of the KKK—were "wrought up" about Smith's religion. The women asked about the vandalized banners. "Oh, some boys, I guess, trying to break up things," Senator Hawes told them. "Just kids romping around."

The women were hustled into the auditorium, but by 8 p.m., the time for the speech, only a handful of attendees was seated. The women could hear people yelling outside the hall. Frances heard men shouting about "tar-and-feathering" and what they would show the "smart girls from New York." Democratic officials came and went, whispering anxiously in Senator Hawes's ear. The women learned that no minister or priest in town was willing to open the meeting with a Christian prayer, so a Mormon preacher would give the blessing.

Finally, it was time to go out onstage.

"Now, girls, hold your horses," Hawes said. "Don't show any fear. . . . They may begin to throw things. . . . Tomatoes, eggs."

Frances was shocked. She had not seen hecklers pelting opponents with produce since her suffrage-marching days. She also felt a "depth of violence" unlike any she had encountered. "It was full of threat—just full of threat."

At last the meeting got under way. Hawes rose first to speak, and Frances followed. Spectators split into screaming factions, turning on each other. Hawes decided to end the meeting, just as the rival sides turned to fisticuffs. "All bedlam broke loose," Frances said, and the police rushed in. Hawes and the other men hustled the women to safety. Frances later recounted a pelting with tomatoes and eggs. Webb remembered the day as tense and menacing, but recalled no produce being thrown.[13] Local newspaper accounts did not mention any rotten vegetables, either. The incident may have been another illustration of Frances's willingness to construct a dramatic story for herself.

In the crowd that day was Harry S. Truman, a Missouri judge and local government official. He had helped organize the meeting, and standing in the front row, he had watched Frances face the rowdy crowd. He knew the seriousness of the potential threat: The Klan had recently threatened to kill Truman, too. From the first time he saw her, and whether produce was lobbed at the stage or not, Truman recognized Frances from the beginning as a loyal Democrat who was willing to face fire for her beliefs.[14]

Despite her devotion to Smith, Frances now knew his chances of election were slim. She sat with Belle Moskowitz one night back in New York, listening to Smith via radio broadcast from Helena, Montana. He expressed support for all the concepts dearest to Frances's heart—regulating work hours, limiting child labor, requiring employers to provide safe and sanitary workplaces. Her heart sank as she listened. She'd realized his raspy voice, so familiar to New Yorkers, sounded harsh and alien to people in other parts of the country. His labor views, easily comprehensible to workers in big cities, struck a dissonant chord in more rural areas where industrialization was only a distant dream.

Belle listened intently. "That is wonderful!" she told Frances.

Frances disagreed. "Belle, I just don't think this will go in the country."

Belle contradicted her sharply. "You're quite mistaken," she said.[15]

Al Smith was equally oblivious. Heartened by the roaring approval he had received in New York and other cities, he was convinced he would win, with Roosevelt riding to victory on his coattails.

But a few hours into election night, Smith's defeat became apparent. His eyes grew glassy as he steeled himself to face it. Hoover got 21.4 million votes; Smith received only 15 million. Normally ebullient and resilient, Smith's face was plastered in a rigid smile. His wife looked ready to break into tears. She'd heard how she was viewed in many parts of the country as a coarse, beer-drinking tart. Campaign workers roamed the halls, weeping. Smith conceded to Hoover early in the evening and departed for home in bitter humiliation.

"Smith was never the same after November 6, 1928; that day was his Gethsemane," Robert Moses said later.[16]

With the presidential race now decided, Frances turned her attention back to the contest for governor. She wandered over to the Roosevelt headquarters at the Biltmore Hotel, where the crowd was thinning. FDR had gone home. Only a handful of devout supporters remained—Democratic activist Jim Farley watching the wires, Nancy Cook and Caroline O'Day, two former suffragists who had led a women's campaign caravan in New York, and Roosevelt's mother, Sara. Newspaper reporters asked Frances if she intended to stick around after Smith's concession, and Frances said she would stay until the outcome was final. She joined Sara, who was then seventy-four, to wait it out. "I'll stay with you," Frances told her. "I don't think it's over by a long shot.' "[17]

Hotel managers turned out the ballroom lights, and the small corps of diehards went into the corridor to wait. Around 2 a.m., they started to receive scattered reports of small wins for Roosevelt—six votes from Cattaraugus County, a few more from elsewhere. By 4 a.m., FDR had squeaked to victory and become the new governor of New York.

By dawn, Frances and an ecstatic Sara Roosevelt realized that Franklin had won. They telephoned Hyde Park, found that FDR knew the outcome, and offered their congratulations. The two women wanted to celebrate, but most establishments were closed. They went together to the nearby Commodore Hotel to drink glasses of milk and unwind.

Frances had made a point of cultivating Al Smith's mother. Now she did the same with Roosevelt's.

Chapter 12

WITH THE ROOSEVELTS
IN ALBANY

few weeks after his election, FDR summoned Frances to Hyde Park. They drove around the estate in an automobile. Roosevelt told her he planned to promote her from her oversight role on the state industrial board, which supervised the state industrial commission, to the role of actually running the department herself. She would oversee one of the state's largest agencies and supervise hundreds of employees, including factory inspectors. Her salary would be $12,000 a year, a welcome increase from the $8,500 she received as board chairman. The job would make her one of the state's most powerful and highest-paid appointed officials.

Frances told him she believed she would accept the job, but if the appointment proved problematic, she would step aside. In the meantime, she wanted to keep quiet about the offer, giving FDR time to change his mind if he so chose. Her lack of ego impressed FDR. He later told people it showed him Frances wouldn't be "greedy" and that she would "make things easy" for him.[1]

FDR's decision represented one of his first disagreements with Smith, Frances later learned. He had told Smith about the plan to elevate Frances, and Smith advised against it. Though he had high regard for her work, Smith proclaimed that men would never take orders from a woman. He predicted a revolt among factory inspectors and other male government officials if she were appointed. Roosevelt nodded at the advice but persisted in his plan.

Frances believed that one reason Franklin gave her the high-ranking job was that it allowed him to surpass Smith as a pathbreaker in his appointments. Roosevelt seemed determined to shake his image as a Smith protégé: ". . . one of the reasons Franklin Roosevelt thought of it, and he often said so, was 'Al would never have thought of that. Al would

never have thought of making a woman the head of the Department,' "
Frances recalled. "Franklin was quite vain about how much better he
was than Smith."[2]

While most women would have been distressed to learn that a former supervisor and dear friend had recommended against their promotion, Frances took a more detached view. In her mind, it actually had
taken greater courage for Smith to appoint her as an industrial commissioner in 1919, when women could not vote and held no such jobs, than it
did for Roosevelt to give her a slightly elevated post in 1928.

Roosevelt distanced himself from Smith in other ways. Smith offered to visit Albany several days a week to provide guidance, but Roosevelt's obvious lack of enthusiasm chilled that idea. FDR was already
demonstrating the ruthlessness a successful politician often has in personal relationships.

A few days after assuming office, Roosevelt asked Frances to meet
with him. He told her he had rejected Smith's advice to keep Robert
Moses on board because he didn't trust him; in fact, Frances knew that
Moses had privately spoken of Franklin as "not quite bright." Roosevelt
then questioned her closely about Belle Moskowitz. She told him that
Belle was a fine and capable woman.

Roosevelt told her he had wanted to keep Moskowitz on as his assistant, but that Eleanor, who was a close friend of Belle's and had worked
with her during the campaign, had disagreed. Eleanor said that while
Moskowitz was competent, farsighted, and reliable, she would likely exert too much power over the state government if she remained.

" 'You have to decide, and you have to decide it now, whether you are
going to be Governor of this state, or whether Mrs. Moskowitz is going
to be Governor of this state,' " he said Eleanor told him. " 'If Mrs. Moskowitz is your secretary, she will run you.' "[3]

Listening to him relate Eleanor's opinion, Frances saw the sway his
wife had over him. Eleanor had convinced her husband that his illness
made him vulnerable to a strong force like Moskowitz. With a few words,
Eleanor had killed Moskowitz's career. Frances was becoming increasingly aware that Franklin was a man who could be manipulated.

Recognizing the sensitivity of the situation, and unwilling to cross
the governor's wife, Frances backed away. "You're not going to ask me,
are you, to advise you on this matter?" she asked.[4]

"Oh, no, no," the governor said, pulling his lip down. It was an unusual but meaningful gesture Frances was already beginning to recognize. On the surface it appeared to be an unconscious indication of someone lost in thought, but Frances was noticing it also signaled a certain evasiveness, an unwillingness to share the full details. He paused. "Right at this moment, as I am now, I know I can't be bossed around," he said. "I mustn't allow myself to be pushed around, because I might get into the habit. It would be easy because I haven't got my full strength."

Frances soon discovered that Roosevelt's loyal assistant Louis Howe also opposed Moskowitz, seeing her as a rival.

Frances again found herself pulled into the fray when Smith asked to speak with her, ostensibly to discuss workplace codes for industrial diseases. The conversation soon turned to Moskowitz. Frances realized that part of the reason Smith wanted Moskowitz as Roosevelt's secretary was so he could continue to exert influence in the governor's office. Frances decided not to tell Smith anything more about the selection process, worried that it would add to mounting tensions between the families.

Roosevelt ultimately heeded Eleanor's advice. He told Smith he planned to hire as an assistant a physically strong man who could discreetly help him get around. Smith, who had been calling Roosevelt almost every day, thought this was a dreadful mistake. Frances privately agreed that the talented Moskowitz would have helped Roosevelt's effectiveness. But she also suspected that Moskowitz might have placed Smith's interests above Roosevelt's.

Roosevelt's decision exacerbated an already acrimonious split between the Smith and Roosevelt camps. Moskowitz despised Howe; Howe detested Moskowitz. Moskowitz, now embittered, pointed out to Smith every Roosevelt shortcoming, and Howe began erasing every mention of Smith's accomplishments from campaign literature. Moses, an important power broker, spread his negative impressions of Roosevelt among influential people whose help Roosevelt needed. Smith stewed in a sea of resentment, angling for the Democratic nomination for president in 1932.

Smith could not accept that he, a poor boy from the slums who had strenuously climbed to the top, had lost out, while the rich boy, with fewer credentials, had won. Stripped of both his job and the executive mansion, Smith, at fifty-nine, had little to show for his hard work.

The man once dubbed the Happy Warrior now brooded darkly on his loss, blaming his defeat on deep-seated prejudice against Catholics: "To tell you the truth, Commissioner," he told Frances a week after the election, "the time hasn't come when a man can say his [rosary] beads in the White House."[5]

Smith fell into a state of near-despair. A few nights after the election, he was invited to a victory dinner for FDR and the new lieutenant governor Herbert H. Lehman, at the Lotus Club in Manhattan. It was an all-male event with guests that included real estate entrepreneur Henry Morgenthau, financier and Democratic Party backer John Raskob, Vincent Astor, journalist Herbert Swope, and political activist Frank C. Walker. Smith grew maudlin. Eddie Dowling, an actor and Smith supporter, went to the men's room. Smith followed him.

"Eddie," he said, "I could cry."[6]

"What about, Governor?" Dowling responded. "You've had a wonderful career. You came up out of the sidewalks of New York, the Fulton Fish Market. You're the greatest governor New York ever had. . . . You will be in the hearts of your people forever. Don't worry about this," he said.

But Smith was inconsolable. "Eddie, I haven't got a five-cent piece," he said. "But I've got children. I'm a poor man. My God!"

Then Raskob, a wealthy General Motors executive who pioneered the concept of selling cars on credit, entered the men's room. He listened to Smith sharing his woes with an actor and admitting he had made no provision for his family's future. He offered a solution: "Some friends of yours and myself have assembled a plot at the corner of 34th and Fifth Avenue," Raskob told Smith. "There we are going to build the tallest building in the world. We're known as the Empire Realty Company. It's for you, Governor. You're going to be the president of the Empire Realty Company at a salary three times what you ever got as Governor, and it's your job for life."

Frances lamented Smith's failure to rebound from defeat and make a fresh start in politics. In her opinion, his lucrative job with the Empire State Building was only a "place to hang his hat" for a man with a true gift for administration: "I've never known a person who had such sagacity and ability in the field of government," she said.[7]

Compounding Smith's estrangement was a sense that Roosevelt had breached some fundamental values.

"The friendship between Al Smith and Roosevelt was, I think, political rather than personal, but Smith, essentially a warm-hearted man, threw into it a real emotional attachment," she wrote later. "He understood loyalty, both politically and personally, as a virtue, and he didn't separate the two in his mind." Smith missed his political career dreadfully. [8]

Moskowitz and Howe stoked the embers of the conflict, Frances believed. Advisers, after all, typically want to curry favor with the boss and secure their own futures, and this makes them especially prone to exploiting hostilities by sniping at rival camps and their opposite numbers there. The bitterness increased when the men became direct political rivals.

Admiring Smith as she did, but committed to advancing her program of reforms in state government, Frances agonized about the rift between Smith and Roosevelt. Smith had allowed her to advance in public life, and she hoped to avoid falling on his bad side, even as she rose along with Roosevelt.

Frances regretted these turns of events, but she was never one to dwell on the past. She was eager to move ahead with her work. As she had done when she moved into the sphere of Tammany Hall, she accepted the good with the bad and embraced the checkered relationship with the Roosevelts. This was a major turning point in Frances's life. She walked away from Smith to join FDR, even seeing his limitations and personally preferring Al Smith.

Over the next four years in Albany, Frances worked as closely with Roosevelt as she had with Smith. In some ways, communication between Frances and FDR was easier because they shared the same cultural history and viewed past events from the same perspective. Gradually, Frances grew so close to the Roosevelts that she would often stay with them in Albany, as she had with the Smiths, and she was drawn into their circle.

Franklin and Eleanor were naturally sociable, which proved politically advantageous to them. They held lunches and dinners in Albany with people of varied ages and occupations, building networks. FDR's secretaries, Grace Tully and Missy LeHand, were always on the scene, along with his assistant Louis Howe. Eleanor, with her thick mane of long hair coiled atop her head, performed perfectly as the mansion's gracious hostess. She had a gift for making people feel welcome and appreciated.

"It was like a constant house party," Frances recalled.

FDR had hesitated before reentering public life, but now he embraced it with gusto. His popularity grew, and soon their home became a political mecca.

The Roosevelts often asked friends and associates to stay overnight, and the mansion's bedrooms were filled with guests. Sometimes Eleanor would give up her impressive quarters to visitors and sleep in a more modest room, a move that also underscored her physical distance from her husband. When the mansion was crowded, she and Frances would sometimes bunk together, sharing a small third-floor room.

"You don't mind rooming with me, do you?" Eleanor would ask, and Frances would assure her that she didn't.

An intimacy developed between the women—not the intimacy of true friendship but the kind of closeness that results from physical proximity. Brushing their hair, preparing for bed, sitting in their twin beds dressed in their nightgowns, talking before they drifted off to sleep, the two shared stories and learned about one another.

During Frances's early years in New York, she had known Eleanor as a timid, diffident, and serious woman, always eager to please. Eleanor had done volunteer work for the National Consumers League in New York City and had become active in the Junior League, which had been founded by Frances's friend Mary Harriman. The Junior League connected affluent young women, who ordinarily would have little contact with the poor, with social service groups they could assist and finance, particularly settlement houses.

Their lives had been very different. In stark contrast to Frances's demanding activity on workplace legislation, the women's vote, and her obligations as the breadwinner for her family, Eleanor, a wife and mother, lived comfortably with her husband and his mother at their Hyde Park estate overlooking the Hudson. In a throwback to feudal times, FDR served as young lord of the dominion, and Eleanor, a descendant of the wealthy Livingston family, was his consort and future lady of the manor. Eleanor had few financial worries. In 1917 she told the *New York Times* that she was contributing to the nation's war effort by asking her ten household servants to economize in their use of bacon and laundry soap. She had limited the menu to two lunch courses and three at dinner.[10]

Although Frances admired many things about Eleanor and publicly praised her elegance, in private she tended to view Eleanor condescendingly and questioned why such a handsome man had married such a homely woman. She felt that it could only be a deliberate act by a man who wanted to ensure he would always be the one most admired.

During these evenings in the governor's mansion in Albany, Frances learned that Eleanor was haunted by the melancholy of her childhood. She had grown up in relative splendor, a debutante, but she still grieved over the fact that she had never really had her own home. Her father, whom she adored, had been an out-of-control alcoholic viewed by his family as a disgrace. Eleanor's mother was beautiful and died young, when Eleanor was only eight years old, and her father died soon after. Eleanor and her brother, Hall, had inherited money and were never mistreated, but they moved among various relatives and lived precariously as orphaned guests in other people's homes. Eleanor was shipped to boarding school in England when she was in her teens; it was the happiest home of her childhood. After she married Franklin, his mother controlled their household. Sara Roosevelt furnished a set of rooms for the young couple within her own Hyde Park home. Then, to provide them with a proper New York residence, she built a house on 65th Street for the couple and built another one for herself next door, breaking down walls to connect them. She furnished both houses, leaving Eleanor to choose not so much as a teacup.

"Then we moved up here to the Executive Mansion," Eleanor continued to Frances that night. "This isn't my home. It belongs to the State of New York. It's furnished by the State of New York. It's furnished in the official taste of the State of New York. Even the servants are civil servants hired by the State of New York. Nothing belongs to me except my maid."[11]

Even when they vacationed, they went to Sara's home in Campobello. It made Eleanor feel powerless.

She clearly thought of herself as a rather pathetic figure. Although Frances responded sympathetically, Eleanor's willingness to share the private grief of her life struck Frances as rather inappropriate, and Eleanor found Frances strangely cool. She had reached out to Frances and must have expected a warmer reception. Frances, however, conducted her life behind a veil and was not inclined to respond with an equally personal tale. But Frances did find Eleanor's story moving. "I never had thought before what it means to a child to be pushed around from house to house, from one member of the family to another, always being expected to be so polite, so excessively polite, with no time for the sulks and tantrums that children were allowed to have under the shelter of their family," she recalled.

Part of Frances's wariness stemmed from observing Eleanor's treatment of Belle Moskowitz. She knew that Eleanor and Belle had been close friends during the 1928 campaign, but in the end Eleanor had cut Belle off without a backward glance.

Frances realized she must handle not just the governor but also his wife, who was both fragile and capable of making trouble. Eleanor struggled with feelings of inadequacy, a problem exacerbated by her husband's infidelity. He had a long affair with a former secretary of Eleanor's, Lucy Mercer, and it was clear that his current secretary, Missy LeHand, was engaged in some kind of a romantic relationship with him, even as she lived in the mansion with his family.

Though Eleanor and Frances had similar values and many common friends, their differences kept them from becoming true friends, and they never really did do so. For Frances, managing the boss's wife became an unspoken but demanding task.

Even so, a mythology arose, a "newspaper person's fiction" that Eleanor and Frances were close friends and that the president had appointed Frances to state government, and later to the Cabinet, to please his wife.[12] Both women denied the report, but the story had remarkable staying power, probably because it let people explain things to themselves without rethinking any old assumptions. Few women had climbed as high in public life as Frances, and many were reluctant to attribute her rise to the simple fact of her proven competence. The public often assumed sex was involved when women took over important posts. The Eleanor connection offered a similar but less-salacious explanation, which still accounted for Frances's success without acknowledging her abilities.

In time, Frances developed a deeper friendship with Franklin Roosevelt than with Eleanor. Indeed, Frances had set out very purposefully to learn how FDR thought and to maximize her effectiveness. Smith had been rather simple for her to understand, but FDR was not. Roosevelt "appeared extremely complicated from the very first conversation you ever had with him," she said.

She made a practice of conferring with him for about an hour every ten days or so. "I suppose it was partly then, as well as later when he was President, that I learned the trick of repeating things to him—telling him three times—because I discovered that that held it in his memory. If I wanted to present a subject, I would begin by telling him what I was going to tell him.[13]

"Now I want to tell you about the hazards of dust in materials that up to date we thought were non-explosive," she would say.

"Such as what?" he would say.

"Well, such as the dust that comes out of pearl buttons, such as the dust that comes out from an aluminum grinding operation. We had known that there were explosive elements in gasoline and things like that. We had known that there were explosive elements in some kinds of other solid chemicals."

Then she would tell him about a specific case.

"There's been an explosion in a small plant that's not in the state of New York—fortunately. The report on it is this: It seems to be that it's the proportion of air to the proportion of dust that does it. Any little spark will set it off and sometimes it appears to be spontaneous."

Then he'd usually interrupt and divert Frances, asking something like, "Was it anything like Massena?," a city with an aluminum plant. And she'd agree there was such a plant there, but a different one. He'd interrupt a dozen times with questions. "How many people did you say were hurt? Where were they?" She came to realize he wanted not just the point but the story. He read a lot of fiction and always enjoyed a good tale. But these stories also became the most effective kind of political communication, enabling FDR to clearly explain the underlying issues to reporters and the public.

After Frances told the story, she would recommend action, and usually he would agree. She would ask a legislative committee for a specific bill, or she would launch a "trial balloon in the newspaper," to test reaction. Before long, Roosevelt would line up the political backing, a bill would be passed, and she would administer it.

There were practical reasons for this approach as well. While Frances might take Al Smith to see children working in a factory, Roosevelt couldn't get to these places and needed the vivid mental picture she could paint. Eleanor, of course, had long served as her husband's eyes and ears.

Sometime during this period, Frances made yet another adjustment to her public identity. She had already changed her name, her religion, and her appearance. Now she started presenting herself as a Boston Brahmin, sometimes referring to her boarding school years when she had in fact attended public schools.

She kept quiet about her own difficult family situation. In 1929, at a luncheon to honor her at the Hotel Astor in New York City, she talked about her private life: "I have had the greatest blessing any one can have, man or woman. I have had a happy personal life. I have had the friendship of a husband who had put a brilliant mind to work on some of my knotty problems, and let me have the praise. I have had a good daughter, who has grown to girlhood without being a troublesome child. And I am thankful indeed for the women who have helped me bring up my child and take care of my home. There is no coin in which I can repay those fine and loyal helpers who have worked with me in that intimate way."[14]

Frances had also reinvented her age, making herself two years younger. In the mid-1920s, Frances reported her birth year as 1882, two years later than the 1880 that had always appeared in her records before. Whether it was female vanity or unusually bad arithmetic remains unclear. The age adjustment made her the same age as Franklin, rather than two years older, and put them on a more equal footing.

Chapter 13

FDR Becomes President

$\mathcal{F}$ranklin Roosevelt's ascent to the New York governorship coincided with one of the most buoyant periods in American history. Under a string of Republican presidents, the economy was booming, with soaring real estate values and a surging stock market that turned many investors into paper millionaires.

Everywhere, it seemed, people were richer and flashier. Girls were flappers, men wore raccoon coats, and nightlife brightened as speakeasies made a mockery of Prohibition. The old conservatism dropped away. New York's mayor Jimmy Walker, after reconciling with his wife on the churchyard steps, openly cavorted with chorus girls amid a pack of merrymakers rumored to have their hands in the till.

A culture of immediate gratification sprang up, as Americans with newly electrified homes stocked up on toasters, irons, refrigerators, and vacuum cleaners. Automobile production jumped from 4.3 million cars in 1926 to 5.4 million in 1929. Everything was available for purchase on credit, payable with interest.[1]

Homes rose markedly in value, especially in hot markets like Florida and New York City. Borrowers believed that home purchases were no-risk ventures certain to escalate, and they went out on a limb to buy. Lenders who had once required large down payments now permitted home purchasers to combine two and three loans to buy a home. People took out what were called "bullet" loans, which were interest-only loans that buyers were told they should refinance in three years or five years. Lenders told home buyers not to worry; homes were rising so fast in value that it would always be easy to refinance into another loan. Developers built larger houses. Why not? Borrowers wanted larger homes. They needed the space to hold all the things they were buying.[2]

The pursuit of pleasurable living became an end in itself as Ameri-

cans shook off their deep-seated cultural prejudices against material-
ism, previously anathema to the Puritan work ethic. Music, art, theater,
and retailing flourished. It was intoxicating.

Frances, living and working in vibrant New York City, was perfectly
situated to watch it all.

"Everybody was enjoying himself," Frances recalled. "Everybody was
thinking he was richer and richer. Everybody was spending money. For
the first time, the strange puritanical American attitude relaxed. We began to import a lot of plays from Europe. We began to import a lot of
luxurious habits. . . . A lot of people moved in [to New York] to enjoy
the fun, make more money, deal on the stock market, go up with the
bubble."[3]

Frances's own standard of living rose, thanks to her lucrative new
job as state industrial commissioner. In November 1929, she moved into
a beautiful apartment at 1239 Madison Avenue, a few blocks from Central Park, with three bedrooms, a maid's quarters, and a dining room. A
charming birdcage elevator took people up to their floors, and a doorman was available to help with errands.

Presiding over it all was Republican president Herbert Hoover, a true
Horatio Alger character. An orphan, he had grown up on an Iowa farm
and earned an engineering degree at Stanford University. While still
young, he became an international mining expert and multimillionaire
and played a heroic role in a 1914 Belgian relief effort. When the United
States entered World War I, he took charge of protecting America's food
supply as food administrator. Afterward he took the same job to Europe,
helping the reconstruction effort. Returning home decked in laurels,
Hoover was appointed Warren Harding's secretary of commerce and
transformed the department into a center of technical competence.

After handily defeating Al Smith, Hoover entered the White House
with some concern about the speculative boom. As time passed, however, his anxiety subsided.

Then the free fall began. Real estate values dropped, employment
fell, and the stock market went into a spin. The *Great Gatsby* era disintegrated into the misery of *The Grapes of Wrath*. "In our own country,
at least, most people were too busy being prosperous to do more than
glance up abstractly when the rather more than occasional job seekers
first began to knock at the door about two years ago," Frances wrote in
1930. "Then gradually they found themselves feeling that this discon-

tented fellow was forming an annoying habit of knocking; and then, suddenly, there he was—a whole, long, haggard line of him—the bread line!"

As a top New York economic official during the Smith and Roosevelt administrations, Frances was well placed to observe these developments from a unique position. She had entered public service shortly before the 1921 recession, sought solutions for joblessness, then watched the economy rebound and soar for the next eight years. But from her perch, talking to businessmen and workers and tracking state unemployment statistics, Frances also realized that the 1920s boom years were not really that prosperous for all that many people. Many people had gotten rich, but many more approached the 1930s with high hopes but empty pockets.

Many companies, she believed, had earned record profits but spent much of the money on new machinery that boosted worker productivity and allowed firms to operate with fewer employees. The downsizing left a large and growing pool of workers marooned in outmoded occupations and viewed as too old to adapt to the new higher-paid jobs, and when the new jobs started disappearing, much underlying unemployment was exposed.[4]

Frances later took the position that the Crash of 1929 was just a symptom of underlying problems, not the cause. Beneath the superficial prosperity of the 1920s, large economic problems had simmered, and early responses to the problems only made them worse. Interest-only loans had fueled real estate speculation, and home prices had soared, but in about 1925, first in places like Florida, housing prices had started to fall and families began to lose their homes. Each foreclosure affected the surrounding neighborhood, and even workers who kept their jobs found their primary asset was worth only a fraction of what they had once believed.[5]

According to Frances, worsening all aspects of the situation was the lack of accurate information. For example, there was no centralized source of reliable data on joblessness. "All sorts of amateurs were putting out estimates of unemployment on a given day and predictions of what it would be one month later," Frances wrote.[6]

In time, wage cuts and layoffs were apparent everywhere, even in the financial hub of New York. The stockbrokers had no choice but to join the ranks of unskilled or manual workers hunting for jobs, while real estate, the supposedly safe investment—something that one could always count upon—went on the market everywhere. Facing a national disaster, Americans agonized over what to do. Jobs for able-bodied men were so scarce that a backlash developed against working women. Early in the Depression, Frances, whose income supported her family, openly criticized married women who were working for income she called "pin money." As time wore on, she grew alarmed at the broad and exclusionary nature of some federal and state legislation that was passed to restrict employment of married women. She publicly criticized these measures, saying it was unfair to dismiss women workers unless they were inefficient or unneeded. Many working women lived in poverty, she said, and many supported infirm husbands or aging parents.

But from crisis, opportunities emerge as well. Frances came to realize that the Great Depression could make it possible to take dramatic action on issues she had pondered for two decades. Joblessness and despair had penetrated middle-class society. She realized a consensus for action could be close at hand. Robert F. Wagner had been elected a U.S. senator, promising that labor issues would be his central focus in Washington. And if Roosevelt could be elected president, she thought, much could finally be accomplished. "The political impact of the Depression, with millions of people unemployed and still many millions of others adversely affected in one way or another, was that it was a situation which was so universal in its application—by that I mean, it affected people who were rich, who had been rich and people who had been poor."

Frances soon began to push a reform agenda at the state level. One of her principal tools was a state employment service that helped workers connect to available positions without paying fees to employment agencies. She also convinced Roosevelt to appoint a state commission to study unemployment. This allowed New York officials to spread the word about the innovative steps some companies were taking to protect their workforces, by using work-sharing arrangements so that more people could remain employed.

Frances also pushed FDR toward some more far-reaching social programs. In October 1931 she asked the governor to invite states surrounding New York to participate in an unemployment insurance system. She envisioned a multistate operation similar to what the Port Authority had done in New Jersey and New York. She explained that this was neither a draconian idea nor a panacea for recurring woes of the business cycle. Instead, she said, unemployment insurance would extend a "well-known principle to offer some protection for the individual against the hazard of unemployment, which as an individual, he can in no way prevent. . . . It will ease the burden of the individual in the face of this industrial hazard, and it will immensely relieve the community of the cost of poor relief and charity in periods of unemployment."[7]

Frances went to England to study the country's unemployment compensation program and came back with a strong vision for how a system should be constructed. The British system involved a staggering amount of manual record keeping of workers' wages. Boxes of paperwork rose to the ceilings of an enormous warehouse, and clerks used rickety ladders to pull down specific boxes for review. On her return she told FDR that it was possible to duplicate the system, but that in the more populous United States the process must be mechanized. She suggested referring the project to an up-and-coming New York firm called International Business Machines, or IBM, to see if it could develop a paperless system for tracking workers' claims.

Frances also helped FDR assume a leadership role in developing plans for rebuilding the nation's economy. On March 30, 1930, FDR became the first American governor to stress that unemployment was a major national risk. In a press statement, FDR promised to confront unemployment in the same way a "scientist faces a test tube of deadly germs, intending first to understand the nature, the cause and effect, and finally the method of overcoming and the technique of preventing its ravages."[8]

Roosevelt announced that he would appoint a committee to stabilize employment, and he urged state and local organizations to join. Heading the new enterprise would be his industrial commissioner, Frances Perkins. In June 1930, he advanced her recommendations in a widely acclaimed speech to the governors' conference in Salt Lake City. He vowed to consider some kind of "unemployment insurance," as well as an old-age pension plan. He also urged government officials to face unemployment squarely and to report numbers honestly, rather than "distort facts."

In Washington, President Hoover, once known for his energy and determination, had frozen into inaction. Faced with massive joblessness, he had wanted to boost employment with public works projects, but he worried about the negative effects on the federal budget. As conditions worsened, Hoover actually reduced government expenditures at the same time that private lending activity was violently contracting.

Unable to face the unfolding economic deterioration, Hoover tried to reassure the public with wishful pronouncements about the economy. In January 1930 he issued a press statement asserting that the Depression was almost over. He cited a specific statistic, noting that employment rates had risen 4 percent in the previous month.

Frances exploded when she heard the president's statement. She knew the 4 percent increase reflected only Christmas hiring, not permanent jobs, something the U.S. Bureau of Labor Statistics should have made clear to him. She also knew that Hoover, a quick study and a good mathematician, would have known he was using the statistics improperly.

Frances pounced on Hoover in the most visible way. She double-checked the U.S. employment figures, then called the news services to publicly dispute the president's facts: "The President of the United States has deceived the people about this matter of employment," she told a cluster of eager reporters at a press conference. "It is worse, not better. It's a cruel deceit, because people will believe it. Mother will be mad when father comes home and says he can't get a job because the President said that employment is going up. The tragedy of families who still hope that father will get a job is just terrible when this kind of thing happens."[9]

After she had issued her statement, she suddenly realized that she should have told Roosevelt first as a courtesy. She called FDR to alert him of the possible implications.

"I have done something that you may think is very wrong," she said. "I'd like to tell you about it. Are you feeling amiable?"[10]

Yes, he was.

Frances told him she had sent out a statement disputing Hoover's comments that would soon appear in numerous newspapers.

"The hell you have!" Roosevelt burst out.

"Are you going to kill me, or fire me?" she asked.

Roosevelt burst out laughing. "It's bully!"

Still roaring with merriment, Roosevelt said he thought it was wonderful—though if consulted first, he probably would have told her not to do it. He would do nothing to reprimand her but told her she was out there on her own. Fortunately, Frances was right.

The next morning, the story ran on the front pages of newspapers across the country. From then on, whenever Hoover talked about the economy and unemployment, reporters would call Frances for the countervailing comment. Suddenly, she became a sought-after speaker, which gave her a platform for talking about needed changes of all kinds. Within the Roosevelt presidential campaign, Frances's gutsy stand against Hoover was regarded as her "great political service" in the coming months.

Frances's position on the numbers was bolstered by the chief of the Bureau of Labor Statistics, Ethelbert Stewart, who echoed her opinion that Hoover's figures were inaccurate. He told Hoover that the numbers were false, but the president continued to glibly cite them. Stewart resigned in protest, ending his own career. Hoover partisans portrayed him as an old crank who had reached his dotage, and the Labor Department officially declared that he had retired because of his age.

Frances, however, was uninjured by her bold stance and became an important weapon in Roosevelt's battle against Hoover. Roosevelt prodded her to continue: "Frances, this is the best politics you can do," he told her. "Don't say anything about politics. Just be an outraged scientist and social worker."

Frances continued to play this part, the avenging statistician against Hoover's economic misrepresentations, up until the election.

"We kept him on the run," she said.[11]

Frances established herself as a foremost national authority on unemployment statistics. She appeared as a witness at a hearing called by her old friend Senator Wagner, pointing out a phenomenon that no one had previously noticed. She testified that the Depression had spawned additional unemployment. As main wage earners, mostly husbands and fathers, lost their jobs, their wives and teenage children looked for work, perhaps unsuccessfully, and instead of one unemployed person, soon there were two or three or four. In other words, the loss of one well-paying job created joblessness in even more people.

In the hearing room that day was a merchant's son, coincidentally also from Worcester, Massachusetts. He was a young economist and statistician from the Brookings Institute who would later become one of Frances's closest allies, Isador Lubin. "She pointed out something which is so accepted today but at the time was in a sense heresy, in the sense that she claimed as you went further into a depression, unemployment

ABOVE: The Brick House, the Perkins family homestead in Newcastle, Maine. *(Courtesy of Tomlin Coggeshall)*

LEFT: Fannie Coralie Perkins at approximately six years old. *(Courtesy of Tomlin Coggeshall)*

ABOVE: Fannie Perkins (Frances Perkins) at Mount Holyoke. *(Mount Holyoke College Archives and Special Collections)*

TOP RIGHT: Susan Bean Perkins, Frances Perkins's mother. *(Courtesy of Tomlin Coggeshall)*

BOTTOM RIGHT: Frederick W. Perkins, Frances Perkins's father, about 1912. *(Frances Perkins Papers, Rare Book & Manuscript Library, Columbia University)*

Frances stands next to a fire escape as she investigates working conditions during an inspection for the New York Factory Investigating Commission.
(Frances Perkins Papers, Rare Book & Manuscript Library, Columbia University)

ABOVE: Paul Caldwell Wilson and Frances Perkins soon after their marriage. *(Courtesy of Tomlin Coggeshall)*

LEFT: Husband and daughter: Paul Wilson and Susanna Wilson in Newcastle, Maine. *(Courtesy of Tomlin Coggeshall)*

RIGHT: A family Fourth of July parade in their yard at Newcastle, about 1925. Paul, Susanna's governess, Frances, and Susanna. *(Courtesy of Tomlin Coggeshall)*

Frances reading aloud to Susanna at their home in New York City,
1921. *(Courtesy of Tomlin Coggeshall)*

RIGHT: John Mitchell, former head of United Mine Workers and close friend of Frances Perkins. *(The Library of Congress)*

BELOW: Frances playing in the yard with family dog, Balto, in Newcastle, 1930. *(Courtesy of Tomlin Coggeshall)*

The first woman to serve in a presidential Cabinet: Frances Perkins is standing at far right. Others pictured, seated left to right: George H. Dern, secretary of war; Cordell Hull, secretary of state; President Franklin D. Roosevelt; William H. Woodin, secretary of the treasury; and Homer S. Cummings, attorney general. Standing: Henry A. Wallace, secretary of agriculture; Harold L. Ickes, secretary of the interior; Claude A. Swanson, secretary of the navy; James A. Farley, postmaster general; Daniel C. Roper, secretary of commerce, 1933. *(AP Images)*

Frances shares a secret joke with incoming president Franklin Delano Roosevelt, January 1, 1933. *(Frances Perkins Papers, Rare Book & Manuscript Library, Columbia University; MPI/Getty Images)*

Eleanor Roosevelt presents a gold medal to Frances, who has just been named Outstanding Woman in the Field of Civic Achievement by Chi Omega sorority, December 1934. *(AP Images)*

increased because a lot more people become available for employment," Lubin recalled. "She made a tremendous impression on me at the time; in fact, she impressed everybody, all of the Senators who were there."[12]

By early 1932, FDR's political team began to develop a sense of its own destiny.

On March 4, 1932, one year before the formal presidential inauguration day, Frances sent Roosevelt a telegram: "This day next year will be interesting," she wrote.[13]

"I applaud your faith," the governor shot back, also by telegram.

And her faith was justified. On the night of November 4, 1932, after another long run on the presidential campaign trail, Frances found herself once more at the Democratic campaign headquarters on election night, this time at the Biltmore Hotel in New York City. The festive mood grew ever more buoyant as the evening progressed and it became apparent that Roosevelt was winning a decisive victory over Hoover. Women hugged each other in excitement. Frances mingled with a group of women campaign workers who decided on the spur of the moment to rush up to Hyde Park to be at the center of the action.

It was a jubilant train ride to Poughkeepsie, the closest big city to Hyde Park. One of FDR's assistants met them at the station and drove them to Roosevelt's estate on the Hudson. There they gathered around the telephone, continuing to monitor the election returns. Roosevelt eventually captured 57 percent of the vote. As word spread, neighbors clustered at the gate and gathered on the house's broad lawns.

Enjoying the merriment and excitement, she stayed until late that night, catching a 2 a.m. train back to the city. Bedraggled, exhausted, and radiantly happy, she made her way home. With Roosevelt headed to Washington, she began contemplating a very different future for herself as well.

Chapter 14

FRANCES BECOMES
SECRETARY OF LABOR

$\mathcal{A}$s Roosevelt rested in Warm Springs after the election, speculation focused on his likely Cabinet choices. Amid rampant joblessness, the appointment of a strong secretary of labor was considered a key to the success of his administration. Though Frances had served with FDR in this capacity for four years in New York, at first her name circulated as a slim possibility. After all, no woman had ever been named to the Cabinet, and Frances told people she considered a job offer unlikely. Frances publicly denied her ambitions as she campaigned quietly for the job.

She traveled to Washington for a dinner meeting with a group of possible supporters, including Clara Beyer, a Labor Department official. Beyer arranged for Frances to appear at a gathering at the home of a wealthy Democratic activist, to meet with Supreme Court Justice Louis Brandeis, and to dine with women journalists. She assured Frances that the meetings were merely a "tribute" to her past leadership in New York, not to advance her as secretary of labor.[1]

Grace Abbott, head of the Labor Department's Children's Bureau and an influential Hull House alumna, took another step to raise Frances's profile. At her urging, Frances addressed a conference on the impact of unemployment on the nation's youth. Abbott made sure the audience was stocked with female reporters, all of whom had been tipped off about Frances's potential importance. They hung on her words and sat "scribbling away."[2]

Abbott also arranged Capitol Hill meetings with senators and congressmen closely identified with labor issues. She scheduled a photography session to shoot the requisite publicity head shots of the photo-shy Frances.

Frances professed surprise at the attention she received in Washington, calling herself as "innocent as a child" at the time she received

Abbott's invitation. She claimed the same naïveté as the photographer snapped her picture.

Suddenly her name appeared more frequently in newspaper columns, with Frances's friends nudging along the efforts. Beyer sent letters asking other labor advocates to support Frances as labor secretary.[3] More support for a draft movement came from Felix Frankfurter, a Harvard law professor who had served as legal counsel to the National Consumers League after Brandeis left for the Supreme Court.

Democratic official Mary Dewson, another friend from the league, orchestrated a national letter-writing campaign on Frances's behalf. Dewson worked her own political and activist network, supplemented by a list of names Frances provided.[4]

Hundreds of endorsement letters flooded FDR's office. Petitions arrived bearing dozens of signatures. "I need not recite any of her qualifications, for it is a wonderful coincidence that the woman best equipped for the post should have sat in the previous cabinet of the President of the United States," wrote Jane Addams, from Hull House, in December 1932.

The exiled commissioner of labor statistics, Ethelbert Stewart, as well as a handful of businessmen, echoed Addams's view. Lincoln Filene of Filene's department store wrote: "I hope that it may be true that you are seriously considering her. She is the best equipped MAN for the job that I know of."[5]

Beyer, Dewson, and others feverishly consulted about how to push Frances's candidacy: "Is there anything that I can do to help make Frances Perkins Secretary of Labor?" Beyer wrote to Dewson. "She is just the person for the job and so terribly needed at this time. . . . How can we bolster up the Governor's hands? I feel sure that he wants her if he can possibly put her across."[6]

In January 1933, Justice Brandeis met with Roosevelt at Washington's Mayflower Hotel and urged him to name Frances secretary.[7]

Mary Harriman Rumsey, by now a key campaign contributor to the Democratic Party, told Frances she knew she would be chosen. By mid-February her appointment was beginning to seem inevitable.

Amid this avid politicking, Frances still played coy in public, partly because of her own uncertainty as to whether FDR would choose her. She hedged her bets and cultivated Lehman, the new governor of New York, hoping that he would retain her as industrial commissioner if FDR did not take her to Washington. Keeping a job was imperative to maintain the fragile balancing act of her personal life. Lehman made clear that he gladly would keep her on, and, as she had done with both Smith and Roosevelt, Frances began studying Lehman's operating style so that she could serve him effectively and stay in his good graces.

Around this time, Dewson called on Frances for a heart-to-heart talk. She told Frances that she had gone on record in support of her nomination, and she didn't want to "make a fool" of herself pushing something Frances didn't want. Frances murmured that she didn't think Roosevelt wanted her. Dewson brushed aside her objections, telling Frances that the job offered the chance, perhaps the only chance she would ever get, to enact the legislative agenda they had all espoused for twenty years.

Dewson had an even more convincing argument. In February 1932, Florence Kelley, the inspiration for a generation of young reformers, had died at age seventy-four. The fiery founder of the National Consumers League had spent her life laboring for workplace reforms, but her victories had been few and hard won. In the last decade of her life, she had made little progress on her pet causes, including the abolition of child labor. Her efforts had been stymied by the growing clout of the National Association of Manufacturers, which adamantly defended the right to employ children. Having Frances as labor secretary battling the issue on the federal level would vindicate Kelley's work.[8]

Frances felt deeply responsible to Kelley's legacy. When she had become New York industrial commissioner in 1929, Kelley wrote "there will be less death, misery and poverty because you are at the helm."[9] Frances had written back to tell Kelley she had been her most important mentor: "Darling Mrs. Kelley:—It is a shame that you weren't here on my induction into office," she wrote. "You were the only person whom I particularly wanted to be here and so stated, but they couldn't find you at the moment . . . I would have given a great deal to have you here for I regard you as the head of the family in this enterprise which binds us all together.

"Thank you for believing that I shall accomplish something. To the very last of my ability I shall try to do what you expect of me, and partly I shall try because it is you who is expecting so much. Your demand for good work and results has always been an inspiration, quite as much of an inspiration, I think, as your continual stream of new ideas!"

Dewson and Frances both knew that the best way to honor Kelley's memory was for Frances to win the appointment. Dewson insisted that they float another trial balloon to gauge public reaction—a press statement announcing Frances's imminent appointment. Frances reluctantly agreed, hoping that FDR would disapprove. Instead, he gave it an enthusiastic nod. The ploy inspired positive comments from around the nation. The only hostile reaction came from top union officials, who wanted one of their own men in the post.

Newspapers began reporting on Frances's probable nomination. Her friends, especially her old league allies, grew jubilant in expectation. Yet Frances couldn't help feeling some reluctance about the post. As a wife and mother, she knew the timing was terrible. Paul had returned to the mental hospital, and Susanna was a strong-willed teenager entering her last years of high school. Frances still adored New York City life. Her work was satisfying, and she enjoyed her home, the theater, and a circle of longtime friends from church and discussion groups and clubs. She feared she would never recapture her comfortable lifestyle if she left.

The prospect of moving to Washington "horrified" her. She needed to supervise Paul's care, yet she knew that a Cabinet post would be all-consuming and would open her personal life to scrutiny. In an era when mental illness was stigmatized, she feared embarrassment for herself and her family if Paul's problems were exposed.[10]

She also knew from her own family's history that the risks of public service could be great, particularly when the work was controversial. Her ancestor attorney James Otis won glory with his no-taxation-without-representation cry, but died ignominiously. Her grandmother's cousin Oliver Otis Howard had been attacked as corrupt for trying to advance the cause of freed slaves after the Civil War.

The job also would be physically exhausting. A year earlier, her friend Margaret Bondfield, the first female labor minister in Great Britain, collapsed and was hospitalized after her political party was defeated in the national election.[11]

Then there was the gender issue. She knew that being a woman in a man's job would subject her to particular ridicule.

In public, Frances usually brushed off questions by calling gender irrelevant. "Does it hold you back?" she was asked. "Only in climbing trees," she quipped. Occasionally, she spoke her mind freely, as a male reporter learned when he needled her by asking if she knew that men laughed at women among themselves.

"Why, certainly I know they laugh at women," Frances responded.[12]

"Doesn't that make you angry?"

"No, not particularly, because it isn't anything like [when] women laugh at men," she said. ". . . All women laugh about all men. No two women ever get together really that they don't have some little joke to pass between them about the inadequacies of men or the stupidity of men, or the self-deceit of men."

She decided to squelch the recruit-Frances drive by telling Roosevelt she wasn't interested in the job. She advised him to appoint a union official to build labor support. She added that her "grave personal difficulties" would likely impair her effectiveness in such a job.[13]

Her letter prompted a call from the president-elect's office, asking her to meet with FDR at his home on 65th Street the following day. Frances called Dewson to see if she knew why she was being asked.

"Sure, I know what's it's all about," Dewson said. "You do, too. Don't be such a baby. Frances, you do the right thing. I'll murder you if you don't!" [14]

Frances confronted the reality that FDR likely would ask her to become secretary of labor. Over the next day, she compiled her to-do list. She had been accumulating ideas from around the world for some time. She had written them on individual slips of paper, storing them in the lower right-hand desk drawer.

Frances wondered whether it was even possible to implement some of the ideas in light of Supreme Court rulings. In 1905, the Court had said that restricting bakery workers to a ten-hour workday violated workers' rights to contract for their own work hours. In 1918, the Court had ruled that federal restrictions on child labor violated states' rights to regulate production. In 1923, the Court ruled it was illegal to set a minimum wage for women regardless of whether or not they were earning enough to live on.[15]

More pressingly, the country's economic distress made it hard to imagine taking steps that would cost money before they delivered benefits. Frances wasn't even sure whether FDR shared her goals. Despite their amicable relations, she viewed him as an elusive figure, ultimately a politician, who might not follow through on what they started. Although he had said the right things about workplace reforms, there were times when he could not fully empathize with workers' plight. She remembered a time when she had argued that women workers needed seats with backs to support their spines and Roosevelt had roared laughter at her idea. Frances had been incensed, and told him so. don't know anything about women's backs," she told him. "They a like thunder from sitting up perfectly straight at a machine with no support for the small of the back."[16]

And Frances knew that FDR had no real action plan once he took over the White House. "Nobody knew, least of all the President-elect, whether the most important thing was to balance the budget, to conserve the trees out in the wilderness, or to feed the unemployed in the Bowery mission. That's literally true. There was no conviction about which things came first and which things second," she said later.

Instead, Frances had developed her own views on needed action. She ranked unemployment first and wanted to provide immediate relief through measures that would mitigate the extreme economic cycles that led to joblessness. Before long, she could tick off a list of priorities.

On February 22, 1933, a week before the inauguration, Frances headed over to her appointment with the president. She arrived to find the house littered with debris from countless meetings held there over the past few weeks. What had been a quiet family home had been transformed into an encampment for reporters, politicians, policemen, detectives, and the Secret Service. The little hall was piled high with overcoats, hats, umbrellas, briefcases, notebooks, and sheaves of paper. A handsome Chinese rug was rumpled and left in a careless heap.

Frances was directed upstairs to wait outside the president's study. A plump, bespectacled blond man waited in another chair. He didn't look up or greet her, and she had no idea who he was. She sized him up as a rather rustic out-of-towner, probably from Syracuse or Buffalo.

The door opened, and the governor greeted them both. Seeing the pair standing awkwardly, FDR asked Frances if she knew the man, whom he called Harold. No, she told him. The strangers bowed stiffly, and the man was ushered into FDR's study, while Frances waited. After a long while, the man emerged and put on his coat. They exchanged their only words: "Good evening." Then he left.[17]

Frances was led into Roosevelt's office. To lighten the mood, she asked who Harold was. Harold Ickes, FDR told her, with some surprise that she didn't know. Roosevelt had just offered Ickes, a progressive Republican from Chicago, the post of secretary of the interior.

"He looks like an American, but how do you spell his name?" she asked. They laughed, and he wondered about the name's origins. "Polish?" she said. She later learned it was English.[18]

Roosevelt got down to business.

"I guess you know what I want you here for," he said. "Did Molly Dewson tell you what I have in mind?"

"Well, I never know if Molly is speaking the truth or just reflecting her own hopes and aspirations," Frances said, laughing.

"I really mean it, Frances," he said. "I think you'd be a good Secretary of Labor, and I'd like you to come along and be Secretary of Labor. Molly must have told you. We had discussed it before she spoke to you."

She feigned surprise, said she was honored, and thanked him.

"Oh, come on now," he said. "You're no fool. What did you think I wanted to see you for when McIntyre telephoned you to come up today?"

"I thought you might just want to say good-bye to me," she joked, then acknowledged she had given it some "offhand consideration."

Then she proceeded to lay out her dramatic plan of action.

The Labor Department, she told him, needed an overhaul. It had a $3 million budget in 1932 but was overwhelmed by its largest single operation, immigration, which devoured two-thirds of its budget. That left only $1 million to enforce labor laws and address working people's problems. She'd been told that the department was riddled with corruption, with inspectors and other officials on the take. She also reminded him of the Wickersham Commission report, conducted during the Hoover administration, which had examined problems in law enforcement generally, given the sharp rise in crime under Prohibition. The commission had detected many specific problems in immigration. It found that inspectors were deporting foreigners on flimsy grounds, citing spurious immorality claims, often without permitting them to defend themselves. Foreigners, particularly labor leaders, who offended powerful people were likely to be forced out of the country. She thought the department needed a thorough cleansing.

The minuscule Bureau of Women in Industry was handling the only real workplace reform. Another part of the department was the Children's Bureau, but while it did good work, it wasn't particularly focused on working people. Another agency, the Public Employment Office, "did nothing," she said, serving merely as a sinecure for Republican cronies. Frances proposed dismissing poor performers, then improving the service to help the jobless find work. The Bureau of Labor Statistics, which had produced the dubious employment figures used by Hoover, needed serious revamping. She wanted to make it a source of dependable statistics for planning.

Tragically, she said, nothing had been done to create a national labor policy, leaving workers to the vicissitudes of their individual states. "Although the State of New York has pretty good labor legislation, and Wisconsin has good labor legislation, California has some, Massachusetts has some, the other states of the union, and the people who are in the other states of the union, have practically no protection or very meager protection," Frances told Roosevelt.

She reminded him of the practical difference between the workmen's compensation laws in New York and neighboring Pennsylvania, which had much weaker protections. When a truck driver got hurt driving close to the state border, the employer would invariably claim the injury happened in Pennsylvania so that he could pay less.

When FDR asked her what she thought should be done, Frances produced her notes: "Unemployment is the present pressing issue," she said. "The first thing I think we should do, and this should emanate from the Secretary of Labor's office, although it's a general problem, is to find some way of general relief and to do public works. . . . They should be thought of as temporary. There are plenty of public works in different parts of the country, and we'll have to devise a fiscal arrangement whereby the federal government can assist the states."

The strategy would hold the wolf at bay, she said, while the federal government pushed ahead with a program to reduce unemployment more significantly. Child labor should be prohibited, not just because of its damage to young people, but also because it drove down wages and caused adults to lose jobs. Working hours, which had stretched to twelve hours or more a day in many industries, should be reduced to spread work among more people and to prevent workers from being crushed by fatigue. An eight-hour day would be preferable. A minimum wage needed to be established.

"Can that be done constitutionally?" FDR asked.

"It's very doubtful, but I want to say now that we should try," Frances said. "I would like to try and would like to know now if you would back me in trying."

"Sure," he said.

She intended to start with one particular approach, which had been Felix Frankfurter's idea. Frankfurter thought the government could set wage and hour restrictions on the manufactured goods it bought—something the federal government could clearly do under its right to define its requirements on its own purchases. Since the federal government was the largest single purchaser for many industries, she said, these changes would affect many workers immediately. It also would help boost the money in circulation in the economy, a theory being promoted by economist John Maynard Keynes.

"Yeah, that's interesting," Roosevelt said. "Surely, anyhow, we ought to peg wages at a living level."

She moved to workers' health. Workers' compensation must be imposed across the country, Frances said, so that workers maimed on the job would not fall into desperate poverty. Workers in some southern states received no guaranteed compensation for a workplace injury, even a broken back or an amputated hand. Frances didn't think she could do anything directly about poor working conditions in those states, but she could try to convince individual states to institute reforms of their own.

Roosevelt laughed at what he thought would be a phenomenal bit of salesmanship. "How will you promote it?" he asked.

"Well, you can persuade people to do a lot of things," Frances said. She explained she would seek to build better relations between the federal government and state labor agencies and would need Roosevelt's help there.

"Part of your genius has been that you've been able to establish good relations where there were poor relations," she told him. "With your help, if you're willing to take a hand with the governors, then I think that I can follow through.... All I expect from you at the beginning is that you call a governor's conference and that among the items mentioned will be some of the things that I have in mind," she said. "I'd like you to lay the path, to make it possible for the Secretary of Labor to approach the departments of labor in those states."

Ever mindful of the Triangle fire, she said she also would push for safety regulation in states across the country. Roosevelt nodded.

She then spelled out a plan for a national system of unemployment insurance, which would reduce the financial distress of laid-off workers and which also would keep money circulating in their communities. This would involve a system of worker contributions during their employment so that they could collect some income during hard times. Unemployment insurance, Frances said, was a way to mitigate the worst effects of capitalism's natural down cycles.

While a national plan was under development Frances would promote private unemployment insurance, such as the systems voluntarily established by companies like Eastman Kodak, Procter & Gamble, and the Manning-Adams Company. She would also highlight efforts some companies had made to stabilize employment. As an example, garment manufacturer Hickey Freeman had shifted to a non-fashion-dependent, "evergreen" product line, the Chesterfield coat, when demand for its other goods dried up.

The largest item on her agenda was an old-age pension, a minimum allotment to the elderly so they would not burden their families. She envisioned it operating something like unemployment insurance, with people paying into a system when they were young and receiving payments years later.

At this point, FDR objected. It reminded him of the English system he knew as the "dole," in which people received handouts for doing nothing. He was already worried about the growing popularity of the Townsend Plan, a harebrained scheme circulating around the country that guaranteed large monthly payments to the elderly, without making provisions for funding. Roosevelt thought an old-age pension plan might reward older people who no longer wanted to work.

Frances asked whether she could at least study the issue to look for ways to avoid the pitfalls of the English system. FDR agreed.

"Are you sure you want this done, because you won't want me for Secretary of Labor if you don't want these things done," she told him. "I'd be an embarrassment to you because when I start a thing, I round up the cohorts. I get out advisory committees who really become supporters of the idea. You get a public demand for it the next thing you know. You wouldn't want me if you didn't want that done."

FDR told her he would back her; he had promised the American people he would improve their lives, and he intended to do so.

The president-elect waited for her answer. She asked instead for time to tell Paul.

"I must consult him," she said. "I cannot let him read in the paper that I have been appointed to something and have accepted something he doesn't know about. You understand that?"

"All right," he said. "Let me know tomorrow night."

As she rose to leave, Roosevelt spoke again. "I suppose you are going to nag me about this forever," he said, referring to the program she had just laid out. He knew her well enough to know that she would not back down. "He wanted his conscience kept for him by somebody," she thought to herself.

Discussing the matter with Paul was an obligatory but meaningless gesture. He hadn't worked for four years and was severely incapacitated. Frances knew it would likely be eight to ten months before he would be released from his most recent hospitalization. Still, on some level, she needed his support, an affirmation that she still had a life partner.

"I knew that my husband's view on the matter would be what I told him it was, because he was in no state of mind at that time to have an independent analysis of anything."

She told him about the offer. His first reaction was to think of himself.

"Well, I won't go to Washington," he said. "That would be horrid." He asked her where he would live instead. Knowing he was too ill to go in any case, Frances had already made a plan. She said she would keep the New York apartment and commute to the city every weekend. She thought Susanna, a high-school junior, should finish up at the Brearley School rather than moving to Washington.

"You'll be up every weekend, will you?" Paul asked plaintively. Of course, she said, since it was her habit to visit him every Saturday afternoon. She told him that accepting the job was an obligation to other women who aspired to similar roles.

"I told my husband all of this," she recalled some years later. "He was very nice about it. He was happy that I had been asked. He was having a good day."

Back home, she suddenly found herself crying, racked with sobs, walking from room to room with tears streaming. She debated whether she could accept the post, knowing instinctively that the work would tax her more than anything she had ever done and that she would have to give up her life in New York to attempt it. She was filled with dread, even terror.

She knew Susanna was watching with astonishment and fear, but Frances couldn't stop herself. "That evening I cried all the time," she said. "I just couldn't stop. . . . I just didn't want to venture out into this great sea of the unknown."

The fifty-two-year-old woman finally comforted herself by remembering her grandmother's advice: "If somebody opens a door for you, my dear . . . walk right in and do the best you can," she would say. "Do the best you can, for it means that it's the Lord's will for you."

A month later, some eight hundred friends saluted her at a testimonial dinner at the Hotel Commodore in New York City. A procession of friends and allies rose to praise her accomplishments. Political activists applauded her role. "When I think of all FP has done, I feel obliged to shake her hand," said Caroline O'Day, a wealthy widow active in the Democratic Party. "Women love her, that she is a woman more worthy than any man; men, that she is the fairest of all women. I would like to ask for a blessing among her own people. The blessing of Providence on you, Frances Perkins, and may the Lord take cognizance of you, but not too soon."

Her words drew hearty laughter and applause.

Then Mrs. Louis Slade, former chairwoman of the League of Women Voters, spoke. "I come here tonight as a Republican." More laughter and applause. "She has taught us all to hitch our wagons to stars, to know that where something needed to be done, if it was impossible, it should be done."

Marion B. Folsom, assistant treasurer at Eastman Kodak, spoke of Frances's help to Rochester businesses and urged her to establish uniform federal workplace standards that would prevent an inconsistent profusion of state laws. Jesse Isidor Strauss, head of the retailer Macy & Co., praised her for her leadership in New York.

He also, seemingly in jest, raised a delicate point:

"Miss Frances is going to make such a fine record in the job that some of us, particularly the married men, may possibly have to look forward to the time when all the Cabinet positions and possibly the Presidency too will be filled by women, and what then?" Strauss asked.[19]

Chapter 15

THE PIONEER

$\mathscr{A}$mong women's groups, Frances's appointment as secretary of labor brought pure joy. Flowers and congratulations streamed into her apartment. "This is a red-letter day for women," said Nellie Tayloe Ross, vice chairman of the Democratic Party. League of Women Voters president Belle Sherwin declared that her group was "delighted that the first woman appointed to a cabinet office is so exceptionally qualified."

Not everyone was pleased, however. William Green, president of the American Federation of Labor, issued a statement that union officers were "keenly disappointed" over the president's choice: "Labor has consistently contended that the Department of Labor should be what its name implies and that the Secretary of Labor should be representative of labor, one who understands labor, labor's problems, labor's psychology, collective bargaining, industrial relations and one who enjoys the confidence of labor. . . . In the opinion of labor, the newly appointed Secretary of Labor does not meet these qualifications. Labor can never become reconciled to the selection made."[1]

Green's dismay may have been compounded by the fact that he, too, had wanted the position. Some labor leaders wanted Green out of command of the AFL, and getting him the secretary's job would have removed him from their path.[2]

Some male Labor Department staffers threatened to resign rather than report to a woman. Other outside observers took a dim view of a feminist victory. An editorial in the *Baltimore Sun* read: "A woman smarter than a man is something to get on guard about. But a woman smarter than a man and also not afraid of a man, well, good-night."[3]

Frances declined to spar with Green or other critics, and she strove to take the high road at her first press conference. About twenty newsmen crowded into her Industrial Commission office, more reporters than she had ever faced. Prodded to respond to Green, she called him a "man of great integrity, vision and patriotism." If labor leaders "cannot find time to come and see me," she said, "I will hasten to see them."

But Frances grew testy when the reporters' questions focused on Paul or sixteen-year-old Susanna. She had no intention of discussing her marriage, both because of Paul's illness and the active movement to ban married women from employment. Questions about Susanna terrified her because she planned to leave the girl with family friends in New York City to finish high school, and the Lindbergh kidnapping a year earlier had instilled fear among America's prominent families.

"Is this quite necessary?" she snapped. Normally personable and described as delightful by those who knew her well, Frances developed a reputation among reporters as being "schoolmarmish and stuffy."[4] In fact, many of her public comments came across as dry and fusty, designed to deflect attention from herself rather than attract it.

Part of her problem was that her nomination came so late in the process that she had little time to prepare for the move and the new job or to ponder how best to present herself to the public.

Her friend Margaret Poole rescued her on the wardrobe front. She sent dresses to Frances for inspection, and the new secretary selected a simple black dress, a suit, and a black velvet gown with iridescent sequins for evening wear. Eager to claim credit for outfitting the secretary of labor, clothing stores sent seamstresses to make sure the garments fit perfectly.

Amid the chaos of the times and the usual commotion entailed by a change of administration, the incoming Cabinet officers found that little had been done to help them manage their arrival in Washington. The Democrats had not won the presidency in two decades, and the inauguration committee failed to make lodging or transportation arrangements for Cabinet officers.

The outgoing administration, meanwhile, was "bitter, sour, mean," Frances said later, and quite unwilling to facilitate the transition. Frances was disappointed when not a single Department of Labor official contacted her to prepare for a transfer of power.[5]

With inauguration day rapidly approaching, all the good Washington hotels were completely booked. The Roosevelts were ensconced in the Mayflower Hotel's lavish presidential suite, but Frances couldn't even find a simple hotel room for herself and Susanna. Growing desperate, she turned to longtime friend Henry Bruere. Bruere served as president of the Bowery Savings Bank, which held a mortgage on the dilapidated Willard Hotel on Pennsylvania Avenue. Bruere leaned on Mrs. Willard to make sure Frances and Susanna had a place to stay.

Frances and Susanna took the train to Washington with a small group of friends and supporters, including a cousin and his two sons. Arriving at Union Station the day before the inauguration, they entered a scene of "perfect bedlam." [6] The building was packed with Republicans leaving town and Democrats arriving. Streets were gridlocked and sidewalks jammed with pedestrians. Frances and her party rushed into the streets to hail taxicabs, but they ended up walking to the hotel, a long winter mile from the station. The hotel room was large but old-fashioned, with high ceilings, a floral carpet, wardrobes rather than closets, and an ornate Victorian brass bed. The decor was so unstylish that Susanna burst out laughing when she saw it. The room became Frances's operations base for the next few hectic days.

They had no communication with the White House or with Roosevelt until much later that night, when they returned to the hotel after a tiring evening trying unsuccessfully to get to a party at the Pan American Union. They missed the event while their taxi inched through the clogged city streets. Arriving back at the hotel after midnight, they found a note on the door asking them to call a Mr. Early. Frances wasn't sure who he was but called immediately. The man was Stephen Early, a new aide to FDR.

"For heaven's sake, where have you been?" he asked impatiently. She explained their foiled effort to celebrate at the Pan American Union. Early scoffed. She had wasted her time because only the "riff-raff" had been invited to that function, he said.

He told her that FDR wanted all the incoming Cabinet members to attend services with him the next morning at St. John's Church in Lafayette Square near the White House. They would go from the church to the Capitol Hill inauguration ceremony.

Frances rose early so that she and Susanna could prepare for the important day. But outside the hotel, they again found themselves stranded without a vacant taxi in sight. The doorman suggested they walk the four blocks to the church, so they set off on foot in the unfamiliar city. Worried about getting lost, they stopped for directions several times.

Finally, they found the small church with its dark medieval-looking chapel. The pews were filled with people Frances recognized from newspaper photos. There was no time for formal introductions. Soon the president and his family entered and took their places in front. Endicott Peabody, founder and rector of Groton School, which FDR had attended, conducted the service, using passages from the Book of Common Prayer. The group sang two of FDR's favorite hymns, "Faith of Our Fathers" and "Oh, God Our Help in Ages Past." To Frances, a devout Episcopalian, both the service and the hymns were familiar. The faith she shared with Roosevelt was a bond between them.

When the service ended and the clergy departed, Roosevelt remained seated for some time, praying silently. The Cabinet officers and their families waited quietly. Finally he rose, turned, and smiled at the congregation in a fatherly way. He left through the side door and entered a waiting car.

The inauguration was scheduled to begin within minutes on Capitol Hill. The Cabinet officers had been assigned special seating, directly behind the president.

But when churchgoers exited, they confronted the same traffic-jammed streets. Those more familiar with Washington had arranged for limousines to pick them up. Cordell Hull, the incoming secretary of state, climbed into a car with his wife. Another limousine swept away Navy Secretary Claude Swanson and his wife. Wealthy Dan Roper, who would head the Commerce Department, found his own limousine waiting. Harold Ickes and his wife had hired a car, and they, too, were whisked away. A few other Cabinet members dashed into the street and snagged the only available taxis for themselves and their families. Finally, only Frances, Susanna, and one other couple were left standing helplessly outside the church.

"You're Miss Perkins, aren't you?" asked a tall, handsome man standing with his wife. Perkins recognized him as the incoming secretary of agriculture, Henry Wallace.[7]

"Yes, and you're the Wallaces," Frances said, turning to introduce Susanna to them.

"We better make common cause, get the first cab we can, and all go together, don't you think?" he said. Frances gratefully accepted, and the four started off together. No cabs were to be seen. They darted toward the nearby Hay-Adams Hotel, but the doorman offered no help. With the clock ticking, Henry Wallace staked out one corner and Frances another, finally attracting a passing driver who agreed to take them as far as he could. He warned them that the streets were so crowded that they probably couldn't make it all the way to the Capitol.

Luckily, they came within sight of the building, only to find a wooden barricade blocking further passage. A policeman stopped them. Wallace told him they were Cabinet officers and that their presence was required, but the policeman wouldn't budge.

"Nope, can't be done," he said. "Nothing can go beyond this point. You should have gone some other way or come earlier."

Not to be deterred, Frances noticed a trail of outgoing Cabinet officers entering the grounds. She and the others climbed out of the car and started walking up the hill. Then they started to run. With Wallace leading the way, they pressed through the crowd.

"Henry was very bold, saying 'Will you be good enough to let us pass? Kindly make way. I'm sorry, Madame, but it's essential that we go through. Will you be so good as to let us pass here?' " Frances recalled.

In those moments, a fast friendship was forged between the two families. Finally they reached an expanse of lawn roped off to protect the grass from the milling crowd, and realized their destination was on the other side. Wallace and Frances saw that they would need to duck under the ropes and run across the lawn like tardy schoolchildren if they were going to make it to the reviewing stand on time. Wallace's wife agreed to watch Susanna. It was an overcast and misty day, and the grass was cold and wet.

"I hope you've got your rubbers on," Henry said with a laugh, noting Frances's formal dress heels. The two scampered across the lawn, making their way to the Capitol doors, arriving on the reviewing platform just after the ceremony began. They found places to sit and watched as the new president took the oath, his hand placed firmly on an old Dutch family Bible.

Hoover shook hands with Roosevelt and left the platform with a few friends. Frances walked over to the wall to watch Hoover depart. She'd publicly sparred with him for months, attacking his veracity on the employment numbers. Still, she felt compassion as she saw Hoover and his friends shake hands and depart in separate cars, headed for Union Station.

Frances turned back to listen to Roosevelt's speech and noticed with surprise that it had changed substantially from an earlier draft. The tone was inspirational, calling for courage and optimism in the face of despair. His hopeful message was delivered with stark honesty about the nation's fiscal crisis:

> This is preeminently the time to speak the truth, the whole truth, frankly and boldly. Nor need we shrink from honestly facing conditions in our country today. This great nation will endure as it has endured, will revive and will prosper. So, first of all, let me assert my firm belief that the only thing we have to fear is fear itself—nameless, unreasoning, unjustified terror which paralyzes needed efforts to convert retreat into advance. In every dark hour of our national life, a leadership of frankness and vigor has met with that understanding and support of the people themselves which is essential to victory. I am convinced that you will again give that support to leadership in these critical days.[8]

Frances listened, entranced, as Roosevelt described a national emergency and his plan to seek "broad executive power" to tackle pressing problems. She sensed that Roosevelt must have had a religious revelation, that he was exerting a spiritual leadership that seemed divinely inspired. "It was a revival of faith," she said. "He said, 'Come on now, do you believe?' They said, 'Yes, we do.' "[9]

When the speech concluded, the crowd surged back down Capitol Hill into the city's commercial area. Frances found a taxi but soon found herself in gridlock again. Katharine Lenroot, a Labor Department employee, met Frances for the first time that day. Lenroot was on foot, walking with Grace Abbott, her supervisor at the Children's Bureau, and the two stopped to chat with Frances in her immobilized car. Lenroot had been stirred by Roosevelt's speech, and looked at Frances intently as they spoke.

Lenroot thought Frances looked "rather slight and feminine," and too small to carry such a large share of responsibility for Roosevelt's agenda in solving the problems facing the nation. She wondered how she would handle it.[10]

The new administration voiced enormous aspirations. Frances was amused by the irony of undertaking huge challenges without knowing how to conquer even simple things in Washington. Sitting paralyzed in

Washington traffic was the first of many indignities she would suffer from not knowing the rules in the nation's capital.

She made another misstep that night. Invited to the White House for dinner, she arrived with Susanna at the East Gate, as the invitation stated, checked her coat, and got in line to enter. The extremely long line included faithful Democrats from all over the country. She slowly made her way toward the main hall, when she was spotted by Missy LeHand, FDR's faithful secretary.

"What are you doing here, Miss Perkins?" LeHand said. Frances explained that the line had been long. LeHand laughed. Cabinet officers didn't need to wait, she said. They could enter the White House through the front door as though they were family, and a military aide would have quickly escorted her to the president. LeHand motioned for help, and soon Frances and Susanna were escorted in high style on the arms of uniformed young men.

Learning Washington etiquette would clearly be essential to functioning in the city. Her schoolgirl friend from Mount Holyoke, Elizabeth Rogers, now Mrs. Owen Roberts, wife of the Supreme Court justice, gave Frances a book that explained Washington's arcane protocol. She needed to study quickly, because soon invitations to teas, dinners, concerts, and art gallery openings flooded into the Willard Hotel.

One difficult question surrounding her newly elevated post was where she should sit at official functions. Under long-established protocol, the secretary of labor would be seated among the high-ranking officeholders. But as the only woman, she raised a special question. Frances decided to ask that she be seated among the Cabinet wives, as if she were the wife of the secretary of labor.

Frances did it to avoid what she called the "Dolly Gann-Alice Roosevelt Longworth type of dispute." Soon after Hoover took office, a famous feud erupted between two prominent Washington socialites, Dolly Gann, the sister of the vice president and his regular escort at events, and Alice Roosevelt Longworth, the daughter of Teddy Roosevelt, who was the wife of the Speaker of the House. Gann's situation was irregular, since she was not the vice president's wife, so the question arose: Who outranked whom? It became a delicate dilemma, and the subject of much frenzied speculation, mostly among male reporters, who saw it as a catfight over who deserved the better seat. The brouhaha went on for months and left both women looking petty.[11]

So Frances gave up her assigned position to avoid creating jealousy. "I knew intuitively, and having heard and read about what was said about that row, that any effort on my part, or any insistence by anybody, that I should precede anyone would stir up agonies in people's breasts," she said. ". . . It's really the best way. That meant that at ladies' luncheons you didn't precede Mrs. Hull. You didn't have to sit on the hostess's side at a ladies' luncheon. You sat down where the wife of the Secretary of Labor would be seated. It's fairly far down the table, but still it's a good seat. That was a much better arrangement."[12]

She also made no objection to the custom of the ladies retiring after dinner for a rest while the men smoked cigars and talked politics. She joined the women in the drawing room rather than staying with the men, although sometimes the men discussed important business. Frances found being with the women more pleasant because they talked about family and personal issues.

Frances plunged into both the work and social aspects of her new life—and more quickly than she had expected. She needed to wrap up some important work in New York for the Industrial Commission, and so she assumed that she would return home to New York City for at least a short period after the inauguration. She planned to travel that Sunday, since Susanna was due back at high school on Monday. But Stephen Early informed her the Cabinet would be sworn in immediately, leaving Frances no time to finalize her affairs in New York.

Frances protested. The president had said the swearing-in wouldn't occur for at least two weeks. She was also surprised that the Senate, driven by the Democratic majority, already had confirmed their nominations.

The president had decided to install the Cabinet quickly because economic conditions were deteriorating so rapidly, and he wanted to reassure the American public that competent hands were at work. Banks were failing at an alarming rate while the nation's top financiers were being exposed as inept and corrupt.

Frances knew all too well the human toll it was taking. Relief stations were shutting down, food riots were becoming common, and petty larceny was on the rise as desperate people turned to crime to feed themselves. Once-secure families who had been evicted from their homes were living in the streets or squatting in city parks, taking refuge in makeshift tents.

Frances reluctantly agreed to start work immediately. She sent Governor Lehman a telegram resigning her job as state industrial commissioner and apologizing for the short notice.

At the White House, Frances was escorted upstairs by aides but, uncertain how to proceed, left Susanna downstairs, mingling in the crowd. Frances found FDR seated at his desk in a study. Other Cabinet members filed into the room, joined by their families, and soon, Susanna, too, flustered and excited, was ushered into the room. Decked out in his judicial robes, Supreme Court Justice Benjamin Cardozo, a New Yorker appointed to the court by Hoover, stood by, preparing to swear them in.

"I hope you don't mind being sworn in on my old Dutch Bible," Roosevelt told the group. "You won't be able to read a word of it, but it's the Holy Scriptures, all right, isn't it, Justice Cardozo?"[13]

One by one, the Cabinet members stepped forward to be sworn in. Frances observed each of them closely, trying to gauge who would support her programs and who would not. She expected little of the new attorney general, Homer Cummings, a New York lawyer and political activist who had agreed at the last minute to fill in for FDR's original choice, Senator Thomas Walsh, seventy-two, of Montana, a former prosecutor who had chaired the Teapot Dome investigation. Walsh died of a heart attack in the night while traveling to Washington in a sleeping coach with his new wife, a Cuban widow thirty years his junior.

At least two of the other new Cabinet members were familiar and friendly faces to her. Jim Farley, who had waited out the election returns with her in 1928, had been named postmaster general. Treasury Secretary William Woodin, an industrialist who headed the American Car and Foundry Company, had been an officer at the Council on Immigrant Education in New York City when Frances worked there during one term when Smith had not been reelected governor. Woodin had been "delighted" by Frances's appointment.[14] (His health soon broke under the job strain, and he was replaced by another man she knew well—Henry Morgenthau Jr., whose father had served with Frances on the Committee on Safety.)

Frances's new friend Henry Wallace, meanwhile, was taking the reins at the Agriculture Department, and a business-oriented South Carolinian, Daniel Roper, was secretary of commerce.

George Dern, the former governor of Utah, FDR's secretary of war, made an immediate positive impression on Frances because of his practicality and humanity. He was so self-effacing that Frances wondered how he had made it so far in politics while lacking the "elbowing" quality she had seen in most elected officials.

Almost from the start she liked Harold Ickes, the rigidly honest progressive Republican chosen as secretary of the interior. He had what she called a "determined pout," which made him appear as though he would accomplish what he had set out to do. It reminded her of the "good Saxon faces" described by Shakespeare. He was witty but also prone to sarcasm and to biting, cruel remarks—including barbed comments directed at Frances.[15]

She knew little of Cordell Hull, secretary of state, or Claude Swanson, secretary of the navy, both of whom she had seen for the first time at the church.

Cardozo swore in Frances after all the others. She came last because the labor secretary was the newest seat on the Cabinet. Labor always came last.

"Roosevelt's Cabinet was a strange assortment," wrote James MacGregor Burns. "Ideologically, it embraced Democratic conservatives and Democratic progressives, a Republican conservative and two Republican progressives . . . Politically it catered to almost every group."[16]

Their average age was fifty-nine—Frances was one of the youngest at fifty-two—or fifty as she presented herself.

She immediately perceived that the Cabinet, despite its bipartisan and diverse character, was prepared to work together. A few days later, on Tuesday, March 7, 1933, the group had its first formal Cabinet meeting. Frances knew she must make a good initial impression.

The Cabinet gathered in the White House in a handsome room with oval windows. FDR walked haltingly into the room, though he would later use a wheelchair for his entries and exits. Sitting down at the head of the table, he introduced the group to his vice president, John Nance Garner, who many of them had not yet met.

Frances assessed Garner as well-intentioned and warm, given to hearty handshakes and backslaps. He had a ruddy complexion with a beakish nose, white hair, and steely blue eyes. A Democratic congressman, he'd competed with FDR for the nomination at the Democratic National Convention. Frances suspected he might prove to be an ally because of his sense that the election campaign had promised to do something for the "poorer kind of people."

Again, protocol ruled. The Cabinet officers were seated and called in order of precedence. Secretary of State Hull, well groomed and fine featured, sat on the president's right; Roosevelt questioned him first. Treasury Secretary Woodin discussed the widening banking crisis.

Secretary of War Dern endeared himself to Perkins by talking about his meetings with army officers who had expressed concern about unemployment among reserve officers. Frances noted his compassion for the jobless.[17]

Finally, it was Frances's turn. The president gave her a brotherly smile.

"Well, Miss Perkins, have you anything to say, anything to contribute?"

Frances had deliberately kept silent while the men spoke, knowing that her very presence probably left them unsettled. Normally loquacious and articulate, she thought she would fare better with the men by keeping her comments pithy and businesslike.

"I could see that they were all looking at me. They didn't stare because they were gentlemen, but I was aware that one by one they turned their attention toward me. . . . I tried to have as much of a mask as possible. I wanted to give the impression of being a quiet, orderly woman who didn't buzz-buzz all the time, who didn't butt in where she wasn't wanted, who could be trusted not to be an embarrassment," she said. ". . . So I kept perfectly still. I knew that a lady interposing an idea into men's conversation is very unwelcome. I just proceeded on the theory that this was a gentleman's conversation on the porch of a golf club, perhaps. You didn't butt in with bright ideas."

She kept her comments brief and to the point. She mentioned the administration's plans to rebuild a federal employment service and to regulate work hours.

She noticed that Garner was assessing her thoughtfully, at one point listening so carefully he forgot to smoke his cigar. Later he told his wife that the new female Cabinet officer had comported herself well. "She didn't interrupt. She didn't butt in. She didn't ask any questions. She kept still until the president asked her what she had to say. Then she said it. She said it loud enough so I could hear. She said it plain and distinct."

Frances approached all of the Cabinet meetings in that same way. She often hid information about her programs, her instincts telling her that some Cabinet members would secretly work against them. She came to wonder whether some had the public interest at heart or were simply advancing their own careers.

Still scrambling to learn the ropes, Frances found herself caught flat-footed on one thing right after the first Cabinet meeting. Frances left the White House accompanied by the speaker-elect of the House of Representatives, Henry T. Rainey of Illinois, who had attended part of the meeting. They were mobbed by newspaper reporters. A reporter asked Frances how they should address her, since there was no precedent for what title to give a woman Cabinet officer. Frances suggested they call her Miss Perkins, but that didn't satisfy the newsmen. Seeking a graceful dodge, she referred them to Rainey, an old Washington hand, who haughtily informed the group that a lady official should be addressed as "Madame," an old literary custom. The term was unfamiliar to the rough-hewn reporters who traveled in packs in Washington, and some of them soon began to refer to her as the Madame Secretary, or even the Madame, with its bordello connotation.

But casual informality made her uncomfortable, too. Some reporters, using the slang of the day, referred to her as "Ma Perkins" or "Frances the Perk," slipping into use of her first name—something the proper New Englander thought was appalling. She thought first names were for personal friends, and she preferred more formal address in business settings. But Roosevelt himself had set the trend, calling reporters by their first names in regular press conferences. He had long called her Frances.

Using first names began a popular craze, and it was difficult for those who disliked it to object. Frances chafed when her ally Senator Wagner started calling her Frances. She considered him "fresh" for doing it.

"I hadn't known him on first-name terms," she said of the man she had known for more than twenty years.[18]

Chapter 16

SKELETONS IN THE
LABOR DEPARTMENT CLOSET

*E*agerly, Frances set to work. As she got dressed on her first Monday morning, she assumed that by 9 a.m. she would receive a call from the department, probably from her predecessor, Secretary of Labor William N. Doak, to arrange for her arrival. Her secretary, Miss Jay, who had traveled with her from New York for the weekend's festivities, waited with her in the hotel. The phone didn't ring. Finally Frances realized she must take the initiative.

"Well, we might as well go right at it hammer and tongs ourselves," she told Miss Jay. "Apparently nobody is going to show us any courtesy or open any doors. I am the Secretary of Labor, and I have not only a right but a duty to take possession of the premises. But let's be more polite than they are and telephone." [1]

She looked up the number and address in the telephone directory and called Doak, who answered after a long delay. After a polite greeting, she asked him if he knew she had been sworn in as secretary. He said he had read about it but assumed she would head home to New York first and assume her duties later. She said Roosevelt expected the Cabinet to begin work immediately. She told Doak she hoped to talk with him *before*—and she chose her words for emphasis—he departed later that day. He agreed, though Frances realized he originally had no intention of leaving anytime soon.

A few minutes later, Frances and Miss Jay headed over to the agency. The department was housed in a decrepit former apartment building ungracefully converted to offices. No one met her at the door. The front desk guard said he couldn't send her up without first getting her name.

"I've already telephoned, but I'm Miss Perkins, the new Secretary of Labor," she said.

"Oh, you are," he said, with dull surprise.

⋏

ℱrances started to realize that reshaping the department would be even more difficult than she had imagined. The Wickersham Report, the internal study commissioned by the Hoover administration, had made clear that the Department of Labor's immigration bureau was plagued with corruption. A week after Frances's selection was announced, a New York City police officer informed her gangsters had gotten control of the agency and were using their enforcement powers to shake down frightened newcomers. They were raiding private parties and arresting those in attendance, including foreigners lawfully in the country, threatening to deport them if they did not pay fines, he told her. Top department officials knew about their activities and were either taking a cut of the profits or looking the other way, he said.

"Wickersham didn't find out a quarter of it," he said. The ringleader, he said, was a devious man named Murray Garsson. The policeman warned Frances to be careful, because the man had friends in high places.[2]

Corruption was one challenge; ineffectiveness was another. The Labor Department had been founded in 1913, after pressure from labor unions and worker advocates who wanted higher visibility for their concerns. It was begun with great promise. It initially encompassed a newly created labor mediation agency, the U.S. Conciliation Service, and three preexisting offices, including the Bureau of Labor Statistics and the Immigration Service. The third component was the Children's Bureau, which addressed many child welfare issues, including maternal and infant death rates, children's health, orphans, and juvenile delinquency. It was placed in the department because research had shown a correlation between a father's earnings and infant mortality rates. When husbands earned little money, their wives and children were more likely to suffer.

On the issues of greatest concern to Frances, however, the department had proven to be, in her words, "almost nothing." There was little actual federal labor legislation for it to enforce, and most states also had few laws in place. The prevailing national sentiment was that any restrictions on employment conditions were unconstitutional because they interfered with a worker's contractual rights. In reality, employers had the upper hand. Three decades of open immigration policies brought a glut of poor workers too desperate to make demands.

Frances had met with Secretary of Labor William B. Wilson soon after his appointment. She maintained a keen interest in the Children's Bureau. The bureau had been created at the urging of Hull House women, including Jane Addams and Florence Kelley, and Frances's work at the Maternity Center Association had made her a natural ally in its efforts. Later, when Frances sought to curtail child labor in New York, the Children's Bureau played a vital role by providing data on children's work hours in various states and foreign countries. Frances consulted regularly with the Children's Bureau before proposing legislation or rule changes.

Frances also had developed important ties to the Bureau of Labor Statistics, a well-meaning but not entirely competent information source on living costs and unemployment rates. She knew many people throughout the department and had interacted with it on the highest levels. She even had an international perspective on it, since she was also an officer in the International Association of Government Labor Officials. Her network of friends there included labor leaders around the world, and they shared with her their knowledge of the department.

And so by the time Frances took over the Department of Labor, she knew its strengths and weaknesses—and how little horsepower she had inherited. In her view, the agency had gone nearly dead under Republican control during the 1920s.

⚜

Upstairs, Frances found a dingy secretary's office suite, with brass spittoons in the corners. Crumpled papers littered the floor. The officials had made no preparations for vacating their offices.

The receptionist was a friendly elderly black man who wore a dirty shirt with frayed shirt cuffs. He bowed politely and took Frances to meet Doak, who greeted the women but seemed clueless about what to do next. Frances solicited his views on the economy and joblessness, but he had no suggestions. She asked him to introduce her to the top department officials.

As lunchtime approached, she asked Doak pointedly if he had a luncheon engagement. He did, so Frances suggested that the receptionist pack up Doak's belongings while he was eating and arrange to have them delivered to his home. He was dumbfounded. While he made a few final telephone calls before departing, she began dictating letters to a stenographer in Doak's outer chamber. Frances was now in charge.

Among the trail of people she saw that day, one official caught her eye—Robe Carl White, first assistant secretary. He was tall, white-haired, and bespectacled, with a tight mouth, and Frances judged him to be both knowledgeable and honest. A Republican appointee, he had prepared his resignation, but Frances asked him to stay for a while. In a private meeting, White confirmed the distressing reports Frances had heard. He called her attention to Section 24, a part of the immigration department, and called its activities "very irregular." The section had been created to prevent abuses of low-paid foreigners who were brought to America for short-term contracts. Congress had given the secretary of labor power to investigate and deport workers brought to the United States in violation of national quotas.

"I don't even like to think what's going on there," White said. He described an unsavory group of men who were being employed as fixers for senators and congressmen—little more than street toughs who did as the legislators told them.

"They're low-lived people," he said. "They'll promise anything to a Senator or Congressman and they'll go and get it done. You want to get rid of them right away."[3]

At one point that day, Frances opened a desk drawer and a huge black cockroach jumped out. The desk was crawling with cockroaches. She wondered what was drawing such huge bugs and discovered that the agency's African-American employees, who were barred from eating at many restaurants in segregated Washington, brought their lunches and ate at their desks. Frances and Miss Jay set to work, vigorously cleaning. Frances gave the receptionist a tin lunchbox to control crumbs and soon ordered the Labor Department cafeteria desegregated so that black workers could use it on equal terms.

Just as she had done at the New York Industrial Commission, Frances went to meet and get to know everyone at the agency.

"Feathers are beginning to fly around the Department of Labor," Clara Beyer wrote to a friend. "The whole atmosphere has changed since March 4th. I wish you could see the men who threatened to resign if a woman was appointed; they are crawling on hands and knees!"[4]

After cleaning out the office, Frances set out to cleanse the department of corruption. White had recommended that she quickly fire the Section 24 immigration staff. This was difficult because Hoover had converted them into civil service employees. White suggested that Frances abolish the section altogether, since funding for it was due to expire in March.

"If you're going to do it, you'd better do it quick, Madam Secretary, because they'll plant something on you," White told Frances. Roosevelt agreed to the plan.[5]

On March 8, just a few days after her arrival, the Section 24 officials, including Garsson, were notified that program funding had ceased for budget reasons and their jobs no longer existed. But the problems reached high into the agency. Doak had become "quite a rich man," as a result of what Frances called his "sinister relationship to these people and their relationship to the gangster world." The links between criminals and the Labor Department also made her wonder about Doak's relationship with Hoover. Although she always considered Hoover honest, she wondered why he had kept Doak in office after the Wickersham report exposed such serious problems in the department.[6]

A few days after the firings, Frances returned to the office at night to work. An aged guard escorted her upstairs. She heard noises on the fourth floor, where Section 24 had been housed. Asking the guard to accompany her, she went to investigate. She found a group of men rifling through government files, their coats off and shirtsleeves rolled up. She'd caught them red-handed stealing records. She asked the guard to stay with her, although she knew he would offer scant protection if the men decided to hurt her.

"What are you doing here, Mr. Garsson?" she asked. "I'm surprised to see you here tonight because your duties ended as of last night."[7]

Quick on his feet, Garsson said he and his friends had come to pick up their belongings.

"These files surely can't be personal," she said. "They look like official files, immigration files, files of investigators."

She asked them to return the next morning, when White could assist them in obtaining their belongings. "I think I'll have to ask you to leave the building now."

For a long moment, the men hesitated. Frances stared at them, until one by one they finally left. Only Garsson remained. Calmly, she asked for his key. When he left, she called for another guard to watch over the files that night. The next morning she ordered new locks made.

Later linked to gangsters Dutch Schultz and Owney Madden, Garsson had attracted some notoriety even before leaving the Labor Department. A congressional inquiry had posed questions about his $9,000 a year income, which Doak had defended as appropriate for Garsson's "special work." Garsson spent much more time in the headlines in coming decades—most notably in 1947, when he and his brother went to prison, along with former representative Andrew May, wartime chairman of the House Military Affairs Committee, for bribery and conspiracy in munitions sales to the U.S. government. Documents related to the investigation were stolen at night from the offices of the Senate War Investigating Committee, but the prosecution proceeded nonetheless.[8]

Dismantling Section 24 was just the beginning. Ultimately twelve government immigration officials were convicted of malfeasance, thirteen more were dismissed for misconduct, and five others resigned rather than face charges.[9]

To establish a new system of immigration procedures, Frances named as head of the immigration service Army colonel Daniel W. MacCormack, a logistics expert who had overseen construction of the civilian quarters at the Panama Canal, enabling the Americans to complete the Herculean task of building the canal, an effort that had defeated the French who had attempted it decades earlier.

She then chose Isador Lubin to reorganize the Bureau of Labor Statistics (BLS), which had been tarnished by the controversy surrounding Hoover's misstatements about unemployment rates.

For his part, Lubin had been impressed with Frances's understanding of unemployment statistics when she had testified at a Senate hearing, so he was thrilled by her call. She asked if he wanted the job. "Yes, I'll take it," he said promptly.[10]

Lubin turned the bureau into a respected source of economic statistics. He quickly improved the country's system for gathering employment and wage statistics, and put systems in place to minimize political pressure to show positive results. For the first time, the federal government tracked hourly earnings and average weekly hours by industry. Lubin also modernized the cost-of-living index. One component in the outdated index was the price of high-button shoes, still included long after people had stopped wearing them. The BLS also tracked productivity, an important gauge of business modernization trends, and it made separate forecasts of growth in different occupations in order to steer workers to new industries.[11]

When Frances hired Lubin, she asked him to always remember that statistics represent real people, coping with conditions as best they can. Roosevelt shared her perspective, and Lubin's humanitarian approach and his ease at explaining the meaning of numbers ultimately won him a place in Roosevelt's inner circle.

Yet another agency, the Conciliation Service, which helped settle strikes, also was faltering. It had been laxly run, with union officials hanging around its offices for hours a day. Mediators sent into the field sometimes failed to report to the central office for weeks at a time, their whereabouts unknown.

The scandal-plagued Employment Service especially needed reform. Doak and his predecessor, James Davis, used it as a patronage shop. In the mailroom, for example, seven sinecures had been created, each paying $3,500 a year, for workers opening mail, a job that previously paid $600 a year.[12]

Its employees, most appointed for political reasons, operated out of far-flung offices, some in remote areas where the staffers lived in semiretirement. With the president's blessing, Frances terminated the agency's managers, telling them it was because they were Republicans and would be replaced by Democrats. Actually she considered them incompetent. She had told Roosevelt she would need to completely rebuild the Employment Service, particularly once the president asked her to staff the Civilian Conservation Corps through the rejuvenated office.

Two departments functioned fairly well: the Children's Bureau, run by Grace Abbott, and the Women's Bureau, run by Mary Anderson. The Children's Bureau had recently suffered a major setback. A successful initiative it had launched to reduce maternal and infant deaths lost its funding after the American Medical Association opposed it as an intrusion into private medical practices.

With the change of administrations, Abbott, a Republican, feared she might lose her job, but Frances hastened to reassure her. Don't even bother to submit your resignation letter, she told her.

These two departments appealed to Frances, but they were not politically powerful. Other department officials saw the women's work as more tangential to the agency's mission. White, for example, accepted the women's work as a given and saw them as relatively unproblematic: "Both of those girls are sensible girls," White said, describing Abbott, fifty-four, and Anderson, sixty. "They haven't got any money to spend anyhow. They tend to business. We never see them. Doak never saw them and I never see them. If I ask for a report, they give me a report and it's all right. I can make it out."[13]

Once Frances gained her footing, she took her overall housecleaning plan to FDR. Frances left the meeting with assurance and confidence. Again, he had said yes to everything she had proposed.

Even with the president's support, however, she confronted a lonely task at the department. Aware of the magnitude of the problems and surrounded by staffers she considered ineffectual or worse, Frances turned to a familiar and loyal face. Miss Jay had worked with Frances for more than a decade as a secretary and assistant. She was a native New Yorker with no intention of moving to Washington. But a day or so after she started work in Washington, Frances asked Miss Jay to stay by her side, and the woman agreed. Frances needed someone who could handle correspondence about Paul's medical treatments and hospitalizations and who could be trusted to cover for her when she rushed off to oversee his care.

Afterward Frances agonized over whether she had selfishly asked Miss Jay to give up her comfortable situation in New York for a pressure-cooker existence in Washington. Miss Jay, then in her early thirties, worked long hours at the department and never married or had children. She reassured Frances, saying that her work in Washington had given her a more interesting life than she would have otherwise had, but Frances still felt guilty about it.

Even with Miss Jay's help, Frances was poorly served by a dysfunctional support staff and she made some early gaffes that had long-term consequences. She invited members of the House and Senate labor committees to visit her department and observe its workings—and many accepted. But Representative William P. Connery Jr., a Massachusetts congressman who chaired the House Labor Committee, was incensed that Frances would ask members to visit her instead of showing proper respect by calling on them on Capitol Hill.

Senator Pat Harrison, a senior Mississippi Democrat who chaired the powerful Senate Finance Committee, did visit but expressed his displeasure in how he was received. Swamped by guests who wanted a peek at the new female Cabinet officer, Frances had asked her staff to keep people at bay so that she could work uninterrupted. Harrison was kept outside her office for some time before someone told her a gentleman visitor was waiting. Frances rushed to greet him, but the damage had been done. He gruffly announced he must return to the Hill. Stories immediately hit the newspapers saying that she had ignored the important senator.

Maurine Mulliner, an aide to Senator Wagner, blamed the incident on Miss Jay, who she said was "rude to everybody." Undoubtedly Frances's guilt toward Miss Jay in some ways made her unduly obliged to her assistant. Miss Jay's abruptness became well-known, and several department officials privately referred to her as Cerberus, the mythical dog guarding the gates of Hades.

Frances's antipathy for the press added to the public relations problem. Many Washington reporters were freelancers, living hand-to-mouth. Quick, superficial stories on a personality conflict or a new evening ensemble put more money in their pockets than the fact-filled economic analyses that Frances admired. Heavily burdened by her work, and trying to promote a new economic agenda, Frances considered the newsmen intrusive, and she would discharge the requisite press conferences in a clipped manner quite unlike her usual demeanor. One reporter cattily said Frances spoke like she was reading a press release, and indeed, Frances often stuck to a prepared text, worried that her words would be twisted.

She had reason to be cautious. In one speech, for example, she explained that providing people with jobs would boost consumer spending. She described how the economy could be stimulated in new ways. Shoes made in New England and sold in the South, for example, produced jobs in one place and generated sales in another. But she phrased her comment as "putting shoes on the South," and reporters hungry for a quick controversy suggested she had implied that southerners were so backward they didn't wear shoes. The offhand comment infuriated southern congressmen, who knew that many in the South, particularly blacks, were in fact so poor they didn't own shoes. Some southerners took grave offense, and never forgave Perkins.

Eager to avoid similar missteps, Frances ordered staffers not to speak to reporters without her prior clearance. The policy caused inordinate delays. She also refused to provide an office to reporters assigned to cover the Labor Department, even as she tried to be more accommodating to the press. She saw this as an improper government expense. Finally she relented, offering a small, badly located press area. Frances failed to realize that making reporters' jobs harder only antagonized them.

And, as she had with legislators Connery and Harrison, she angered some of the more thin-skinned reporters. Badly time-pressed, she refused an interview with Rodney Dutcher because Frances was unaware that he regularly wrote a column for a chain of midwestern newspapers. Soon afterward journalist Ruth Finney warned Frances that Dutcher was furiously bad-mouthing her at the National Press Club, a popular reporters' watering hole. Frances then granted him the interview, but she believed that he never forgave her.

"Although he was very much for everything that Roosevelt was doing, he would write his columns saying that this is a good idea, but he would give a dirty dig at me in the course of saying that what was being done was okay."[14]

Nevertheless it was clear that she would rather suffer with adverse press than deal with reporters as often and as amiably as other cabinet members did. Instead, she simply refused to read press clippings.

Many reporters fed her disdain by writing untrue stories, or refusing to correct errors. *Time* magazine, a publication owned by Henry Luce, a prominent Republican who opposed many social programs, reported that Frances had launched her awkward press relations by telling reporters at her first press conference: "Call me Madam."[15]

Only a handful of reporters gained Frances's respect, but the respect in those cases tended to be mutual. Bess Furman of the Associated Press called Frances's early press conferences "masterly and revealing," in laying out the thrust of the New Deal after only a few days in office.[16]

And Frances sought to cultivate veteran *New York Times* reporter Louis Stark, who was carving out a Washington-based labor beat. He gave her a cordial hearing, even though he disparagingly referred to her as "Fannie" in letters to his wife.[17]

The Roosevelts handled their public relations very differently from Frances. Franklin found dealing with reporters easy and comfortable,

handling his discussions with them with first-name aplomb, and reporters basked in his attention.

Eleanor, meanwhile, used her female-only press conferences to give
women reporters a stronger position in the newsroom. She began holding these conferences after hearing two female reporters describe the
discrimination women were facing as unemployment mounted. Frances grew concerned that Eleanor would embarrass herself, but she soon
realized she need not worry. Eleanor skillfully skirted around conten-
tious questions that would have embarrassed her husband, while still
explaining the programs of the New Deal in understandable terms. Eleanor more effectively touted Frances's efforts to a female audience than
Frances did. Eleanor also was able to inform newswomen that Frances's
husband was ill, and the topic was not to be discussed, sparing Frances
from questions about Paul's mental health.

Frances thought that in their casual dealings with the press, Franklin and Eleanor had unleashed something that would haunt later presi-
dencies. Newspapers are businesses, and reporters write stories that
their editors will publish. Readers do not always have a good independent check on the information reported. But in her view, reporters began
developing a corrosive sense of entitlement that was reinforced by informal access to the powerful.

Focusing on cleaning up the agency and enacting her far-reaching
agenda, Frances wasn't inclined to spend much time worrying about
how she was viewed by the press. But reporters write the first rough draft
of history, and how they describe events is often how they end up being
perceived.

Chapter 17

JUMP-STARTING
THE ECONOMY

*F*rances's enthusiasm for change was part of a feverish spirit that infected the federal bureaucracy in the early days of the new administration. Government agencies bustled with activity until midnight, and workers commonly put in long days and then returned to their offices again on Saturday and Sunday.

Optimism was desperately needed, for economic conditions were about as bad as they could be. Between 13 and 18 million Americans, about a third of the working population, had no jobs. One in six homes was lost to foreclosure. Charitable organizations ran out of resources and turned away the hungry. The sick stopped going to doctors because they could no longer afford medical care; hungry physicians joined the breadlines.

Frances later described it: "We had been seeing hardship and poverty. We had been blaming the Hoover administration for doing nothing. So in the first weeks of the new administration there wasn't much of any doubt but that we would have to do a pure relief program at the same time that we thought we were committed to a public works program—a real public works program—as one of the basic ways of getting money into circulation and stimulating a great variety of industries, as well as giving work at regular wages directly on the location."[1]

Given the nation's distress, one of the president's first official acts was to repeal Prohibition. Drinks started flowing openly once again. First beer and wine with 3.2 percent alcohol content and then harder spirits started bubbling up.

The administration improvised, choosing prominent projects from among the thousands of ideas floating in from around the nation. FDR extended government assistance to banks and then declared a national bank "holiday," a euphemism for shutting down the banks to prevent runs on their deposits until the system stabilized. He took the United States off the gold standard, cut expenditures, and slashed federal pay to balance the budget. He enacted a sweeping agricultural bill to stop the downward pricing spiral. The Securities and Exchange Commission appeared to regulate the stock market and protect investors. And the Home Owners' Loan Corporation was formed to help at-risk homeowners keep their properties.

This "new deal" meant FDR would give each person a fresh start. The administration set out to remove capitalism's worst excesses without destroying its essentially entrepreneurial culture.

Under Frances's leadership the first major public works project, the Civilian Conservation Corps (CCC), kicked off within days of the inauguration. At an early Cabinet meeting, FDR had come up with the notion of sending the unemployed into rural areas to do forestry work. Roosevelt had long supported a universal youth service, and now the time seemed right.

Everybody blinked, Frances recalled, and then several endorsed it as a fine idea. Frances considered it a foolish pipe dream. She wasn't sure what to say, since she tried not to contradict Roosevelt in public.

"Well, Mr. President, what are they going to do when they get to the woods?" she finally asked. He told her they would be doing forest preservation and building dams to prevent water runoff. The exodus of farmers from the Great Dust Bowl in the Midwest had highlighted the nation's soil erosion crisis, and environmentalists had long called for better land conservation practices.[2]

"Yes, I know, but what about the unemployed? Where are they?"

"Well, on the streets of New York," he replied. "You've seen them lining up at the bread lines. Take them right off the bread line."

Frances expressed skepticism. "Take those poor men off the bread lines and take them up to the Adirondacks and turn them loose?"

Work it out, FDR told her. He planned to pay them a dollar a day.

"Well, you've got to have able-bodied people," she said. "You know, an awful lot of these unemployed people have heart trouble, varicose veins, and everything else. Just because they're unemployed doesn't mean they are natural-born lumbermen. . . . How are you going to recruit?"

Use your Employment Service, he said, cheerfully overlooking the fact that just days earlier she had informed him that she planned to shut down the ineffectual Employment Service and fire most of its workers. What remained was only a shell. Create a new one, he told her.

Frances paused. Well, she said thoughtfully, the Forest Service could tell us where work needs to be done. And perhaps the military could set up camps and provide the tents, cots, shoes, and blankets workers would need. Secretary of War Dern agreed that the military had many available resources, and recommended bringing back unemployed reserve officers to administer the camps.

A few days later, Frances testified to Congress about the proposal, stating with assurance that it could be done. Some criticism surfaced: Green of the AFL told a congressional committee the plan smacked of "Sovietism," a Communist blasted it as "forced labor."[3] But Congress received the plan favorably, and by month's end the CCC legislation passed and went to Roosevelt for his signature.

On the day of the hearing, however, Frances got another early reminder of the challenges faced by a woman Cabinet officer. She won a cordial reception from the congressmen and left Capitol Hill with a warm glow. But one lawmaker, a Democrat, left the room and described the scene to others who hadn't been there. Frances had done "awful well, she's an awful smart woman," he said, then adding: "But I'd hate to be married to her."

Frances laughed aloud when female reporter Ruby Black related the comment. But later on she realized the member's comment had a long-term negative impact, because it emphasized her gender rather than her competence.

"The remark in that hearing room was repeated over and over again and was the basis of the stories that appeared [that] the congressmen didn't like me," she said. "A Congressman had said that he didn't want to be married to me. I hadn't asked him. That was the beginning of those rumors."[4]

Frances turned her attention to setting up the CCC. To recruit, she created the National Reemployment Service, which she intended to essentially expand into a revitalized U.S. Employment Service, with a national network of offices to help job-seekers find work. She anticipated that legislation would soon be passed allowing her to do this. She hired Frank Persons, whose work she had known at the Red Cross, at first on a temporary basis until funding was approved.

Initially they sought to confine the roster to young men aged eighteen to twenty-one, a group that social workers considered vulnerable because of the worsening economy. Some families had virtually cast off their older sons because of the stresses of providing for younger children. Living along railroad tracks and seeking shelter in big cities, the boys fell into wayward behavior and faced bleak futures. Persons recommended that they select recruits from families who already had sought relief. Recruits must pass physicals before acceptance, but then they would be provided with food, military clothing, and transportation.

The young men were shipped off to live in tents in army-run camps, and later in more permanent barracks. From this improvised beginning came one of the New Deal's most politically popular programs. It was reauthorized repeatedly and ceased operations only on the eve of World War II. By August 1933, the program included almost 300,000 men. By April 1936, there were 2,158 Civilian Conservation Camps, each with about 157 enrollees. Most were young men, with about 60 percent of them under age nineteen, but about 30,500 were jobless veterans of World War I.[5]

Most enrollees helped support their families back home. Slightly over 85 percent made allotments to their mothers or fathers. The additional income helped: About 73 percent of enrollees came from families on work relief or public assistance and another one-quarter were from families living in poverty.[6]

But the program's benefits were not wholly economic. The young men developed self-pride as they worked for the national good, planting trees, building bridges and fire towers, restoring historic battlefields, and beautifying the country's National Park System.[7] "Its more important service is that of giving immature youths, who stand at the threshold of their vocational years, valuable work habits and useful skills, while building them up physically, and providing, through satisfying achievement in an orderly camp environment, the elements of self-reliance, cooperation and broadened outlook which are important to good morale—either for employees or citizens," Persons wrote Frances.

Not everyone liked the program, of course. "We are obviously opposed first of all, to placing men doing honest labor of a constructive variety in the same category as that large group of loafers now maintained at the taxpayers' expense in the United States Army," wrote one irate citizen, George A. Yager, to the Labor Department in March 1933.[8]

Other problems involved patronage and cronyism. C. M. Brown, a citrus fruit distributor in Redlands, California, wrote to the secretary of commerce to complain that almost all the CCC camp registration officials were Republicans. It's a "darn shame," Brown said, that one Republican official was telling people that to get work they would be expected to vote Republican.

Frances explained to Commerce Secretary Roper that the program was apolitical but put together quickly. She noted that the people determining who was "certified" for duty were volunteers usually working through local unemployment relief agencies. It was one of many management issues that arose in the program.

Early on, Frances and Eleanor Roosevelt sought to promote similar CCC camps for unemployed young women, where they would do lighter horticultural work. But many people were dismayed at the prospect of teenage girls being out on their own, and Frances was deluged with telegrams condemning the idea. Ultimately, only a token group of twenty-eight female camps was established.[9]

But the thorniest problem involved race relations. Throughout the South, most notably in Texas and Missouri, local political leaders objected to African-American enrollment in the program and balked at integrating blacks and whites in the camps. Some communities fiercely objected to having camps with black CCC enrollees located within their boundaries. To ensure the safety of participants, federal CCC officials placed the black camps on U.S. military reservations, but this solution pleased nobody.

Persons wrote to Frances to reassure her that he was doing everything he could to ensure fair treatment for all applicants. The labor department, he said, "is squarely on record in every quarter as being absolutely devoted to the legal mandate, which states: That in employing citizens for the purposes of this Act, no discrimination shall be made on account of race, color or creed."[10]

In many cases, black applicants needed the positions more desperately than others because the Depression hit their families especially hard. By May 1935, 28 percent of the black population was on relief. Some early labor laws offered them no real protection because they exempted domestic and agricultural laborers. Compounding the problem, blacks were now likely to have moved to cities, away from home-grown crops that could feed their families. Between 1910 and 1930, the percentage of blacks working in agriculture dropped from 55 to 36 percent.[11]

Reginald A. Johnson, Washington lobbyist for the Urban League, pushed for greater black participation in the CCC. He said that some black men had spurned the program at first because of fears of entering a new kind of "forced labor." Over time, more of them wanted to sign up.[12] Frances handled this issue cautiously. She disapproved of discrimination—one of her first official acts upon becoming secretary of labor had been to integrate the department's cafeteria. But she was wary of offending southern congressmen whose votes she needed to pass legislation that would benefit all races. She also was unsure whether the president would approve if she forced the creation of more camps or integrated camps, since FDR considered the issue "political dynamite." The military itself was segregated, so it was decided that the camps would remain segregated.[13]

More than 3.5 million Americans participated in the CCC during its nine years of existence.

Simultaneously with the creation of the CCC, a second major relief program was launched. A week or so after FDR's inauguration, Frances received a call from her friend Harry Hopkins, who was frantic over the need for a public works program that would employ people of all ages. He feared that FDR, whom he knew only slightly, would put it on a back burner.

Frances had known Hopkins since he served Mayor Mitchel as executive secretary of the Bureau of Child Welfare. Like other displaced members of Mitchel's administration, Hopkins had been forced to find new work and had joined the Red Cross. In the early 1920s, he was appointed general director of the New York Tuberculosis Association, a prominent job in the world of social work. When the Depression hit, FDR had named Hopkins head of a New York relief organization.

Now Hopkins and another friend, Bill Hodson, were in Washington trying to reach FDR. Rebuffed by White House aides, they learned that Frances was FDR's contact on the public works issues. The men begged her to see them that night.

Frances arranged to meet them, just before a dinner engagement, at the Women's University Club, where she was staying. Every table and sofa in the reception area was taken. Frances and her friends eventually found free space under the stairway, borrowing a bench from the telephone operator. They crowded together, cramped and bent, while Hopkins and Hodson laid out their national proposal for organized relief. It called for a state-federal system that gave states money but left them free to administer it, as long as they met certain federal guidelines. Impressed, Frances said she would ask the president to consider it. But who should manage the program, she asked.

"Well, Bill and I have decided it ought to be one of us," Hopkins told her. "We don't care which. We've decided that there are other people just as smart as we are in this country, but nobody else in this country who is in the relief business, who has had experience as a relief administrator, has given as much time and thought to this particular project at this particular time." [14]

When Frances presented the proposal to FDR, he agreed to it. Then, she took the men to meet with him. On March 21, he asked Congress to create a federal relief administrator with a budget of $500 million to dispense as state grants. By April, the measure was approved by a large margin. [15]

FDR and Frances deliberated over which of the two program originators should manage it. In many ways, they were evenly matched, with similar skills and aptitudes. Hodson was smoother, but Hopkins was more fearless and analytical.

"I guess I prefer Hopkins," FDR concluded. "Anyhow, the [New York City] mayor wants Hodson and has so told me. Hodson's going to be the [relief] administrator for New York City. That's just as important as this. The Mayor wants him and I think that's the best way. So we'll take Hopkins." [16]

It was as simple as that. Hopkins's extraordinary talents, energy, and indefatigable spirit became obvious, and the organization grew quickly. It was named the Federal Emergency Relief Administration. Local and state officials designated projects best suited to their communities—repairing college campus buildings, improving public parks, building playgrounds. Half of the money went to places where local governments matched the funds and half went to places with the most urgent needs. Drought-relief programs were established, teachers were dispatched to reopen schoolhouses in bankrupt school districts, and jobs and housing programs sprang up for unemployed transients. Across the country, workers earned money for their efforts, toiling on projects that improved the lives of their fellow citizens.

Surprisingly enough, Democrats voiced the first real opposition to the program. As with the CCC, they were angry that Republicans and apolitical people were hired to administer the programs. Hopkins looked for competence in hires, not politics.

In addition, relief money was going to the states on the theory that they could best target their needs. But many governors were Republicans, thus allowing the opposing party to distribute goodies and take credit for them.

Postmaster General Farley was placed in the difficult role of placating Democratic allies about the program.

Congressman Bennett Clark, a Missouri Democrat, could not be reconciled. He demanded the ouster of Republican Martin Lewis, the director of the Federal Reemployment Service in Missouri. The compensation was only $1 a year plus expenses, but the post offered public visibility. It entailed establishing a network of local employment bureaus, whose charge was to certify the eligibility of applicants for the 100,000 jobs offered through the new public works agencies.

As his replacement, Lewis recommended a middle-aged Democratic Party activist named Harry S. Truman. Frances agreed to the request, which effectively launched Truman's federal career. Employment offers across Missouri now went out over Truman's signature. Naturally, this allowed him to build loyalty among hungry job seekers, and gave him his first important national contacts and his first official business in Washington.[17]

Frances didn't like replacing people for political reasons, and indeed had hired and retained Republicans on her staff. But she saw merit in Truman, whom she viewed as an "unemployed businessman who was just down on his luck."[18]

By October the effort had expanded into an alphabet soup of relief agencies—the Federal Employment Relief Administration, or FERA; the Civil Works Administration or Program, known as CWA; and the Public Works Administration, or PWA. The programs contained relief features, but, because Roosevelt favored paid work rather than handouts, they involved creating jobs, so that people earned pay for accomplishing tasks. Roosevelt later explained that "to dole out relief . . . is to administer a narcotic, a subtle destroyer of the human spirit."[19]

At first, the programs focused on gardeners and manual laborers, but as increasing numbers came forward for work, it became apparent that many of the unemployed were skilled professionals. Historians, archaeologists, researchers, playwrights, musicians, actors, entertainers, and seamstresses showed up on the breadlines. People considered special projects that would take advantage of unique talents available because of the economic downturn. Historians worked on oral histories, violinists performed concerts, and actors staged plays. An orchestra ser-enaded commuters at New York's Grand Central Station; archaeologists and historians restored old Fort Saint Augustine in Florida; an all-black cast performed *Macbeth* in Harlem.

Frances's daughter, Susanna, who loved art, believed that unem-ployed artists should share in the government largesse. Frances sug-gested that artists could always seek work in road construction. Susanna said road work would ruin their hands. Her mother resisted what she saw as Susanna's "nagging." "She annoyed me so with it, told me so many cases, told me so much of the kind of thing they could do that I finally listened. She told me that all the public buildings of America are so dreary and so gloomy that artists could decorate the walls of these public buildings—the post offices, the libraries and other places—so that they would be interesting and cheerful, and make people happy when they went into these buildings."[20]

Frances discussed the idea with Roosevelt, who liked the concept, just as Treasury Secretary Morgenthau arrived to meet with the presi-dent. At that time, Treasury was responsible for constructing, furnish-ing, and decorating public buildings. The president suggested that the department hire unemployed artists to decorate government structures, even jokingly suggesting they place sculptures on the Boulder Dam.

Morgenthau spoke to an architect who referred him to Ned Bruce, a Washington artist who took the lead on the effort. A set of programs put artists to work across the country decorating municipal and fed-eral buildings and providing art education classes. Soon monumental scenes from American history graced far-flung post offices in places like Berkeley, California; Decatur, Illinois; Abbeville, Louisiana; and Flan-dreau, South Dakota. Sculptures appeared atop Boulder Dam.

Again, job recruits were approved by the revitalized agencies that Frances had created to staff the CCC. They were run by people who themselves had experienced unemployment. When the services were fully funded, Persons took charge under Frances's supervision.

By July 1933, the U.S. Employment Service had expanded to 192 of-fices in 120 cities and twenty-three states, and the National Reemploy-ment Service provided services in still other cities. By June 1934, the U.S. Employment Service had registered 12.5 million people, and by the time the country entered World War II, it had placed some 26 million Ameri-cans in jobs.[21]

But the public works agencies did not prove as popular as the CCC, partially because some projects were viewed as radical or silly. Frances acknowledged that there were "some ridiculous aspects," but said that Roosevelt didn't take the complaints too seriously. He believed that workers needed paying jobs, and as long as some people found their efforts entertaining or worthwhile, he was satisfied.

While Roosevelt supported the cultural projects against criticism of their frivolity, he was careful to keep an eagle eye on expenses in the public works programs. Early on, FDR ripped up a list of Frances's proposed construction projects in front of a Cabinet committee, criticizing many of the proposals, particularly in New York. Ickes recalled feeling a "bit sorry" for Frances during the session, but she held her ground. She dropped the items FDR found objectionable, and by the end of the meeting had won support for the rest.[22]

Many of the public relief programs benefited the poor, but the administration simultaneously took steps to help the country's middle-class homeowners, burdened with debt and facing foreclosure.

The Federal Home Owners Loan Corporation was created in 1933 to help families keep their homes by refinancing them with government backing. Borrowers behind on their payments could apply for the program, which allowed them to pay off their houses at 5 percent interest over fifteen years. The new agency was swamped with applications. About 20 percent of homeowners with mortgages applied for the bailout, and about half of those eventually participated. The government helped more than 1 million people between 1933 and 1936. Seven in ten of the participants had been burned by buying in the go-go 1920s.[23]

Housing had long been a particular interest for Frances. She urged that public works projects include apartment complexes and single-family homes, particularly for lower-income people. Little affordable housing had been built during the 1920s because developers saw minimal profit in it. The urban poor had been left living in firetraps, dangerously heated by coal stoves and lit by kerosene lamps, with no indoor plumbing. Disease ran rampant in the most overcrowded of these slums. Frances saw an opportunity to create jobs by stimulating housing construction. More than a hundred apartment complexes were built with federal money.[24]

The middle class also benefited through a second program, the National Housing Act, passed in 1934. This utilized Frances's favorite tool for reducing the inherent risks of capitalism: insurance. The United States offered loan insurance through the Federal Housing Administration (FHA), which meant that private lenders could once again loan money for home purchase or remodeling with confidence that they would be repaid—if not by the borrower, then by the government. The program introduced a concept that would revolutionize home purchase: 20 percent down payment, fixed rate mortgages, payments lasting twenty years. The risky interest-only loans of the 1920s almost disappeared.

By the end of the first year, nearly 73,000 home-improvement loans had been made, and the building trades had returned to work. In the coming decades, hundreds of thousands of moderate-income people would become homeowners thanks to FHA assistance. "The strongest Cabinet support" for the program came from Frances, according to Henry Wallace and to a federal report written twenty-five years later.[25]

Frances's accomplishments somehow began to get lost amid the swirl of publicity about FDR's initiatives. Part of this was her doing. Soon after Frances's arrival in Washington, she was contacted by a newsman who was preparing an update of a 1932 New York Times piece on Roosevelt's "brain trust," his key advisers.

He told her the piece would include Rexford Tugwell, Raymond Moley, and Adolph Berle—all people Frances viewed as short-termers and fairly insignificant in Roosevelt's New York years. She'd never even heard of Moley or Tugwell until they began writing speeches for Roosevelt in 1932, twenty-two years after she had first met FDR. The newsman asked her for some background information. Of course not, she told him disdainfully. She later thought what a "narrow escape" she had from inclusion on the list, particularly as the pretentious title became an object of scorn in some anti-Roosevelt quarters. The very term Brain Trust set her teeth on edge."[26]

"It was a term of disrepute, or so it became very quickly," she said. "What interested me was that the men to whom it was applied never seemed to think it was."

Indeed, most of those listed had disappeared from the president's inner circle within a few years. For some of them, inclusion in the Brain Trust would be their primary claim to fame—a list so off base that it omitted Frances's name.

Chapter 18

AT HOME WITH
MARY HARRIMAN

*N*o matter what she did to deflect public attention, Frances's unique place in American history guaranteed that the fifty-two-year-old Cabinet secretary was scrutinized wherever she went. Casual observers continued to comment on her appearance, her clothing, and her speech, often noting that she appeared far more attractive in person than she did in photographs. Her lack of conventional beauty remained a recurring theme in her life, another cross for a woman to bear that men do not face.

"She is not a pretty woman in the sense of cameo features and tea-rose complexion, but to those who see beauty in character, Frances Perkins is more than satisfying to the eyes," wrote a *Washington Star* reporter. "She has smooth olive skin touched with a healthy color. Her hair is soft brown with the suspicion of a wave, and she wears it straight back from her forehead, catching it in a graceful knot at the back of her well-rounded head. Her mouth is mobile, turning up at the corners with definite humor. But it is her eyes that tell her story. Large and dark and vivid, they take their expression from her mood. If she is amused, they scintillate with little points of light. If moved to sympathy or compassion, they cloud over. At the slightest suspicion of insincerity or injustice, they can become keen and searching."[1]

Frances strove to maintain her crisp, no-nonsense appearance. She wore tailor-made suits, well-cut jackets, and skirts made of good quality tweed or serge in Oxford gray or dark blue, often with a silk blouse, her trademark tricorn perched atop her head. Her evening gowns were simple, often trimmed with mink or squirrel. She seldom wore jewelry and never wore makeup.

"She is a smallish lady of great force of character, determination and experience; and she is the best of mixers," wrote Sir R. C. Lindsay, the British ambassador, describing Frances to the foreign office in London.[2]

Her secretive nature, however, assured that little was known of Frances's life at work and at home. Her address was kept confidential, even from White House secretaries. But one of her new hires, brilliant young lawyer Charles Wyzanski, the department's new solicitor of labor, kept an interested eye on her comings and goings.

"She speaks fluently and well, but she is so full of energy or nerves that she is constantly adjusting her black hat and simultaneously answering the two telephones on her desk," he wrote to his mother. "While I was there, Mrs. Roosevelt ("dear") to Miss Perkins and Mr. Morgenthau ("Henry") telephoned . . . I must say that Miss P immediately impresses you with her competence, her unceasing energy and her administrative skill."[3]

Frances had always worked hard—so hard in fact that she often collapsed and needed complete rest for some weeks each year in August, the hot and humid month in which it was impossible to accomplish much—but once she got to Washington, her pace became frenetic. She worked from 9 a.m. frequently until midnight, and then would get into bed at night for more reading, keeping a glass of cold water by her side to dab on her eyes to keep herself awake longer. She gave more than a hundred speeches in 1933, working such long hours that her chauffeur quit. She frequently outpaced Wyzanski, an intense twenty-eight-year-old who had earned top honors at Harvard Law School, who panicked over the extreme workload. Exhausted at trying to keep up with her, he even considered resigning but was dissuaded.

Frances's obligation to house her husband and daughter in New York City left her financially strained, and she had difficulty finding a home for herself that she could afford. She evaded talk about her living arrangements, but she briefly found a home at Uplands, an elaborate colonial estate at 1600 Foxhall Road that belonged to a wealthy socialite. Frances began entertaining out of Uplands, hosting Wyzanski and other labor officials at an afternoon tea soon after Wyzanski arrived. It was a temporary arrangement, however, and Frances needed a more permanent solution.

The lack of a fixed address was a social problem for Frances. Washington's rigid social code required that wives of government officials engage in a ritualized system of calling-card exchanges, in which women trekked from home to home leaving cards that indicated their desire to pay respects in person. Women hoping to visit her were forced to take their cards to the agency, where Frances was hard at work with no time to spend on protocol.

A December 1933 article in the *Washington Post* pointed out that Frances was faltering socially with her female obligations. "Capital Has a Rigid Calling Card Code, Social Ostracism Is the Penalty Paid by Women Who Break It," read the headline on a story describing how Frances was failing to measure up.[4]

Frances solved the calling-card problem by moving into a Georgetown house with the charming and wealthy widow Mary Harriman Rumsey, her longtime friend from New York City and the woman who by now had come to Frances's rescue on numerous occasions. Mary had helped finance the Maternity Center Association and the Bureau of Municipal Research, lobbied for Frances to become industrial commissioner of New York, switched her political allegiance to Al Smith, and gave him campaign contributions. She had even once given Frances a home for several months at her Long Island estate when the two women were doing volunteer war work in New York City. Frances had helped Mary, who was chairwoman of a group called the Council of Organizations for War Service. Frances mentioned it only once, and obliquely, but it occurred in 1917 or 1918, when Susanna was still an infant, around the time when Paul had first become ill. It seems likely that Mary had sheltered Frances when Paul lost his job and before Frances found paid employment herself in the Smith administration.[5]

In any case, Mary was easily able to provide her with refuge. She was the daughter of railroad tycoon Edward Harriman, who had died in 1909, leaving Mary's mother the wealthiest woman in America. Mary had been Harriman's favorite child, and he frequently took her on business trips, traveling in personal railroad cars on rail lines they owned and meeting business leaders across the country. They had even embarked together on a famous expedition to Alaska. Mary, bubbly, vivacious, and warmhearted, was not just known to America's economic elite, she was beloved by them.

She had grown up as a Gilded Age princess on the family estate, a hundred-room French Renaissance–inspired mansion on twenty thousand acres in upstate New York, with its own railroad to transport them to the city. In winters, the family lived in a townhouse on 55th Street in Manhattan, and society reporters followed Mary's daily activities breathlessly. Quick-witted and energetic, Mary thrived at doing many things simultaneously, and great wealth allowed her to multiply her efforts. When she attended Barnard College in Manhattan, for example, she commuted to school in a beautiful carriage, driving the team of horses herself, dictating notes on her lessons to a secretary sitting beside her on the bench.[6]

Mary shared many of Frances's progressive leanings. In 1901, when she was a nineteen-year-old debutante, she used that position's visibility to found the Junior League (originally known as the Junior League for the Promotion of the Settlement House Movement), inspiring affluent young women to help the poor and needy. She had permanently changed New York City's landscape by helping establish five hundred playgrounds for children.[7]

Mary had made her debut the same year as Eleanor Roosevelt, and she had been one of the most toasted of the young eligible women. Pretty and popular, Mary's marriage prospects were bright, and newspaper accounts frequently linked her name to the man believed to be America's richest young bachelor. But her father contracted for a sculpture to be made of Mary, and during the sittings she and the young artist fell in love. Mary and her new husband, Charles Cary Rumsey, an avid polo player and horseman who came from a prosperous upstate New York family, soon had three children. Charles was a bon vivant with a serious alcohol problem, and he died in an automobile accident at age forty-three, leaving Mary a widow. Mary had decided to forge a new life for herself, and the excitement in Washington after Roosevelt's election made that seem like a good place to start.[8]

Mary was an invaluable ally for Frances, a newcomer to the city trying to quickly build a social network. The women leased a spacious and tree-shaded Georgetown row house at 3304 O Street NW that had served as the art gallery for the larger home next to it. It contained both formal and informal areas for entertaining, including space to dance, with a ground floor beneath that was decorated with a tropical mural and Javanese batik wall hangings.[9]

"Slim, dark-haired, with sympathetic brown eyes," Mary made friends easily, and even the fiercest doyenne of Washington society, Alice Roosevelt Longworth, acknowledged Mary's adroit social skills. In an article in the *Ladies' Home Journal* titled "Lion Hunting in the New Deal,"

Alice noted that Mary had succeeded in the "most wholesale roundup of the lions of the New Deal, big and little."

Her homes, Alice said, "have become meeting places, almost recreation centers, for professors, brain trusters and bureaucrats of every degree, who are indeed fortunate to have found someone as hospitable to them and to their ideas as she is. She is in her element in the confusion and scurry and experimentation of the New Deal, and I do not know anyone in Washington who fits into it better."[10]

*H*aving Mary in their lives allowed Frances and Susanna a lifestyle they had never before enjoyed. Frances shared with Mary the services of a French maid, which Susanna thought was wonderful. Mary found time to spend with Susanna when her own harried mother could not, and Susanna visited Washington frequently. Susanna considered Rumsey a "second mother." Both women had teenage daughters: Mary's daughter got along well with Susanna. The seventeen-year-old girl flourished in this atmosphere, maturing into a young woman whom even the erudite Wyzanski considered surprisingly "well-informed."[11]

Mary had been trained from girlhood to serve as a trusted assistant to a successful executive, her father, and now she stepped into the role of helpful helpmeet once again. She also shared Frances's values, and was eager to help her advance her agenda. Now she took over all household details, leaving Frances to focus on her work, assistance that she desperately needed. With Mary's support, Frances functioned more efficiently and with fewer distractions, and Mary was able to draw top names to her table because of the lure of a presidential cabinet member living there. Frances got yet another chance to develop her social network. The two pursued a far-ranging array of interests—art, classical music, scientific advances—and made a point of inviting entertaining guests, which made their invitations coveted by Washington insiders, who found both women charming. "[Perkins] had a warm, outgoing personality," recalled Katharine Lenroot, who worked with Frances at the Labor Department. A dinner guest at one party, Lenroot recalled, was a man collecting folk songs throughout the South, and he sang some of the pieces he had discovered.[12]

Frances and Mary got on splendidly, sharing a whimsical but pragmatic approach to life. Mary was not an intellectual, but she was intelligent and idealistic and had enormous personal energy. She seldom wrote letters because she preferred quick telephone communications. She loved to have fun, and had a good sense of humor.

Mary's status among America's financial elites was invaluable to Frances, who was trying to steer business executives toward a more neutral stance on organized labor. In August 1933, for example, while Frances was orchestrating labor codes for the steel and coal industries, she called top industry leaders to a conference in her office. The industries were then almost completely non-union, so Frances invited AFL president William Green to sit in on the talks as a representative of workers. When industry leaders saw Green, they were repulsed and moved as a group to a distant corner of the room. Frances pleaded with them to sit down and talk, but the executives told her that even speaking with Green would strengthen the hand of workers who wanted to organize. The meeting collapsed.

Soon after, Frances and Mary held a dinner party with twelve to fifteen guests, including Green and his wife, and the telephone rang. Mary answered the phone, speaking casually to a familiar voice. "Oh, how nice," Frances heard her say, urging the caller to join them for dessert. Frances didn't think to ask who was coming, but soon the door opened and in walked Myron Taylor of U.S. Steel and his wife. Green and Taylor were startled to see each other, but knowing they were in safe company, they soon drifted in each other's direction. When Frances next looked up, they were deep in conversation. Not long after, Taylor agreed to unionization, and soon after that, Roosevelt named him ambassador to the Vatican.[13]

"Washington itself, particularly in 1933, with all sorts of people coming to help, was a strangely effective melting pot," Frances said.[14]

As she had feared, Frances didn't really like life in Washington, and as Wyzanski casually noted to his mother, "she hate[d] her job." Mary eased life for Frances in many ways and also forced her to confront things she preferred to avoid. Mary, for example, encouraged Frances to read some hostile newspaper articles, helping her find ways to improve her handling of both reporters and prickly senators by being less "tutorial."[15]

Life in a fishbowl wasn't easy, and even a poor word choice could result in negative press. But in those early years, Frances accepted almost every speaking engagement, even though it sometimes drove her to exhaustion: "I felt we had a major responsibility to explain to the people of the United States what we were doing, why we were doing it, what the objectives were, what the hazards were."[16]

She had to continue to live down the offense she had created by implying that southerners were too poor to own shoes. The story had circulated widely, and after that, whenever she traveled to a southern town, she gritted her teeth and smiled at the jokes. On a visit to Atlanta, for example, a chorus sang "All God's Chillun' Got Shoes" as a play off the gospel classic "All God's Chillun' Got Wings."[17]

Mary's presence in Washington made the stresses more bearable.

Frances kept quiet about her privileged life, fearful that it would tarnish her image at a time when much of the country was so poor. She described her home with Mary as merely a wing of a larger house with a handful of rooms, including three bedrooms, not at all "ornate," she hastened to add.[18]

It is probably impossible to know whether Frances's relationship with Mary was also sexual or romantic. Certainly it was much more than an ordinary friendship. The women lived together during the week, often spent weekends together at Mary's estates on Long Island or in Virginia, and entertained as a pair. They got two puppies and raised them together, which suggests they saw a shared future.

Frances pointedly noted that they shared expenses, emphasizing a roommate-style arrangement, but Harriman family financial records showed that Mary essentially supported Frances. Mary spent $13,187 in 1933 on household expenses in Washington, and paid the salaries of three maids, a butler, a cook, and a houseman. Entertainment expenses, including free-flowing champagne, were lavish. Frances paid $450 that year. In 1934, Mary paid $22,081 toward their basic expenses, and Frances paid $800.[19]

Their life together was pleasant and elegant, and Mary was an attractive social partner. A reporter who profiled her around this time described the woman's animated brown eyes and dark hair, set off with a red-and-white-striped blouse and pearls.

"Her beautifully simple home in Georgetown, Washington, is shared by the labor defender, Frances Perkins," the reporter wrote. "It is difficult to believe that the severe, just and practical Secretary of Labor and the petite, artistic dreamer, Mrs. Rumsey, could sit down in harmony amid the Chippendale, the Chinese art objects and the bowls of spring flowers. Yet they do so because of unity of purpose . . . Mrs. Rumsey has the ideas of a leader but she dallies with beauty, art and luxury on her way. If she did not have that softening, feminine spot in her makeup, she, too, might be a maker of history."[20]

The women clearly knew each other well, but some secrecy surrounds the relationship. Frances said little about Mary publicly or privately, and in fact neglected to mention her even when it would have been appropriate. Mary, however, admired Frances so greatly that she often asked friends whether Frances would approve before she made major decisions. She held Frances in higher esteem than anyone else, even asking her to review letters before she sent them to make sure they had the right tone.[21]

No personal letters between the women have come to light. The few letters that survived are pleasant business letters and somewhat distant. Frances destroyed her most personal letters, and Mary's correspondence burned in a warehouse fire.

Frances was comfortable with the idea of lesbian relationships and nonjudgmental about them. She exchanged letters with Jeannette Marks, the longtime lover and partner of Mount Holyoke president Mary Woolley, that show that Frances recognized Marks as Woolley's life partner. Marks wrote to Frances confident that her letters would be seen as the thoughts of a loving spouse, speaking of the profound disappointment that Woolley suffered when Mount Holyoke decided to appoint a male president, partly because of concerns that the school was developing a reputation for being run by lesbians.

Some of Frances's closest friends appear to have been bisexual or exclusively lesbian. Some were engaged in what were called "Boston marriages," when two women resided together and shared their lives. One such couple was Mary Dreier and Frances Kellor. Eleanor Roosevelt, a mother of five, meanwhile, was engaged in a relationship with reporter Lorena Hickok that has appeared to some scholars to have been more than a flirtation. Molly Dewson had a lifelong relationship with heiress Polly Porter; the women referred to themselves as "partners."[22]

These tight alliances sprang up frequently among the first generation of professional and college-educated women, who were sometimes seen by men as unappealing marriage partners. Jane Addams shared her innermost thoughts with Mary Rozet Smith. Some of these relationships were sexual; others were platonic. But for many women of the era, finding a compatible female partner seemed a prelude to success and contribution. Heterosexual relationships seemed to stifle their professional development, as many employers routinely fired women who got married.

On the other hand, it is possible to overstate these implications. Women often engage in close, sisterlike friendships that have absolutely no sexual component. Women at that time had few avenues to power, and it is possible that an heiress seeking to influence policy would cultivate a relationship with such a prominent woman as Frances. Frances maintained unusually close ties with many women over her lifetime. When someone married, she wrote about the wonderful strength of the bond; when someone had a family death, she found special words of consolation. Her suffrage-era friends remained her closest allies, frequently rallying around her when she was publicly attacked. Her female friendships also helped fill the gap in her life left by her ailing husband, who could not be a true life partner because of his unreliability.

Mary, however, was an attractive and immensely wealthy widow who could easily have found male suitors. She did not choose to do so, and appeared at their dinner parties as Frances's partner rather than in the company of a suitable man. Her social comings and goings continued to be chronicled in the society pages, but there is no mention of any men paying court to her. Mary was making a deliberate choice to ally herself with Frances rather than to seek a husband.

Alison Bruere Carnahan, a longtime family friend, thought that Frances engaged in a sort of trade with affluent women to buy herself some respite from her financial troubles. Recalling Mary as rather "empty-headed," Carnahan thought that she might have been "delighted to have a celebrity in her home."[23]

"A lot of rich women wanted her as a jewel in their crown, that they could present themselves as deep thinkers," Carnahan said. "They wanted to be friends with her—and Frances Perkins traded on that." Carnahan thought Frances might accept such an unusual relationship because she was often in difficult financial straits.

"She had to live by her wits," Carnahan recalled. "A lot of it was to create a beautiful life for Susanna. She wanted Susanna to have the life of an upper-class New York girl, for her to have a golden life."

Family friend Jane Gunther, wife of travel writer John Gunther, also believed that Frances allied herself with Mary to bolster Susanna's prospects. Frances "was worldly enough to want to launch Susanna," she said.[24]

Susanna, who spent her childhood and most of her adult years traveling in avant-garde circles in New York City, was irritated in her later years by biographies that sought to identify lesbians in the Roosevelt administration. Mary Dewson was indeed a lesbian, she said, but most other women in those circles were not, including her mother and Eleanor Roosevelt. She thought biographers didn't understand the nature of female bonds and the fact that in the early 1900s it was fashionable for women to write "very flowery" letters to each other.[25]

Frances was not wholly dependent on Mary. She also received assistance from other sources. In 1933, an anonymous donor gave $1,000 for an honorary life membership for Frances in the prestigious National Women's Democratic Club at Dupont Circle.[26]

These contributions helped Frances greatly. With secure financial footing, besides providing for Paul, she was able to prepare Susanna for a proper New York debut in December 1934. Mrs. Caspar Whitney hosted a dinner at the Rainbow Room at Rockefeller Center, with Susanna Wilson as her honored guest, marking her formal entry into New York society.[27]

Regardless of the exact nature of the relationship between Frances and Mary, there is no question that heartfelt emotions were at play. Mary became the key to reaching Frances with requests. When Mary Dreier's sister, Margaret, sought federal help to turn her Florida home into a nature preserve, she and her husband exchanged letters about how they should contact Mary to "influence" Frances.[28]

And Frances, in turn, influenced Mary and her family and friends. Mary's younger brother, Averell Harriman, joined the women in Washington in 1933, and soon he began working for the Roosevelt administration. "She had a great influence on Mary and on my father," recalled Kathleen Mortimer, Averell's daughter.[29]

Around this time, two separate books hit the stands that cast doubt on Frances's public persona as a middle-aged mother of impeccably correct appearance and rectitude.

In 1934, Matthew Josephson's scathing critique of American industrialists, *The Robber Barons,* became a bestseller. The book chronicled how financiers rigged the stock market for their own gains. It had obvious parallels to the 1929 stock market crash, which most people saw as the start of the Great Depression.

A central figure in Josephson's account was Edward Harriman, Mary's father, who was described as "brilliantly deceptive," orchestrating schemes that made him immensely wealthy while injuring workers and small-business owners and throwing other investors into bankruptcy. Frances must have known controversy would erupt if her opulent living arrangements, comfortably ensconced in Mary's home, living on Harriman largesse, became publicly known.

The second book was written by Frances's longtime friend and rejected suitor Sinclair Lewis. He became enormously famous in the 1920s with novels, some made into popular movies, that painted a vivid picture of shallow American entrepreneurship and the narrow provincialism of its small towns. His negative depiction of American life caused Lewis to be denounced as a traitor in the United States, while Europeans delighted in tawdry anecdotes about the once-backwater country that had grown into an important actor on the world stage.

But fame wanes, and by the 1930s, Lewis was worried about maintaining the spectacular trajectory of his success and wanted to write an epic story about American labor. He ultimately gave up, proclaiming labor leaders a "dreary and futile lot," and turned instead to a racy novel, titled *Ann Vickers*, about the sexual and professional travails of a New York City social worker.

In a letter to his second wife, journalist Dorothy Thompson, Lewis said he was modeling the heroine on her, Shakespeare's Portia, Susan B. Anthony, Sarah Bernhardt, Catherine the Great—and Frances Perkins. The book was released in 1933, the year Frances became secretary of labor. It had little in it of the other famous ladies, and according to Dorothy Thompson's biographer, Peter Kurth, "it bore only a minor resemblance to Dorothy's experience."

Frances's friends quickly spotted the closer similarities to her. In a letter, Mary Dewson, head of the Women's Division of the Democratic National Committee, playfully began with the salutation: Dear Ann Vickers. Another letter contains a pointed reference to the book.

The book opens with the account of a young girl playing "pretend" with three boys, re-creating the discovery of America, unable to decide if she wants to be Queen Isabella or Christopher Columbus. Her eyes, "dark, surprisingly large and eager," are her one beauty, Lewis notes. Bright and resourceful, she "lies like a gentleman," Lewis wrote, noting she well conceals her deepest emotions behind a wall of pleasantries.[30]

In the book, Ann Vickers attends a women's college in New England, reminiscent of Frances's time at Mount Holyoke. There she finds herself an important person on campus, preparing to become class president. A student athlete, she shares an apartment with a wealthy female classmate who loves her and who attempts to kiss and embrace her. Ann rebuffs the advances, but not decisively, and is left confused.

After college, Vickers becomes a social worker and suffrage organizer. Then she takes a job with a "committee investigating conditions" in the textile and garment industries in New York, where she spends time with settlement workers and crusaders, including Upton Sinclair.

Vickers goes to live in Greenwich Village, Frances's old neighborhood, which Lewis describes as replete with "poetic editors of trade journals, nymphomaniac and anarchistic lady managers of tea-rooms, reporters who were continually out of jobs." Though Vickers "hated to be pawed," some fifty or so "kissed her lingeringly, male and female," Lewis writes.

The book's sexual content drew outrage in some circles, but it became popular and was soon made into a movie starring the famous actress Irene Dunne. Lewis frequently took inspiration for his novels from the women in his life, and there was a real risk that the connection could be made, but few people in the general public recognized the parallels between the lead character and their middle-aged secretary of labor.[31]

There is no record of Frances's reaction to the book. Recent communications between Frances and Lewis had been amicable. Frances knew he often handled things badly and recognized his alcoholism and pitied him for the ways he damaged his friendships.

In the early 1950s, when Lewis died, Frances wrote a letter that gave his son, Michael, from whom he was estranged, great comfort. Thompson told Frances the letter finally helped him cry. Michael wrote to her, thanking her for the letter. "I see that you knew Father well, and understood, as did so few people, his vast loneliness."[32]

Chapter 19

Blue Eagle:
A First Try at
"Civilizing Capitalism"[1]

*O*ne day at a Cabinet meeting when Frances was making one of her standard pitches for a job-creating public works program, she was interrupted by an enthusiastic Henry Wallace. The secretary of agriculture had just heard of a "very brilliant scheme"[2] that might turn around the whole economy without requiring an expensive public effort. Budget director Lewis Douglas, who wanted to rein in expenditures and opposed costly public works projects, said that he, too, had heard the idea and planned to talk to Roosevelt about it.

Douglas's interest put Frances on full alert, and she knew that she had better hastily learn all she could about these new ideas. It turned out that two groups of Washington insiders were developing competing proposals in hopes of winning presidential support. Both involved more collaboration among competing industries, and they reflected growing worldwide experiments in fascism, a political ideology that specifically tied together government and business interests.

Frances convinced FDR to dispatch her to investigate these plans on his behalf, a move that both rival groups greeted with consternation. She wanted to attend the groups' working sessions, but the participants were reluctant. Rexford Tugwell, a member of one of the groups, said she wouldn't find the meeting interesting because it involved "delicate, detailed thinking-out."[3]

"I'm not coming for interest," she said. "The President wishes to know what's going on and what you're thinking about, and I'll come over."

She arrived at what she'd been told was the starting time, only to find the meeting well under way. The men, including a more congenial fellow named Donald Richberg, plotted strategy around a circular table. Their goal was to set aside federal antitrust laws and allow competing firms to reach industry-wide agreements on prices that would reduce competitive pressures. Intense competition had driven down prices and caused employers to cut wages and lay off workers; such industrial planning would permit them to retain more people and pay them more.

Some worried that the Supreme Court would quickly invalidate the concept. A beefy, red-faced man presiding over the group waved away their concerns. He sat nervously in his chair, then paced the room, then sat on his feet and leaned over the table, sweating profusely. Frances noticed his "curiously restless, uncontrolled, undisciplined kind of face."[4]

"Well, what difference does it make anyhow because before they can get their case to the Supreme Court we will have won the victory," he said confidently. "The unemployment will be over and over so fast and no one will care. We'll go on doing it somehow under some other name because this is the answer."

The man's vow to proceed with the plan regardless of its legality startled Frances. It proved a fitting introduction to Hugh Samuel Johnson, a West Point graduate who had risen to brigadier general during World War I. He had helped to manage the army's purchase programs and draft administration from Washington, and then had worked for multimillionaire financier Bernard Baruch.

"He has the military type of mind, which brushes aside obstacles and ignores precedents," a British official told Sir Anthony Eden in a confidential report on America's leading political figures. "In addition, he has a great flair for publicity and a command of language which is both unorthodox and vigorous, and which frequently verges on the blasphemous or obscene."[5]

Meanwhile, a rival group headed by Senator Wagner was developing its own plan. Frances found the members of the group "full of jealousy and animosity," squabbling over who would earn credit for an intellectual contribution. This group, too, hoped to get companies to voluntarily operate under agreements forged within specific industries, as an exception to ordinary antitrust principles.[6]

With Frances's prodding and the president's backing, the two groups slowly coalesced around one set of ideas. Frances privately considered the industrial plan "somewhat exotic and thoroughly experimental," even reactionary. The plan's price-fixing aspects undid decades of antitrust law that had maintained a competitive marketplace.[7]

Still, she saw ways to use the plan to accomplish her own agenda.

Perhaps what couldn't be done by law could be accomplished instead by agreements reached by corporate participants. The plan also provided her with a fresh opportunity to get a bigger public works program by simply attaching it as a side provision to a proposal rapidly gaining traction. Moreover, an expansive public works program would produce jobs that would help the other economic aspects of the proposal succeed, she thought.

Of course, it was essential that businesses voluntarily participate in the plan, but industry leaders already were promoting something similar. As early as 1932 two top U.S. Chamber of Commerce officials privately visited President Hoover to urge him to consider some form of industrial planning to save the economy. Hoover had derided the proposal as "sheer fascism."

Rebuffed, the officials met privately with Roosevelt in Albany and began making the same suggestions to the incoming president, who listened with more interest. At the Chamber's twenty-first annual meeting in May 1933, Roosevelt was keynote speaker, and eight members of the president's Cabinet attended the dinner. When he entered the room, Roosevelt won a standing ovation, and when Roosevelt described the industrial plan, those present enthusiastically applauded.[8] For that reason, Roosevelt knew he had enough business support to launch the project.

When Roosevelt asked Frances who should head the new National Recovery Administration (NRA), she recommended Donald Richberg because he strongly shared her commitment to public works. But since Richberg was virtually unknown, FDR saw the gruff and difficult General Johnson as the frontrunner. Frances set out to cultivate him. She laid it on thick, referring frequently to his "great mind," a tactic the egotistical man found impossible to resist.[9] She invited Johnson for dinner at the home she shared with Mary, and he soon developed the habit of dropping by almost nightly to discuss his grand plans.

Under her influence, Johnson came to see public works as an indispensable part of the program, the carrot to dangle in front of industrialists' noses so they would agree to restrictive codes.

As Johnson visualized it, with some prodding from Frances, individual companies within an industry would adopt a government-backed agreement permitting them to obtain an exemption from antitrust laws. The agreement would allow them to avoid cutthroat competition by sharing markets, guaranteeing them a certain profit margin and protecting their investments, which in turn would allow them to offer good wages and working conditions. Public works projects would ensure there was work for the companies to do. Johnson thought the program's director should dictate the terms of the agreements, preferably by government fiat, with the director deciding whether the companies were efficiently run and deserving of protection. Johnson clearly visualized himself making those determinations.

His enthusiasm was boosted further when he read some of the material that had inspired Benito Mussolini, who had assumed control of Italy and merged political and business forces there. Fascism was growing in popularity in Europe because people believed it would allow institutions to operate more efficiently. In these corporate states, governments would work cooperatively with businesses and direct their operations. Johnson, Frances thought, was captivated by the idea of a central authority empowered to make important decisions. His frequent references to the "war against depression and poverty" struck her as forceful, though unsettling, rhetoric.

Another important supporter for the effort was Nelson Slater, a leading textile manufacturer and the scion of one of the nation's longest-standing textile empires. Nelson's ancestor, Samuel Slater, a young Englishman apprenticed to a textile mill, had decided in 1789 that the British textile industry was heading for a collapse because of ruinous competition. He emigrated to the United States with crucial plans for textile machine designs stored safely in his head, and struck up a partnership with American textile manufacturers. Together they built a mill in Pawtucket, Rhode Island, that became profitable and Samuel Slater became known as the father of the American Industrial Revolution.[10]

In the United States as in England, success spawned imitation. In 1806 there were fifteen cotton mills in the United States. Three years later, there were sixty-two, with twenty-five more under construction. Increasing competition drove down prices. As prices dropped, so did wages, and the mills began hiring less-educated workers. In the early years, Slater Mill's employees were local people who were literate. By the 1830s the company hired immigrants who signed their names with an *x* because they could not read and write.[11] Then textile companies moved south in search of workers who would accept even lower wages. Nelson

Slater felt responsible for workers employed by his family for generations, and he wanted to stop the downward economic spiral in the textile business.

Slater began collaborating with Johnson, seeing the NRA and industrial cooperation as a potential solution to textile industry woes. Textiles became the first of many industries to undergo the process of obtaining government approval for a wage and hour code.

In the code's development, Frances scored an enormous victory almost right away—attaining something that her mentor, Florence Kelley, had sought unsuccessfully for decades. The textile manufacturers were asked to eliminate child labor. At first the firms objected; then, eager for a deal, they agreed. By this time, only about fifteen thousand of the industry's six hundred thousand workers were children, so the prohibition actually had little practical effect. But removing child labor from such a large industry became "moral dynamite," according to *Time* magazine. It forced other employers to consider whether they, too, could operate without children in their factories.[12]

Frances wanted to give workers a formal place at the table in this new orchestrated arrangement between government and employers. Johnson and Slater were paternalistically attentive to workers' welfare, but they considered it ridiculous to include labor representatives in the negotiations. Even Frances agreed that the existing textile union, the skeletal United Textile Workers, was a "set of lunatics and grafters," and many of the other unions were too feeble to be effective.[13] So Frances suggested they set up a labor advisory committee. With the backing of the AFL, Frances appointed the labor representatives and found substitutes if no legitimate unions could be found to represent worker interests.

In this way, the right of unions to organize originated in the NRA bill, and almost by accident. In drafting the legislation, Frances and Richberg decided to insert language to ensure a role for the workingman in the talks, wording that would permit workers to organize into unions more easily. They reasoned that the NRA cleared the way for business to return to sustainable profitability. It didn't seem fair that employers who cooperated with their unions should suffer an economic disadvantage from having to pay union wages, while those who simply intimidated, fired, or locked out union organizers did not.

Frances privately met with Green of the AFL to discuss the proposal.

He, too, liked the idea and applauded Roosevelt for thinking of it. Frances didn't tell him that Roosevelt didn't even know about the provision. Green normally agreed to Frances's suggestions, but this time he asked for time to consider the provision. After conferring with other union officials, he returned to suggest refining the language to include: "Employees shall have the right to bargain collectively . . . free of interference by employers. . . ." To Frances, it didn't seem much different from the original suggested language. Richberg, Johnson, and Wagner also saw it as an innocuous change. The clause became known as Section 7(a).

In other words, Frances said later, the exact wording of Section 7(a) was "almost an accident . . . You see, the labor movement at that time was dead," she explained. The drafters also saw no need to give federal officials any particular power to enforce workers' rights. According to Leon Keyserling, Wagner's legislative assistant, the drafters assumed that employers would cooperate willingly, given their support for the overall concept of the NRA.[14]

Johnson, Slater, and George Sloan of the Cotton Textile Institute agreed to the clause, mainly because they considered unions ineffectual. Frances remembered them saying: "Well, of course, that won't mean anything because there isn't any labor to be represented in most places. There isn't any organized set of workers. If any committee from the local plant wants to come in and talk about things, they surely can. That's all right. Nobody denies them that so long as they don't try to push into any agreements and put a rule on them."[15]

When the draft was completed, Frances arranged for its presentation to Roosevelt, who was pleased. They had emphasized the president's emergency powers in justifying the setting aside of antitrust laws. The sole sticking point was whether the bill's public works section would be included. Frances, of course, favored it, but budget chief Douglas argued that it would increase federal spending. FDR waffled.

"Well, now, do you want public works, Mr. President, or don't you?" she asked.[16]

He stalled. "Well, we'll see," he said.

For the next few days Frances worked on sewing up the president's support. But she was shocked when she saw the bill in its final formulation—neatly cut in two. The new National Recovery Administration was a freestanding measure, and public works were addressed in a second, separate bill—a bill that might never be passed. She recognized the split as Douglas's work. Angry, she quietly arranged a Saturday afternoon meeting with the president, knowing he would be seeing Douglas earlier in the morning. When the meeting began, Frances explained again about the multiplier effects of public works—how building a bridge gives work to brick makers, steelmakers, engineers, and everyone in between. She reminded Roosevelt that he had loudly endorsed public works projects as a way out of the Depression when he was governor. It's now or never, she said.

"You've got to decide it right now, Mr. President," Frances said. "Here on this beautiful sunshiny afternoon, we have to decide if we shall put it in or leave it out. If we leave it out, I know we'll not get public works this year. If we don't get it this year, it'll be too late to do any good." [17]

The president hesitated and asked more questions. After several hours, he agreed. He told her to put public works back in the NRA bill and to tell Senator Wagner that's how he wanted it done.

Frances jumped, eager to act on Roosevelt's commitment before Douglas got to him again.

"Wouldn't it be all right if I used your telephone now and tell him, because he may get away from the place where he is?" she asked. All right, Roosevelt said. Frances called Wagner, and in the president's presence told the senator that Roosevelt wanted to restore the bill's public works portion. Then she put the president on the telephone, and Wagner voiced his agreement. The deal was done—and in a way that would be almost impossible for Douglas to unravel between late Saturday afternoon and Monday morning, when the bill would be introduced. [18]

To have prevailed on the issue, it was essential that her voice was the last one that Wagner and the president heard.

Frances was a little ashamed of her maneuvers and admitted that she would have much preferred to have beaten Douglas openly or to have been beaten by him. Yet she understood that was the only way to get the public works bill introduced. The bill ultimately passed by overwhelming majorities in both the House and Senate in 1933. The two-pronged measure allocated an initial $3.3 billion for public works, and it permitted trade groups to establish codes for business operations. Businesses were required to abide by Section 7(a), the labor provision, as part of those agreements. The measure drew favorable publicity, as commentators painted it as a brilliant solution to a deep problem.

Johnson became more convinced than ever that he would run the NRA. During his evening visits with Frances, he talked at length about how he would administer the agency. She saw he was erratic, excitable, but at times touched with "streaks of genius." [19] In a comfortable setting, he expanded, almost physically, and was magnetic in his charm and energy. But in a conference room, he huddled down, stubborn, sullen, and intractable, and his natural brilliance would fade.

One hot summer night, Frances and Mary were at the Middleburg farm when Baruch, Johnson's former employer, unexpectedly showed up. At first, Baruch seemed to be making a social call, and being a little deaf, he urged Frances to sit by his good ear. When the others were talking among themselves, he asked Frances whether she thought Johnson might be named to head the NRA. She said she believed so.

"You'd better interpose," he told her. ". . . Hugh isn't fit to be head of that." He told her that Johnson had many weaknesses, although he would not be more specific, and could not be relied on to head a project of such great importance. He urged her to tell the president.[20]

FDR, however, had already decided that he wanted Johnson and would not revisit the decision, and, as he often did with unpleasant tasks, he told Frances to keep a close eye on Johnson and the NRA. Frances didn't like the idea of crossing lines of authority, even if her boss had ordered her to do it. She began monitoring the NRA, but cautiously.

Baruch's warning made her feel uneasy enough about Johnson that she persuaded FDR to split the job at the NRA by putting the public works portion under the management of Interior Secretary Ickes. Ickes had impressed her as punctilious, even fussy, which she thought was an essential characteristic for someone overseeing expensive and controversial government construction projects. Frances also thought he would make good practical decisions about which projects to undertake. The president agreed.

A day or so before Ickes's appointment was to be announced, however, Frances learned the president had not told Johnson he planned to divide the NRA's responsibilities, or that he had asked Ickes to handle public works. FDR had procrastinated, dreading Johnson's fury when he learned of the shift. He asked Frances if she had ideas on how to handle the situation. Frances felt awkward because she had sought Johnson's help in getting the public works provisions included and had listened as he shared his plans for the job.

She suggested FDR call Johnson to a Cabinet meeting. There, FDR could announce Johnson's appointment in a safely public setting. Then he could say that the Cabinet had suggested the job be divided to ease the burden on Johnson. Meanwhile, FDR left it to Frances to tell Ickes that FDR was giving him the real duties. Ickes exploded.

"The hell he is!" the irascible interior secretary said.[21] Ickes eventually came around, however, and in fact, his successful administration of the Public Works Administration (PWA) cemented his reputation. The PWA handled large-scale projects, and was an entity separate from the Works Progress Administration (WPA), the Hopkins-run project targeted to smaller relief projects. The PWA eventually would build thirty-four thousand projects, including the Grand Coulee Dam on the Columbia River, the All-American Canal in Southern California, the Triborough Bridge and the Lincoln Tunnel in New York City, the road linking the Florida Keys, the Blue Ridge Parkway from the Shenandoah to the Great Smoky Mountains, and scores of hospitals and public schools. It helped create the infrastructure that allowed the U.S. economy to expand dramatically in future years.

When the Cabinet meeting opened, Roosevelt announced that the NRA had passed, that he would be signing it, and that Hugh Johnson would be administrator. Public works would be handled separately, he added. Frances sat silently while the men discussed it. One by one, the other Cabinet officers agreed that the public works portion required separate, special attention. Bolstered in his opinion, Roosevelt then called Johnson into the room and named him head of the NRA. Johnson preened, but his face darkened when the president said that public works would be administered separately.

Johnson turned red, then purple. Frances fancied she could even see his hair standing on end. But Roosevelt blandly persevered, telling the group he had chosen "that fellow down there," pointing to Ickes, to help share the burdens, which drew a laugh and served to cover Johnson's discomfort. Johnson said nothing at first, then responded woodenly with a "little patriotic speech" that portrayed him as a loyal soldier.

Frances realized Johnson was still wild with rage, and after the meeting, she told the president so.

"Stick with him, Frances," Roosevelt said. "Don't let him talk to the press. Get him over it."[22]

So Frances accompanied Johnson, who was muttering to himself, out the door and ushered him into her Labor Department limousine. At first he was in a fog, but as the haze lifted, he cursed and gesticulated. She instructed her driver to cruise over to Haines Point and up Rock Creek Park, to keep Johnson confined until he calmed down. After several hours, they drove him home. As they approached his house, it occurred to Frances that Johnson's wife would be naturally sympathetic to her husband's point of view, and would likely stir things up again with pointed questions. Frances suggested he tell his wife that he had initiated the separation of the two roles so he could give his undivided attention to the main NRA code. The next day, that was the story he gave to the Washington press corps as well.

The tempest passed without attracting attention. Johnson embarked on the task with his characteristic enthusiasm, drive, and skillful public relations. He infused dynamism in others as well, and the new agency catapulted into action. Its emblem—the blue eagle—became a patriotic symbol that companies flaunted to demonstrate their participation. The NRA's launch was greeted by a huge parade reminiscent of the celebrations that had greeted the end of the war, with thousands of marchers filling Manhattan's streets, accompanied by corporate-sponsored floats festooned with flowers.

"The NRA burst on the American scene like a national call to arms," wrote James MacGregor Burns.[23]

The Chamber of Commerce sent out bulletins to trade associations urging them to participate.[24] And certainly the early economic signs inspired hope—a new textile mill opened in Georgia, workers in Savannah bought express train tickets to a seaside outing. It seemed that money was moving again.[25]

Problems, however, emerged almost immediately. Too many industries sought codes; federal officials became involved with minute detail inside each industry. Hundreds of issues came up for review, leading to administrative gridlock and confusion.

In the textile industry, for example, the NRA's compliance division had to decide whether a mill that gave its workers a 5 percent bonus was violating the industry code. It had to define whether the job description for a "cleaner" applied to bobbin cleaners, quill cleaners, and harness cleaners or just to workers who clean floors and machinery.[26]

Workers were befuddled by their new freedom to organize. "We have in Winooski at the present time a man who claims he is from the textile union, who is trying to organize a union here," wrote Albert Therrien of Winooski, Vermont, to Johnson. "Do you think it is perfectly alright for us to join?"[27]

Some unions gouged workers, requiring steep fees to secure employment. A nonunion picture show operator, J. B. Butler, of Attalla, Alabama, complained that he had to pay $250 to join the union, plus $5 a week out of his $20 salary.[28]

Employers wrestled with new issues too. The textile industry code impressed an eighty-hour-a-week limitation on machinery use, to stem overproduction. Medical products manufacturer Johnson & Johnson sought permission to run longer hours, and the textile industry went into an uproar.

"The change as suggested by Johnson & Johnson will disrupt labor most seriously in most sections," wrote the American Cotton Manufacturers Association, apparently straight-faced in its unfamiliar role as the champion of labor interests. Johnson & Johnson's request was approved because the company also proposed paying workers more for shorter shifts.[29]

A bizarre corporate-state scheme, with the government as puppet master, appeared to be emerging, and this worried Frances. Government oversight seemed to be introducing new economic inefficiencies, as companies shifted the way they handled production and allocated their resources to fit into new governmental straitjackets.

Seeking more balanced input for the NRA's decisions, Frances urged Johnson to establish three advisory committees—representing labor, employers, and consumers. Her primary interest, of course, was the labor committee, but she had become alarmed that consumers could be injured as companies and the government set up codes that suited them. She had noted "nobody gave a tinker's damn for the public in the whole thing."[30]

The secretary of commerce selected the Employers Committee. For the Labor Committee, Johnson wanted a marquee name, and he picked as chairman Senator Wagner, who had introduced the NRA bill. Frances tried to dissuade him from this choice, worried that the role would only feed Wagner's ego. Johnson was adamant.[31]

Johnson balked at creating a consumer's committee, but later he relented, and Mary Harriman Rumsey was appointed to the job of overseeing consumer interests. The office she created became the government's first foray into consumer protection.

While the NRA's underlying problems festered, the president sought to maintain some control of the agency's activities through a Cabinet committee that met with Johnson regularly. The group included Frances, Ickes, Commerce Secretary Dan Roper, and Attorney General Cummings.

Frances was seen as the committee chairwoman because of her closeness to Johnson. The exuberant general once called her the "best man in the Cabinet," which, though intended as praise, embarrassed Frances and irritated the male members. Roosevelt, however, saw it as humorous and repeated it frequently.[32]

Although the oversight meetings kept a positive focus, doubts were spreading about both the NRA and Johnson. Small business owners angrily reported to Roper that matters were being decided only by the "big boys in the industry, that the little fellows weren't being consulted."[33]

The frantic pace of code creation made the NRA's process seem more like a mania than an orderly plan. Hundreds of new codes were created, and, observers noted, they often had the effect of favoring the big firms that negotiated the agreements while squeezing little firms out of business. Howls of criticism erupted. Senator William Borah of Idaho said the NRA was controlled by "combines, trusts and monopolies," and that it had become a "travesty upon justice." Business opposition to the program grew as well. And the Federal Trade Commission, the agency that enforced antitrust laws, prepared to take action against business maneuvers its officials viewed as unlawful.

At Mary's urging, Frances convinced Mary's brother Averell to join the NRA to help administer the industry codes. He did well in the job—his first stint in a long career in the federal government—but problems were mounting and Johnson was raging out of control.

Frances also began hearing alarming reports about Johnson himself. In late summer 1933, Johnson began going on drinking binges, disappearing for days at a time. When he was around, he often forgot what he had done while he was on a bender, sometimes refusing to sign documents that he had negotiated only days earlier, and was intransigent about correcting errors. Meanwhile his faithful staff concealed what was happening from the press and outsiders.

Finally a report reached the president that Johnson had done something "disgraceful and slightly obscene" while he was intoxicated. Roosevelt called Frances.

She hadn't heard of the particular incident, but she shared what she knew about the state of the NRA. Roosevelt decided he needed to get rid of Johnson, and he would do so by offering him a high-profile post examining the progress of economic recovery in Europe—England, France, and Belgium but emphatically not Italy, where Johnson's national planning schemes would look too close to the corporate-state system undertaken by Mussolini.

Using Baruch as an intermediary, Roosevelt broached the idea with Johnson, then he invited him to his office to finalize the plan. Somehow, Johnson came out of the meeting convinced he had not been asked to go. He emerged "wreathed in smiles," reporters said, twirling his hat. "The president told me I could not get away from the NRA," Johnson said. "He wants me to stay right here in Washington with my feet nailed down to the floor."[34]

Frances read the newspaper accounts but was determined to take a vacation to visit friends in Cooperstown. She drove all day to get there. When she arrived the family rushed to the car to say the White House had called and the president needed her in his office by 10 a.m. She had a quick meal, washed her face, left Susanna in the care of friends, and drove back south. She drove through the night to reach the White House on time. There she found that Richberg had also been summoned.

Then Johnson arrived, "very red in the face and very puffy"; he had been drinking heavily. The three looked at each other questioningly. No one knew what the president wanted. An aide ushered them into the Blue Room, and Frances could see Roosevelt bracing himself. No small talk, no smiles or pleasantries. Without delay, he told Johnson he was sending him to Europe, and that if he would not go, he needed to resign—immediately. The president had brought them there as witnesses to make sure Johnson heard what he was telling him.[35]

Meanwhile, the constitutionality of the NRA was being questioned. A case brought by the Justice Department against the A. L. A. Schechter Poultry Corp., alleging wage and hour violations, the filing of false reports, and the selling of unfit chickens, proceeded through the courts. Wyzanski, the Labor Department's solicitor, considered the case a poor vehicle to use to defend the NRA, saying that its specific facts put the federal government in a bad light. However, Attorney General Cummings insisted it be pushed to the High Court because it was the first one up. Richberg, the NRA official, also defended the decision to fight the case because the paperwork was complete and the employer had simply refused to do what the code required. An example needed to be made to deter similar intransigence.

The Schechter decision came down in May 1935, with the Supreme Court ruling unanimously that the NRA code system was unconstitutional because it gave the president too much power. Wyzanski was traveling to Europe, but he quickly cabled Frances that based on what he was reading, he did not believe the Supreme Court had intended to wipe out the NRA entirely. Attorney General Cummings had a different interpretation, saying publicly that the ruling spelled the end of NRA.

"Do not agree with Cummings," Wyzanski cabled Frances. "Believe something can be salvaged. Hold on."[36]

She rushed over to the White House with Wyzanski's cablegram, but by the time she arrived, Cummings was already there and had convinced FDR that the NRA had been eviscerated. He seemed different that day, Frances thought, than the friendly person he had always been. Standing in the White House, a pince-nez perched on his long nose, he seemed to be looking through Frances rather than at her. He dismissed her comments and Wyzanski's opinion out of hand.

Frances realized that Roosevelt was eager to see the end of the NRA. He viewed it as spiraling out of control, with too many small industries demanding codes. Frances felt that Roosevelt was "very glad to be rid of the whole thing."[37]

Cummings then launched into a full-throated damnation of the Supreme Court.

"Mr. President, what can you expect?" he asked. "This decision of the Supreme Court is absolutely unnecessary. They could just as well have decided the other way."

He denounced each individual justice. McReynolds was disagreeable; Van Devanter was "dead from the neck up"; Butler and Sutherland were too old. The rest, he implied, were simply going along with the other reactionaries.

Frances again tried to intervene, urging the men to reconsider saving some part of the NRA, but they would not hear of it. She approached Cummings several times in the next week, but he refused to listen. Instead he repeatedly blamed the Court for destroying a key part of Roosevelt's New Deal program.

Justice Harlan F. Stone later told Frances the justices were startled by the administration's decision to jettison the program based on a single ruling. "Why did they jump to the conclusion it was all over?" he asked, shaking his head about what he viewed as a lack of "intelligence and imagination" in the White House.

Indeed, what Frances had seen that day in the White House seemed odd, and in the coming months she grew increasingly uneasy. Cummings's behavior was out of character, and she came to believe he was using the incident to advance a goal he had long sought. A second-rate attorney from upstate New York, Cummings had apparently decided that the one way to cap his career was to win appointment to the Supreme Court.

"The so-called Supreme Court fight started that day," Frances said, adding that Harold Stephens, the assistant attorney general, came to share her suspicions. "He knew certain things I only suspected," she said.

Chapter 20

REFUGEES
AND REGULATIONS

*I*n addition to helping restore the economy and initiating new labor policies, Frances also had responsibilities in an entirely different arena as well. The nation's primary immigration agency was located within the Labor Department, and Frances early on had reason to believe that it might present new and unprecedented challenges.

In early 1933, Frances had given a dinner party that included Sinclair Lewis's wife, reporter Dorothy Thompson. Thompson had just returned from Germany, and she electrified the guests with her stories about a maniacal politician named Adolf Hitler. He had become chancellor that January and had consolidated his power when the Nazi Party won the Reichstag election in March. Nobody in America had heard much about him. Thompson launched into an intense monologue about Hitler's background and the danger he posed to liberals, intellectuals, trade union leaders, and Jews, many of whom she believed were at mortal risk. The cheerful table banter slowly died as the guests listened, "absolutely silent, stricken," Frances recalled.[1]

After Thompson left, they talked. It couldn't be true, they said to themselves. The Germans aren't that kind of people. Frances, who was assuming control of the Immigration Service, the government entity that decided who could enter and stay in the United States, carefully noted Thompson's words.

There was more bad news as well. Frances had become acquainted with European labor leaders through the International Labor Organization (ILO), an international agency that promoted workplace improvements. The Germans held particular sway at the ILO, since they had invented many worker benefit programs and their country boasted the world's largest single trade union movement. The Great Depression and widespread unemployment had weakened and demoralized Germany's union movement, as had happened in the United States. By 1933, when the jobless rate in Germany was 40 percent for industrial workers, union membership had plummeted.

Hitler, a militant nationalist and decorated war veteran, had a personal grievance against unions. He considered them complicit in what he saw as Germany's national shame: the country's decision to sue for peace in November 1918. Mired in a war with casualties of five thousand people a day, union officials had joined forces with sailors and soldiers in a revolt to end it. In one of the key turning points leading to the armistice, embittered and malnourished German sailors in the port city of Kiel, Germany, allied themselves with unionized dock workers against continuation of the war.

To Hitler, the union leaders were cowards and shirkers. He linked them to two other groups he despised: Marxists and Jews, also referring sometimes to union leaders as "Jewish-Marxist wire-pullers." On them he also placed the blame for Germany's postwar economic woes and rising unemployment. On May 2, 1933, soon after Hitler's ascension, Nazi storm troopers invaded and occupied the offices of the three major German trade unions, seized their property, and confiscated their pension and benefit funds. Hundreds of union officials and their secretaries were brutalized, arrested, and imprisoned.[2]

A few months later, reports of scattered sightings trickled in: In July, a refugee who said he had escaped from Nazi captors claimed to have seen Herr Schmaus, an elderly trade union official, at a prison in Köpenick. He and a nineteen-year-old girl, both naked, had been beaten unconscious. In an account published in the *New York Times,* the witness said they had then been dragged away. The body of another of their allies, a man who had been president of a veteran's group, was found in a sack in a Berlin canal.[3]

Theodore Leipart and Peter Grassmann, both prominent labor leaders in their sixties, had been tortured in bizarre ways, AFL officials in the United States learned. They were forced to sing Nazi hymns and spend hours performing gymnastics, although one of the men was recuperating from an automobile accident. At gunpoint, another trade unionist was forced to serve as a mock drillmaster, marching the two collapsing men around the barracks courtyard.[4]

Immediately after the assault on the trade union offices, Nazi loyalists took over the positions of the deposed union leaders. Collective bargaining, established by law in Germany in the 1860s, was declared illegal. A new Nazi-controlled labor union governed by Robert Ley, a Hitler acolyte, became a gigantic propaganda machine churning out re-education materials.[5]

No major German industrialist opposed Hitler's attack on orga-nized labor, and instead they questioned why the Nazis permitted the unions to continue to exist at all. Elsewhere in Western Europe and in the United States, the overthrow of the democratic trade union move-ment in Germany drew surprisingly little criticism. In England and the United States, many people had been fearful of the spread of Marxism since the Bolshevik Revolution in 1917, and some praised Hitler's action in ridding Germany of a movement they considered closely associated with communism. The anti-Semites among them, inclined to harbor suspicions about the role of Jews in organized labor, likewise were qui-etly supportive.

William Green, president of the AFL, protested the German ac-tion to the U.S. State Department. But generally, the American labor movement, basically conservative and organized to promote better pay and conditions for specialized craftsmen, felt little solidarity with the more broad-based and politicized European unions, although some labor groups in the United States and abroad pushed for a boycott of German-made goods. About a year after the German unions were taken over, a group of New Yorkers formed the Jewish Labor Committee, which sought to publicize Germany's problems. By that time, however, the Ger-man labor movement had been destroyed.[6]

European labor issues were not on Roosevelt's radar screen at all. In his diary, William E. Dodd, newly appointed ambassador to Germany, recounted that during his first official meeting with the president, on June 16, 1933, Roosevelt gave him explicit marching orders. He instructed him to push for repayment of the large debts owed by the Germans to U.S. creditors, including many small investors who had bought bonds in the 1920s to help rebuild Germany after World War I. While he told Dodd he thought Hitler's discrimination against the Jews was "shame-ful," Roosevelt said that nothing should be done publicly to interfere with German internal affairs.[7]

As head of the Immigration Service, Frances followed the move-ments of German union leaders who had avoided being caught in the dragnet. Some sought safe harbor in other countries. Under U.S. immigration law, immigrants were required to obtain visas from consular officials located in U.S. embassies overseas, a State Department function, but once they arrived on American soil, they came under the control of the Immigration Service, which was part of the Labor Department. The Immigration Service ultimately decided whether to admit an immigrant. However, highly restrictive immigration laws imposed in the United States in the 1920s made it impossible for Frances to do much for the fleeing trade unionists.

Meanwhile, the worsening plight of the 525,000 German Jews was becoming apparent. Frances was visited by a number of prominent Jews, fellow New Yorkers, including Supreme Court Justice Benjamin N. Cardozo; Judge Julian Mack, a Jewish leader who was a founder of the *Harvard Law Review;* and Joseph Proskauer, a former New York state judge. The Nazis were boycotting Jewish businesses and had begun dismissing Jews from their jobs. About thirty-four thousand Jewish wage earners lost their livelihoods and fell into poverty. Half of Germany's seven thousand Jewish doctors were prohibited from practicing medicine, and about twenty thousand merchants and workmen were jobless. The group that met with Frances wanted to see more refugees offered shelter in the United States, but nobody knew how many actually wished to move.[8]

The crisis in Germany came up in April 1933 at a Cabinet meeting. Most of the officials in attendance supported increasing immigration quotas, and Frances advocated it. Roosevelt considered speaking out on behalf of the German Jews. George Dern, Homer Cummings, and Secretary of State Cordell Hull agreed that something needed to be done. Dan Roper and Claude Swanson said nothing.[9]

But the fact remained that in spite of Secretary Hull's support, State Department officials advised the president against speaking out about conditions in Germany. Ambassador Dodd said German officials had reassured American diplomats that Hitler would soon soften his stance against the Jews, and things would improve—as long as Americans did not aggravate tensions.

The Roosevelt administration's failure to act "grieves me beyond words," Felix Frankfurter, who was Jewish, wrote to Frances that month. He predicted that the Germans would grow more aggressive toward Jews because the State Department was so timid.[10]

And as summer passed, matters indeed grew worse in Germany. By fall, Frances urgently wanted action, but her job as labor secretary required her to enforce the laws on the books. Political opposition to immigration had been growing for decades. In 1930, during the Hoover administration, more restrictive immigration laws had gone into effect. People could immigrate only under a country-based quota proportionate to their share of the U.S. population. The State Department also issued a limited number of work visas through its embassies. The Immigration Service admitted only immigrants with the proper paperwork who were deemed literate and of good character.

By 1933, the year Frances took over, economic conditions in the United States were so desperate that new entry hit a hundred-year low. U.S. immigration basically halted during much of the 1930s. More people left the United States than had entered.[11]

Frances knew restrictive policies were politically popular. "It is generally recognized that the United States can no longer absorb annually hundreds of thousands of immigrants without serious economic and social dislocations," she wrote. "Certainly the present restrictions can not be relaxed while millions of workers are unemployed and maintained at public expense."[12]

In fact, Frances had to spend much time reassuring disbelieving citizens that immigration had indeed been curtailed. Many refused to believe government statistics, and they circulated reports alleging that 1 million foreign sailors jumped ship in the United States each year, or that five hundred thousand Mexicans strolled across the border in the previous decade. In her annual report in 1935, Frances blasted these accounts as "fantastic exaggerations."[13]

But the situation in Germany called for extraordinary measures. Behind the scenes, Frances looked for ways to relax the formal requirements so she could bring German refugees to safety. She faced tough legal obstacles. In addition to restrictive laws, Hoover had issued an executive order requiring that U.S. consuls block entry by any people "likely to become a public charge." And a 1924 immigration law did not allow prospective entrants to arrange for employment before they arrived.[14]

Within these constraints, Frances immediately did what she could. Foreign students attending American schools and colleges previously had been required to post a $500 bond to ensure they would not become public charges. Under Frances, the bond was cut to $150. She also set aside a 1932 order forbidding foreign students from working for hire or for room and board.[15]

She loosened another rule as well. U.S. citizens who had foreign relatives could bring them into the country without applying for a quota visa. Under Hoover, such petitions were accepted only if the relative was living outside the United States; under Frances, relatives already in the United States also could petition to stay. Relatives no longer had to return home to a danger zone to petition for U.S. entry.

By October, with Congress opposed to increasing quotas, Frances looked for alternative ways to permit more immigrants to enter. On October 25, 1933, she asked Wyzanski to devise a "plan to admit German Jews to this country" and recommended creating a delegation to lobby on behalf of German immigration. She suggested it include a prominent Jewish-American who would represent Jewish organizations, an official from the Labor or State departments, and a third party, perhaps someone, she suggested, like internationalist Elihu Root Jr., former secretary of state, who she called "conservative in form but liberal in heart," Wyzanski wrote.

Wyzanski thought the best strategy was to experiment with existing quotas, embracing Jews with "special vocational aptitudes such as chemists, doctors, economists or metallurgists," and providing for settlement "in the interior of the country."[16]

Indeed, many scientists and professors in Germany were interested in migrating. A Rockefeller Foundation study found that more than 1,600 university professors and teachers lost their jobs in Germany in the early years of the Reich and would presumably have considered employment in America. U.S. Ambassador Dodd, stationed in Berlin and growing more depressed by the day, encountered a steady stream of intellectuals pleading for help.[17]

On November 4, Wyzanski presented his plan. He proposed permitting the secretary of labor to admit political and religious refugees to the country on public charge bonds that guaranteed they would not become public burdens. In the past, consuls had turned down many aliens because of the risk they might become indigent. The attorney general reviewed Wyzanski's proposal and found it legal. Frances called Wyzanski to her office.

She wanted at once to entertain applications from anyone to the full limit of the German quota, twenty-six thousand, by making use of bonds. Wyzanski, however, warned that precipitous action was "unwise." He suggested she first discuss the matter with the Cabinet and the president because of its dangerous political ramifications. Wyzanski, a Jew of German descent, pointed out the potential problems with the plan, then came to the point that he was "particularly hesitant to discuss: the effect of the admissions upon Jews already here and upon the increasing wave of anti-Semitism," which he told her he and many other American Jews considered a "serious concern."

By the next morning, Wyzanski heard from Roosevelt strategist Raymond Moley, who said that public-charge bonds would cause controversy unless "sparingly exercised."

Colonel MacCormack of the Immigration Service said he believed that Congress was "unsympathetic to the refugee crisis," and that the AFL was likely to oppose anything that would expand the workforce.

Within days, various patriotic societies had signed declarations objecting to changes in the immigration policy. This forced the issue into the political arena, where it became mired in controversy. Frances was singled out for blame for her "lack of empathy with the policy of Congress and of the United States."[18]

The State Department vociferously opposed the bonds proposal advanced by Frances. C. Paul Fletcher, a supervisor, warned that when "ships begin to arrive in New York City laden with Jewish immigrants," the "sleeping" State Department would be blamed for failing to exclude them.[19] State Department officials said they would do as directed only if it were made clear to the public that the Labor Department was to blame. The internal skirmishing stretched for eighteen months.

The bond program went into effect in 1935 but lost some effectiveness because the U.S. Foreign Service sought to evade it.[20]

Frankfurter thanked Frances for her "alert and courageous attitude" on the charge bonds, but realized that the State Department was creating a barrier nonetheless.[21]

"Frankly I expect next to nothing from the State Department except timidity and non-action, couched in the wooden language of polite courtesy," he wrote her.[22]

As he predicted, State Department officials abroad, including many who were personally disinclined to take an activist role in saving lives, adhered rigidly to the letter of the immigration laws. The U.S. consuls in Germany used whatever means they could to deny visas to desperate Germans fleeing the Nazis, according to Holocaust scholars.

FDR, however, was not ready to challenge the State Department bureaucracy. He was appalled by the situation in Germany, but he chose for political reasons to generally follow the State Department's advice. Not personally anti-Semitic, anti-labor, or anti-intellectual, Roosevelt still looked squarely at what he considered to be the reality of the situation, which was that 30 percent of Americans were unemployed.

So Frances found herself combating the State Department and FDR, as well as much of the Cabinet. Only a handful of others—Ickes, and later, Morgenthau, himself a Jew—joined her in sticking up for the refugees.

Even proposals to admit German Jewish children met widespread resistance. Frances had sought entry for two hundred fifty children, proposing that the German Jewish Children's Aid provide backing for their care, but negotiations between Jewish leaders and the governments dragged on for a year. Again, the State Department opposed the plan, and even some Labor Department officials delayed action. Meanwhile, political opposition grew: Captain John B. Trevor, spokesman for an alliance of American nativist associations, called for a congressional investigation of the immigration department, attacking the Labor Department for its cooperation in the "systematic importation of indigent alien children." Trevor later insinuated that the children came from communist families.[23]

When the German Jewish aid group was able to find families for only one hundred of the two hundred fifty children, Frances pressed for legislation that would permit minors to be admitted outside the normal country quota system. That effort was blocked in Congress. Ultimately, about four hundred children were rescued.[24] And by 1937, Frances admitted 50,255 immigrants for permanent residency, including almost eleven thousand Germans, two-thirds of whom were Jews, and 231,884 foreign "visitors."

This last category was a particularly important subterfuge on Frances's part. While she couldn't change the formal quotas, she did have some discretion in applying them. She used this to admit endangered refugees on temporary tourist visas, knowing full well that many would quietly stay on in safety, and indeed, some people managed to disappear within the United States once they arrived.

Combined, these various efforts were an improvised but initially sufficient response to the looming threat in Europe. Viewed from the vantage point of the mid-1930s, the horrors to come were unprecedented and could not have been fully anticipated. Frances's measures were able to bring to safety many of the German Jews who wished to leave that country, and at that time, the Jewish populations of other nations appeared to be beyond the Nazis' reach.

⚜

$\mathcal{T}$he immigration issue wasn't the only international area that was preoccupying Frances. She also wanted to see workplace standards applied internationally and saw the International Labor Organization as the answer. If the United States would join the ILO and participate in the passage of substantive rules, for example, that limited work hours, gave maternity protection, and restricted night work for children and women, then it might be effective. It would be acting by treaty and compact—agreements that were unequivocally permitted under the U.S. Constitution—and she might be able to accomplish overseas what couldn't be done in the United States. In other words, treaties would be less vulnerable to the kinds of hostile, conservative court interpretations that had outlawed the regulations as soon as they were imposed at home.[25]

Moreover, the ILO needed an American presence more than ever. Germany was withdrawing from the organization, and the Italian delegates under Mussolini had stopped attending meetings.

But convincing Congress to join would be no easy task. Americans had felt burned by the senseless slaughter of World War I, and they feared European entanglements. They saw the League of Nations as such an entanglement, and the country had soundly repudiated President Woodrow Wilson's initiative in advocating it. Frances's task would be to bring the United States into the ILO, a League of Nations affiliate, without attracting much attention.

In June 1934, Senator Joseph Robinson introduced a draft resolution to allow the United States to join the ILO. It had been prepared by Labor Department staffers. On Roosevelt's advice, Frances gathered support and thought about timing: "In the excitement over more dramatic matters, it may be that it can be slipped through without opposition in the closing days of the session," Wyzanski wrote. "If so, it would be an important step toward international cooperation in raising labor standards throughout the world."[26]

A last-minute hitch emerged when Republican George Holden Tinkham of Massachusetts prepared a speech that would bitterly oppose the

ILO. Wyzanski heard that Tinkham planned to attack as well the "communist Secretary of Labor," Frances Perkins. Wyzanski rushed to Tinkham's office to ask him to temper his remarks, reminding him of his friendship with Wyzanski's father, who had recently died. Tinkham still spoke in opposition to ILO membership but toned down his remarks.

Amid a flurry of other legislation that attracted much more congressional scrutiny, Frances and her allies succeeded. The House of Representatives endorsed joining the ILO on a 236 to 110 vote; the Senate embraced it unanimously.[27]

Jubilant ILO Director Harold Butler wired Frances: "Official notification of United States entry to International Labor Organization will cause intense satisfaction in these difficult times to all who cherish ideals of social justice and security."[28]

Frances sent top-notch delegates to the next ILO conference, including Wyzanski and Grace Abbott, recently retired from the Children's Bureau. Wyzanski worried to Frances that he should perhaps not attend because he might attract controversy because he was Jewish, but she told him he was "over-sensitive." Another friend asked him if he was trying to apply a "Harvard quota" to himself, referring to the limitations on admission of Jews to the college.

The U.S. delegates were received enthusiastically in Geneva. They talked comfortably about the American successes with the forty-hour workweek and the child labor ban, and this made it harder for businessmen from other countries to say such rules were unworkable.

Frances's struggles with the State Department nonetheless continued without a break, originally over the refugee question and now over the ILO. Wyzanski had written a memo to her, outlining specific ways the Labor Department could assert itself in relations with the ILO. Later, when State Department officials complained they were not being informed about ILO activities, she fended them off.[29]

But her internationalist efforts were creating powerful enemies who would use her benevolence—what critics had called her "sentimentality"—as a new club to try to destroy her.

Chapter 21

Rebuilding the
House of Labor

*B*y the time the Roosevelt administration came to power, the labor movement had disintegrated, with union membership falling to 5 percent of the workforce. The American Federation of Labor had more than 4 million members in 1919 but fewer than 2 million in 1933. Companies in the 1920s had set out to break the unions, and succeeded. As joblessness mounted, the remaining workers faced falling wages and lengthened work hours. Union leaders had to fight the insurmountable combination of implacable employers, a receding economy, and hostile courts. Many lost hope.[1]

Frances faced a conundrum. She hoped to boost the union movement to create a counterbalancing force on behalf of workers. But her position with union leaders was weakened when from the start AFL president Green protested her appointment. He decreed that labor unions should "boycott" her.[2]

Frances didn't permit herself the luxury of being insulted by Green. She chalked it up to what she called the "deep, lower endocrine excitement" that men experience when they hear of a woman's elevation. Frances quickly turned the other cheek, refusing to let reporters goad her into saying anything derogatory about Green.[3]

She also refused to let the rude statement interfere with her relationship with the AFL. Within ten days of taking office, she called its headquarters and asked Green's secretary for a 2 p.m. appointment. It placed her in the awkward role of a supplicant, when in fact labor leaders generally hastened to meet any new labor secretary.

Green was polite, and the two chatted casually about unemployment and their hopes that it would drop. Soon Frances left, having established an amiable relationship with him that would last throughout her Cabinet tenure.

To underscore her support, Frances called a conference of labor leaders, the first time such an event had taken place so early in a presidential administration. Even deciding who to invite was complicated because of political affiliations, jealousies, and animosities. Some union leaders also were hostile to the new administration: Mountainous "Big Bill" Hutcheson, head of the United Brotherhood of Carpenters and Joiners, with 322,000 members the country's largest single union, was a Republican who had campaigned against Roosevelt.[4]

Many of the other men were presiding over deteriorating unions, their memberships diminished, and so they tried to make up for it in ferocity, combativeness, and ego. John L. Lewis, the squat, broad-shouldered president of the United Mine Workers of America, viciously attacked his rivals and was unpopular with other union leaders. Lewis demanded a meeting with Frances soon after she became secretary. He strode into her office and gave a long oration in his usual salty way. Tired of standing, he grabbed a chair and spun it backward, straddling it like a horse.

Lewis presided over a tattered union, with only three regional branches still operational, but most people didn't realize it. As a young coal miner rising in the union, he learned to put on a good front by studying George Baer, the owners' representative in the 1902 anthracite strike. The striking miners had been led by John Mitchell, Frances's "intimate friend" during her New York labor commission days. Baer famously told local residents not to worry about the strike: "I beg you not to be discouraged," he said. "The rights and interests of the laboring man will be protected and cared for—not by the labor activists, but by the Christian men to whom God in his infinite wisdom has given the control of the property interests of this country."

Lewis set out to imitate Baer's sense of iron certitude, and it made him an intimidating figure. Most people were physically afraid of Lewis, an effect heightened by the rumor that he had once killed a man.[5]

Frances also invited Sidney Hillman, a tenacious Jewish Lithuanian immigrant with a strong Yiddish accent. Hillman gained the enmity of the American Federation of Labor when he successfully rebelled against the former leaders of the United Garment Workers union and took over its leadership. He pioneered member recruitment strategies, opened a bank to serve members' needs, and set up an unemployment insurance program. The AFL, however, expelled his union from membership because they believed Hillman had stolen control of it. Now, in the face of the Depression, membership in his Amalgamated Clothing Workers of America had dropped from 177,000 members to about 7,000.[6]

Hillman, Lewis, and other critics viewed Green, and the AFL leadership in general, with contempt. They saw Green and his team as stale and unimaginative in defending the labor movement, when its very future was at stake. Plodding, kind, and easygoing, Green had become head of the AFL after Samuel Gompers's 1924 death because its Executive Council viewed him as unlikely to exert control over the independent fiefdoms that these unions represented.[7]

And so it was that one afternoon in early 1933, these men and about seventy-five other labor leaders gathered for Frances's conference. The meeting was held in her office, cleared of furniture for the occasion. It was spring, and the room grew uncomfortably warm—an atmosphere made more unpleasant by the presence of so many hot-tempered and physically intimidating men perched precariously on small folding seats.

Dan Tobin, head of the International Brotherhood of Teamsters, looked particularly ill at ease. He'd thought he was a contender for the job of labor secretary, and instead, he sat awkwardly in a little chair in the female secretary's office. He suggested they move the meeting to AFL headquarters. Frances declined. There was a murmur of discontent. Lewis rose in her support, and in an unctuous tone told the gathering that a government conference should rightly occur on government property. Others agreed, but Tobin left and didn't return until afternoon, somewhat calmer after downing a few beers.

Frances invited the group to discuss the country's economic problems and to brainstorm solutions. George L. Berry, of the printers' union, advocated immediate financial assistance to the states to provide jobless benefits. They all wanted some limitation of individual work hours to share the work around. Perkins told the group about Felix Frankfurter's plan to set workplace standards on products purchased by the government, and they also liked that idea. They endorsed many proposals that Frances had promoted for years, but from then on she called these ideas the "labor proposals" for the economy, giving the recommendations more strength than plans advocated by intellectuals and social workers. To smooth over differences, Frances arranged for Tobin to be delegation chairman when the men presented their recommendations to the president.[8]

Frances did not embark on this course because she was a passionate labor supporter. She saw union leaders simply as representatives of particular interests, just as she viewed company presidents as representatives of other interests. She saw the labor movement as a "natural and good institution," important in a modern, industrial world. But she harbored no illusions. She knew that unions seldom pushed for social advances and, like all other institutions, often suffered incompetent or dishonest leadership.

Sometimes, she watched unions explicitly fight against reforms that would have been beneficial to nonunion workers. Most unions excluded women and blacks, even as these groups increasingly entered into the workforce. She had known Gompers from the Factory Investigating Committee and knew he played a minimal role in promoting new labor legislation in New York. And around 1910, when she pushed for a worker's compensation bill, the labor unions opposed it so adamantly that she and colleague Paul Kennedy were nearly "run out" of a union meeting. Union attorneys already represented unionized workers who got hurt on the job, and they did not want government assistance for unorganized workers if it might mean less money for their members.

"They didn't care about the thousands of men who didn't belong to trade unions and the thousands of men who were injured under circumstances where they could not bring a suit against their employers," she recalled.[9]

In her opinion, labor leaders were seldom the selfless people that liberals imagined them to be. Generally speaking, the labor movement suffered from a lack of charismatic and visionary leaders. Frances regularly attended AFL meetings, which had given her a window into the labor movement, and she thought union officials often seemed more like depressed bureaucrats than rebels with a cause. In fact, the AFL's leaders often found themselves in the dark when significant labor events occurred. In Lawrence, Massachusetts, for example, a communist-inspired group, the Trade Union Unity League, was successfully organizing workers who either did not belong to unions or whose unions were ineffective. Scuffles erupted between workers and police.

"The AF of L didn't know anything about it," Frances recalled. "The AF of L didn't deny that it was their strike at first, because they always went and took care of the strike if there was one. After some time, they began wondering who these fellows were, who it was who was telling them what to do. The regular walking delegate of the AF of L went up to take charge of the strike. He held a meeting and told them what to do. The next day they did the opposite. He didn't know who had countermanded his orders. Then he'd run across one of these people that he called a foreigner horning in."[10]

In most places the labor movement was so weak or splintered that it was just ineffectual. Farm workers in California's fertile Imperial Valley—the kinds of people depicted in John Steinbeck's *Grapes of Wrath*—were in desperate straits. High unemployment left many families unable to purchase vegetables grown in California, and as their purchases fell, farm businesses cut back on wages and workers, just as waves of dispossessed farmers from the drought-stricken Midwest arrived to seek work in the Golden State. Pay plummeted even further, leaving families starving, living in tent cities.

Left-wing groups, including many inspired by communist ideals, tried to organize the workers and spot strikes broke out. The landowners wanted the army to force people back to work and sent vigilantes to beat union organizers. Church ministers who visited to inspect the situation were threatened with guns. A civil rights attorney who called a meeting to discuss the situation was kidnapped, beaten, and abandoned in the desert without shoes. He managed to walk to help and survived.[11]

Frances decided to hire a military man to make order out of chaos. She had long admired General Pelham Glassford, a retired brigadier general who had behaved honorably as District police commissioner when returning World War I veterans looking for promised bonuses marched on Washington during the Hoover administration. Frances named him a departmental conciliator and gave him the duty of trying to make peace in the Imperial Valley. He drove a Ford to the West, traveling through California's lush fields and stopping in towns to hear anyone willing to talk. Glassford decided the region's core problem was that wages were continually being undercut. He issued a U.S. Department of Labor proclamation defining what the correct wages should be. Then he had it printed on posters and tacked it up across California's heartland.

Unprecedented and completely illegal, his action was extraordinary because in some ways it worked. It established a wage baseline respected in the agricultural community. Known as the "Glassford wage," the calculation reflected the advice he had heard in his interviews in small towns across the valley.

Soon California political and business leaders sputtered with indignation. James Rolph Jr., Republican governor of California, sent an
angry telegram to FDR asking why Glassford had come to the Imperial
Valley to stir up communists.[12]

Frances privately thought Glassford's action was not only inspired
but also testament to his "courage and vim and vigor." She heard from
church groups that conditions radically improved after Glassford's
arrival. Glassford soon left the post, disgusted by the behavior of the
grower-shippers, who he said had used terrorism and intimidation
against the workers. He hadn't ultimately solved the problem, but his
intervention in California signaled to employers that the federal government was adopting a different approach to labor disputes.[13]

It was one of many occasions in which Frances intervened on behalf
of workers, with varying degrees of success. "For years, labor never had a
chance," Frances told a *New York Times* reporter in 1934. "Then in March
a year ago a vast change came about. In the midst of the catastrophe to
our economic life the New Deal was inaugurated. A different point of
view was established. Labor and capital were put on an equal footing and
a new technique was worked out to settle the differences which might
arise between the two great classes which go to make up industry."[14]

Glassford's work was just one example of the unusual strategies she
employed. With the labor movement so weak, Frances found unconventional solutions to workplace disputes again and again.

She discovered that she could use people on one side to later battle
the other. Walter Chrysler, head of Chrysler Corp., for example, had been
out on strike with Eugene Debs, the socialist presidential candidate, at
an earlier stage in his life. He told Frances about it one day, sitting in his
beautiful office with paneled walls lined with his collection of mechanical penny savings banks. He said he had been arrested with Debs at the
Pullman strike and spent two days in jail.

"I was a red hot labor man and I was a red hot striker," he told her.
But he had been more interested in the mechanical end of the railroad
business and had focused on learning to be a machinist and then moved
into the automobile business. Frances turned to him for help in getting
other automakers to agree to settle strikes with their workers.[15]

There were three labor leaders whose careers she promoted by ar-
ranging for Roosevelt to nominate them to an NRA advisory board, con-

vinced they showed promise for the future. They were Lewis, Hillman, and her old friend Rose Schneiderman, president of the Women's Trade Union League, the woman who had spoken out so angrily after the Triangle fire. In this way, Frances made sure the feisty immigrant who had felt she had been unheard was now given a formal role in government.[16]

In the Roosevelt administration's early years, Frances often stood as the only person representing workers. In late July 1933, she toured steel plants in the northeastern United States—McKeesport and Homestead in Pennsylvania and Sparrows Point in Maryland—to underscore support for including workers' opinions in the NRA codes. She talked to laborers and visited their wives at their mill-owned housing. If no union officials could speak for labor, then the secretary of labor did it herself.

While visiting Homestead, the town where Henry Clay Frick broke the steelworker's union in 1892, Frances stopped to meet the town's burgess, John Cavanaugh, a cordial man who had assembled the city's foremost citizens to meet with her before she visited the mill. A crowd gathered outside, with other people asking to meet with her. The mayor blocked their entrance, calling them troublemakers who had been laid off from the plant. Frances asked to speak with them anyway, but the burgess declined. Frances responded that they could always talk in a nearby public park.

"You can't do that," Cavanaugh said. "It's against the law. There's a law in this town that there's to be no public assembly in the parks, no street meetings, no public assembly permitted in this town." [17]

Just then Frances spotted, from the corner of her eye, an American flag flying just down the block at a post office.

"Very well," she said. "There is the American flag. There is a federal building. I have the right to receive in a federal building."

She headed to the post office, with an audience trailing behind. Frances explained the situation to the local postmaster, who welcomed her. She then stood on a chair to address the group. The crowd continued to stream in, filling the corridors and the steps. Several workers complained about problems at the mills, and she thanked them for coming. She made it clear that the administration was paying attention.

"I have come to the conclusion that the Department of Labor should be the Department FOR labor, and that we should render service to the working people, just as the Agriculture Department renders service to the farmers," she said in a hearing soon afterward. "That is why I speak here today—in order to render a service to wage earners who have no particular representative to speak for them."[18]

When strikes broke out and her other strategies failed, Frances turned to a final line of defense—a handful of men who would privately intervene to move warring sides toward industrial peace. Through the 1930s, there were three people to whom Frances turned frequently, and privately, for assistance.

Postmaster General Farley enjoyed a network of contacts he had developed as chairman of the Democratic National Committee. No matter where a dispute arose, he knew someone on the ground who could mediate between workers and employers. Farley would place a call to a Democratic colleague, who would in turn contact the employer and ask if perhaps a meeting between the parties could be arranged.

Jesse Jones, a Houston builder and businessman, had valuable financial contacts around the country. In the Roosevelt administration's early years, he chaired the Reconstruction Finance Corp., and then became secretary of commerce.

The third man was Thomas Lamont of J. P. Morgan & Co., the man who had famously tried to play down the stock market crash by calling it "a little distress selling." A successful businessman, he was also a compassionate person. Frances knew Lamont and his wife, Florence, socially, and she learned she could prevail on him to resolve disputes.[19]

Frances's role as the strongest and most effective promoter of the labor movement within the Roosevelt administration was a bit incongruous, since she actually disliked most of the labor leaders with whom she dealt. She didn't idealize them, and in fact she respected them very little as a group. In time, Frances resented it when the union movement sought to take credit for advances that had really been won for it by middle-class social reformers.

Fundamentally she lacked a deep rapport with most labor leaders. The labor movement typically did not admit women, and it was unlikely that people who were so essentially sexist could appreciate her contributions. Some union leaders felt more comfortable dealing with Eleanor Roosevelt, who was a sympathetic ally but who played an acceptable female role as wife to the president.

"The president had great confidence in her," said labor economist John Dunlop, who worked with Frances and later served as labor secretary himself. But that relationship seemed suspect to men who couldn't imagine hiring a woman, or having a woman in their union brotherhood, Dunlop noted. Sometimes they mused aloud about what they suspected to be a sexual relationship between Frances and Roosevelt; her close friendship with the president made her character somewhat questionable to them.[20]

Chapter 22

Labor Shakes Off
Its Slumber

On a spring night in 1933, when the National Recovery Administration was just getting off the ground, a fateful meeting occurred at the grand St. Regis Hotel in New York City. John L. Lewis of the United Mine Workers was meeting Green, head of the AFL, who had used his own membership in the UMW to catapult himself to leadership of the labor federation. The two men, allies and rivals for decades, exited the hotel and strolled down Fifty-fifth Street discussing the potential of the NRA's labor provision, Section 7(a), which gave unions the right to organize. In their lifetimes, they had seen the labor movement shrivel. Lewis had given the matter much thought, and as they walked he spilled out to Green a grand vision of how Section 7(a) could be turned into the labor movement's golden opportunity.

Green listened. He was a cautious man, and he had seen unionizing workers jailed, deported, even murdered; he feared what could happen if the effort failed. The courts had come down against the labor movement over and over, and Green worried that trying to expand unionization to include unskilled or semiskilled workers would prove impossible. Over the years, the labor movement had been most successful in unionizing specialized craftsmen who had more bargaining power with employers. Lewis, on the other hand, argued that the movement would never be strong unless it was more broadly based. He offered to throw $500,000 into the effort, money he planned to raise by mortgaging the UMW's headquarters building in Washington.

"Now, John, take it easy," Green said. It sounded too risky to him.

The conversation proved a defining moment for Lewis. He fell asleep that night and awoke the next morning determined to go it alone. Lewis planned a huge nationwide campaign, first to reorganize his own industry and then to reach out to other workers. Lewis mortgaged the building and devoted the entire treasury of the United Mine Workers to the effort. He bided his time while the bill was considered, saying little, but within twenty-four hours of its passage in June 1933, he'd arranged for posters to be plastered over every mining community in America. Each poster contained the smiling visage of Franklin Roosevelt with the headline: "The president wants you to join the union." Lewis dispatched a hundred paid union organizers and volunteers across the mining region to convince new recruits to sign up with the United Mine Workers.[1]

Frances heard rumors of this activity and called Louis Stark, labor reporter at the *New York Times,* to see what he knew. He packed his bags and hit the road. After he'd written his story, he described to Frances what he had seen: "It was the most remarkable thing I ever saw," he said. "Those miners came out of those towns . . . They just came out of the mountains by the thousands. It was just like an Army moving out of the mountains. Anybody that the United Mine Workers could get hold of made a speech, but they had all the papers there for them to sign and they signed up by the thousands, which showed that they always did really want to belong to a union, that they had drifted out of the union because they were forced out. The mine owners had forced them out."[2]

By September, Lewis reestablished unions throughout Pennsylvania, West Virginia, and the Midwest and won collective bargaining agreements for thousands of miners. He had saved the United Mine Workers and built a base for future expansion of the labor movement.

The impression soon spread across the country that Roosevelt wanted workers to join a union, and hundreds of thousands responded to the call. Section 7(a) had tapped into a reservoir of anger about working conditions. Even people with marginal employment—part-time and unskilled workers, often with scanty or nonexistent savings—risked their security in hopes of a better future with a union.

The Labor Department's once-somnolent Conciliation Service was called on again and again, even as Frances remade it into a more efficient and effective organization. She later likened the process to a kitchen renovation project: "You have to cook the dinner while the kitchen's being painted."[3]

Other unions replicated Lewis's strategy. In Philadelphia, the American Federation of Full-Fashioned Hosiery Workers posted signs emblazoned, "President Roosevelt Has Endorsed—Congress Has Passed

These Workers Rights . . . Join the Union and Insist on Your Rights in This Bill." The poster made it appear that the government was endorsing unionization.[4]

Across the country, workers of all kinds scrambled to join new unions, but most lacked experienced officials to steer them. There simply weren't enough trained organizers among labor's decimated ranks. Left on their own, workers tried to force their employers to negotiate on wages and work hours, but in many cases they were rebuffed by startled employers who didn't want to negotiate. Instead, companies fired agitating workers, and the firings led to strikes and work stoppages that paralyzed factories stumbling back to life after the Depression. These uprisings led to violence, injuries, or deaths. Soon both sides—workers and employers—screamed for federal conciliators, and Frances frenetically dispatched mediators all over the country.

Both sides were unfamiliar with the process of labor negotiation. Veteran labor reporter Mary Heaton Vorse described a typical scenario: Workers would make demands and then quickly go out on strike when employers balked. Employers would panic and press local officials to use police powers to get people back to work. Local governments didn't have police forces big enough to handle such disturbances, so they would deputize other local men, often area shopkeepers fearful for their own businesses, to serve as backup. These inexperienced policemen confronted workers who had never before raised their voices but who were now taking to the streets in pent-up rage.

"Each side was scared to death of the other," Vorse recalled. "They had deputized lots of scared white collar workers and put guns in their hands, and of course, among those scared people, you know, they shoot."[5]

The Labor Department was so busy handling strikes, day blurring into night, that officials barely noticed the change of seasons, Wyzanski wrote home in August 1933.[6]

Frances and Roosevelt saw the upswing in strike activity as a positive development. "It is [a] pretty encouraging thing to see people who have the guts to stand up for their own rights and it means that they feel that they can get employment somewhere else if they are thrown out," FDR told reporters.[7]

The textile industry, the first to get an NRA code, was also among the first to be affected by strikes. The industry had the nation's lowest wages, and the leadership of the ragtag United Textile Workers union was superseded by a young union official named Francis Gorman. Gorman employed a radically new organizing technique called the flying wedge. Organizers arrived at a mill in a cavalcade of five cars with one in the lead and two others in a V-shaped formation behind it, and two more behind them. They approached with horns blaring, singing and shouting. Naturally, workers ran out to watch, and the organizers greeted them with posters, flags, and banners announcing their new right to organize. Sometimes, catching the guards flat-footed, organizers ran through the plant, capturing the attention of even more workers. They passed out papers asking people to sign to show union support. Then they got back into their cars and drove away.

The tactic was exciting but also disruptive. It caused many textile workers to become enthusiastic about joining a union before there was any mechanism in place to create a real functioning organization. Often, partially organized but without leadership, the workers went on strike within a few days, unsure of exactly what concessions they wanted but bringing work to a halt. During a single week in September 1934, some 376,000 textile workers around the country went out on strike. It was a dramatic display of discontent over the stretch-out system, in which workers were asked to work longer and harder for less money. But the union's efforts ultimately faltered in the face of aggressive action. Southern business owners and state officials sent in the national guard to subdue workers. Unlike the coal mining industry, efforts to unionize less-skilled textile workers failed, as Green had warned.

As disturbances flared, many people clamored for the secretary of labor to do something. Some people mistakenly believed the department could intervene and force people back to work.

Another dramatic face-off occurred in the automobile industry in the mid-1930s. Union organizers previously had been rebuffed by the workers because the auto workers tended to be well paid (Henry Ford had set the bar high with his $5-a-day wage) and viewed union leaders as lazy wastrels. They also tended to be native-born Americans who disdained the immigrant leadership of other unions. The industry was also new. Many of its corporate chieftains had come from worker ranks themselves, meaning that workers identified with management. Many hoped to become managers themselves, in the way Walter Chrysler was a machinist before becoming a millionaire.

The auto industry was entering a turbulent period. Several companies failed, and others took over their production. Johnson had sought to get the auto industry leaders to consider creating a code, but the larger companies wanted the freedom to swallow the weaker ones and were reluctant to agree to a set pattern of conducting business. Meanwhile, auto sales dropped during the Depression, and employers cut pay and reduced their workforces. Once-happy workers grew restive and confrontational. Frances told Walter Chrysler and Alfred Sloan, of General Motors, that they should blame themselves, since they had compounded their problems by their practice of hiring only the young.

"The companies had a positive rule against hiring anybody after 40 and of keeping anybody in their employment after 45," Frances said. ". . . They had hired deliberately a large group of people at the peak of their physical powers and at the peak of their recklessness."[8]

The auto workers soon picked up a new technique that was cropping up in other workplaces, the sit-down strike. First used by rubber workers in Akron, then by department store clerks in Paris, the sit-down strike, where workers simply sat down on the job and refused to work or to leave the premises, came to be viewed as a tactic that gave even relatively powerless, unskilled workers leverage.

A wave of sit-down strikes began roiling the auto industry. The most famous occurred soon after Christmas 1936 in three General Motors plants in Flint, Michigan. About one thousand of seven thousand workers decided they would remain in the plant rather than leave when their shifts were over, refusing orders to vacate. The strike spread. By mid-January, fifty General Motors plants were shut down, and the sit-down strikes spread to other auto plants as well.[9]

Fearful of violence, Frances tried to bring the disputants together to discuss a settlement, but Sloan proved intransigent. She talked with Michigan governor Frank Murphy about developments there almost daily. The sit-down method raised difficult legal questions. In one sense, workers were trespassing and preventing normal business. But was it really trespass if the workers had essentially been invited onto the premises by their employers when they were hired?

Many businessmen were clamoring for federal intervention. Vice President John Garner, a Texan, took umbrage at Frances for what he perceived as her failure to act, and in a Cabinet meeting in early 1937, he called the sit-down strikes "just terrible." He insisted that Murphy be urged to use the state militia to turn out the workers.

Pressure on the president was mounting, too. In a news conference, he was peppered with questions about whether he thought the striking workers' behavior was "reprehensible." In a private meeting, he asked Frances about it again. They agreed it was reprehensible, but knew that if troops were dispatched to the plants, many workers would be injured or killed. They decided not to intervene militarily.

Governor Murphy backed the workers and didn't call in the troops. Lewis helped conciliate, the strike ended, and the United Auto Workers solidified its industry position. But the strike was so long and so disruptive that Frances suspected that it, indeed, had been inspired by Communists eager to make problems, not solve them.

Frances was urged to take more drastic steps against strikers in other cases. When merchant seamen on the S.S. *California* went out on strike while they were at sea, Joseph P. Kennedy, head of the Maritime Commission and father of the future president, urged that they be charged with mutiny. The sailors realized their lives were on the line but persevered. Joseph Curran, a strike instigator, recalled that the California newspapers called for the men to be executed. The main question the newspapers raised, he said, was where the executions should occur. Should they hang the men on the roof of the post office or some other government building?

"Anybody who would say he wasn't frightened" would be crazy, Curran said later. The men called Frances for help. Taking one officer as a hostage so they wouldn't be killed, a small group of sailors went ashore and called her from a telephone booth.

"Well, Joe, what do you want?" she asked.[10]

They told her they wanted a wage increase, and she promised to help them negotiate. She also assured them that no criminal charges would be brought against the sailors. Convinced that they could trust Frances, the men returned the ship to port, and although many were discharged, none was sent to jail.[11]

Sometimes Frances intervened directly with employers to resolve disputes. Les O'Rear, an official of the Packinghouse Workers in Chicago, recalled that workers at one plant had won a union election, but that management refused to recognize the union and begin bargaining. The union seemed headed toward a strike, but it wasn't yet strong enough to survive an extended walkout. Frances, who had worshipped with the Armour family at the Church of the Holy Spirit in Lake Forest, arranged for Armour executives to meet with the workers in Washington, and soon the dispute was settled. "Frances Perkins saved our skins," O'Rear recalled. "We appreciated Ma Perkins."[12]

One dramatic strike, however, had the most lasting effect on Frances's life. She had heard about trouble brewing on the West Coast from maritime workers. New loading machinery had increased dockworkers' productivity without increasing their compensation, and they objected to low pay, long hours, and the "shape-up," the dehumanizing slave-market manner in which they were hired each day. The shape-up had spawned corruption, as foremen doled out jobs to men in return for kickbacks. The San Francisco longshoremen wanted the system replaced with hiring halls where dockworkers could wait indoors to be matched with jobs. Small work stoppages cropped up at various docks, usually for a few hours, but sometimes for two or three days.

Then, in May 1934, longshoremen up and down the West Coast went on strike, and about two thousand miles of coastline shut down, with no cargo moving. Maritime executives infuriated longshoremen by hiring replacement workers to break the strike and load the cargo, paying them well, housing them shipboard, and providing free room and board. The longshoremen attacked scab workers who stepped outside of police protection. When they captured a scab, they kicked out his teeth or laid his legs over a curb and jumped on them, maiming some 150 strikebreakers.[13] The ports stayed shut, and other maritime unions, whose work conditions mirrored those of the longshoremen, also went out on strike. The Teamsters joined in, too.

Ship owners were reassured when Joseph P. Ryan, president of the International Longshoremen's Association, arrived in San Francisco to settle the strike. Ryan was known for his lavish lifestyle. He exemplified both sides of what Republican labor secretary John Dunlop once described as the two different kinds of union corruption: when unions steal from their members directly and when employers bribe or blackmail union leaders into accepting low pay and long hours so the employers can steal from union members indirectly. Ryan brokered a sweetheart deal with employers, only to find the agreement rejected by his members, who then rejected his leadership as well. Instead they turned to Harry

Bridges, an Australian from a comfortable middle-class family who had shipped out from home for adventure and had worked the San Francisco docks as a longshoreman for more than a decade. Personally committed to substantive change, not just for longshoremen but for all maritime workers, Bridges proved to be a brilliant tactician.[14]

With Bridges leading the cause, the longshoremen's strike continued. Shipping companies in Seattle brought in strikebreakers, with police guards. Officials in Alaska demanded federal action. Some navy ships were affected as well, because the longshoremen also loaded their vessels. To naval officers, such slowdowns were tantamount to treason. Businessmen on the West Coast demanded action.[15]

A simmering situation reached the boiling point. A well-funded group of employers created an organization called the Industrial Association to break the strike. It hired a trucking company to haul goods from the warehouses along the docks, protected by seven hundred men armed with tear gas and riot guns. On July 3, the first trucks moved out from the piers, and rock-throwing strikers and sympathizers blocked them. The police responded with tear gas and bullets, and then the police closed in with their billy clubs. The strikers fought back. The next day's newspapers listed two people dead, both workers, and at least sixty-seven wounded. Joe Rosenthal, a newspaper photographer who would later win fame for his picture of the flag raising at Iwo Jima, said the fighting in San Francisco that day seemed as bad as what he witnessed in the Pacific war.

Governor Frank F. Merriam called out the national guard, and soon about 5,100 soldiers patrolled the streets. San Francisco canceled all police vacations, sent seven hundred officers to the port, deputized an additional five hundred, and ordered $59,000 worth of extra ammunition.

But ordinary workers in San Francisco viewed the situation differently. A massive funeral procession was organized, with thousands of people marching eight or nine abreast down San Francisco's Market Street to honor the slain. Sympathy washed over the city, and rumors spread that soon union organizers would call a general strike, something that had almost never happened in American history.[16]

The next day, Monday, business activity ground to a halt. The marine unions and the Teamsters were already out. First the taxis disappeared, and then the trolleys stopped. Many small shops shut down.

Most restaurants closed. About 130,000 workers stayed home that day. On Tuesday, some workers returned to the job, including some ordered to do so by the unions' strike committee, but many others refused to work.

San Francisco newspapers reacted with outrage. Roger Lapham, chief of the American-Hawaiian steamship lines, called Frances to tell her that California wanted action, warning ominously that "some bloodshed might be desirable to bring the matter to an end." (Frances later remarked to Wyzanski that she hadn't bothered to ask Lapham if "his own blood was offered as the sacrifice.")[17]

Frances monitored the situation constantly. Cross-country communications were difficult because of the time difference. The situation was bad, she learned, but not yet a crisis, and observers told her they expected it to blow over soon. Federal negotiators were working hard to make peace.

Roosevelt was out of reach that week, on a tour of the Pacific fleet. On the third morning of the work stoppage, Secretary of State Hull, who was standing in for the president, called Frances soon after she arrived at the office. His tone made clear he considered the problem very serious.

She attempted to soothe his concerns. "Yes, it's unfortunate, Mr. Secretary, but we have good reports," Frances told him. "We think that it will soon be over and that there's not much more to it."[18]

Hull said he viewed the events as very serious, and as acting president, he intended to take "very severe and drastic steps immediately."

Frances grew alarmed. It was clear that he intended to use the army to put down the strike. She asked to see him immediately. He told her he was in the attorney general's office deciding how to proceed. She rushed over to the Department of Justice and found Hull and Attorney General Cummings holed up in the law library.

She tried to assure them the situation was headed toward resolution, but Cummings told her she was mistaken. He told her a general strike was an effort to overthrow the government. "My information," he told her pompously, "comes from the district attorneys and from the United States Attorneys, who are in that district. We have been in telephonic communications."

Frances retorted that these men were probably well-to-do gentlemen who likely had little personal contact with the bakery wagon drivers, printers, and streetcar operators who had staged small sympathy strikes for the longshoremen. It also deeply irritated her that Hull and Cummings, who had no experience with strikes, took it upon themselves to intervene in a matter that she had well in hand.

"Surely one can say that local law and order has broken down," Hull said. "I think that we should prepare to send in the federal troops. We have a very sizeable body of federal troops right there at the Presidio."

Frances continued to hold back her reaction. "How would they break it up, Mr. Secretary?" she asked.

"By military means," he said.

"You mean force men to get on the bakery wagons, force them to drive them?"

"Yes, or drive them themselves, with armed guards, so that if any group of bakery wagon workers attempts to stop them, they can be—"

"Shot at?" Frances asked.

"Yes, shot at," he said.

Frances explained the whole situation again, that the Labor Department official Thomas Eliot was there, that a panel was mediating, and that experts on the scene expected the workers to return to work soon.

"Mr. Cummings, I think I do see it seriously," she said. "I see the military moving in there from the Presidio. You can send a message to the Presidio and alert them at once. In an hour, they'll be out and armed and equipped. There will be all kinds of trucks, all kinds of motor vehicles, all kinds of . . . weapons. . . . It will create the most terrible resentment and all the trade unions who are not out now will go out. . . . There will be public gatherings. They'll gather in crowds to hoot and jeer at the soldiers driving a bakery wagon through the streets. You know what'll happen. The soldiers will fire. Somebody will get hurt. The mob will attack. There will be some regular shooting and a lot of people will drop in the streets. I call THAT very serious."

She insisted they consult the president immediately, before calling out the army. The men finally agreed.

Quickly Frances rushed to naval communications to get a message to the president, eager to make sure her opinion got to FDR before he heard from Hull. Waiting nervously, she finally learned that her message had arrived first. FDR had responded with a complicated answer about how arbitration with the strikers should be handled.

For Frances, this "answer was almost perfect." It offered a sop to

Cummings and Hull because it urged they be consulted if food supplies in San Francisco were affected by the strikes. It made clear to the men that they needed to give arbitration a full try before resorting to violence. And it made clear, once again, that Frances was in charge.

Meanwhile, Louis Howe, the president's adviser, urged the president not to return until the problem was resolved, so that he would not be drawn into the dispute. Roosevelt remained at sea, fishing and playing cards and sending occasional messages back to Washington.[19] It became Roosevelt's established practice to avoid dealing with strikes personally, when possible, and the president frequently referred reporters to Frances for questions on progress.

In a day or two, as she predicted, the workers in San Francisco returned to their jobs. On Friday, the employers gave in. They agreed to arbitrate their differences, and Bridges was forced to agree as well. Ultimately the longshoremen won their hiring hall, better wages, and improved working conditions. Face had been saved all around, but the balance of power had shifted, not just for Bridges and the longshoremen, but for workers throughout the West Coast.

But Frances's role in holding back the army had also changed the dynamics of national politics. "Marxism predicted that in crisis the state would support the dominant class," wrote Irving Bernstein. "Public officials in San Francisco and Sacramento had behaved as they were expected to; but those in Washington and on the high seas had not. In fact, if Roosevelt and Perkins had thrown their weight to the employers, which they did not do, the longshoremen's union and Bridges could hardly have survived."[20]

Incredulous and outraged state officials and business leaders blasted the labor unrest. "A more active and intensified drive to rid this State and nation of alien radical agitators should be undertaken by the workers themselves if they are to enjoy the confidence of the people," thundered Governor Merriam in a radio address.[21]

But Bridges did not behave like a dangerous radical to Frances. In her experience Communists fomented unrest but often avoided workable solutions to problems. Their goal, after all, was to overthrow the system, which usually required breaking the system so that people believe it had ceased to function. But according to her conciliators in San Francisco, Bridges was circulating through the city in the weeks following the strike with clear solutions. His ideas for handling workflow and labor issues were so insightful that the presidential board decided to compile them into a single document.

Frances grew curious about Bridges and asked more questions about him. Labor Department conciliators described him to her as a modest man, poorly dressed with rough clothes, but with a logical way of speaking. He always consulted with his colleagues before answering questions. He wasn't argumentative and didn't make broad charges about the evils of the steamship companies. Instead he focused on the injustice of management demanding higher work productivity with no increase in pay. The police report Frances requested said he had been with one shipping line for more than a dozen years, and that he was "a quiet, orderly man." Bridges was married with a child. His only diversion, said a former landlady, was a mandolin that he played in the evening. The report confirmed that he was indeed Australian, not American.[22]

Soon after, Frances met Bridges at an AFL meeting in San Francisco. She was introduced to him backstage at the auditorium. She found him to be a rather ordinary-looking fellow, tall and very thin, somewhat stooped over, wearing a poorly fitting jacket held together in front with a safety pin. In his hand he held a cloth cap of the kind typically worn by British workmen, twisting it in an embarrassed way. Something about him conveyed the physical attitude she had seen in England, the way working-class people comported themselves when speaking to the county squire.

Frances thought Bridges looked shabby and subservient, hardly the type to lead a dynamic and growing union. If anything, he seemed rather passive, she recalled later. But in coming months, he somehow managed to coordinate the unions into a smoothly working group, and he played a role in the creation of hiring halls, which permitted workers to sit comfortably and with dignity while awaiting assignments.

That is why she found it so surprising in coming years when the waterfront employers in San Francisco began spreading the story that the Australian was a dangerous anarchist working to undermine America. It was hard to square the man she had met with the man his critics detested. Even more surprising to her was how much her fate became entangled in his. "He was just an inexplicable man who had appeared from the mist," she said.[23]

———————————⟩⟨———————————

Chapter 23

THE UNION MOVEMENT
REVITALIZES AND
SPLITS APART

*F*rances presided over the Labor Department at a time when momentous changes were reshaping the American labor movement. In 1935, new legislation passed that enshrined a more comprehensive set of workers' rights and an enforcement mechanism. That same summer, a civil war erupted within the ranks of organized labor that pitted union brother against union brother.

The impetus for both events had been Section 7(a) of the NRA bill, which, as Lewis had predicted, had unleashed enormous pent-up demand among workers for unionization. Although many employers maintained peace and production by negotiating with their workers, many others vowed to fight, even to the death, against unionization. A gun battle in Trion, Georgia, left two textile strikers dead and fifteen injured; six more died in Greenville, South Carolina. Riots erupted in Minneapolis after truckers went on strike, leaving several dead and dozens injured. In San Francisco, troubles on the waterfront turned so violent that some believed a revolution was brewing.[1]

Senator Wagner was asked to chair a committee that would resolve labor disputes. In his new role, Wagner grew increasingly angry at what he saw as employer intransigence in negotiating with workers. Employer opposition was "virulent," recalled his legislative aide, Leon Keyserling.[2] A week after the Pulp Sulphite and Paper Mill Workers won a union election in Covington, Virginia, for example, the company closed the mill, putting fourteen hundred employees out of work.[3]

After five years as a U.S. senator, Wagner was unaccustomed to open opposition of the sort he was now seeing among employers. He grew more irate. He decided that legislation must be written to require employers to deal with unions in collective bargaining, with legal penalties if they refused.

Frances tried to argue Wagner out of forcing the issue with legislation, saying that people could not be forced to accept what they instinctively opposed. "This is an educational process that we must go through," she told him. "It's just possible that no law could make them do it. A bargain to make a bargain by collective means, or even between individuals, requires and implies some voluntary action. People may be made to go into the same room, but they can't necessarily be made to agree. Be patient, Senator, this is an educational process." [4]

Wagner insisted that further delay would be an injustice to employers who had agreed to work with their unions. "It isn't fair that those who are good citizens and trying to cooperate should be made to deal with their unions collectively, whereas those who are just recalcitrant and stubborn don't have to."

In January 1934, Wagner called a meeting to discuss what to do. His aide Keyserling, Green, Lewis, and Labor Department solicitor Wyzanski joined him. They drafted a measure that included provisions guaranteeing the right to organize, collective bargaining, majority rule on union elections, the employers' obligation to bargain, and workers' right to strike. The bill also called for a special board to investigate disputes and issue findings. [5]

The concept of union elections had been invented almost accidentally by an employer. Gerard Swope, a General Electric executive who served on the panel with Wagner, had been called to mediate a dispute at a Pennsylvania hosiery mill operated by a German-born American who refused to meet with his unionizing workers. Swope was no stranger to union difficulties, since GE had long been plagued by the conflicting aims of several different unions operating at its plants. Swope didn't want to travel to Pennsylvania to discuss the problem, so he and Frances convinced the man to meet at her Washington office.

Frances had expected the mill owner to be impressed by Swope, a leading industry figure, but she quickly saw that he didn't even recognize the man. As the conversation continued, it became apparent that the hosiery factory owner simply couldn't believe that his employees actually wanted to join a union. Finally Swope had an idea.

"Why don't we agree to let them take a vote—a secret vote—to see how many of them want to belong to the union and how many don't?" Swope suggested. "I assure you that if a vast majority doesn't want to belong to the union as you say they don't, we will take that into consideration and that will certainly be held to relieve you of any necessity of dealing with a small minority."[6]

The man rose up in his seat, his eyes bulging, and he said scornfully in a heavy German accent: "Vote? Vy should they vote? Vy should they vote?"

Frances bristled at the man's contempt. Swope, the son of German-Jewish immigrants, spoke forcefully: "Because that's the way WE do things in America. We take a vote on things that we are uncertain about, and we let the majority control."

It was a new concept—that union representation could be determined by an election. At the meeting's end, Frances called the hosiery strike leaders and they agreed to an election. Frances insisted that it must be a secret ballot so that no one would suffer retaliation. Swope suggested that they use the town's regular polling places and ballot boxes. Frances called the town's mayor, and he agreed to help.

Swope went to Walter Teagle, Wagner, and the other NRA arbitrators and found enthusiastic support. The tactic solved the problem of determining union legitimacy, an issue that had cropped up at many newly organizing establishments. Soon after, the union won a victory at the hosiery factory, and the company organized.

The experiment impressed Wagner, then busily drafting the new labor law, which would become the National Labor Relations Act. Wagner wanted to set up a labor board that would compel employers to negotiate with their workers by requiring them to accept collective bargaining. Initially Wagner conceived of it as a board within Hugh Johnson's NRA.

Frances privately thought the idea was wrongheaded. She considered it "hazardous" for labor's future for it to rely on a governmental body operating under administrative law. She questioned whether, over time, a political system could be made to operate fairly for workers. It could easily become a tyrannical administrative body where the government would "have the final word," in which labor unions "would just be kind of pawns pushed around," she said.[7]

Wyzanski also considered the proposal flawed. It called for creation of a board with powers so sweeping, as "judge, arbitrator and conciliator at its choice," that it would create confusion and lead to a backlash. He thought the new board should instead be patterned after the Federal

Trade Commission, with power to intervene in "unfair labor practices" just as the FTC intervenes to correct "unfair" commercial practices.[8]

Roosevelt, according to Frances, also quietly opposed the creation of the National Labor Relations Board. "He never lifted a finger to put the act through the Congress," she said. "He never did a thing . . . he hoped it wouldn't pass."[9]

Frances in public appeared neutral, but later she admitted she tried to squelch the bill: "I did all that I could to slow the idea down and perhaps to persuade, without opposing, Wagner out of it. I even talked to certain labor men about it, although that was later, because at the beginning there was no great enthusiasm for it among labor men."[10]

More experienced labor leaders shared her wariness about relying on political support on labor issues. Gompers, former head of the AFL, had believed that an increased federal role on behalf of workers would erode the appeal of labor unions because people would place their trust in government instead.

But gradually, Wagner persuaded Green, Lewis, and other leaders to support his idea. He also effectively shepherded his legislation through the Senate, according to attorney William Davis, not because he was "brilliant," but because he had an "almost uncanny ability to pick good assistants" and because he had such congenial relations with fellow senators.[11]

Wagner ultimately introduced his bill on February 21, 1935. Almost all business groups opposed it as unconstitutional and injurious to the nation's economic recovery. Almost all the nation's newspapers editorialized against it, but still the measure was signed into law on July 5, 1935. About one month earlier, the Supreme Court had ruled harshly against the NRA in the Schechter decision, so Wagner's bill had the effect of preserving the Section 7(a) labor provisions that might otherwise have died.

Once the bill's passage became clear, Frances dropped her opposition to it and lobbied strongly to have the NLRB placed in the Labor Department. She worried that otherwise intellectuals with little real understanding of employment economics would control the board. Some of the board's duties would conflict with the work of the Labor Department's Conciliation Service. Moreover, the board would set policies that Frances must consider expanding to the wider workforce and that people would mistakenly think emanated from the Labor Department. When she tepidly testified in support of the bill, she spoke strongly only on the point that it should be placed within her agency.

Wagner ended up opposing Frances on this. Egged on by his assistants, Boris Shishkin and Leon Keyserling, Wagner decided that the NLRB should be independent for the stated reason that if the agency were placed in the Labor Department, it would be viewed as pro-labor in orientation.

Others believed that he may have had different motives. Wyzanski thought Wagner, like the labor leaders, simply couldn't conceive of a woman governing labor disputes, especially a woman whom he still thought of primarily as a social worker, as a result of the days they had worked together on the Triangle fire committee.[12]

At one point, according to Frances, Roosevelt told Senate Majority Leader Joseph T. Robinson that the board should be placed under her control, then took no action on her behalf.[13] Someone at the White House gave Wagner a private memo Frances had given the president, asking that the board be placed in her department. Clearly someone within the administration was trying to sabotage her effort.[14]

Possibly to help Wagner win passage, Roosevelt accepted the board's creation as an independent agency. By now, he had surely begun to notice that he could pick up votes among southern Democrats, even for measures they did not ideologically agree with, if the action included a ritual public humiliation of Frances. Losing the new labor-oriented agency was that kind of an embarrassment for her.

Then, adding insult to injury, the president let Frances know he shared her worries about the NLRB, instructing her to "keep very close" to it. Knowing that NLRB officials would be reluctant to report to her, Frances asked the president to tell board members that they were expected to give her regular reports.[15]

Once the board was created, Wagner took no interest in its actual operation. "From the time the Act was signed by the president, Wagner, to a considerable extent, washed his hands of it," recalled Joseph Warren Madden, the first NLRB chairman.[16]

Keyserling, ever loyal, interpreted Wagner's inaction more generously, convinced that the senator truly believed the board should be independent, even of his own review. Still, it couldn't create itself. Frances scurried around to find people to fill the board seats, a job she quickly found "thankless."

The new board was viewed as a questionable creation, and many established scholars and lawyers backed away from participation. Frances contacted more than two hundred people to find three for the well-paying jobs. She rejected some candidates because they seemed too emotional to rule dispassionately on labor-management disputes. She even asked Wyzanski if he would do it—and he flatly and firmly refused.[17]

Frances finally settled on Madden, law school dean at the University of Pittsburgh, Edwin S. Smith, whom Frances knew from his tenure as labor commissioner of Massachusetts and as a former personnel director at Filene's department stores, and John Carmody, a well-known labor mediator. On August 27, 1935, Roosevelt announced the appointments.

As Frances had asked, the president wrote to Madden and asked him to report regularly to Frances. She in turn would report on the board's doings at Cabinet meetings.

Madden amiably started off making reports, but soon the flow of information dried up. Staff members told him he had no responsibility to Frances and that he should resist her supervision. When Frances protested, Madden asserted that the NLRB was independent agency with no obligation to report to Roosevelt. As a quasi-judicial body, moreover, the board needed to be free of executive interference.

More a legal scholar than administrator, Madden set rigid rules that were hard to enforce and easy to criticize. For example, the NLRB ruled that it was an "unfair labor practice" for employers to tell workers they did not want them to join a union. Practically speaking, it was almost impossible for employers to avoid communicating that feeling. Frances understood why the NLRB made the rule. But forbidding employers from expressing opinions sounded like censorship to many observers, including Roosevelt.

NLRB officials, meanwhile, wined, dined, and flattered Wagner, giving them an important ally on the Hill. Madden said that after the board's work became the subject of criticism, however, Wagner seemed to view his creation as a "political handicap" and sought to avoid public association with it.

Internecine strife within the labor movement compounded the early woes of the NLRB. Lewis, now with a formidable membership roster and bulging war chest, grew even more arrogant and clashed with other AFL leaders. The other leaders, most representing traditional craft-based unions, opposed the idea of organizing industrial, or mass-production, workers. Lewis saw opportunities to organize everywhere, especially once the National Labor Relations Act passed. To him, the AFL was mired in the past. Lewis's heated exchanges with Green and other AFL executive council members succeeded in further alienating them.

Then, in October 1935, at an AFL conference in Atlantic City, the conflict burst into the open. Lewis and his allies, most of them the movement's Young Turks, proposed resolutions expanding organizing efforts in mass-production industries. Some of his words were persuasive. "The labor movement is organized upon a principle that the strong shall help the weak," he said.

At other points, however, Lewis insulted people from whom he needed cooperation. He threatened to "rend . . . from limb to limb" his fellow delegate Matthew Woll, a more traditional union leader, adding that he meant this only "figuratively." Soon the resolutions were rejected.

And then the delegates came to blows.

During the debate, the industrial-organization activists tried to raise the issues, but the AFL traditionalists called for points of order to limit their remarks. Lewis told "Big Bill" Hutcheson, head of the carpenters' union, that his objections were "small potatoes." Hutcheson defiantly stood across from Lewis, blustering that he had been raised on such "small potatoes." Hutcheson called Lewis a bastard, and Lewis hit Hutcheson. Hutcheson fell back on the table behind him, then jumped up and rushed Lewis. As the argument descended into a fistfight, Green looked on helplessly.

"Will the delegates please be seated?" he repeated as the crowd thinned.[18]

And Lewis was not alone in his disaffection. Another AFL critic was James Carey, who believed it was time to broaden the movement's base. Carey had organized many electrical workers, only to find their membership applications rejected by the AFL. Carey argued that the economy was changing, and that only by organizing by broad industry rather than by particular craft could the union gain enough members to exert negotiating power.

Carey used the example of a rheostat, a piece of polished metal that adjusts the volume on a radio. "Three unions could claim jurisdiction over the worker who made that single part": the Metal Polishers, the Machinists Union, and the International Brotherhood of Electrical Workers, he told them. Meanwhile, Carey noted, the part was actually made by women workers, adding pointedly that neither the IAM nor the IBEW nor the Metal Polishers would accept females as members. So who, he asked, properly had jurisdiction?[19]

Carey grew so angry at the intransigence of the older officials that when reporter Louis Stark asked him how the meeting was going, Carey arranged to be photographed holding a dead mackerel, with Carey trying to talk to it. Stark roared with laughter.

At the same meeting, longtime unionist John P. Frey made himself a laughingstock among younger delegates by referring to a man he said he had known since 1811. He had meant to say 1911. Soon the younger workers streamed into the street. They ran into the lobby of the Chelsea Hotel, and Carey yelled out: "I want to nominate someone I've known since"—and his friends yelled back, "1811." Next, they ran over to the Ambassador Hotel, where most traditionalists were staying, and Carey repeated his performance. They gained more recruits among the people in the lobby.

The growing crowd surged to a nearby nightclub, and Carey again made a speech about choosing one kind of worker over another. Carey shouted that the floor show, featuring scantily clad women, was discriminatory, with men the beneficiaries. Who is responsible, he shouted? The crowd shouted back: the master of ceremonies. So the group hauled out the emcee and forced him to engage in a striptease act out of solidarity with the downtrodden women workers. They required him to remove his tuxedo piece by piece, while the orchestra, joining in the merriment, offered musical accompaniment.[20]

The next month, on November 9, 1935, Lewis met with seven other leaders at United Mine Workers' headquarters in Washington. They formed a group that they called the Committee for Industrial Organization, or the CIO. They leased offices in the Rust Building at Fifteenth and K Streets Northwest, with start-up money pledged by several unions, including the UMW.[21] Not surprisingly, Carey and his new union, the United Electrical and Radio Workers of America, soon sought affiliation with the CIO, as did the United Auto Workers and a number of other locals led by upstart newcomers.

In January 1936, the AFL's executive council, hoping to quash the insurrection, ordered the CIO to dissolve. In August 1936 they kicked out ten CIO-affiliated unions. Lewis defied them by adding to his CIO roster two new unions, the United Electrical and Radio Workers and the Industrial Union of Marine and Shipbuilding Workers, groups that had been claimed by two AFL unions, the IBEW, and the Metal Trades.

Then Lewis completed the breach: He expelled the mineworker Green from membership in the UMW for his role in "fraternization with avowed enemies" of the union. From then on, the officers of the AFL and CIO spent as much time fighting among themselves as they did fighting on workers' behalf.

Frances was caught between the two warring factions—both of which wanted her support. They were jealous siblings, and their nasty feud spoiled worker discourse for twenty years. The split was "largely an internal fight for control" of the labor movement, Frances believed.[22]

The rival organizations competed viciously for members, taking their problems to the fledgling NLRB. The CIO moved restlessly from place to place, using confrontational tactics that gained members but also stirred new opposition among businessmen.

But through such means, the CIO had extraordinary success at bringing novice members into the fold. Stanley V. White, an employee of the Works Progress Administration, reported that a "contagious enthusiasm" for the CIO swept through New England in 1937. In Providence, Rhode Island, department store workers went out on strike, quickly winning raises. In six weeks, the Woolen and Worsted Workers union gained thirty-five hundred new members in Lawrence, Massachusetts. Close to ten thousand members were recruited by the Shoe Workers Organizing Committee, after strikes in Lewiston and Auburn, Maine. The rubber workers' union membership tripled in a few months.[23]

The CIO also made recruiting runs at workers who were already organized into AFL-affiliated unions. Employers who agreed to union contracts suddenly found the contracts voided when the workers abruptly joined another group and went out on strike again. The AFL wanted employers to be able to tell workers to remain with the union rather than joining another one. Sometimes the AFL colluded with employers, positioning themselves as the "lesser of two evils."[24]

At this point, employers poured into Frances's office, desperate for help handling the situation. Others became belligerent. Some reported that the NLRB was coaching unions on how to prepare their cases so that when disputes arose, they would be more likely to prevail over employers.

The NLRB seemed to favor the more radical CIO over the AFL.

Negative reports about the NLRB mounted, and the president decided to fire Madden. He also chose not to extend Edwin Smith to another term. Frances had to deal with both men. She felt that the president had unfairly tarred Madden, and she helped him find a post elsewhere. But she had to tell Smith that she agreed with the president because the former personnel manager had ended up allying himself strongly with the union movement's most radical elements.

"You can't do the kind of work I've done, see what's been going on in American industry, without feeling differently about the rights of the working man, feeling more wrought up over it," he told Frances. She found it a "very painful interview."[25]

Frances replaced Smith and Madden with Gerard Reilly, who had been her solicitor of labor, and William Leiserson, a labor relations expert and mediator.

Frances came to believe the NLRB had been influenced from the start by Communists. One key NLRB official, Nathan Witt, was widely believed to be a Communist. The CIO, meanwhile, also became riddled with Communists as Lewis looked for help staffing the newly formed locals. One of his most important new hires was Lee Pressman as general counsel for the CIO. Pressman later admitted that he had been a Communist. Consequently, the businessmen's fears of Communist agitation had some basis in fact.

With little oversight and a strong Communist contingent working inside the NLRB, the board soon came to be viewed as unfair to business. NLRB officials sometimes did little to disguise their jubilation when workers voted to organize. Paul M. Herzog, NLRB chairman in the late 1940s, said that the perceived "pro-labor bias" eventually injured the board and later resulted in restrictive new rules being written by Congress that impeded future union organizing efforts.[26]

While Roosevelt had permitted the NLRB to be stripped from Frances's domain, he continued to expect her to monitor it, and he consulted with her privately about its leadership. When the head of the board presented a list of possible new members, FDR sent it to Frances for comment, adding this notation: "Please treat it as highly confidential. You have never seen it." Frances was expected to solve the agency's problems without being given any formal authority to do so.[27]

The public held her responsible for administrative failures over which she had no control. Her friends watched with dismay, aware that she was receiving little praise and much abuse.

"I think Miss Perkins has not been well treated and that anyone who had been Secretary of Labor during this insurgent period would have been blamed for all the excesses of labor," wrote Lloyd K. Garrison to Burlingham. "She was particularly easy to pick on, being rather easily agitated and not too tactful. But I think she has done a fine job, for which someday she will be given credit."[28]

Amid the sound and fury, an important point was often missed. By 1937 some 6.2 million members were affiliated with the two major union movements—with the AFL boasting 3.2 million members and the CIO claiming 3 million. Union membership had more than tripled in five years. By 1945, 35 percent of the U.S. workforce was organized. When Frances ascended to power as secretary of labor, the union movement had been almost dead.

Some workers found this change a mixed blessing. While many greeted unionizing with open arms, some unions quickly started bullying workers or holding them up for dues they did not want to pay.

Some labor leaders flexed their muscles simply to prove they could. The Teamsters' union, for example, hijacked the delivery trucks of farmers bringing their produce to market. The farmers would be removed from their trucks or forced to pay fees for carrying their own merchandise into the city—simply so the union members could pad their income, said attorney general Robert Jackson.

"The leadership took it as unqualified license to get whatever they could out of the economy," Jackson said. "They felt that the old restraints which had been imposed on them in times past were all off and the sky was the limit."[29]

Women workers in Allentown, Pennsylvania, complained to the White House that they were compelled to make charitable contributions to a German refugee fund, with money either deducted from their pay or taken out in unpaid overtime. A Labor Department investigation found that the plan had been devised by officials of the International Ladies' Garment Workers' Union, headed by David Dubinsky, a Jewish labor leader active in promoting the refugee exodus from Germany. Although this appeared to be an illegal and forced contribution by workers, nothing could be done by the federal government because the workers feared antagonizing the union or their employer and were unwilling to make their claims public.[30]

Though neither Roosevelt nor Frances had pushed for the NLRB, the board's creation shifted the unionists' political allegiance leftward, away from Republicans and toward the Democrats. Even so, union leaders continued to vilify Frances when it suited them. They were never really able to reconcile themselves to the presence of a woman in the Labor Department—even though she turned out to be the most important political benefactor labor had ever had.

Chapter 24

SOCIAL SECURITY

*J*oblessness. Strikes. Immigration. Huge new public works programs. By 1934, Frances certainly had a full plate. But instead of conserving her strength or allowing herself to become distracted by the whirl of issues she confronted daily, Frances now began to turn her attention to solving some of the larger societal problems, including unemployment and care for the aging, that had been of concern to her since her settlement house years.

The problem of the indigent elderly had been brought into stark relief with the onset of the Great Depression. Few of the nation's 6.5 million people who were sixty-five and over had made provisions for their golden years. Even those with savings saw their hard-earned dollars dissipate in failed stock and real estate investments. Only about three hundred thousand had public pensions, through the states or federal retirement systems. Another one hundred fifty thousand received pensions from their private employers or unions. The rest were on their own.

Some 30 to 50 percent of the elderly sought support from friends or relatives, and adult children often found this burden unendurable. Humiliated seniors turned to charity, and around seven hundred thousand obtained federal relief.[1]

Physician Francis Townsend, who worked for the health department of Long Beach, California, looked out the window one day and saw three elderly women rummaging in a garbage can for discarded food. Townsend bellowed with rage about the world's injustices, and his wife begged him to quiet down. "I want all the neighbors to hear me!" he shouted. "I want God almighty to hear me. I'm going to shout till the whole country hears!"[2]

And so he did: Townsend started a grassroots political movement, urging the federal government to provide seniors with $200 a month in spending money. Townsend Clubs, operating like old-style Baptist Revival meetings, spread everywhere.

Frances thought Townsend's plan was foolhardy. Where would that kind of money come from? Its popularity, however, meant that the momentum for solutions was growing. Frances pondered the options. She looked to Europe, where old-age pensions were common, and wondered how best to adapt them to the United States.

In other countries, while employees and employers contributed to the pension system, the central governments also made significant contributions from general funds. In the United States it would be difficult, if not impossible, to convince citizens that the government should somehow become the primary supporter of people's older years. She focused on ensuring that people could contribute substantially to their own accounts. She looked to the insurance model, in which people pay in when they are employed, so that they can get money back when they are not.

During Roosevelt's first year, officials had been too busy to launch either unemployment or old-age insurance programs. Now, a year had passed, and Frances insisted that the time was right. She nagged the president to get it started. "It is probably our only chance in twenty-five years to get a bill like this," she told Roosevelt.[3]

Finally, Roosevelt gave her the nod. With joblessness rampant, Frances decided to go for unemployment insurance first. If such a program went through smoothly, then perhaps old-age insurance could be next. She was uncertain about the outcome. Even the piece that seemed the most likely to pass—unemployment insurance—seemed radical to many Americans. Few employers supported the idea. Some scholars had written books about it and Wisconsin had enacted its own state version, but the concept was still widely ridiculed. Just a few years earlier, Thomas Eliot, assistant solicitor in the Labor Department, had attended a play in which cartoonish characters walked onstage carrying placards reading "We Want Unemployment Insurance," which, he recalled, drew a "big laugh from the audience."[4]

U.S. representative David Lewis, a former coal miner from Cumberland, Maryland, took on the job of handling the legislation. He introduced an unemployment compensation bill written by Eliot. The House Ways and Means Committee held hearings on it in March 1934. Frances testified in support, and the bill seemed likely to sail toward easy approval.[5]

But suddenly Roosevelt held back. He decided to capitalize more directly on the successful Townsend activism and the populism of Senator Huey Long's "Every Man a King" campaign. It occurred to him that by presenting more moderate programs in several areas simultaneously, more might be accomplished in total. Roosevelt would assemble a package of programs under a single label of "economic security." But this would take time. Meanwhile, he decided, the unemployment insurance bill would have to be put on hold.[6]

Roosevelt told Frances of his decision indirectly. He called Representative Lewis and told him he thought it needed more study. Lewis told Eliot, and Eliot told Frances. She hit the roof. "That man, that man!" she muttered.[7]

She ripped over to the White House. The next day, FDR told the press conference that he was "tremendously" for the bill.

Back on track, Roosevelt and Frances instead began considering programs far more sweeping than just the unemployment insurance bill. They would initiate a much more expansive version of an "economic security" package that would cover people from cradle to grave. The concept included not only unemployment insurance, which would tide over the jobless workers who were the primary source of support to children and old people, but also old-age pensions, which Frances was eager to promote; health insurance, so people would have medical care, even when they had no money; and financial assistance for the handicapped and for widowed women with children. Many women earned so little money that losing their husbands meant that they must put their youngsters to work or place them in orphanages.

Roosevelt and Frances set up a Cabinet-level economic security committee to do the groundwork. The two of them shared a predilection for creating committees or boards to get things done: during her tenure as secretary of labor, Roosevelt named Frances to eighteen separate committees.

Sometimes the committees they formed were little more than window dressing to gather support for a predetermined position. These ruses could be successful only if they were well managed by a director who kept the committee members busy and presented the group with small, easily resolved questions that permitted little debate and precluded members from developing their own agendas. Frances would set the agenda for the outcome she wanted, and the president would lend his prestige to the effort by ceremoniously appointing the people Frances had picked.

Roosevelt liked to have committee deliberations led by a Cabinet officer and handled with little publicity. "Remember, Papa wants to know first what you're thinking about," he told his Cabinet officers. "I don't want to wake up and read in the paper what this committee is about to report."[8] When there was a big splash to be made, he would make it and take credit for it.

Some committees, however, were designed to be more substantive and influential. The committee on economic security was one of those, and in this one Frances used all the tricks she had learned over a lifetime. Roosevelt named her as the chair. Giving the program priority over her many other duties, Frances drafted letters appointing the members, then had FDR sign them. She chose the members carefully: Harry Hopkins, who had become Federal Emergency Relief Administrator; Secretary of Agriculture Wallace, by then her closest friend in the Cabinet; Treasury Secretary Morgenthau; and Attorney General Cummings. Not everyone would be willing to work hard on it or even be that interested in it. Frances was determined to hold their feet to the fire on this one. In a meeting with Roosevelt present, she went around the table and extracted from each of the major members of her committee a pledge to support the program being prepared by the committee. Publicly obligated, they could not back down later.

On June 8, 1934, Roosevelt formally unveiled the plans. He said he intended to create a program that would provide "security against the hazards and vicissitudes of life." His plan would include both state and federal components, with funds raised by individual payroll contributions rather than from general taxes.

In late June, the Committee on Economic Security was created, and FDR and Frances looked for experts who could support its work, along the lines FDR had set down. She loaded the staff with allies, including Labor Department official Arthur Altmeyer, and she tapped another Wisconsinite, Edwin Witte, chairman of the University of Wisconsin economics department, for the job of executive director to oversee the daily operations. But she soon found that Roosevelt's support remained equivocal. He had tested the waters by making his announcement, but he had allotted no money to launch even the study group. Frances went hat in hand to raise money and borrow staff from other departments.

The Federal Emergency Relief Administration, under Hopkins, came up with an initial $87,500 and then another $57,000.

Assembling the technical experts soon turned into an unexpected melodrama. Frances, Witte, and Altmeyer tried to avoid people so committed to one concept that they couldn't be open-minded. They also worried about adversarial personalities who might alienate potential supporters. Two well-known experts, I. M. Rubinow and Abraham Epstein, who were abrasive and publicly feuding, were not invited to participate. Epstein's absence was awkward for Frances, since she had written the foreword to his book, which described social insurance schemes in the United States and around the world. And in return Epstein couldn't forgive Frances for excluding him from the study group and subsequently published articles denouncing the economic security proposals as misguided. Their friendship ended.

Many of the staff members ended up being ineffectual. Some people accepted offers but had previous obligations that kept them away for weeks. Some theoreticians who had spent decades developing what they viewed as ideal programs were reluctant to give them up, even if it became clear that the president and Frances had found it necessary to devise specific plans that could draw enough political support to pass.[10]

Many academics turned out to be both arrogant and impractical, eagerly writing reports but unable to figure out how to take action to implement them.[11] Barbara Armstrong, a California law professor, redhaired, beautiful, and argumentative, turned out to be a particularly unfortunate selection—even though many of her ideas were incorporated in the plan and others were more far-sighted than the politically necessary compromises being crafted. Armstrong undermined Witte by calling him, behind his back, half-Witte. She further complicated matters by leaking stories to the press about what she perceived as Frances's duplicity or lack of interest in enacting a meaningful national program.

Despite all the challenges, ultimately a core of specialists began working in concert on the program.

Constitutional issues were delegated to the twenty-six-year-old Labor Department's assistant solicitor Eliot. The Supreme Court's recent hostile decisions about workplace regulations gave Eliot's job particular importance. A group of four hostile Supreme Court justices—McReynolds, Butler, Van Devanter, and Sutherland, with occasional support from Roberts and Chief Justice Hughes—were known as the "battalion of death" for worker-friendly legislation. Unemployment insurance and old-age pensions looked especially vulnerable to judicial disapproval. On the other hand, the Court previously had upheld the federal government's right to make grants to the states for child-welfare programs, so that approach was viewed as less vulnerable.[12]

Two Supreme Court justices provided crucial guidance behind the scenes.

Paul Raushenbush, a young economics professor at the University of Wisconsin and a proponent of unemployment insurance, came to Washington for a visit along with his wife, Elizabeth, who was also an economist. They stayed with Elizabeth's father, Justice Louis Brandeis, who had had an interest in social insurance programs since his days as a lawyer for the National Consumers League. The young couple discussed Wisconsin's new unemployment insurance program and asked Brandeis whether he thought a similar federal program could pass constitutional muster.

As a Supreme Court justice, Brandeis could not publicly promote specific legislation, but he privately supported unemployment insurance. He told them of a device that he believed would put a state-federal measure on solid constitutional ground. Brandeis suggested a plan in which contributions to state unemployment reserves could be offset against federal payroll taxes, thus avoiding any problematic direct taxes for this purpose. Later, at a dinner party attended by Frances and Senator Wagner on New Year's Day 1934, Brandeis's daughter explained to them her father's tax-offset suggestion.

The next morning Frances, "full of enthusiasm," sat down with Wyzanski and devised a plan calling for Wagner to introduce a tax-offset bill in the Senate. Brandeis virtually dictated the legislation's shape, believing it improved its chances of passing the scrutiny of his conservative colleagues on the Court. Within the month, Raushenbush and Tom Eliot had drafted the measure to his specifications. Not surprisingly, it mimicked aspects of the Wisconsin plan.[13]

Meanwhile, Justice Harlan F. Stone had whispered some words of advice as well. At an afternoon party at Stone's home, Frances was drinking tea with the justice when he asked her how things were going. She told him they were wrestling with how to establish an economic security program. Stone looked around to see if anyone was listening, then leaned in toward Frances. "The taxing power, my dear, the taxing power," he said in quiet tones.

With two justices suggesting similar ways around the constitutional difficulties, Frances believed that the legal problems could be solved if she did as they directed.[14]

Work moved ahead quickly. In November 1934, Frances called a National Conference on Economic Security at Washington's Mayflower Hotel, hoping to continue building support. Normally Frances tried to control such events with careful planning, but this time she outsmarted herself, and the event turned into a debacle.

First, the organizers were startled by the conference's surprising popularity. More people than expected chose to attend at their own expense and many had to be turned away. Participants had been asked to write papers describing their proposals and grew angry when they realized that important decisions had already been made. Some attendees, even people who had been friends of Frances for years, perceived the tenor as Machiavellian rather than Democratic.

Then the president threw gasoline on the fire. During a speech, using words to some extent written by Frances, Roosevelt publicly took a more cautious stance, saying he supported unemployment insurance but was uncertain "whether this is the time for any federal legislation on old-age security." With prodding from several disaffected experts, reporters at the *New York Times* and Associated Press interpreted FDR's statement as a retreat from his earlier support for the entire program. The *Baltimore Sun* reported that one participant called it the "kiss of death."

Louis Stark's piece in the *New York Times* portrayed the president as callously abandoning the effort. "The whole economic security thing is a fiasco," Stark wrote home to his wife that night. Stark wrote that he knew the administration wouldn't like the article, "especially Fanny Perkins who harbors grudges and is vindictive."[15]

Indignantly, Frances called a press conference to say that listeners had misinterpreted the president's words and that FDR actually supported the full range of proposals being considered. An article in the *New York Times* said that Witte was responsible for the flawed language; the *Washington Post* blamed it on Frances.[16]

After the conference concluded, Frances named an advisory council to offer more perspective on the process and build support in other quarters. She tried to keep the roster small, perhaps seven people, to avoid further communication problems, but the list expanded as interest groups demanded representation. Ultimately twenty-three members were named.

Some members attended only a few meetings, but others took their advisory jobs so seriously that they grumbled to newspaper reporters that they had been brought together to act as "fronts" for the administration's preconceived plan. Some, including Barbara Armstrong, wanted a national system, saying that a state system would allow employers simply to move to less costly states, promoting a race to the bottom. They were unaware that the justices had suggested the state-federal plan, and that FDR specifically wanted a system that would give states, such as his own home state of New York, the option of developing more generous programs of their own design.[17]

As the advisory council and various subgroups finalized their proposals, the work shifted back to the larger Cabinet committee. It found itself stymied by the magnitude of the tasks and the difficulty of deciding how to administer these new programs. The Cabinet committee met once a week through the fall. Only Frances attended all the meetings, although Hopkins, Morgenthau, and Wallace were there frequently as well. Cummings always sent a subordinate.

Roosevelt had set an arbitrary Christmas deadline for completing the committee's work, but as the holiday approached, many details remained unresolved. On the night of December 22 or 23, committee leaders were called to the Georgetown house Frances shared with Mary Rumsey. She led them into the dining room, placed a large bottle of Scotch on the table, and told them no one would leave until the work was done.[18]

On December 24, just barely meeting the presidential deadline, she and Hopkins presented the committee's findings and recommendations to Roosevelt. He accepted them, saying he would promptly send a message to Congress.

Then new opposition cropped up. Rexford Tugwell, undersecretary of agriculture, and others in the Agriculture Department voiced their dislike of the state-federal plan for unemployment insurance, urging a national system instead. The group agonized over the report's final wording on New Year's Eve 1934 but failed to reach final agreement. Frances finally settled the matter by going over Tugwell's head to her friend Henry Wallace and secured his consent to a state-federal plan without any difficulty.

Serious fissures developed in the Treasury Department as well, even though Morgenthau had initially agreed to the plan. Department conservatives criticized its expenditures and the risk of "alarming business," while liberals asserted the provisions were so weak they had "little value."[19]

At a meeting attended by Eliot, Morgenthau "thundered" that the old-age pension plan was not an insurance scheme but a disguised federal handout. Frances tried to explain the risk of placing too heavy a tax burden on individual taxpayers. "But Henry! But Henry!" she started off as he interrupted.

The man who once had been a junior assistant in her office now got on his high horse. "This is Henry Morgenthau, Jr., speaking and these are his opinions," he shouted. He won that round, and the president sent word later that day that taxes would have to be increased so that the reserve fund would have enough money.

Incensed, Eliot asked Frances how Morgenthau had succeeded in unraveling months of planning: "Oh, I can guess," she said cheerfully. "Right after breakfast, Henry's sure to appear in the president's bedroom, insisting on this change. The president tells him to go away. He comes back to the White House at noon and tells his story again. And then about four o'clock, when the president's getting tired, he puts his head in the door again, and the president says, 'Oh, all right, Henry, all right!' "[20]

So Frances agreed, and after that, the committee released a unanimous report.

On January 17, 1935, about ten months after the process began, Roosevelt proudly presented the economic security legislation and urged Congress to pass it. At first all went well. But then reporters interviewed the experts from the advisory council, outside advisers, and support staff, all eager to expound on their dissenting views. Many newspapers counseled a delay.

Louis Stark, using Professor Armstrong as an unnamed source, wrote an article calling the program a "debacle" and blamed Frances. Frances had been so removed from the process that she had failed to meet with "one of the foremost social insurance experts," clearly Armstrong, from July to November, "even socially," it added. The article implied that Frances, who had worked to advance social insurance since Armstrong was still in graduate school, was less committed to the program than the technical advisers.[21]

Fueled by negative press reports, Congress reacted with hostility to some of the proposed legislation. Witte quickly saw the wisdom of the president's plan to keep all the program components together. While the old-age pension system appeared likely to be enacted, the other parts of the program were in danger of falling by the wayside. Eliot boosted the entire package's chances by flipping the components of the bill. He placed old-age insurance as the first section in the legislation, which "had the effect of drawing away opposition from the other titles, which had much less popular support."[22]

Congressional hearings were set for January 22. Frances intended to make opening statements to the House and Senate. She had a long-scheduled appearance at the Southern Labor Conference on January 21 but thought she could easily return by the next day. But House leaders, hoping to upstage the Senate, decided to move their hearings forward one day to January 21, which meant Frances couldn't attend. Instead, Witte made the opening statement in the House, and Wagner did it in the Senate. All in all, Witte spent two days testifying in the House and another two in the Senate. In the House, he explained the bill's philosophy fairly well, but in the Senate, subjected to constant interruptions, he was less successful.

"No systematic explanation of all provisions was ever presented to this committee by anyone," Witte later recalled.[23] Frances followed up with the legislators later to describe how age discrimination made it essential to provide a pension to people whom employers did not want to hire.[24]

Witnesses lined up to discuss the bill. Academics and theoreticians who had long advocated forms of Social Security spoke, but many were irked that the plans did not incorporate their personal visions.

Employer testimony was mixed. The National Association of Manufacturers vehemently attacked the bill, calling it the "ultimate socialistic control of life and industry."[25] The president of the Chamber of Commerce suggested some amendments but generally favored it.[26] Many businessmen, however, wrote to Congress saying that while they supported the concept, they rejected the proposed taxes.

The measure again looked like a failing proposition. Witte had come to the reluctant conclusion that few legislators actually wanted the bill but that they did not want to anger the president by expressing opposition publicly. A *New York Times* headline of March 30, 1935, said it all: "Hopes Are Fading for Security Bill."[27]

Recognizing that the bill was at risk, Frances rushed to rally other supporters. She secured fifty signatures of prominent people in a letter urging prompt passage and slowly the tide began to turn.

Legislators were also influenced by a rain of letters from supporters of the $200-a-month old-age payment plan proposed by California doctor Francis Townsend. Congressmen generally thought the Townsend bill "utterly impossible," so the economic security measure began to emerge as an acceptable compromise.

Final passage in the House came on April 19, on a 10-to-1-vote margin, with one significant change. The Economic Security Act had become the Social Security Act, possibly because of the references to "social security" in Epstein's landmark book. Ironically, while the term worldwide continued to refer to a comprehensive system of economic security programs—from maternity care to unemployment, welfare, and old-age pensions—in the United States the term came to refer only to payments to the elderly, and most of the other programs generally slipped from the forefront of public consciousness.[28]

Opinion in the Senate seemed even more unreliable than that in the House, however. Members of the Senate Finance Committee, which handled the bill, were mostly conservative southerners with high seniority. Ultimately they approved the measure—but with one important and malicious caveat. They added an amendment placing the Social Security Board, which would administer the old-age and unemployment programs, inside the Labor Department but said that the secretary of labor should play no role in hiring its personnel. Senator Pat Harrison, the committee's chairman, whom Frances had offended by making him wait in her office, helped direct the bill to the floor but made sure to deprive her of any control over the program she had championed. In the final version, the Social Security Board was made entirely independent of Frances's department.

In the end the Senate passed the bill overwhelmingly.

The compromise measure approved by both houses evolved during debates in the conference committee. Unemployment insurance was established as a state-federal collaboration, with a federal reserve fund established to provide financial assistance but with state governments given much latitude in designing their programs. The decision was controversial, but the Wisconsinites carried the day, not wanting their plan diluted, and the president's backing of a state-based system proved to be the determining factor.

As Barbara Armstrong predicted, however, the state-federal system contained real weaknesses. Many states had little commitment to unemployment insurance and quickly began whittling away their programs to attract migratory firms looking to lower their wages and tax burdens. Altmeyer, the Labor Department official and Wisconsin academic who later headed the program, came to believe he had committed something of a "sin" by pressing for a plan that proved to be so worker-unfriendly in many states.[29]

The old-age insurance program ended up covering more retirees than originally envisioned because people started living longer. But at the time, a critic of the Social Security system drew laughter on a radio program by noting that workers started receiving benefits at age sixty-five, when actuarial statistics showed that most men died at sixty. The program had other imperfections. Agricultural and domestic workers were exempted, against Frances's wishes, because Treasury officials said collecting their taxes would prove overly difficult. Therefore, blacks and Hispanics, who were more likely to be farm workers or domestic servants, were disproportionately excluded, even though most earned such low wages that Social Security would have been their only source of retirement income.

And low-wage church employees, such as secretaries and janitors, also found themselves without retirement assistance. Church officials had obtained exemption for their employees, partially because retired clergymen mistakenly believed they would lose their church pensions if they were included in Social Security.

Congressmen then and later created further problems by allowing the Social Security trust fund to become underfunded. Workers initially paid in at a rate of a 1 percent tax on employers and 1 percent on employees, but the rate was supposed to be gradually raised to 3 percent by 1949. But Congress had no appetite for raising taxes even slightly, even though their calculations said it would be necessary. Consequently, within a few decades, large shortfalls in the program's funding emerged.

Another misjudgment caused other serious social consequences.

The old-age assistance called for payments of $30 per month. But mothers, under the program that came to be known as Aid to Dependent Children, got shortchanged from the start. Congressman Fred Vinson said that grants to mothers should be limited to the amounts payable to veterans' widows, or $18 for the first child and $12 for additional children. The bill was so amended. Vinson, however, forgot that pensions for veterans' widows would pay an initial $30 for the mother, with the children's amounts on top of that.[30]

Frances tried to eliminate Vinson's amendment when the bill came before the Senate, but Senator Harrison, who pretty much opposed anything that Frances initiated, said the aid could start at this low amount, since it could easily be increased in the future. Fearful of losing the bill if they pressed the issue, Frances, Witte, and the others decided to accept the terms rather than take the risk. They knew that families' needs were acute: About 20 percent of urban families receiving benefits were mothers with children; only 3.8 percent of children in female-headed households were illegitimate in 1930, with most mothers having lost their husbands through death or desertion. Frances believed that women needed and deserved reliable support to raise their children and that child rearing is itself a full-time job. She never guessed that there would later be an explosion of out-of-wedlock births because she had grown up believing the stigma of bearing illegitimate children would far outweigh any economic incentives that were built into the new legislation.

Over the next few decades, however, impoverished women found that they could get more money from the government by having more children while households in which a man was a full-time resident got no aid at all. This perverse policy had been intended to encourage men to seek gainful employment and support their families, but it had the side effect of discouraging marriage in the first place, spurring even more illegitimate babies, and removing adult men from households that needed them.[31]

Other provisions were tacked onto the bill: funding for Maternal and Child Health; up to $1.5 million for Child Welfare Services, including programs to aid homeless, dependent, and neglected children; and $8 million for public health services. A program to aid crippled children was the brainchild of Grace Abbott, the head of the Children's Bureau. She told key employees that it would be so difficult for legislators to oppose help for such a pitiable group that this plan could become the "entering wedge for medical care."[32]

A lobbying campaign promoting vocational rehabilitation was successful as well. A statement by blind and deaf disability advocate Helen Keller to Robert Wagner was all it took to garner support—and pensions—for people who could not see.[33]

But amid the new benefits, an important part of the original vision was abandoned. National health insurance was dropped altogether, a major disappointment to Frances. She had initially been optimistic and had written to a friend in confidence, saying that she had "made some real progress" in convincing the "most eminent members of the profession" to back the plan. Harry Hopkins told his friend Kingsbury that FDR "would not ignore" health insurance but was watching for political reaction.[34]

But the American Medical Association mobilized such intense opposition that backers of the economic security bill believed they would scuttle the entire program to avoid creation of a federal health plan.

At a Harlem Medical Association meeting in January, Dr. Morris Fishbein, editor of the *Journal of the American Medical Association,* labeled the health-insurance plan "socialized medicine," saying that the profession would decide on its own how care should be provided. He ridiculed the Roosevelt plan, saying it came from "Eleanor advising the President in night conferences," after Frances advised him during the day.[35]

Frances and the committee decided to bury even the report that had laid out their health insurance proposal. The president finally pulled the plug on it himself. Instead the American Medical Association endorsed voluntary health insurance, under which its members would prosper for decades. Private employer-backed plans proliferated for people who were relatively young and healthy.[36]

But the core of Frances's legislation survived. On August 14, 1935, the president signed the measure into law, and the Social Security Act became effective immediately. FDR said it had been constructed in a way that no future politician would be able to tinker with it because it would be funded by workers' own contributions.

The "New Deal's Most Important Act," proclaimed the *Washington Post* that day. "Its importance cannot be exaggerated . . . because this legislation eventually will affect the lives of every man, woman and child in the country."[37]

Many people would later claim credit for the creation of Social Security, but to those closest to the process, Frances was the one most responsible.

"The one person, in my opinion, above all others who was responsible for there being a Social Security program in the early 30s was Frances Perkins," said Maurine Mulliner, an assistant to Senator Wagner, who left his office to join the Social Security Board soon after it was created. "I don't think that President Roosevelt had the remotest interest in a Social Security bill or program. He was simply pacifying Frances."[38]

"She deserved much of the credit for getting this legislation through," said Marion B. Folsom, an executive at Eastman Kodak who served as conduit to the business community. She "virtually forced the President to have a Social Security program," Wyzanski recalled later.[39]

Frances gave credit for the program to the economic events that started in the 1920s: the Great Depression. "Nothing else would have bumped the American people into social security except something so shocking, so terrifying, as that depression."[40]

On the day the bill was signed, Frances issued a statement hailing "one of the most forward-looking pieces of legislation in the interest of wage earners" in history.[41]

In public, she hid her feelings of disappointment about being blocked from administrative control of the agency and never blamed anyone but herself for that decision.[42] Still, she ended up naming most of the agency's top officials, who were then formally appointed by the president.

By 1936, Frances could report that nearly 1 million people were receiving benefits. Nearly three-quarters of a million were old people, 184,000 were dependent children, and nearly eighteen thousand were blind. She also said that all the states were now enacting unemployment compensation laws, including fifteen that had done so since the Social Security Act was passed.

But on that day in August, when she achieved a life dream, Frances found only a moment to savor her success. In pictures taken that day, she is smiling but looks slightly anxious. While she prepared for the presidential bill-signing ceremony, she learned that Paul had escaped from his nurse's care and was roving alone in New York City. She attended the White House ceremony and then immediately slipped from the room. She found Paul later that night, unharmed.[43]

Frances had dropped from the economic security plan the one provision that would have helped her personally: national health insurance, which might have covered her husband. Perhaps the thought occurred to her as she traveled to New York that day.

Chapter 25

FAMILY PROBLEMS

As Frances labored over the Social Security bill in the fall of 1934, juggling the numerous egos at play, she once again found herself tugged at by the needs of her personal life.

Frances had kept her beautiful apartment in New York City for Susanna's use and provided the young girl with a fashionable wardrobe that allowed her to be named one of New York City's best-dressed women. Susanna also was a good dancer, slim and lithe. Frances's daughter was every bit the lovely ingénue her mother had dreamed of being, and Frances held the highest hopes for Susanna's future. In June of 1934, Susanna finished high school at Manhattan's exclusive Brearley School, living with family friends and visiting Washington frequently. She had good grades and was easily accepted at Bryn Mawr College, a school that her mother had long admired for its socially progressive curriculum.

"She is a perfectly fascinating girl, lovely to look at, really intelligent, talented in painting and especially able in mathematics and science. She has seen a great deal of older people and is mature in her interests, her reading and her speech," a Bryn Mawr administrator wrote.[1]

William Astor, by now a longtime friend of Frances's, visited America, and attended a tea at which Susanna was also a guest. He wrote her mother, who he was planning to see in Washington, to say that Susanna had "kept everybody enchanted."[2]

At Bryn Mawr, Susanna was attractive and popular. She dressed in Brooks Brothers Shetland sweaters, tweed skirts, and saddle shoes, wearing jaunty silk Liberty scarves at her neck, as the other girls did. But Susanna's frame had become pencil thin, which worried one classmate and childhood friend from Brearley. Rather plump in high school, Susanna began "looking like a wraith," her classmate recalled.[3]

Some of the girls who lived in Susanna's dormitory at college also noticed something seemed amiss. While many girls leaving home for college have a bad case of nerves, Susanna seemed more irritable, more easily agitated than the others. On the day Susanna arrived at the college with Frances and was unpacking, they overheard her speaking sharply to her mother. Frances responded to her quietly, in a calming tone of voice, they recalled.

Within a month of her arrival, Susanna developed a bad cough that turned into bronchitis and then whooping cough. It became evident to school nurses that Susanna's resistance to illness had most likely been lowered by her excessive dieting to maintain a trim figure. To protect other girls from exposure in these pre-antibiotic days, Bryn Mawr planned to quarantine Susanna in the infirmary for three weeks. Instead, however, Frances took her seriously ill child back to Washington and tended her there, something that her critics did not know.[4]

At the same time, her husband Paul suffered a serious relapse. He had been in a mental hospital when Frances consulted him on taking the job as secretary of labor, and had been expected to remain hospitalized another eight months, or well into the fall of 1933. Eventually he was released into a boarding home that cared for the mentally ill. But in 1934, Paul became ill again. Frances sought help from Paul's brother, Harlan Wilson, a banker in Upland, California. Harlan at first questioned whether Paul was really as sick as Frances claimed. He arranged for an independent medical evaluation of his brother. In September 1934, Dr. Charles I. Lambert reported back that Paul indeed showed signs of manic depression and suggested that he be hospitalized, "against his will if necessary."[5]

Harlan forwarded the evaluation to Frances, along with a letter acknowledging that she had been correct. Paul was again placed in institutional care, this time for nearly a year. There was little doctors could do to help Paul cope with his symptoms; lithium would not be approved for use in bipolar disorder until 1970.

Susanna, meanwhile, recovered from her whooping cough and returned to Bryn Mawr in the late fall of 1934. She did well in her classes, studying biology, French, art history, and English composition. Frances visited the campus from time to time and took groups of Susanna's friends on outings, including trips to the theater or to the cinema—things she managed to do despite the crushing work burden imposed on her as she maneuvered the Social Security bill to passage.

Frances had just gotten Paul and Susanna back on an even keel when disaster struck from another direction. One Friday night in November 1934, Mary left Washington late one evening so she could get away to Middleburg to join a fox hunt the next morning. She was tired as she joined the hunt. Approaching a stone wall, her horse abruptly stopped short. Mary fell to the ground, and the horse fell on top of her. Her riding companions rushed her to the hospital. Mary had suffered a fractured hip and several broken ribs, but her spirits were good. At fifty-two, in excellent health, Mary was expected to recover quickly, and soon she was drafting letters to her staff from her bed. Mary's wealth made her a celebrity, and her injury and its aftermath were chronicled in daily news articles. But Frances, of course, had no official relationship with Mary and no one mentioned the connection between the two women.[6]

Mary was given several blood transfusions to speed her recovery, but instead she developed pneumonia, and soon it became apparent that she might not survive. Ironically it was during this time, with Frances spending hours at the hospital each day tending to Mary, that Frances's colleagues began carping about her failure to meet socially with people on the Social Security task force.

On December 18, 1934, with Frances and Mary's three children at her bedside, Mary died. Mary's children believed she died of internal injuries from the fall, but Frances privately blamed a tainted blood transfusion. Doctors denied they had made an error. Physician Dana W. Atchley told Mary's brother Averell that her death was a fluke, a "tragic and mystifying affair."[7]

Frances was devastated by Mary's death, Susanna recalled. Wyzanski told his mother he didn't know if Frances would even remain in Washington with Mary no longer at her side.[8]

The service was held at St. Thomas Episcopal Church in Washington. Frances was acknowledged as a primary mourner. Eleanor Roosevelt attended, and many of the other luminaries who paid their respects were friends of Frances, including Henry Wallace, George Dern, and Jim Farley. Mary's children escorted the casket out the church door, followed by Mary's siblings, and then ten or more servants from her various estates. Last came Mrs. Roosevelt and Frances.[9]

Several letters found among Frances's papers suggest that friends viewed her bereavement as more profound than simply losing a dear friend. "You are going through one of those tremendously alone experiences, yet lacking in importance outside yourself," wrote a friend named Elizabeth, on Christmas Eve.[10]

Frances's friend Mary Dreier sent a thoughtful letter: "From the depths of my heart I send you my loving sympathy in this hour of grief caused by dear Mary Rumsey's death. It must be a heartbreak for you to whom she meant so much and with whom you had such a close and beautiful friendship. Dear Frances life can be so incomprehensible and full of sorrow at times and I stretch out my hands in fellowship and love."[11]

Dreier's life partner, Frances Kellor, organized a memorial service for Mary in New York City.

Yet there was no respite for Frances. Her life's work would go down the drain if she did not push ahead on the Social Security bill. The night she brought the Social Security committee to her home, slapped the bottle of Scotch on the table, and told them they could not leave the room until the deal was struck, Mary had been dead less than a week and Frances had no place to go.

For not only had she lost her closest friend, Frances had lost a home as well. Mary's estate was quickly settled to maximize income for her children. Averell, administrator of his sister's estate, shut down the house, canceled the lease, stored Mary's furniture and artworks, and sold her farms and thoroughbred horses. It was all done so hastily that decades later, a pair of modernistic sculptures by the artist Brancusi were found in a warehouse in New York City's suburbs because neither Averell nor bank trust-department officials had recognized their value and simply packed them away.[12]

But Frances always had a remarkable survival instinct, and somehow, when she most needed something, a solution would materialize. Within days of losing her home with Mary, another wealthy widow came forward who would similarly help subsidize her life. Caroline Love O'Day, whose husband had been a key associate of John D. Rockefeller, had just been elected congresswoman-at-large for New York state. In early 1935 she was moving to Washington to take office. She approached Frances to find out if she would be interested in sharing a house with her and her daughter Elia.

It was another compatible match. The two women had known each other for more than a decade through their various civic, political, and philanthropic pursuits. Caroline shared Frances's most pressing interests, supporting almost all of FDR's policy proposals. She was also a close friend of Eleanor's, having joined her in a furniture-making business they operated in Hyde Park. Eleanor had promoted Caroline's congressional candidacy.[13]

Frances and Caroline soon found a home together and by the end of January 1935, just a month after Rumsey's death, the two of them entertained together, just as Frances and Mary had done. They invited Wyzanski to dinner one Saturday night, and Susanna, who was there for the weekend, joined them. On March 12, they hosted the unlikely combination of the German ambassador Hans Luther, who had previously been chancellor, as well as the Soviet ambassador, Alexander Troyanovsky, and his wife.[14]

That summer the women leased a home on California Street, in Washington's elegant Kalorama section. By mid-1936, they moved again to a more settled house described by a *Washington Star* reporter who visited it as a "charming, red brick house in one of the swankiest sections of Georgetown. [O'Day's] house has the quiet, gracious charm of its occupant, is filled with almost priceless paintings, including many from the ancient Chinese, and there's a splendid library."[15]

In the same way she was close-mouthed about her life with Mary, Frances almost never mentioned her relationship with Caroline, and only a handful of letters between the women survived. They make it clear that Caroline was a faithful friend to Frances, and one of the few people she could trust in Congress.

In the early fall of 1935, Susanna, a sophomore at Bryn Mawr, suffered what friends later described as a nervous breakdown. Frances herself referred to it as a "psychiatric episode." Susanna was almost exactly the same age that her father had been when he suffered similar problems at Dartmouth.

Susanna withdrew from her classes "on account of illness" and was hospitalized in Philadelphia, while Frances anxiously sought and obtained the best psychiatric care for her. Frances managed to visit Susanna frequently. Many evenings after work, she took her limousine from Washington to Philadelphia to stay with her and then returned late at night. Reports of Susanna's inconsistent behavior toward her studies, one moment hardworking, the next filled with apathy, had deeply worried Frances. She hoped that Susanna would shake off the disorder, and by the end of October she was relieved to tell school officials that her daughter was a "great deal better and is making rather steady improvement." But less than a month later, Bryn Mawr officials wrote Frances to say they were sorry that Susanna was not well enough to return.

Frances asked whether Susanna might keep up with her course work by doing reading at home. Over Thanksgiving weekend, Frances decided to keep her out of school until after Christmas, since the doctors agreed that she was not quite strong enough.

Trying not to sound too desperate, Frances pleaded with the school to keep Susanna on, even if she couldn't maintain a regular schedule. "I suppose other people have taken five or six years to go through Bryn Mawr without ruining their lives and I'd much rather she would do that than get too tired."[16]

The simultaneous hospitalizations of her husband and daughter left Frances strapped for cash, and family friends thought she might have had to turn to Caroline O'Day for financial help from time to time. Ashamed to show weakness or share any vulnerability, Frances was obliged to write to Bryn Mawr to ask if they could reduce the bill because she was under "heavy additional expenses on account of Susanna's illness." Bryn Mawr officials agreed to refund part of Susanna's room and board.[17]

Upon Susanna's release from the hospital in December 1935, she needed a peaceful place to recover but also required medical supervision. Frances searched for a spot big enough to house both Susanna and a full-time nurse. But here, too, money was a factor. Susanna's physician, Frederick Peterson, suggested that Frances contact a well-regarded state public health doctor in Connecticut whose room-and-board charges would be "reasonable." Susanna ended up in a private home elsewhere.[18]

Susanna's relationship with her mother had soured during her illness. Although somewhat overindulged, Susanna had previously been a docile girl who sought to please Frances. But now she grew more assertive and sometimes actively hostile. Some friends thought that Frances was overly controlling, doting obsessively. Susanna sometimes felt overwhelmed by the magnitude and depth of Frances's love.[19]

And Frances was not an easy mother for a person like Susanna. She was a self-controlled perfectionist raising a daughter who could not complete tasks and lacked social reserve. Frances liked to present a flawless facade, and having a mentally ill daughter allowed her life to be questioned in disturbing ways. At that time, mothers were viewed as culpable when their children developed mental illness and working mothers were viewed as especially blameworthy, particularly at a time when many people thought married women should withdraw from the workplace entirely. It was a double-edged sword: Frances's earnings were needed to pay for Susanna's care, but the fact that she had earnings at all would make Frances a target in the psychiatric sessions she was funding.

Soon the conflicts between the two women grew volcanic. Jane Gunther, a family friend and contemporary of Susanna, recalled explosive exchanges. "Frances Perkins was a very dominant person, strong-willed, with a strict sense of how Susanna should dress and Susanna was highly volatile and would get awfully angry," Gunther recalled. "They screamed at each other. . . . Susanna was terribly opinionated and sometimes completely in the wrong but vociferous."[20]

Susanna sometimes went out of her way to aggravate Frances, either because she chose to do so or couldn't help herself. For example, Frances invited Susanna and a friend to attend a reception for Princess Juliana of the Netherlands and asked the young women to wear simple black gowns with pearls. Susanna's friend did as directed, but Susanna donned a watermelon-colored skirt with ballet shoes tied to her knees, with garish red roses festooning her hair and neck.[21]

Some animosity between them would have been a predictable facet of Susanna's disease. Her mother vigilantly monitored Susanna for recurring mental illness, behavior that was both infuriating and humiliating to Susanna.[22]

Susanna finally returned to Bryn Mawr and finished her sophomore year, but she had decided she wanted to be free of her mother's control. Soon after, she told Frances she had fallen in love with a childhood friend, David Hare, and that they would marry. David was a flamboyant and talented young photographer. Frances knew his mother, Betty Sage Hare, a wealthy divorcée who had been a director of the Maternity Center Association with her. Mrs. Hare had caused a scandal by divorcing her first husband, Walter Lippincott Goodwin, a publishing heir and great-nephew of J. P. Morgan, to marry Meredith Hare. While still married to Goodwin, she bore a child who resembled Hare. Betty outlived her second husband, and as a widow she continued her philanthropic pursuits. Among other interests, she was a patroness of the American Museum of Natural History.[23]

This was hardly the match that Frances wanted for Susanna. David had been spoiled by an indulgent mother. He represented the polar opposite of the diligent, conscientious, and erudite men who had played important roles in Frances's life. David was wild, energetic, and irrepressible, with a shock of white-blond hair, a pointed chin, and a gamin face. "It is neither senility nor drunkenness which accounts for my miriad mistakes," he wrote in one letter. "I can neither type nor spell, prehaps too much progressive education or prehaps mere indolence."[24]

Hare also was viewed with disdain by the boys who had grown up with him. Peter Poole, the son of Frances's friends Ernest and Margaret Poole, recalled him as a thin, high-strung boy whom the others delighted in teasing. "He wasn't a rugged sort of person," Poole recalled. "Artistic."

David also engaged in showy antics that sometimes went awry. At a crowded party, he demonstrated what he considered an amusing trick. He began whirling a glass soft-drink bottle by sticking his finger in the neck of the container and gyrating it, but the bottle flew out of his control and hit Susanna in the head, breaking two of her teeth and casting a damper on the remaining festivities.[25]

Frances tried to talk Susanna out of the relationship, telling her she feared David would not prove to be a "solid citizen." She wanted Susanna to finish college, so she tried to distract her with a trip to Europe. The vacation was lavish and glamorous, and Susanna visited all the favorite tourist spots. Together they visited England, France, and then Switzerland.[26]

A highlight of the trip for Frances was her visit to the Geneva headquarters of the International Labor Organization. This was a kind of victory lap because she had successfully convinced the United States to join the organization. While Frances attended meetings to discuss brewing international hostilities, she arranged for Susanna to be safely chaperoned. Frances did not explain why Susanna needed supervision.

Drawing the short straw for this assignment was Carol Riegelman, a young American woman working at the ILO. She was a Smith graduate educated in Switzerland, fluent in French, who had done graduate study on the ILO. Clearly Frances had hoped the serious young woman would introduce Susanna to suitable young men, but it was midsummer, and the city was empty. "[Susanna] couldn't have been more bratty and demanding and more unpleasant," Riegelman recalled.[27]

Upon returning to the States, Susanna dropped out of college, but she wasn't able to make it on her own. In summer 1937, her still-hopeful mother placed an advertisement looking for a German-speaking companion who could watch over Susanna and tutor her, since German was a required language for advanced studies in art history. "I want someone who will act as a companion and tutor in German for my young daughter—not so very young either—20—for about six weeks, beginning the first week in August. We go to a rather quiet country place in Maine and she is anxious to make a real headway start on first-year German," she wrote.[28]

Frances got an enthusiastic response from a young Ohio woman and made arrangements to meet. But tutoring did not pave the way for Susanna's return to college. Instead, Susanna got a job at an art gallery in Washington where she worked for free.

Newspaper reporters found it curious that the daughter of such an intellectual woman, who was such a strong advocate of higher education for women, had dropped out. Susanna replied that she had left Bryn Mawr because she found it "pointless." She said that her mother didn't mind that she had dropped her studies to pursue her interest in art. "Mother does not care a bit what I do," she told reporters.[29]

Susanna's comments must have been acutely embarrassing for Frances, who had been engaged in a public skirmish with Mount Holyoke over the need to appoint a woman as president of the school, and who was hopeful of getting a job herself as dean of some prominent women's college when she left government life. The previous year, Frances had presented diplomas to the young women graduating from Wellesley.

Despite Susanna's behavior, Frances continued to support her daughter in a comfortable manner. Susanna's stylish wardrobe continued to be the subject of interested attention on the society pages, and she was spotted waving cheerily out the window of a limousine. She was a bridesmaid in several high-society weddings, and her mother financed a lavish party for her—a dance for sixty-five—at a mansion in the District of Columbia that had been turned into a private club.[30]

Susanna never completed her degree, and her heart remained set on marrying David. Worn down, Frances announced their engagement around Christmas 1937.

The pair married on March 12, 1938, at Frances's beloved Church of the Resurrection in Manhattan. The *Washington Post* called it "one of the most important weddings of the early Spring." Susanna wore a white silk gown with a short veil and carried a prayer book instead of flowers. Her attendants included her lifelong friends, Alison Bruere Carnahan and Jane Gunther. Hare's best man was Medill McCormick, son of a former Illinois congresswoman, Ruth Hanna McCormick, and grandson of Mark Hanna, an industrial baron who had bankrolled the Republican National Committee. A reception with three hundred guests was held at the Cosmopolitan Club in New York City, Frances's long-favorite haunt. Another article noted that the bride and groom were toasted with the "finest champagne."[31]

Though invited, the Roosevelts did not attend.

Susanna Wilson and David Hare embarked on a bohemian lifestyle in New York. Socially active, the couple drank heavily and traveled in a fast set. They moved into a beautiful apartment on 64th Street, and traveled frequently to the Southwest. In late 1939, Susanna, described as the "most striking blonde" at a fashion designers' gathering in New York, worked as a designer with Muriel King, a Hollywood costume designer who designed gowns for movie stars, including Rita Hayworth, Greta Garbo, Ginger Rogers, and Katharine Hepburn.

Without the need to work, David pursued his photography career, experimenting with color techniques. In the late 1930s, Hare obtained assignments photographing top American officials, including Henry Wallace, opportunities that presumably involved Frances's help. Hare's greatest interest was in surrealism, an innovative art form then sweeping Europe.[32]

At last, Frances breathed a sigh of relief, knowing that her daughter was financially secure, settled, and traveling comfortably in the elite social circles that Frances herself had had to breach with cordiality and cunning.

Chapter 26

COURT-PACKING,
WAGES, AND HOURS

By early 1935, Frances found the early excitement of Washington life had faded, and she was discouraged. She was two years into a grueling round-the-clock job, and Susanna's health problems had been draining. Mary had been dead for six months, and the additional strain of maintaining a household, even with Caroline's financial assistance, was showing.[1]

Two interrelated problems were making her work life especially difficult. The Supreme Court slapped down the NRA, which had introduced new workplace rules, and remained hostile to labor laws. FDR was angry at what he saw as the intransigence of the conservative judicial body and he soon began toying around with a plan to fight the court by undermining it. Nobody wanted protective workplace legislation more than Frances, but she feared that FDR's proposed solution would cause a political backlash.

Frances faced this new set of problems at a time when her energy was flagging. Constant public criticism was taking a toll. Several longtime colleagues had denigrated Frances for her role in steering Social Security to passage; they were angry at being slighted. She continued to be the focus of negative, anonymously sourced newspaper articles. Predicting that her Cabinet days were numbered, many reporters curried favor with their employers by pillorying Frances. Industry officials had gone to the mat with the Roosevelt administration to block unionization. The National Labor Relations Board had ruled against the Associated Press, an organization owned by its newspaper members, and rather than accepting the decision, the AP fought the case to the Supreme Court. Some reporters and editors, no doubt worried about their own job security, would have been eager to demonstrate solidarity with their employers' concerns.

Frances was still having trouble finding support among her fellow

Roosevelt insiders. In the 1930s and 1940s there was no language yet for the sexism she experienced daily in the Cabinet because there had never before been a woman serving in the Cabinet, or indeed, in any prominent government position. She thought she had successfully adopted male patterns of communicating, but she still couldn't suit the men.

Her job security irked the men as well. Many other Cabinet officials came and went, but Frances remained at FDR's side.

Occasionally the men exchanged childish notes about her while she was talking in Cabinet meetings. She could be long-winded when she was talking about subjects she thought were important. In May 1940, for example, Frances spoke on a topic for twenty minutes, but Harold Ickes, secretary of the interior, made no mention in his diary of what she was saying, only that she again talked too long. Harry Hopkins, who often feuded with Ickes, passed him a note suggesting that Frances was lecturing from "4 to 5," then passed the note to Jesse Jones, secretary of commerce. Ickes noted that Jim Farley's eyes were closed, Hull looked like an "early Christian martyr," and Wallace was "contemplating the ceiling."

"And, as usual, only the President listened to her," Ickes noted.[2]

In fact, Roosevelt often sided with Frances against others. He had backed her instead of Vice President Garner on the response to sit-down strikes, and in one Cabinet meeting the president pointedly reminded Garner of it. The president told him that if he had taken the action "urged upon him" by Garner, to call out U.S. troops, the situation would have been aggravated. Instead, Roosevelt said, the "whole matter had been worked out amicably" because he had followed Frances's advice."[3]

On another occasion, Ickes wanted a moment of time to ask the president's permission to use a navy plane to fly to Pittsburgh. Frances, however, got to Roosevelt first and spoke to him privately for about five minutes. When she exited, she saw Ickes and pleasantly asked him about his recent Maine vacation, but Ickes burst out that he was furious at her. He felt she had butted into his time with the president.

As Ickes noted with satisfaction, Frances hastened to make conciliatory conversation with him at the next Cabinet meeting. This relieved his mind, since he had been concerned that perhaps he had offended her "very deeply" with his earlier criticism. Ickes, sixty, who had recently married a twenty-five-year-old woman, later noted, "there is something to the old adage, 'A woman, a dog and a walnut tree, the more you beat them, the better they'll be.' "

Then, at the next meeting, Frances slipped in ahead of Ickes again, once more getting to the president first.[4]

With negative views of her seeping out from her fellow Cabinet officials and into the press, even longtime supporters of Frances accepted the popular perception that she was fumbling in her job. Supreme Court Justice Louis Brandeis, an ally for decades, asked Wyzanski to visit him at his home, making it clear he wanted to discuss Frances's disappointing performance. It was almost perverse. The month before, Frances finalized a project dear to Brandeis's heart, shepherding unemployment insurance legislation to passage. The Social Security Act was the greatest single victory of the progressive movement, and yet now, with the ink on it barely dry, Brandeis mulled over Frances's inadequacies. He told Wyzanski that she was overextended and lacked the time to properly think things through, and Wyzanski found himself compelled to defend her.[5]

But somehow, despite the pressures, Frances found the will to persevere, a sentiment that was undoubtedly bolstered by the president's enduring fondness for her. He continued to consult with her about his thorniest problems—and increasingly they revolved around the High Court.[6]

In one session, Frances and Roosevelt discussed how best to recover from the demise of the National Recovery Administration (NRA). Roosevelt was discouraged. "Never mind, I have something up my sleeve," she told him. She said she had prepared two pieces of legislation, a public contracts bill and a wage-and-hour bill, that could be proposed to replace the NRA.

"You're pretty unconstitutional, aren't you?" Roosevelt said with a laugh, Frances recalled. Then he mused: "You know, I have been in office for two years and haven't had an appointment for the Supreme Court.... What the Court needs is some Roosevelt appointments."[7]

In many ways, the justices, comfortable in the life tenure of their own jobs, did appear sadly out of touch with the experiences of normal Americans. During oral arguments in one case in 1937, Justice Pierce Butler, a Warren Harding appointee, was widely believed to have disparaged the growing hordes of jobless, having reportedly said unemployment was caused by workers' "unwillingness" to work.[8]

Roosevelt already had suggested a plan to expand the Court, and Frances had advised against it. FDR's loyal aide Louis Howe had recently died, and few others in the president's circle consistently looked out for his best interests.

"The only member of the Cabinet who expressed a contrary view on this matter was Miss Perkins, but I suppose that was to be expected of a woman," Ickes noted in his diary in 1937. "Apparently she thinks we ought to pussyfoot on the Supreme Court issue and not present anything, if possible, that is likely to elicit adverse opinion."[9]

The Court's philosophical beliefs were in fact crucial to the country's future direction. Almost as soon as the Social Security bill passed, conservatives backed by the Republican Party launched legal attacks on its constitutionality. Robert Jackson, as assistant attorney general in charge of tax issues, was charged with defending the law. He became a busy man. In one case, for example, the trustees for a bankrupt milk company sought a court order to avoid paying unemployment taxes for 110 employees, alleging that the Social Security Act was unconstitutional.

Jackson soon had a valuable ally on his side: Charlie Wyzanski moved to the Justice Department. The president had been impressed by Wyzanski's lightning-swift mind and cogent analysis of the court's NRA decision, and he decided the young lawyer would be a valuable addition to the attorney general's staff. FDR invited Wyzanski to lunch and asked him a few pointed questions. A few months later, Frankfurter called Wyzanski to tell him a new position was being created for him. He would serve as a special assistant to the attorney general, defending legislation he had helped to write.[10]

Frances had early spotted Wyzanski's potential and had made sure the brilliant young lawyer was given opportunities to shine before the president. She was sorry to see him leave the Labor Department and she missed him dreadfully, but he would prove useful in his new role. She was already pushing her agenda on the state level, looking to get state minimum wage and maximum hour laws and seeking bans on child labor and home-based work of the kind common in tenement houses.

It happened as workplace conditions began worsening again. As soon as the NRA was dismantled, some companies increased their market share by cutting prices, which they accomplished by drastically cutting wages.[11]

The NRA experience, however, had proved that work-hour limitations and minimum-wage requirements would work. Frances needed to devise a plan that could gain political support and pass constitutional muster.

The first part was easy. It was clear that wage-and-hour limitations *were* workable. Employers could no longer argue that a minimum wage would destroy their businesses because many of the NRA trade groups imposed minimum wages on themselves—salaries they viewed as acceptable, practical, and profitable. Almost six hundred such industry codes had been established under the NRA. Consequently, about 40 percent of the workforce became entitled to a minimum wage of at least 40 cents an hour. An additional fifty-three industries, covering another 16 percent of the workforce, imposed on themselves a minimum wage of 45 cents an hour. Many also had voluntarily restricted work hours, finding that this caused only minor business disruptions. Others voluntarily restricted child labor.[12]

But finding a constitutional way to require a wage and hour policy, on a comprehensive national basis, was more difficult. Characteristically, Frances considered several levels of attack.

One approach was political. In 1936, with Roosevelt sailing to an easy victory, Frances went to the Democratic nominating convention in Philadelphia to try to build her ideas into the party platform. She pushed hard for health insurance but quickly realized that the prospect of national health insurance was temporarily stymied because of disagreements within the medical industry over what form, if any, it should take. So Frances concentrated her efforts on a proposal for wage-and-hour protection for both men and women, with a provision banning child labor and ended up with a platform plank she found "really very satisfactory."[13] She defined the minimum wage as a living wage, or the amount it would take to feed and house a person, provide an education for his children, and leave him enough to enjoy some entertainment. She relied on Father John Ryan's book *The Living Wage in America* for the definition.[14]

The first steps she took on the federal level were limited. The first requirement for a minimum wage occurred with passage of the Walsh-Healey Public Contracts Act, which required that a minimum wage be paid to people manufacturing goods for government purchase. At the time, it was thought that this was the only context in which wages could be federally regulated.

She continued on a second line of attack: state legislation. The Supreme Court viewed state wage-and-hour laws as more acceptable under the Constitution's division of authority—and many states were enacting them. In Pennsylvania, for example, the state adopted a forty-four-hour-a-week limit for women. Ohio, North Carolina, New Hampshire, Vermont, Illinois, Nevada, and Arkansas also shortened their working hours. New minimum wage laws, meanwhile, were passed by New York, Massachusetts, and Oklahoma. Many such laws benefited only women because the courts had shown themselves inclined to accept such workplace restrictions on the grounds that they protected the health of mothers and potential mothers. Frances wanted men to benefit from shorter hours, too.

Frances promoted state legislation by holding annual conferences of state labor regulators, giving out awards for those who had managed to get new laws passed in their states. She had found that some officials would enact rules in which they had only tepid interest if they foresaw the prospect of getting a blue ribbon before their peers for their accomplishments. Such competitive spirit enabled her to give out many ribbons, and workers in those states were the real beneficiaries.[14]

Over time, however, Frances became increasingly convinced that federal laws were needed because of what she called the "runaway shop." When New York enacted workplace regulation, such as the ten-hour-a-day work limit for women, companies simply moved across state lines. Oppressive work conditions simply shifted elsewhere, and jobs in the first "reform" state were lost. Now, however, the Supreme Court began attacking state laws as well.

*R*oosevelt got angrier but Frances thought time and persuasion would bring the Supreme Court around.

In 1935, she received a dinner invitation from an unlikely source, Justice James McReynolds, who was adamantly opposed to Roosevelt's policies. Frances accepted. During the meal the southern gentleman turned to her and asked with a chuckle whether the president was considering "breaking up the Supreme Court."[15]

"Well, Mr. Justice, I haven't heard that," she said. "I'm sure I don't know how he would do it. Perhaps you could give me a hint."

He laughed at her comeback but pressed on, Frances recalled.

"Oh well, there are some of them who would be glad to retire . . . if they felt sure they were going to get their salaries for life . . ." McReynolds said.

"Oh, Mr. Justice, really? You wouldn't do that, would you?" Frances responded with exquisite politeness and feigned regret.

"Certainly not!" he said. "I will never leave the court until I'm carried out."

Frances recognized McReynolds as a crafty old fox who was using her to deliver a message. The Depression had put real pressure on the federal budget and some justices believed their pensions were not secure enough to retire. If they could be reassured, they might step down, and then they could be replaced. She hustled back to the White House with this news.

Oddly enough, Roosevelt didn't leap at the chance to resolve the Supreme Court dilemma. It became apparent to Frances that a more radical plan was afoot. Frances thought Attorney General Cummings had persuaded the president to force a confrontation. Cummings undoubtedly knew that if only nine posts were available on the Supreme Court, he had little chance of being selected, but if the Court were to be expanded he might have a shot, particularly if a grateful Roosevelt wanted to thank him for dramatically changing its composition. She became convinced that Cummings was the "author, instigator and persuader of this whole Supreme Court plan."[16]

Frances watched helplessly as the ill-fated political foray to pack the Court proceeded. She believed Cummings attempted to stir the president to rage against the Court and eventually succeeded. She had made it clear to FDR that she opposed his plan. But while many saw the Roosevelt court-packing plan as evidence of megalomania, Frances saw it as proof of how easy the president was to manipulate.

"I have never been one who believed that Roosevelt loved power for its own sake. He was too lazy. A lazy man never really loves power. Lazy men get on a track where they can't pull back and in order to keep on they've got to have some power, but if they had realized all that it led to, they might never have gotten on track. Roosevelt was really lazy."[17]

On this issue, Roosevelt allowed Cummings to lead him, Frances believed, because the president "wasn't a good lawyer" and didn't really comprehend what he was doing. By blaming it on Cummings, Frances may have been subconsciously trying to exculpate the president. The episode represented a troubling failure of "political judgement" that left her dismayed.[18]

Roosevelt kept quiet about his planned counter-assault on the Supreme Court until he had won reelection in 1936. Then, in February 1937, he unveiled the plan to Democratic party insiders, including Cabinet officials. Frances recalled that Cummings rose to describe the plan, and she noticed that FDR had that odd look on his face and was pulling his lip down over his teeth.

Under the proposed court reorganization plan, the president would be given the power to add up to six additional judges to the Supreme Court if seated justices declined to retire at age seventy.

In a fireside chat the next month, FDR told his listeners that "new and younger blood" was needed on the court, particularly because, he said, the justices had placed the country at economic risk by opposing New Deal legislation.

Congressman Hatton Sumners, chairman of the House Judiciary Committee, tried to dissuade FDR, Frances recalled. Sumners had been told privately that if judicial pensions were assured, two or three justices would retire. He had been pulling levers to pass such a bill and ease the justices out gracefully, without the need for a public confrontation. On March 1, a bill guaranteeing full pensions for the justices became law. Roosevelt praised it, but persisted in his plan.

This time, however, Frances's advice to the president fell on deaf ears.

The court-packing bill, in fact, caused a firestorm of controversy. It gave Southern conservatives a good reason to part ways with the president, whose liberal policies had made them increasingly uneasy. Even Roosevelt supporters saw it as an attack on the constitutional separation of powers. Wyzanski wanted to resign from the Department of Justice immediately—but Justice Augustus Hand persuaded him to stay. Roosevelt, however, dug in his heels and lost much political goodwill.

And simultaneously, for reasons that remain not entirely clear and that have much been debated by scholars ever since, the problem was quietly resolving itself. Frances called what happened that year a true "historic event." [19]

Within months, the court decided a wage-and-hour case arriving under a state law. Frances had not even been aware the case was on the docket. But when she reviewed the decision, she realized that lightning had suddenly struck. The Court sustained the state's labor law by a 5–4 vote. Both Chief Justice Charles Evans Hughes and Justice Owen Roberts had voted for it. When Frances learned what had happened, she immediately realized that Roberts, the husband of her girlhood friend Elizabeth, had been brought around. Delightedly, she rushed that afternoon to Roberts's home. She threw her arms around the man and hugged him.

"Owen, I am so proud of you," she said. "I'm just so delighted to know you. I'm proud of you. I think this is marvelous. A man of your standing and intelligence who is not afraid to change his mind!"

He looked at her sheepishly, a little embarrassed by her display of affection.

"Really, do you think so?" he asked. She told him she believed he would be widely praised for his decision.

"You know, it was very possible to differentiate between this case and some of the earlier cases," he said. "I can explain it to you. They were not exactly the same."

Frances said she believed him but never asked exactly how he had come to make the distinction because she couldn't see the legal distinction herself. What mattered was that the votes had changed. A rhyming jibe encapsulated the episode: It was the "switch in time that saved nine."

Owen's wife told Frances that her husband had been visited that summer at his farm in the Pennsylvania Dutch country by Chief Justice Hughes, who engaged him in a heart-to-heart conversation over several days, poring over Court decisions together. Frances had also been talking frequently with Roberts about the legal issues while visiting his wife at their Washington home. In that informal family setting, Frances had explained her New Deal goals to the justice.

Some people believed that Roosevelt's threats to pack the Court had intimidated the justices into ruling differently. Frances, on the other hand, thought a few had retired and others had simply come to shift their views. Her opinion was shared by Robert Jackson, the assistant attorney general, who was himself elevated to the Supreme Court in 1941.

"I think that the Court in the early days had felt that the New Deal was a sporadic and passing thing; that the people of the country hadn't really in 1932 given a mandate for it," Jackson said. "I think that when the 1936 elections came about, Justice Roberts, and perhaps some of the others, felt that such measures were a real-felt necessity on the part of the people of the country and that the Court ought not to strive to support objections to it."[20]

In Jackson's opinion, the court-packing plan began dying when the Supreme Court handed down opinions favorable to administration policies. After that, Jackson said, "it seemed pretty clear . . . that the court plan wouldn't have any popular appeal."

Soon all of the Court decisions rolled their way. Wyzanski defended the Wagner Act—the National Labor Relations Act, which Wyzanski hadn't really supported—before the Supreme Court and did such an admirable job that the opposing attorney, John W. Davis, said it was the "most virtuoso performance" in the High Court. Then Wyzanski and Robert Jackson together argued in defense of the Social Security Act. Both innovative measures were upheld.[21]

With the Court now viewing cases in a new light, Frances turned her attention back to her substantive plans, working swiftly to develop wage-and-hour legislation. She prepared a draft and took it to Roosevelt for review. His presidential campaign had included a plank supporting wage-and-hour laws. Roosevelt clearly liked the law she had crafted, but when Frances asked when it would be introduced he said he preferred to "let it ride a while."[22]

Time passed. The president did nothing to push the bill forward. Frances mentioned it at Cabinet meetings to enlist support from other officials. She also mentioned that Senator Wagner would sponsor it. But she noticed that FDR was once again pulling his lip down over his teeth. He told her to wait.

Another month passed. Frances raised it with him again privately, urging him to get it to Congress before the session adjourned.

"Mmm, well perhaps, but not too early, Frances, not too early," he said.

"What do you mean?"

"If you get it in too early, they forget about what you've done for them when they come to vote," he said. He laughed as Frances recoiled. He had decided to put it off for a year so that he could reap maximum political gain. He wanted to win passage of the bill closer to the 1938 midterm elections.

In May 1937, Roosevelt finally sent the wage-and-hour bill to Congress. As Frances wanted, it restricted hours and limited child labor. It also called for minimum wages to be set within industries, varying by region, with advisory boards calculating what the amounts should be, based on the cost of living in those regions and reflecting the wide variation in industry operating costs. The minimum wage could be lower in places where the cost of living was lower, and should be higher where it cost workers more to live. Frances opposed the idea of a flat minimum wage to be set by Congress because it lacked adequate flexibility to reflect regional differences.

Reaction to the proposal was dramatic. The National Association of Manufacturers strongly opposed it. A group of conservative southern congressmen, including a Democrat from Texas named Martin Dies, sought to trap it within the rules committee so it could not go to a vote.[23]

Northern congressmen, meanwhile, worried that permitting a lower wage in the South would contribute to job flight south, as employers relocated to find a hospitable workforce. They had already seen many jobs migrate south as they instituted workforce protections, such as unemployment insurance and higher wages and benefits.

Moreover, the recent experience of the NRA—bureaucracy run amok—made other congressmen worry about wage levels being set by government boards. Senator William Borah, for example, a Republican populist supporter of the minimum wage, said he would be wary of any NRA-like boards being named to "deal with the most vital matters of human life."[24]

The AFL's Green, meanwhile, lobbied for a flat minimum wage nationwide with a forty-hour workweek. Other union leaders, however, who were wary of federal largesse that could undercut the movement worked to block the bill's passage.[25]

Times were changing. Roosevelt had alienated some of his previous allies, such as Vice President Garner and Congressman Sumners, and he had fewer competent hands in the legislature to shepherd his New Deal legislation. Many southern Democrats had become increasingly disaffected. Some of the idealists who had surrounded Roosevelt in the early days had dropped away from his administration or had died. Some newcomers, particularly Tom Corcoran, were inclined, in Frances's view, to enjoy the sport of "playing politics" rather than trying to craft the best legislation on behalf of workers.

Assistant Attorney General Jackson testified in support of the wage-

and-hour bill, in the face of opposition from his boss, Attorney General Cummings, who thought that FDR's support for it weakened the chances of the court-packing bill he so badly wanted. Jackson was finally permitted to testify only after Congressman William Connery specifically pressured Cummings into allowing it.

The first labor standards bill was defeated, but when Congress reconvened in January 1938, Roosevelt took it up anew. FDR decided that the bulky legislation had been defeated in part for the simple reason that it was too long to be easily read. He asked Frances to get it compressed, and she turned over the job to her new labor solicitor, Gerard Reilly. Together they took the condensed bill to the president for review on a Saturday afternoon in 1938.

Frances, Reilly, and FDR sat together in the president's upstairs study deliberating over the measure. Frances had a deciding voice with the president, with whom she was clearly on close terms, Reilly recalled. FDR would suggest things but if Frances disagreed, "she didn't have to say very much before he would back off," Reilly said later.[26]

The bill suffered a setback when Congressman Connery, a New Deal stalwart, died and was replaced by Congresswoman Mary Norton of New Jersey, who had not so far played a large role in labor legislation. She was a compromiser, not an idealist, and the final bill reflected it.

To please the southerners, Norton agreed to a minimum wage too low to be anything but subsistence pay, and to please the northerners she established a single national wage, so that northern business interests would not be disadvantaged. The minimum wage was set at 25 cents an hour, lower than most industries had voluntarily imposed on themselves during the NRA era. The wage increased by 5-cent increments each year for the next five, and rose to 40 cents after seven years. The workweek was set at forty-four hours each week in the first year, forty-two hours in the second year, and forty in the third. To discourage overworking employees, the bill required employees to pay 50 percent premium pay—or time and a half—for any hours worked over those limits, a provision Frances thought sensible. Granting workers the ability to extend their hours was viewed as giving additional flexibility to employers during rush times, while also offering additional pay for workers were willing to put in the extra time. Congress decided not to have wage boards setting minimum pay but to set the minimum wage itself.[27]

The legislative process was a cliffhanger, according to Rose Schneiderman, who said later that she had been "terribly worried about the wages and hours bill and hope[d] desperately that Miss Norton will finally succeed in getting enough names to bring the bill to the floor of the House."[28]

The Fair Labor Standards Act passed in the Senate by a voice vote on June 14, 1938, and in the House by a vote of 291 to 89. Roosevelt signed it on June 25, 1938.

Soon, there was no constitutional threat to face.

The Supreme Court was a very different group than the one that had considered Frances's bills in the early years of the New Deal. Justice Willis Van Devanter retired on June 2, 1937, and Justice George Sutherland retired on January 17, 1938. Pierce Butler died in office on November 16, 1939. Even McReynolds retired, on January 31, 1941. Roosevelt appointees who were more inclined to a worker-friendly viewpoint replaced them. Among those moving on to the High Court were Hugo Black, the vocal proponent of the thirty-hour workweek in 1933; Robert H. Jackson, a friend and admirer of Frances; and Felix Frankfurter, her old ally and colleague from the National Consumers League. In a 1941 ruling, *United States v. Darby,* the newly constituted Supreme Court voiced clear support for the Fair Labor Standards Act.

It was far from the living wage model that progressives had sought. The final bill offered an annual minimum income of $572 a year, when the maintenance level for a family of four was $1,261 in that year.

Many industries were excluded, but the new bill covered 11 million workers, including some three hundred thousand who were earning less than twenty-five cents an hour at the time of adoption.

Passage of the Fair Labor Standards Act ushered in a new way of life for many workers, permitting them an opportunity for rest and relaxation. Harry Kelber of Brooklyn, a young retail clerk, later recalled the shock he felt when he first had an eight-hour workday, after years of working twelve hours on weekdays and seventeen hours on Saturday. "I remember walking out of the place in the daylight," he said. "When the hours were reduced, people were amazed, almost felt guilty to leave after only eight hours. I couldn't believe it."[29]

But Frances's success proved to be another step toward her undoing. Many Republicans opposed the minimum wage, as well as maximum hour limitations and restrictions on child labor. Southern Democrats, including Dies, shared the same perspective. They had gone along with the early Roosevelt initiatives because of the desperate conditions in the Great Depression. But at heart they were opposed to much of the program. From this point on, Republicans and many conservative Democrats allied in opposition to the woman they saw as the agent of unacceptable changes.

Chapter 27

IMPEACHMENT

*I*n 1939, Frances achieved another, less desirable historic first. She also became the first female Cabinet officer that Congress sought to impeach. Impeachment is such an extraordinary tool that the U.S. House of Representatives launched such proceedings only about sixty times between 1889 and 2001. Usually, it occurs only in the gravest cases of wrongdoing, or when one political party hopes to pull down another.

The charges against Frances arose from the successful waterfront strike in San Francisco that took place in 1934. Harry Bridges, the Australian longshoreman she once called the "inexplicable man who came from the mist," had led the city's workers to an unprecedented general strike, bringing workers together across the traditional lines of particular industries. Mass worker actions, the unionists' dream, became a reality, and labor conditions improved across the board. Businessmen, however, immediately called for Bridges's deportation as a dangerous Communist. While it was legal for an American to be a Communist or run a campaign on the Communist ticket, foreigners who had pledged to work for the overthrow of the capitalist system were subject to deportation.

Bridges denied being a Communist, but he admitted that he had worked with Communists and relied on their help. Frances asked her department's immigration officials to investigate. The reports seemed inconclusive to her. Some of the most damning accusations against Bridges were made by people who were paid by employers' groups. Other accusations came from rival labor leaders and those reports also were questionable. Some accusers were AFL partisans, while Bridges had allied himself with the upstart CIO.

Frances wanted to ensure that Bridges got a fair hearing. She refused to be stampeded into deporting a successful labor organizer on specious charges. She knew the Immigration Service had been used to get rid of "militant and effective" labor leaders.[1] George Woodward Wickersham had told her privately that the practice of deporting foreigners on flimsy grounds was more widespread than anyone realized. Frances recalled the night when she had seen immigration officials surreptitiously disposing of documents a few days after her inauguration. She knew that corrupt officials had been on the payroll then, and though she had cleaned house, she suspected some might remain.

Frances knew of one specific deportation case designed to stall a union drive. Under pressure from employer groups, her predecessor, Labor Secretary William Doak, deported labor leaders who led silk industry strikes in Paterson, New Jersey. In her opinion, Doak ordered them out of the country "merely because they had been active and successful in leading labor movements and in leading strikes."[2]

Frances also was skeptical about efforts to deport people who did not seem to have a real allegiance to communism or who had been duped into joining. The Immigration Service had handled one such case before her arrival. A Hungarian-born miner in Harlan County, Kentucky, who spoke no English, was convinced by a Hungarian-speaking Communist Party organizer that joining the party was equivalent to joining a union because it would help the working people. He signed up, paid a few dollars in dues, and then got exposed as a Communist. He was ordered deported. His lawyer appealed, but the court supported the deportation, and he was sent back to Hungary. Frances thought the penalty excessive for what she called a "trifling" involvement with a political movement dedicated to overthrowing the U.S. government.[3]

For these reasons, Frances tried to slow the pace of deportations. "We have virtually decided to let left-wing trade union people stay here, and cancel deportation warrants," Wyzanski explained.[4]

As allegations against Bridges intensified, Frances conducted a private inquiry. In 1935 or 1936, while visiting San Francisco, she called on Archbishop Edward Hanna and asked his opinion of Bridges, who she was told came from a devout Roman Catholic family. Hanna said that Bridges's daughter was enrolled as a day pupil in a Catholic convent school and that Bridges met regularly with a priest on the waterfront. Frances thought it unlikely that a true Communist would be that religious or spend money to send his daughter to parochial school. She thought Bridges's views reflected the more politicized European-style labor activism, uncommon in the United States but not dangerous. She did not particularly like Bridges, and she found some reports of his behavior distasteful. Officials in Portland, Oregon, eager to find evidence of Communism, tape-recorded Bridges while he was committing adultery with a fellow union member's wife.

"Personally she detested him," Wyzanski wrote later. "She would have been glad for the sake of womankind he was not on the scene, but she thought there was nothing to the suggestion that he was deportable."[5]

She encountered Bridges a second time during another visit to San Francisco. She had made an unannounced visit to a hiring hall, an important gesture, since the creation of these halls had generated fierce debate during the 1934 strike. She was swarmed by men who told her how much its existence had improved their lives. Many of the men did not own telephones, and the hiring hall managers scrambled to relay messages when they got a shot at a job. It was a lot better than standing on a cold pier begging for day labor.

Word of the secretary of labor's visit soon spread to nearby restaurants and saloons. Before long, Bridges arrived. This time, Bridges sported a necktie and looked more like an office manager than a longshoreman. Bridges's rapidly growing union was gaining power up and down the West Coast, and he had moved into the CIO leadership. Even so, Bridges maintained the same modest lifestyle. They had a short, pleasant, unremarkable discussion and Frances left.

Then, in the summer of 1937, more troubling allegations about Bridges surfaced. Raphael Bonham, who headed the Seattle immigration office, gathered affidavits from four witnesses who swore that they had seen Bridges engaged in Communist activities. They provided a copy of a Communist membership card issued to Harry Dorgan; Dorgan was Bridges's mother's maiden name. Labor Department solicitor Reilly went to the West Coast to investigate. Harry Lundeberg, president of the Maritime Federation of the Pacific, confirmed accounts of Bridges coordinating Communist Party members and giving them secure longshoremen's jobs. It wasn't an open-and-shut case. Lundeberg was also a Bridges rival. Under oath, Bridges denied that he was a Communist.[6]

The allegations in the Seattle report struck Frances as "mostly hearsay, vague and indefinite." Nevertheless, she decided to consult Roosevelt. She went to Hyde Park on a Saturday, lunched with the family, and toured the estate with Roosevelt driving a car that had been specially altered to accommodate his withered legs. They stopped on a promontory, and the president turned to her.

"What's the problem?" he asked. Frances explained the situation and described Bridges's unionizing success. FDR's first reaction was that of the "ordinary American liberal," Frances recalled, inclined to discount the dangers of Communist thought. He laughed at the account of this allegedly dangerous radical playing his mandolin at night. She also described the more serious charges made against Bridges and told Roosevelt she was weighing these allegations against Bridges's obvious success as a labor leader.

"Has he done anything to overthrow the government?" Roosevelt asked, and Frances said he had not. "Then why in the world should a man be punished for what he thinks, for what he believes? That's against the Constitution."[7]

Frances explained that immigration law required deportation if he were, indeed, a Communist. She asked how to proceed. Roosevelt told her to carry out the law but not too aggressively. Within a few months, in March 1938, her agency began proceedings to deport Bridges, with the hearing set for April.

Then a federal appeals court overruled a deportation order involving another foreigner accused of Communist affiliation. The case was remanded to the lower court. The decision threw into question twelve ongoing Communist-linked immigration cases, including the Bridges matter. Department solicitor Reilly suggested they ask the Supreme Court to resolve the question, and the attorney general agreed. Frances put all the cases on hold until the Court clarified the matter.

The delay drove critics wild. In early 1938, the House of Representatives had created a Special Committee to Investigate Un-American Activities, led by Texas Democrat Martin Dies. It generated publicity by charging that Communism posed more danger to the United States than Nazism. An early committee witness charged that Ickes, among other federal employees, was a Communist. Ickes wanted to respond forcefully to Dies, but FDR asked him not to do so, saying that Dies had become too powerful to confront head-on. The public bought into the committee's allegations, and its work was extended for another year. Soon the committee put Frances in its sights, and conservative newspapers fanned the flame with stories about her plot to protect known Communists.[8]

Dies attacked Frances specifically for refusing to deport Bridges. His public denunciations came as the Democratic Party was splitting in half. Southerners had grown increasingly indignant at Roosevelt's policies. Frances garnered hatred in the South because of her sex, her active support of the Fair Labor Standards Act, and her unfortunate reference years earlier to southerners not owning shoes.

Warfare between the AFL and the CIO also played a role. Bridges was affiliated with the CIO, which gave an AFL partisan, John Frey of the Metal Trades Union, an opening to prod Dies to push the investigation. Frey wanted Bridges deported because it would be a blow to the rival movement.

External events also came to Dies's aid. With tensions mounting in Europe, anti-immigrant sentiment escalated. Frances noted that it had become customary for people to associate two words—*undesirable* and *alien*—and, indeed, a growing number of Americans considered aliens undesirable. Conservatives opposing labor union growth were irritated that aliens active in unions could remain in the United States. And Frances developed a reputation for supporting aliens because she pushed for European refugees to enter the United States to escape Nazism.

American patriots couldn't understand why Bridges, a U.S. resident for more than twenty years, never became an American citizen. Frances, an Anglophile, thought it understandable that an Australian might have a sentimental connection to the mother country that would make him reluctant to drop his citizenship. She even thought Bridges's failure to become a U.S. citizen made it less likely that he was a Communist because U.S. citizenship would have allowed him to do mischief more easily. For his part, Bridges said his efforts to become a citizen had been delayed, partly because at some points he did not have the money to pursue the process.

As the debate intensified, Frances herself became the subject of investigations. Her long-ago decision to alter her age meant that the official records did not match the year she gave as her birth, and some suggested that she was an imposter. Conservatives whispered that Frances was really a Russian Jewish immigrant named Mathilda Watsky, masquerading as Frances Perkins. A genealogist scouring court records found a marriage license in Newton, Massachusetts, that listed a wedding of a

Paul Wilson to a woman named Watsky. There were obvious discrepancies: Watsky's birth date was 1892, making her twelve years younger than Frances, but that didn't discourage her opponents. After a while, the Newton court clerk realized something was amiss and contacted Frances to warn her that the license was being misrepresented as evidence of her supposed foreign identity. But by then even some longtime Republican friends had come to believe the preposterous story was true.

Anti-Semitism, meanwhile, grew more visible. An anonymous flyer bearing a Star of David showed up around the country. It featured a list of names, including Frances's, implying she was Jewish. Frances was incredulous, then infuriated, by the tactic. The false reports "proved that I was a Jew, and that if I were a Jew, I was also a Red, and if I were a Red, I was protecting Bridges," Frances said later.[9]

Another rumor suggested a personal relationship between Frances and Bridges. By one account circulating in San Francisco, Bridges had visited Frances at her Virginia estate. In truth, Frances had never met with Bridges in any home setting and didn't own an estate. Wilder fantasies circulated that Bridges was married to Frances's niece or her daughter or that Frances was Bridges's secret bride.

She finally decided to directly address the question of her identity. To handle the matter, she responded to a letter from a friend, then arranged for it to be distributed to anyone asking the question. In it, she laid out the details of her New England ancestry, tracing both her paternal and maternal ancestors. "All of the people were Protestant Christians, most of them members of the various denominations found in New England during the 17th, 18th and 19th centuries," she wrote. "There were no Jews in my ancestry. If I were a Jew, I would make no secret of it. On the contrary I would be proud to acknowledge it."[10]

She listed her marriage date as September 26, 1913, and spelled out her marriage to Paul and his Northern European ancestry. She noted that the rumor about her background "appears to be political as those who have been circulating it do not know me and therefore can have no personal ill will toward me. The utter un-Americanism of such a whispering campaign, the appeal to racial prejudice and the attempt at political propaganda by unworthy innuendo must be repugnant to all honorable men and women."

She ended by asking the friend to tell anyone who seemed similarly confused the facts of the matter. In the letter, however, Frances perpetuated another fiction about herself—her incorrect birth year—an action that made her other statements subject to continuing questions.

By early fall of 1938, four years after Bridges led the San Francisco strike, conservative anger reached a boiling point. On September 9, Dies gave a speech at New York's Plaza Hotel, at a meeting Frances believed was funded by the German Bund, charging that Frances was "flirting with impeachment" if she didn't deport Bridges.

Frances had never heard of a Cabinet officer being impeached, and she asked the solicitor if it were even possible. "Oh, they can't impeach you," she was assured.[11] It wasn't surprising they didn't know. The last impeachment attempt against a Cabinet officer had occurred in 1876, when Secretary of War William W. Belknap faced impeachment charges after resigning amid allegations he had accepted bribes.

An avalanche of criticism descended on Frances, with many commentators attacking her for protecting Bridges. Frances herself was baffled by Dies, wondering why the Texas Democrat attacked her so personally. She wracked her brain to see if she had inadvertently offended him, as she had Senator Harrison, but she couldn't recall any incident.

As a woman, Frances understood, too, that she attracted different kinds of comments, often more malicious ones, than her male counterparts. Visiting Chicago, Margaret Bondfield, the former British labor secretary, attended "I'd Rather Be Right," a political satire spoofing Roosevelt and his Cabinet. It was presented as good-natured satire, and many Cabinet officials attended. But the tone of the jibes about Frances was distinctive. "There is a strain of venom in the portrayal of Frances Perkins, which is absent in the others, suggesting that she is sour, silly and sloppy—attributes which definitely do not fit," Bondfield observed in her diary that night.[12]

In Washington, Frances shared her feelings with Bondfield, the only other woman in the Western world who had held such a lofty government position. "America gives lip service to democracy, but is far from practicing it," Frances said in December 1938. That same week, at a buffet dinner with female American labor officials, Bondfield asked why they weren't speaking out more forcefully for Frances. She received no good answer.[13]

In January 1939, the blow fell. Congressman J. Parnell Thomas, a Republican from New Jersey, introduced an impeachment charge against Frances, and also against several other top Labor Department officials.

It alleged that they "had failed, neglected and refused to enforce . . . the immigration laws of the United States; and have conspired together to violate the immigration laws of the United States; and have defrauded the United States by coddling and protecting from deportation certain aliens," namely, Harry Bridges. The charge alleged that Bridges, a native of Australia and a British subject, was admitted to the United States on April 12, 1920, and filed two declarations of intent to become a U.S. citizen, which he allowed to expire. It charged that he was affiliated with the Communist Party that "believed in, advised, advocated or taught the overthrow by force or violence of the Government of the United States."

Thomas charged that Frances had protected Bridges because of liberal activist pressure. Thomas had Dies and other Democrats on his side. "Many Democrats as well feel that this woman ought to get out of the Cabinet," Dies told reporters.[14]

The House "sat in unusual silence as the clerk read the measure," said the *Washington Post.*[15]

Newspaper headlines around the country trumpeted the impeachment charge, and Thomas and Dies scored political points. Humorists, meanwhile, portrayed Frances as a foolish old woman. A cartoon in the *Miami Herald* showed a matronly lady throwing her hands out to protect a beady-eyed crouching man labeled "communist Bridges," a hulking unshaven man labeled "undesirable alien," and a lazy-looking lout labeled "sit-down strike." The caption across the top said: "Don't You Dare!"[16]

Kinder critics depicted Frances not as a Communist enemy but as a dupe. Her activities were monitored by the Justice Department under FBI director J. Edgar Hoover, and they cited an analysis, by reporter Benjamin Stolberg, in the *Saturday Evening Post* in July 1940: "Miss Perkins is not a Communist, not even remotely a Communist sympathizer. She is as true a Democrat in her convictions as I have ever known. But she represents the classic type of soft-minded liberals whom the Stalinists behind the scenes know how to exploit for their own purposes."[17]

But even in a Congress dominated by Democrats, almost no one rose to Frances's defense. Her only supporters were the crusty Irishmen of Tammany Hall, often tainted by corruption themselves.

"The Congress was full of men of breeding, intelligence and education, many of whom I had come to know socially and in political relationships somewhat," Frances said. "When these things were said, they all sat in their seats, except for a few. Who do you think were the people who got up and shouted, demanded the floor, accosted the speaker, screaming, 'I claim personal privilege!' which is the one thing that will get you your turn out of order? It was the Tammany Hall delegation, so help me God. Bless their souls. . . . I just cannot forget that. Nothing ever touched me so in this world."[18]

Part of the problem was that few Washingtonians at that time recognized the new threat posed by men like Dies, and they tended to think Frances was overreacting. Thomas I. Emerson, with the National Labor Relations Board, said most young New Dealers thought the committee's charges were "without substance . . . They tended to treat the whole thing as a laughing matter more than anything." Soon they would better understand Dies's tactics, which would be duplicated in later years by Senator Joseph McCarthy.[19]

Roosevelt never mentioned these events to her, nor did he take action to publicly support her. He gave not even a "sympathetic word," she recalled.[20] She persuaded herself that, because of his own New England blood, he knew that discussing it would only make it harder for her.

In fact, FDR made light of the impeachment attempt in his press conferences. Asked to comment on the "possibility of impeaching Secretary Perkins," FDR pretended he hadn't heard and innocently asked, "Increasing what?," drawing laughter. Asked for additional comment, he said it was "not yet" time to discuss the matter. Finally, he avoided mentioning Frances at all. In 1939, her lowest point, he mentioned her in press conferences only four times—a stark contrast to the first couple of years of his presidency when he referred to her frequently at these events.[21]

Frances's personal friends rallied around her during these months, but she found their commiseration too much to bear. She grew remote because their condolences added to her distress. She seemed cold, but her ability to surround herself with a steel wall and deflect the outside world carried her through.

"Of course, if I had wept at all, or if I'd let myself down at all, I would have disintegrated," she said later. "That's the kind of person which we New Englanders are. We disintegrate if we do these things. All the quality in us of integrity and the ability to keep our heads clear and make decisions and take actions which are uninfluenced by our personal suffering, or the personal effect on ourselves, that integrity would have scattered, and I would not have had that inner core within myself which makes it possible for me to rely upon myself under the guidance of God to do the right thing and make the right decision and take the consequence."[22]

Shaken to her core, Frances turned once again to her grandmother's teachings: Take the high ground. Avoid doing things that will make you appear silly or cheap. Frances remembered this advice and comported herself politely and courteously, hiding the rage she felt underneath. She went to church each morning to help her face the ongoing ordeal and seek assurance of the support of a higher power. She prayed for her enemies, including Dies, Thomas, and their associates. Since she found it hard to mention their names in her prayers, she prayed for them as a group: those who make false accusations.

Frances also made frequent visits to the All Saints Convent in Catonsville, Maryland, a stone structure where semicloistered nuns devoted their lives to prayer, meditation, and service to handicapped children. The nuns wore traditional long black gowns and wimples on their heads, and gathered for services up to five times daily. They grew their own food, ate simple meals, and observed vows of silence. Each weekend, the nuns hosted a small number of women on spiritual retreat. All were expected to follow their schedule and refrain from speaking.

Even before the impeachment, Frances would stay there two to three days at a time. She had visited so often that she had become an associate, wearing a modified white cap to signify her close association with the group. It was ironic that Frances, who drove men to distraction by talking too much, actually retreated into complete silence regularly.

Frances had formed a close bond with Mother Laura, the Mother Superior of the convent at the time, and spent hours pondering spiritual issues and how to lead a godly life in a secular world. She and Mother Laura discussed social welfare legislation. Frances worked on drafts of the Social Security Act and Fair Labor Standards Act late at night at the convent. The nuns found her in the early morning hours in the chapel, praying on her hands and knees for guidance. If they were cleaning the room, they sometimes needed to mop around her because she was so consumed in her thoughts. In the afternoon, she often worked in the gardens, tending a lovely grouping of irises at the convent's entry. She tried to maintain her anonymity. "We always tried to protect her privacy," recalled Sister Virginia. "We called her Mrs. Paul Wilson."[23]

But Frances could disappear into the convent only from time to time, and for the remainder of her life, she existed in an often-unpleasant reality. Ickes urged her to respond forcefully to the charges, and so Frances repeatedly asked when the impeachment hearing would be held, so that she could prepare her defense. Congressman Hatton Sumners, like Dies a Democrat from Texas, chaired the House Judiciary Committee. He had soured on the administration after the court-packing effort. Sumners was always polite and courtly to Frances, and he told her not to worry. The time isn't ripe, he would say. Then he told her not to worry about a hearing at all.

Frances grew nearly frantic as the relentless attacks continued, calling Sumners almost daily. "I came to realize that he was playing a delaying game, which made me very nervous," Frances said.[24]

She turned to Wyzanski to draft a response to the charges. By then, he had returned to his Boston law firm, Ropes & Gray, after his disappointment with Roosevelt's court-packing plan. But he spoke frequently with Frances about the impeachment case.

Finally, Sumners picked a hearing date. Frances asked that it be public so that she could make her response before an audience. The committee opted instead to conduct it behind closed doors. Sumners told her he had no power to change the decision, and he added that members had at first opposed the idea of even permitting her to speak. She asked if she could have anyone with her, and the committee reluctantly permitted Gerard "Gerry" Reilly, the department's solicitor, to join her.

On the hearing date, Reilly and Frances went together to the Hill. Many Labor Department employees stopped by her office before she left, wishing her well. When they arrived at Sumner's office, they learned that the committee had already started the meeting. Sumners's secretary told Frances that the committee still wasn't sure whether or not Reilly would be permitted to attend. A few minutes passed, but "it seemed like hours," she said later. Sumner's secretary tried to offer encouragement. "I think it'll be all right, Miss Perkins," she said.[25]

Finally, a clerk emerged and said Reilly would be permitted to enter. The man ushered them into a long, narrow room. At the other end, congressmen sat around a raised mahogany dais, arranged like a horseshoe. In the dim lighting, Frances could barely see their faces.

"I remember that I turned to Gerry and said, 'Do you remember the priest that walked beside Joan of Arc when she went to the stake?' "

"Oh, yes," Gerry said softly.

Frances found herself strangely transfixed by a sense that she was entering a "den of lions" but that she should not be afraid. "I had a sense of a spiritual companion," she said. "As the Christians would say, 'My Lord walked beside me to the jaws of death.' I had a sense of the Lord Jesus looking after his people and walking beside them."

Sumners made an opening statement. Frances started by thanking the legislators for "their enormous sense of justice, their great courtesy, their wisdom, their statesmanship and everything else I could think of." She headed directly to the statement that Wyzanski had written.

"At the outset, I want to make clear that whatever action has been taken in Washington by the Department of Labor in the Bridges and in the Strecker case there has been no 'conspiracy,' " she began. She reiterated her belief in and support for the premise that people who pose a "clear and present danger" to the U.S. government deserve no sympathy, and stressed her own opposition to communism.

Frances laid out the facts of the Bridges case as she knew them, including the investigation, the appeals court decision, and the attorney general's decision to hold back until the Supreme Court had ruled. She concluded: "The problems which the immigration laws present are serious, intricate and of the highest public importance. They have a peculiar significance to the future of our country, for it is incumbent upon those who administer the immigration laws to aim at two important goals: First, to preserve this country, its institutions and ideals, from foreign forces which present a clear and present danger to the continuance of our way of living; and second, to show those aliens who together with their families are soon to become our fellow citizens that American institutions operate without fear or favor, in a spirit of fair-play, and with a desire to do justice to the stranger within our gates, as well as to the native born."[26]

From time to time, congressmen tried to break in, but Sumners overruled them. At last, Frances asked if there were any questions. The congressmen began "sharpening their knives" and preparing to dissect her views. Some questions were friendly, but other congressmen could hardly contain their contempt for Perkins, "shaking [in their] wrath and indignation," she said later.[27]

She realized that much of their anger was directed at what they saw as the problem of "undesirable aliens" who were undermining, even contaminating, the American way of life.

She turned to the congressmen who asked the most outrageous questions and mildly asked them to repeat themselves, knowing that "nobody ever repeats a scurrilous thing a second time."[28] It was hard to stick to this tactic in responding to Thomas, the author of the impeachment charge, whose voice trembled with rage as he questioned her, but she maintained her composure.

Leaving Capitol Hill, Frances felt drained but certain she had done the right thing. She didn't think she would be formally impeached, which would require a vote by the entire House. But the hearing had exposed a disturbing split emerging in the Democratic Party. Some members were becoming more conservative, more reactionary than their Republican peers. The splintering made the members' loyalty to the president uncertain and undependable.

"It's just like being tried for any crime before a court," she said. "You don't know what's going to impress the jury . . . You fear that. You see in some of the members of Congress the makings of one of the most prejudiced, ignorant, irresponsible, and inattentive juries imaginable."[29]

On March 24, 1939, the House Committee unanimously ruled that there were not sufficient facts to support an impeachment charge, and the resolution was tabled. That was formally the end of the matter. A minority report prepared by the ten Republican committee members, however, said that Frances's behavior called for the "official and public disapproval of this Committee." Congressman Thomas called the action a "censure" several days later, and Frances was forever tarnished by that lie, which many people believed. In fact, of course, no majority of the committee had condemned her.[30]

In a radio address a few days later, Congressman Thomas reiterated his support of her impeachment anew. He attacked Frances for permitting more people to enter the United States, noting that the number of immigrants had risen from 163,000 at the end of June 1934 to 231,000 in the year ending June 1937.[31]

On June 12, 1939, the Supreme Court sustained the appeals court ruling that had caused the delay in Bridges's case. For the first time, it also set standards for determining if a person was truly affiliated with a communist organization in a way that posed a risk to the U.S. government. The decision meant that the Immigration Department could proceed with Bridges's case, which it did soon thereafter.

To avoid potential conflicts, Frances sought an outside judge to hear the case. She selected James Landis, a young man who had risen meteorically to become dean of Harvard Law School and was believed to be a future Supreme Court nominee. She called Landis to her office to discuss the case, and he decided to accept it. Frances named him a special immigration inspector so he would have the power to conduct the hearing. Throughout the process, she kept Roosevelt out of the loop, so he would not be damaged by association with the case.

Bridges's attorneys, angling to turn the event into a public spectacle, sought to have the hearing in downtown San Francisco. Fearing violence, Frances decided instead to hold the event at the U.S. immigration office on Angel Island in San Francisco Bay. The secure location allowed the Labor Department to control attendance. "Besides, it will be nice and cool on Angel Island," Perkins added disingenuously.[32]

Landis took the case mostly because he had a free summer and thought it would be interesting. He didn't know much about Harry Bridges. He accepted the job under the conditions that his report would be made public, that there would be no political interference, and that he would have control of the hearing room. The hearings lasted eight weeks. Landis found the witnesses for the government's deportation case completely unreliable. Some had prior criminal convictions or ethical violations.

The strangest witness showed up in a light tan suit, with an orange handkerchief in his breast pocket. He wore a small pink rosebud in his lapel, and his socks were gray, embellished with a pink design. He admitted he had perjured himself in previous testimony. He testified he had been a Communist Party officer and had known Bridges as an agent with the code name of Rossi. Under cross-examination, it emerged that the man was taking relief checks while working at a roofing company. His testimony actually injured the government's case.

Without question, Bridges admitted that he had sought help for his struggling union campaign from American Communists. But Landis believed that it wasn't clear that Bridges was a Communist himself.

Landis ultimately ruled that the government hadn't proven that Bridges was a Communist, and he decided against deportation. The backlash was immediate: Landis received thousands of letters, most of them excoriating him. Landis's career went into a semipermanent stall. "Afterward, doors that had been open to him in Washington quietly closed," wrote Bridges's biographer Charles P. Larrowe.

Later, Bridges appeared before another hearing officer and a judge, and was ordered deported, but the board of immigration appeals overturned the ruling. Then Francis Biddle, now attorney general, personally reversed that decision, thus reinstating the deportation order, because, as he told Landis, he believed it was "politically wise." Bridges later faced trial for perjury for his testimony—and was acquitted. The whole mess finally ended up in the U.S. Supreme Court, where it was narrowly decided in Bridges's favor.[33]

Bridges finally became a U.S. citizen in 1945 after responding to a final question: "Are you now, or have you ever been, a Communist?" the judge asked. "No, Your Honor," he responded under oath.

Years later, when the Kremlin archives were opened, documents emerged that verified that Bridges had indeed been a Communist agent, known by the code name "Rossi." Critics had been right about his Communist leanings all along. But there was no evidence that his activities damaged the United States. To the contrary, his work on behalf of waterfront workers did much good.[34]

After protecting Bridges enough to ensure him a fair trial, Frances's reputation was left in tatters. And now she faced another huge challenge: the need to save the lives of another flood of European refugees as the Nazis steamrolled across Europe.

Chapter 28

War Clouds
and Refugees

*A*cross the Atlantic Ocean, the Europeans also dealt with the effects of the Great Depression. Adolf Hitler and Benito Mussolini furiously built up their respective war machines, creating a wealth of jobs and an economic recovery in both Germany and Italy. The growing militarization of their societies heightened the risk that war would erupt once more on the European continent.

As the threat increased, so did the ardor of the pacifist movement in the United States. Many Americans were still embittered by the pointless carnage of World War I and wanted the United States to steer clear of yet another European morass. British Prime Minister Neville Chamberlain, who followed a policy of appeasement toward the fascist powers, was as popular in American circles as he was in British.

Public opinion in the 1930s adamantly opposed overseas intervention. In 1935 some fifty thousand veterans marched for peace in Washington, and the same year, 175,000 students nationwide staged a one-hour strike against war. For the next six years, ordinary Americans wrote to legislators and to the Roosevelt administration pleading not to get dragged into the European conflict.[1]

Frances, too, was deluged with mail. One petition from Columbus, Ohio, bore five thousand signatures. "We are definitely opposed to any measure which would directly or indirectly involve America in a foreign war," wrote one Mr. R. J. Hooffstetter.

The tone was frequently strident: "As a citizen and taxpayer, I strongly protest the apparent policy of the present administration to convoy us into war," wrote Mrs. J. Maloney of San Francisco. Some letters were plaintive: "Ma Perkins, I understand you have lots of influence with the president. Why don't you stop him from sending our boys out on the ocean . . . Do you have any children if so I bet they won't go to war it is just the poorer class of people that have to fight your war. the insane asylum won't hold all these mothers."[2]

Frances's friend and roommate Caroline O'Day was a passionate pacifist. During World War I, she had hosted antiwar meetings, and her house was watched by federal agents. She had laughed it off, once famously taking cold lemonade out to the investigators sitting in the hot sun. Now she watched the unfolding events with dismay, appalled at the "fiendish eagerness" of Europeans to fight.[3]

Though uneasy about Hitler, many Americans saw events in Germany as a predictable reaction to the country's deprivations after World War I. They considered Hitler a bombastic bully who Germans would eventually restrain, through assassination if necessary. Some others thought Hitler and Mussolini were right, that forceful stands must be taken against communism, trade unionism, and immorality.

Frances had known of serious problems brewing in Europe since 1933, when Dorothy Thompson described the threat Hitler posed, and Frances began unobtrusively relaxing immigration limits to permit refugees to enter the United States on various travel permits.

From 1933 to early 1938, Frances had stood almost alone in highlighting the plight of German refugees and in urging U.S. government action. She had foresight that others lacked. But once Germany annexed Austria in March 1938, the president finally announced at a Cabinet meeting that he agreed with Frances that developments in Europe meant more refugees needed to be admitted. Some Austrians had committed suicide because they foresaw persecution under Hitler, and Spaniards, facing vengeance at the hands of Francisco Franco, also needed refuge. FDR suggested that the United States "make it as easy as possible" for refugees to enter and defer the question of whether they were here legally for later regulation under the quota laws. Ickes suggested simply amending the immigration laws. Legislators on Capitol Hill would oppose any efforts to boost immigration, they were warned.

Then came Kristallnacht, or "the Night of Broken Glass," on November 9, 1938. Rampaging Nazis burned two hundred synagogues, killed or injured hundreds of Jews, and sent twenty thousand Jews to concentration camps. Americans began to recognize the magnitude of the Nazi threat.

Frances privately asked Roosevelt to combine three years of German visa quotas into one, to bring about two hundred fifty thousand Germans to safety in one year. Roosevelt turned her down but permitted her to extend the visas of some fifteen thousand Germans and Austrians already in the country.

When the State Department learned of her request, George Messersmith, a State Department official, said that he considered the plan "illegal" and would oppose it. But this time Roosevelt backed her. "It would be a cruel and inhumane thing to compel them to leave here in time to get back to Germany. I cannot, in any decent humanity, throw them out."[4]

On the same day that Frances spoke to Roosevelt, Sir Ronald Lindsay, the British ambassador to the United States and a close friend of Frances, recommended to Sumner Welles, the principal State Department official on European policy and immigration, that the British quota of sixty-five thousand permanent immigrants be transferred to Germany on a one-time basis, permitting more Germans to enter the United States. Welles rejected the proposal and "gave Lindsay a rather pompous lecture" about visas not being used like party invitations.[5]

While the State Department prevaricated and procrastinated, Frances was flooded with desperate pleas for help from the friends and family members of people seeking refuge in the United States. She intervened in hundreds of individual instances. Her friend Edward Bernays believed she had been instrumental in helping his relative, Austrian psychiatrist Sigmund Freud, to escape. Another friend wrote to thank her for her successful efforts on behalf of "that nice Von Trapp family."

In the summer of 1938, Frances had spent several weeks touring Europe, meeting with dignitaries and visiting the ILO, and what she witnessed made her wonder whether America was adequately prepared for what lay ahead. She had many influential European friends who feted her as a visiting dignitary. They told her of their fears. But in talking to ordinary people on the street, something Frances always enjoyed doing, she actually became alarmed.

Hitler was exerting power in many places. His presence was palpable at the summer music festival in Salzburg. He had a mountain retreat just over the border at Berchtesgaden, Germany, on a peak near the city.

At night, a powerful searchlight scanned the sky. The psychological effect, Frances noticed, was "extraordinary," making people anxious that they may have displeased him.

Hitler seemed all-knowing, perhaps invincible. The Austrian economy had been bad for years, and several laborers asked Frances if she had been to Germany. They wondered about reports that unemployment had evaporated there. "Do you think it is better there? Perhaps it is better there," she heard them say.[6]

In England, Frances saw men digging defensive trenches in the lovely gardens in St. James's Park and Green Park. "Up until that time, I and I suppose a lot of other people, thought, 'This will pass. This is talk. This crowd in Germany are just talking, open threats,' " Frances said. "But when I saw British soldiers and park laborers engaged in digging trenches, taking down iron railings that would have impeded the flow of people into the parks to get into the trenches, one realized how serious it was."[7]

What Frances saw in France also left her unsettled. U.S. ambassador Bill Bullitt assured her that France was war ready and could vanquish the Germans, but Frances was not nearly so secure about its psychological commitment. Government scandals had revealed official self-dealing, causing widespread disillusionment. Frances, using her limited but understandable French, heard much that summer, allowing her to form her own perspective.

At military installations she visited, soldiers in training looked like green, raw farm boys. Their officers, born into higher social classes, treated the recruits contemptuously. She thought the French boys looked sullen and angry, perhaps unwilling to risk their lives as much as earlier generations of Frenchmen had done.

At Chateau Montmirail, a seventeenth-century mansion in northeastern France, the duke and duchess de la Rochefoucauld hosted a luncheon in Frances's honor. Several other guests, including the prince de Broglie, assured her that France's defenses were strong.

But Frances noticed the de la Rochefoucaulds seemed to be scanning the horizon. Their home, overlooking the Marne Valley, lay on a traditional attack route for Germans entering France. The duke de la Rochefoucauld told Frances he had stood on this hill and watched Germans squeeze through a gap in the forest during World War I. The invaders destroyed their home and slashed the property's stately oaks. The de la

Rochefoucaulds restored the property, but the striplings they planted still looked frail. The Germans could tear through again if French defenses caved, he told her.

"I never can believe we are safe from them," he said. "I am not a military man, but neither is the Prince de Broglie a military man. Do not believe him either."[8]

While touring the South of France, Frances slipped into her role as social investigator, interviewing cobblers, bakers, and others she met along the way. Passing through one small town, she chatted with a French housewife doing her laundry. Frances started with small talk, asking whether the water was hard or soft. Even these trivial questions elicited vituperation—the homemaker thought the government cared little about the needs of ordinary people. When she asked about the military, the townsfolk used a common expression, "Pfui! Pfui!," suggesting that military leaders were fools.[9]

In Paris she met top French officials and heard their assurances that all was well. At a luncheon served in the gardens of a ruined chateau, Blerancourt, Frances sat near French general Henri Philippe Pétain, the hero of the battle of Verdun and one of France's most respected military leaders. He asked whether the English seemed alarmed by the German situation. She suggested gently that the English seemed more concerned than the French.

Pétain scoffed. "They talk about the French being excitable, but the French are realists, my dear madam," he said. "The English are the excitable people."

She pushed Pétain harder about the risk, but he shrugged. "We are impregnable. We have made the most magnificent defenses. You have heard of the Maginot Line, madam, have you not?" When Frances nodded, he added, "It is stronger than you or anyone knows. Everything's fine."[10]

Pétain's confidence failed to convince Frances, and when she returned to Paris at the end of her trip, she visited the ambassador again. She explained her impressions of the French villages. "Frankly, Bill, this is the way it strikes me: If anybody gave France a good push with a fist, she'd go all to pieces and fall."

"Oh, Frances, that's crazy," he responded. "France was never stronger."[11]

Bullitt said she didn't understand military matters, she didn't know

France well, and that he was convinced of its invincibility. Frances questioned herself and wondered if the issues were outside her experience.

Another stray bit of information kept the question alive in her mind. Myron Taylor, chairman of U.S. Steel, was also in Europe that summer, examining problems of the German Jews. He described strange things happening in Germany, "very great cruelty, bizarre types of cruelty" inflicted on Jews.[12] She asked Taylor his opinion of the French defenses. He knew the French munitions factories operated at full capacity, but he told her he didn't think they had purchased enough raw steel on the world market to build impregnable defenses.

On the ship home, Frances mulled over her impressions of the situation in Europe. She decided to report her observations to Roosevelt. When she met with him, he listened with interest. "Hmmm. Hmmm. That is not Bullitt's story," he said. She agreed it wasn't.[13]

"Well, of course, there are whole areas of human life that are never taken into account by diplomats," Roosevelt said. "They just don't think about it. It's quite true that the valley of the Gironde and such places are where people don't ordinarily go. No diplomat would have any reason for being in that area, or even making inquiries."

He urged her to share her findings with Secretary of State Cordell Hull.

Hull listened attentively, his hands clasped at the fingertips, nodding slowly, but he remarked that Frances's observations were not in keeping with the State Department's findings. He thanked her for her thoughts, but Frances could tell he was unconvinced.

The British and French continued to placate the Germans. At the Munich conference in September 1938, the two nations reached agreement with the Germans on transferring the northern strip of Czechoslovakia—the Sudetenland—to Germany. The territory was inhabited by ethnic Germans, and the transfer seemed appropriate for national self-determination. It also removed the fortified borderland from Czech control, however, leaving the rest of the country militarily indefensible. In return, Hitler pledged to pursue no further European ambitions. Chamberlain went home, calling it "peace for our time."

The Spanish Civil War ground to its dreary end in early 1939, when General Franco captured Madrid and democratic governance ended in Spain. Roosevelt agonized about whether to help the Spanish trying to preserve their Republic, but his ill-fated court-packing scheme left him with little leverage to go against public and congressional sentiments. Meanwhile, London, under Chamberlain, assumed a neutral stance on Spain. Hitler came to believe he could hit hard without risking a counterattack.

Near the end of August 1939, the Soviet Union signed a mutual non-aggression pact with Nazi Germany, and Hitler, with that worry neutralized, quietly prepared for an invasion of Poland, telling his generals that the British and French were "little worms" who were unlikely to intervene.[14] On September 1, 1939, Germany invaded Poland. The attack caught America by surprise as well.

Frances was hosting a party that day, the Sunday before Labor Day. She was visiting the old family place in Maine and holding a dinner for neighbors, an annual affair that brought old friends around for summer's end. Frances oversaw meal preparations in the red brick house. Suddenly, her Labor Department chauffeur rushed in to say he'd heard on the radio that war had broken out in Europe.

"That isn't possible," Frances said. "It's just somebody crazy on the radio." [15]

"You'd better listen to it," he replied. "This is official. The fellow who's talking has a funny name—Kalten-something or other."

"Hans Kaltenborn?"

"Yes, something like that . . . He says he's in London and that the Germans have invaded Poland. You better come and listen, ma'am. I don't know where Poland is, but they've invaded it."

Frances spent the next hour sitting on a stone wall listening to the car radio, since she didn't have one in the house. After a while she told the driver to make sure the gas tank was full, because she realized she would need to get to Boston for the midnight train to Washington. She packed a bag, stopping only to greet her first guests as they arrived. Old Joe Glidden, a family friend and former military officer, was disturbed by the news.

"Now Frances, take it easy," he said. "Don't be rash. Don't go and get us into this war before we've had time to think about it."

Frances laughed to think that her friends imagined she was directly involved in determining the nation's war course. She realized she would probably never even be consulted. Nevertheless, Frances and her driver set off on a dash to Boston, arriving in just four hours after a ride through Maine's coastal towns. She checked in with her agency and found that workers were returning to the office to help out.

All the Cabinet officers convened at the White House. Many of the men were angry, uttering oaths and blasphemies about the perfidy of the Germans—a startling change from the gentlemanly way they usually spoke in her presence, Frances recalled. "God gave them reason," Vice President Garner said with rage. "They're supposed to be good Christian people, aren't they?"[16]

Now the British and French could no longer remain uninvolved. Within days, both declared war on Germany.

Frances sensed that Roosevelt believed it was only a matter of time before the United States would enter the conflict, but he continued to say publicly that the United States would stay out of the war. He chose his words carefully, but he gradually prepared Americans for action. He pushed more strongly for a revision of the Neutrality Laws so he could sell armaments to France and Great Britain. He began rearming the United States. In 1940 the U.S. Army ranked only eighteenth in the world in size, after Germany, France, Britain, Russia, Italy, and even Sweden and Switzerland. Converting America's industrial base for war, and turning an isolationist country into a world-class military power, would not be accomplished overnight.[17]

In the meantime, Roosevelt tried to get a sense of Churchill's character. Roosevelt had met him at a large dinner when he had been assistant secretary of the navy but had talked to him only briefly. They shared a similar aristocratic point of view and even shared some ancestors. Churchill's mother, the articulate Jennie, was American, descended from American Revolutionary War patriots.

People who knew Churchill and FDR wondered how the two men would interact. Both enjoyed being on center stage—FDR with his good looks and charm, Winston with his keen wit. Roosevelt turned to Frances for her impressions. During Churchill's first decade in the House of Commons, when Frances met him while vacationing in Europe, he enthusiastically supported liberal ideas, espousing the eight-hour workday, a minimum wage, unemployment insurance, mine safety, and old-age pensions, ideas that Frances and her friends across the Atlantic Ocean shared with him.[18] Frances met Churchill from time to time afterward, both in the United States and in England. In truth she knew the man only slightly, but people had spoken to her of him so often that she felt confident sharing what she knew with FDR. The poet Rupert Brooke, for example, who died on his way to Gallipoli, told her he considered Churchill one of Great Britain's greatest men.

"What's he like?" Roosevelt asked Frances. She was cautious not to praise Winston too highly. Well, she said, he's "often right and brilliant" but could also be what she called "pig-headed." He could be vain, insisting on running ahead with his own ideas and sometimes refusing to consider other people's opinions.[19]

"Well, what kind of fellow do you think he is? Will he keep his word?"

"Oh, yes," she answered. "I never heard that complaint from any of his friends. As I've said to you before, what they complain about is that he doesn't listen to the advice they give him and that he dashes off and does what he wants to do, what he's determined to do anyhow, that he's not cooperative, that he's a leader rather than a committee man."

Later Roosevelt asked Frances if she knew whether Churchill held grudges or allowed anger to cloud his judgment. Frances simply did not know. But from the president's repeated inquiries, she concluded that the president intended to meet with Churchill and wanted to prepare. When she learned they had privately met off the coast of Newfoundland in August 1941, she was not surprised. Roosevelt came back enthusiastic about Churchill. She thought that the two men together would be stronger than either would be alone.

"Actually Churchill had much more life experience of war, rumors of war, making war, making peace, keeping the world on an even keel than anybody in the USA did, including Franklin D. Roosevelt," she said. She had feared that Churchill might patronize Roosevelt, which would have soured the relationship from the start.

Roosevelt decided it was time to court Republican support. "These are very difficult days," he told his Cabinet advisers. ". . . I think that for this we need to have a situation which is not partisan politics. I think it would be a good idea to have in this post of Secretary of the Navy a Republican."[20]

Ickes and Hull agreed, but Garner, a longtime Democratic speaker of the House before ascending to vice president, was doubtful. "It depends a great deal on what you mean by a Republican, Mr. President," Garner said. "It depends a good deal on the kind of fellow he is. Some of them are very mean."

The president floated the name of Frank Knox for secretary of the navy, an idea that met with "astonished silence." Knox had been a vice presidential candidate in 1936 on the Republican ticket. For secretary of war he was thinking of Henry L. Stimson, who had held that job under the Republican president William Howard Taft and had been Hoover's secretary of state. Frances had known Stimson for three decades, since his presidency of the Committee on Safety. The men joined the Cabinet in July 1940.

By then they were badly needed, because only bad news came from Europe and Asia. In the fall of 1939, Russia joined Germany in invading Poland, Poland was partitioned, and later on Russia attacked Finland. In the early spring of 1940, Germany invaded Denmark and Norway. Later that year, Italy, which had occupied Albania, also attacked Greece. During this time, Japan controlled the conquered Chinese territory, engaging in atrocities in the Far East.

The heaviest blow fell in May 1940. Germany invaded France and the Low Countries of Belgium and the Netherlands. French defenses collapsed, and the British Army narrowly escaped by sea from Dunkirk. By mid-June, Paris was evacuated, and by June 22, France signed an armistice withdrawing from the war. At a Cabinet meeting, Hull acknowledged to Frances that she tried to tell him about France's weakness, but that her words had conflicted with what the diplomats were saying. Frances agreed that her observations were not the ordinary military sort, but the kind of thing a social worker sees, "the elements of disintegration in the social fabric."[21]

Meanwhile attacks against Frances's immigration efforts were growing louder. Roosevelt, now preparing for the 1940 election campaign, was preoccupied by the danger of saboteurs entering the country along with the genuine refugees. State Department officials, who preferred not to deal with refugees in any event, eagerly tried to wrest control of immigration policy from Frances. To some inside the administration, she now seemed out of step with the times. Her opposition to fingerprinting aliens, for example, seemed foolhardy to people increasingly afraid that hostilities in Europe would spill into the United States.

Sumner Welles worked behind the scenes for months to have the immigration department taken from Frances and transferred to the Justice Department. Robert Jackson, who now headed Justice, disapproved and didn't want the additional responsibility. He believed that moving control of aliens to the criminal justice agency had "unfortunate implications." He also believed the transfer would leave the immigration process without the opportunity for independent legal reviews, something the Justice Department did when immigration was separate.

FDR laughed when Jackson voiced his concerns. "Why, Bob, you're the only man in the government that isn't coming to me asking for more employees, more power and a bigger department," he said.[22]

Jackson also balked because he believed the move was unfair to Frances. "I didn't feel that the criticisms of Frances Perkins, and her handling of the Labor Department, were justified," Jackson said. "I had complete confidence in her loyalty and a feeling that the fact that she was not getting a fair deal from the public, the press and Congress for what she was trying to do was probably a foretaste of what would be awaiting me if I took over the bureau."

On May 21, 1940, about a year after Frances's impeachment proceeding was over, FDR abruptly handed Jackson an executive order that transferred the Bureau of Immigration and Naturalization from the Department of Labor to the Department of Justice—no doubt necessitated by the president's reelection campaign.

Jackson's protests fell on deaf ears. The president, Jackson noted, "turned to his soup and left the move to me."[23]

Working under Roosevelt's direction, the Justice Department registered all 4.7 million aliens in the nation and then required them all to be fingerprinted. It was a step Frances had long resisted, but it proceeded rapidly under Jackson's management. When Jackson rose soon after to the Supreme Court, the department quickly shifted into the hands of Francis Biddle, the new attorney general, but the tough policy toward aliens remained. It was Biddle who later urged the deportation of Bridges and only ineffectually opposed the internment of Japanese-Americans.

Roosevelt had called Frances the night before he announced the transfer to Justice. Although Frances didn't believe that immigration belonged in the Labor Department, where it took time and energy away from other work, and had long proposed putting immigration elsewhere, she did object, however, to housing it in the Justice Department and handling it as a law-enforcement matter. Still, with the world at war, she accepted FDR's decision and understood why the move made sense.

FDR announced the move at a press conference just as France crumbled under the German attack. He noted that moving immigration from the Labor Department to the Justice Department had been "talked about a great deal" in 1939. "Today the situation has changed and it is necessary for us, for obvious national defense reasons, to make that change at this time; so it is going up as a Reorganization order, with the hope that it will be definitely approved without waiting for the 60 days."[24]

Frances's enemies rejoiced. "Thank God!" said Sumner Welles. "The Immigration Service has been moved from the Department of Labor to the Department of Justice. This is something which should have been done a long time ago. Francis Biddle is going to have a real job with that outfit."[25]

It was a public humiliation for Frances. Her growing corps of enemies, particularly those infuriated at her failure to deport leftist union officials and her admissions of European refugees, smugly applauded the move. They called the proposed reorganization a smokescreen that allowed Roosevelt to strip Frances of power.

"We are going to vote for this reorganization plan because the President has not the patriotism nor the courage to remove the Secretary of Labor, a notorious incompetent, and one who for the last seven years has steadily and steadfastly failed and refused to enforce the Immigration Law, and continuously admitted and kept here those who were not entitled to stay," said Congressman John Taber, a Republican from New York and opponent of the New Deal.[26]

Even close friends endorsed the transfer, viewing Frances as too stigmatized by the impeachment case to effectively supervise immigration. "I assume that you know all about the transfer of the Immigration Bureau to the Department of Justice," Burlingham wrote to Frankfurter. "I have written the Attorney General that I think it was the right thing to do. F.P. has administered the law most reasonably, but she has got a bad name for herself, C.I.O., communist, anything, everything."[27]

Frances was removed from this task just as the plight worsened for Jews, labor leaders, and liberals. It was, of course, impossible to save them all, or even most of them. But the one person in the administration most sympathetic to refugees now ceased to have the power to help, just as the need was greatest.

As was her practice when it came to topics that caused her personal pain or that reflected poorly on the president, she never said a word publicly about Roosevelt or his relationship to the Holocaust. She remained silent even after the war was over, the concentration camps were thrown open, and the full magnitude of human suffering was exposed.

Roosevelt's administration was later castigated for its failure to do more—for Jews, Spaniards, or many other groups at mortal risk. Another stain on Roosevelt's legacy was the internment of 110,000 Japanese-Americans on the West Coast, two-thirds of them American citizens. Always loyal to Roosevelt, Frances maintained her silence but in private she told friends that she thought it "very wrong."[28]

⚜

*N*ow, with Frances powerless over immigration, and as Europe went down in flames, her beloved International Labor Organization found itself also at risk. The Swiss wanted to expel any organizations that could attract Hitler's animosity. The United States had belonged to the ILO for only six years, but it had an American director, and America seemed to be the only country that could pull the agency to safety.

Frances had groomed John Gilbert Winant, the idealistic former Republican governor of New Hampshire, to lead the ILO. Frances had first met him at a party at the home of Ernest and Margaret Poole in 1929, and she quickly saw his potential. When Winant completed his term as governor, he accepted the presidency of the National Consumers League in 1934 at Frances's urging. This gave him credentials to assume a management role at the ILO. Winant was named assistant director of the ILO but served only a brief stint there before dashing back to the United States to defend Social Security against Republican attack. He chaired the new Social Security Board, lending Republican credibility and bipartisan support to the agency. That done, he returned to the ILO in 1937 and focused on building international relations, shifting the organization's focus toward the Western Hemisphere by "bringing the Latin and Central American nations into the active fold of the ILO." When the ILO directorship came open, it was easy for Frances to champion Winant over candidates with more agency experience, and in 1938 he got the job.[29]

Ensuring the continued safety of the ILO became Frances's responsibility. In April 1939, American ILO officials wondered what the agency should do if war broke out. The Swiss said that the ILO and League of Nations would need to move out, "because their presence might be interpreted as a violation of neutrality by Switzerland."[30]

In November 1939, after the Germans had overrun Poland, the ILO's vulnerability made a move more likely. In every country that Hitler invaded, the Nazis destroyed trade unions as a first priority. In Holland, the Nazis took control of the Dutch Federation of Trade Unions. They seized the union treasuries and pension funds and took over union hotels and health spas. About 150,000 Dutch workers were turned to forced labor in Germany. In Poland, the Germans confiscated assets of union insurance funds and pensions. Hundreds of thousands of Poles were subjected to forced labor. About three hundred Poles were killed in Skarzysk when they went out on strike; another seventy-five were killed for striking in a coal mine. Yugoslav labor leaders, including some active in the ILO, were thrown into prisons and concentration camps.[31]

Despite the threatened destruction of unions in many European countries, the ILO kept functioning and had substantial representation from elsewhere in the world, now mainly in the Western Hemisphere, where Winant had cultivated Latin American membership. The spreading conflict that doomed the League of Nations meant that the ILO was that organization's last functional unit. "The welfare of labor both in belligerent and non-combatant countries becomes doubly important during periods of war," wrote Isador Lubin to the Labor Department.[32]

ILO officials had decided to move to safety in Paris. Key employees packed their bags. But in May 1940, before they departed, France was invaded by the Germans, and by mid-June, ILO officials realized they had to decide what to do next. Agency employees were terrified. As an organization designed to represent labor interests, they knew the Nazis would hunt them down, kill or imprison them. One American on the ILO staff couldn't take the tension and ran into Winant's office. "We'll all be slaughtered; get us out!" he screamed.[33]

Relying on Frances's assurances, Winant decided to relocate them to the United States. He could not bring all four hundred staff members, so he divided the staff into four categories, based on their nationalities, their ability to get visas, and the importance of their work. About fifty ILO employees were designated "A," the top ranking. Some lower-ranking employees feared being left behind in Europe.

Winant soon realized that, contrary to what Frances and Lubin had said, U.S. entry was far from assured. The State Department did not want to risk aggravating the hostile situation. Winant wrote to Hull pleading for reconsideration and begged Frances, Roosevelt, and the State Department to pull ILO employees to safety.

Frances pressed a list of ILO employees who would need diplomatic visas. She called the president to ask him to intervene personally for the group, describing the exchange in a note to herself on Labor Department stationery. He couldn't make up his mind. "Pres[ident] says he is 'stalling' for time for a week at the least," she wrote. "Thinks they are okay in Geneva."[34]

Henry I. Harriman, the Chamber of Commerce executive who was active in the ILO, wrote to Frances in alarm on July 2, 1940, having heard that there was objection to establishing the ILO in the United States. He volunteered to meet with Roosevelt that week. But it was already too late. After discussing it with the State Department, Roosevelt decided to say no. Hull notified Winant in a July 1 telegram:

> Our decision with respect to the proposed transfer of part of the staff of the International Labor Office to the United States was, I wish to assure you categorically, in no sense a reflection upon the Office or upon your administration of the Office. . . . You will appreciate I am sure the urgency and gravity of the issues which now confront us and will understand that all other problems must be subordinated to these issues.[35]

Frances demanded an explanation. Sumner Welles sent her Hull's conclusory telegram, noting blandly that it will "explain fully to you, I think, the views of the Secretary in this regard."[36]

The decision shocked Winant. In a cablegram he told Frances: "Decision may be liquidation of 24 of the best New Dealers in Europe. Deeply disappointed."[37]

The labor secretary had been outmaneuvered by the State Department, said Carol Riegelman, an aide in the ILO office. Frances later adopted a lighter spin. She said that Roosevelt had agreed to take the dying League of Nations onto the Princeton University campus, and that to do more might aggravate legislators.

"We mustn't press the members of Congress too hard," Roosevelt told Frances. "Why can't they go somewhere else? Why not Canada?"[38]

Frances called Canadian officials, some of whom she had met during her Hull House years, and won agreement for the ILO to be housed at McGill University in Montreal. By then, entering and exiting Switzerland had become almost impossible. The country was hemmed in by enemies—Germany, Italy, and now German-occupied France. The German influence was growing, but its control was still not fully consolidated. ILO officials rushed across the continent to Lisbon, Europe's last open exit port. Winant escaped by driving across Europe and abandoning his car at the Spanish border, taking the train the rest of the way to Lisbon. A second group came in another car and a third came by bus. The ILO officials arrived among a flood of wealthy refugees, each eager to pay top dollar to escape. After they reached Lisbon, finding lodging in boardinghouses or hotels, Riegelman called each morning on all the shipping lines to beg for available berths. She needed eight places for one family that had six children. Two other employees married their girlfriends to bring them to safety on spousal visas. Around 11:00 each morning, ILO officials gathered at a Lisbon bar, drinking coffee, while Riegelman described what spots she had secured. One by one, the entire entourage made it to safety. Arriving at McGill, they set up shop in a church on the campus. The ILO was preserved and waited out World War II in safety in Montreal. It became the only League of Nations entity to survive the war.[39]

Winant's heroism did not go unrewarded. With Frances's sponsorship, he replaced Joseph Kennedy as ambassador to England. Winant lived in London throughout the blitz and subsisted on the spartan rations allotted to ordinary Englishmen, growing thin, even though as a diplomat he was not compelled to accept such meager fare. He took refuge with Londoners in the underground when German bombers appeared overhead. "He enormously helped the situation in Great Britain," recalled Sir Arthur Salter, parliamentary secretary to the British shipping ministry. "He typified to the British people the best side of America."[40]

The tattered remnants of the ILO gathered for a joyous conference in New York City in October 1941. Many former delegates were missing. Some were prisoners; some were still hiding in undercover operations; still others had disappeared and were believed to be dead. The organization appeared on the verge of disintegration. The Dutch delegate, from a merchant seamen's union, represented the only surviving union in the

Netherlands. They had been at sea when the Germans raced into Holland.[41]

State Department officials bedeviled Frances by focusing on the delegates' entertainment—the menus, the restaurants, the musical performances to be presented. She wanted to keep things simple: cold sandwiches and pumpkin pie served at an evening reception, opportunities for dining with river views, traditional cowboy music—all classically American but light in spirit. The State Department instead wanted violin solos, pâté de foie gras and petits fours, and luxurious hotel conference rooms.[42]

The newly escaped Europeans gave delegates, including Frances and other Roosevelt officials, fresh proof they had of the atrocities under way on the Continent. They brought photographs of dead Poles hanging from doorways. "They were just horrible sights," Frances said.[43]

At her urging, Roosevelt addressed the group. He described how, as a young assistant secretary of the navy, he had helped find office space, typewriters, and supplies to organize the 1919 ILO conference in Washington. "In those days, the ILO was still a dream," he told the delegates. "To many it was a wild dream. Who had ever heard of governments getting together to raise the standards of labor on an international plane?"[44]

Now, he told them, you have "weathered the vicissitudes of a world at war . . . And when this world struggle is over, you will be prepared to play your own part in formulating those social policies upon which the permanence of peace will so much depend."

The larger question remained unanswered: Should America enter the war? The dispute caused real stress in the relationship between Frances and Caroline O'Day because O'Day was a committed pacifist, opposed to all war, and Frances was beginning to believe that American military intervention would be needed. Caroline drew away from the other New Dealers, straining her friendships with Frances and Eleanor, who both believed they were duty-bound to back the president.

Caroline wrote to their mutual friend Mary Dreier and told her she could not decide whether to support an end to the arms embargo. Doing so would allow the sale of desperately needed weapons to England, but it also risked bringing the United States into the conflict. Her mail from her New York constituents, she noted, was almost perfectly divided between war supporters and opponents. Famous aviator Charles Lindbergh recently had given a speech urging Americans not to be pulled into war again.

"I was immensely affected by Lindbergh's speech," Caroline wrote to Dreier.

> He expressed what I have been thinking for a long, long time and yet I can't bear to line up with Hitler, Stalin and Father Coughlin. And I hate to be against the President. Ugly partisan politics is already showing itself against the president and if I vote to keep the embargo I will be going along with Hamilton Fish and a few other most detestable Republicans whose hatred of the President is vitriolic.
>
> That makes it all the harder to decide how I will vote. Yesterday afternoon I spent long hours at the Lincoln Memorial hoping that would give me guidance. Whatever decision I will make will go contrary to some of my dearest friends.[45]

Caroline voted against removing the arms embargo, infuriating Roosevelt. The stress and sadness undermined her health. O'Day fell ill and left Washington, recuperating at her estate in Rye, New York. She remained there several months. Then, in June 1941, she broke her hip and was hospitalized. She never returned to her congressional position in Washington. Her family recalled that Eleanor dropped out of their lives, but that Frances kept in close and loyal contact with them, as she had done with Al Smith when his friendship with the Roosevelts splintered.[46]

After 1941, Frances found herself alone in Washington again. This time there was no rescuer in sight.

Chapter 29

FRANCES AND FRANKLIN

When FDR became president, he and Frances had known each other for twenty-three years and had been close political allies for almost a decade. They understood each other so well that they could interpret the meaning of the smallest gestures. Frances noticed, for example, that Roosevelt frequently smiled agreeably when asked about an issue, even though he had no intention of committing himself to it. Many mistook his amiability for agreement and later viewed him as duplicitous, but Frances had learned to distinguish between what Roosevelt said and what he meant.[1]

Their bond was unusual for the times, a connection between a man and a woman that was not dependent on a sexual bond or family ties. Not many men in that era could accept a woman as an equal. Roosevelt was different. For some reason, perhaps his close relationship with his mother or his physical dependency on others, he accepted women as confidantes. In doing so, he won their intense loyalty. Frances saw that Roosevelt treated her as a peer, and in return she devoted to him her skills, diplomacy, and remarkable emotional intelligence.

"Franklin Roosevelt's relations with Frances Perkins were very tender and very trusting, and he knew she was his most loyal friend—that she was the only person around him who had no axe of any kind to grind. She would tell him what she thought. If she disapproved, she would say so," wrote Arthur Krock. "But she would do it gently, and he knew she meant it—that she was sincere—so he always stood by her and she by him."[2]

Their familiarity permitted easy teasing. In April 1934, for example, when FDR asked Frances about a deteriorating coal dispute in Kentucky, she responded smoothly. "Well, Mr. President, I think the NRA is handling the matter," by which she implied the NRA had created the mess and was making it worse. "Meow, meow," the president responded.[3]

There was even a slight flirtatiousness between them. A newspaper photograph captured Frances smiling up at Jim Farley, her hand to her cheek. Roosevelt sent her a copy of the picture, along with a note: "After all these years of trusting you I believed that I could let you go to Chicago without a chaperone. You really must not let the camera men catch you when you are so truly coy!"[4]

Frances's verbal deftness, meanwhile, and confidence in her place in his affections, allowed her to parry FDR's barbed jests. Roosevelt enjoyed setting people against each other just to see what would happen. He invited rivals Harry Hopkins and Harold Ickes on fishing trips together, just for the pleasure of watching them squirm trying to make pleasant conversation. "He got a lot of fun out of it. . . . He would remind me sometimes of handling people like pinning bugs to a board to see what would happen," recalled one bemused witness.[5]

Agriculture Secretary Claude Wickard, who took the post later in the Roosevelt administration, recalled that Frances stood up not only for herself, always with humor, but also for others caught in FDR's crosshairs. Their "close personal friendship" gave Frances much latitude, permitting her to "criticize Roosevelt and even to his face," something no other member of the cabinet could do. FDR "clearly loved and admired" Frances, Wickard said.[6]

FDR laughed at the perennial newspaper rumors of Frances's impending dismissal. When a reporter asked in June 1940 if Frances was resigning, the president quickly made light of it. "Oh, I have been reading that for almost every first of July since 1933," Roosevelt said.[7]

Contrary to the reports, FDR frequently pleaded with her to stay. "How little the critics know!" Wyzanski wrote. "Not once but many times, Frances Perkins pressed President Roosevelt to take her resignation. Finally, in despair, she told him that she had canceled her lease, sent back her belongings to New York, and was now going to depart. The President replied: 'Frances, how can you be so selfish?'"[8]

Frances had suspected that Roosevelt intended to run for an unprecedented third term, although he repeatedly denied it. Her initial reaction was that this would be bad for the country. She also feared it would narrow the party's political base because older people would block the advancement of energetic young activists. She had seen the New York Democratic Party weaken during Smith's governorship, after he had held the reins of power for so long, and she wanted the national party kept strong.

Surveying the country, however, Frances saw no one with the stature to replace Roosevelt and continue the New Deal's momentum. She liked Jim Farley but didn't believe he had "presidential timbre." Her experience with Al Smith's 1928 candidacy had also convinced her that the public would not endorse Farley's Roman Catholicism.[9]

She did not trust James Byrnes, a former congressman who had become a senator. In her opinion, Byrnes, a southern conservative who had opposed the Fair Labor Standards Act, was a political manipulator. She thought he was so cynical that he could never appreciate that some people actually worked for higher causes.

She considered Paul McNutt, a former Indiana governor with presidential aspirations, a vain stuffed shirt. She thought Roosevelt bought his support by naming him to head the Social Security Board, telling Frances he gave McNutt "something" to keep him in the president's corner.

"Why do you think he wants it?" Frances asked.[10]

"Don't you know?" Roosevelt said. "His name will be signed to quantities of documents that mean money and good will to the people. He's the head of the agency that gives them their old age wages, their unemployment checks, money to build a hospital with, and all that kind of thing. That is quite a lot of very good publicity."

FDR's decision left Frances feeling that a vital humanitarian post had been used as a cheap political chit. But in this, as in other matters, even when she protested something privately, in public she acceded to his wishes and accepted his decisions.

Meanwhile she probed FDR for information about his plans, using indirect methods to try to find out his intentions. When they were discussing legislation, for example, Frances would ask if they could try to put it through the next year. At first FDR would parry the questions.

"Well, how do you know there's going to be any next year for us?" he'd say with a laugh. "Papa won't be around."[11]

In time she discounted his denials, as it became clear that he meant to run again. Gradually, she decided it would be better for the country if

Roosevelt remained president. World War II was raging in Europe, and Roosevelt's success had made him a respected world figure who could marshal a coalition against the Axis powers, if necessary.

By April or May of 1940, Frances took it for granted that he would run. The unresolved question was who would be the next vice president. Garner, disaffected with Roosevelt's New Deal, objected to FDR's decision to pursue a third term and returned to Texas. Frances decided that the best replacement would be her friend Henry Wallace, a former progressive Republican. Wallace was highly intelligent, made friends easily, and understood agricultural economics, making him attractive in the Farm Belt states. His policy of destroying crops and livestock to reduce oversupply had been criticized, but otherwise he was seen as far-sighted and competent. He had created the food stamp and school lunch programs. If the president were to die, the vice president might step into the post. Frances pondered it all, and her mind inevitably returned to Wallace. In a city where facile self-advancement reigned, Wallace showed an integrity that Frances admired.

"Wallace, if he comes with you, will be absolutely loyal," Frances told Roosevelt. "He will not knife you. He will not let you down."[12]

Frances chose Wallace in her mind for vice president in early July 1940, and touted his candidacy as vice president at the 1940 Democratic National Convention in Chicago, even though Roosevelt had yet to name his own favorite. She worked the floor and tried to help Wallace and his wife, Ilo, circulate effectively. She took a personal interest in Ilo, and she helped adapt the woman's appearance to eastern tastes, to remove what she called the "Iowa look." She convinced Ilo to remove her spectacles and helped her select a new wardrobe. Now Frances and her friends hastily arranged a tea in Ilo's honor so she could meet women delegates. Frances noted with satisfaction that Ilo did well, proving herself "fit to be the wife of a man in high office."[13]

But a grim mood surrounded the convention. Roosevelt expected to be drafted for another presidential run, and had decided not to attend the convention in order to remain above the fray. Instead he sent Harry Hopkins and Frances as his emissaries. But support for the New Deal was ebbing; an undercurrent of resentment about the president's high-handed tactics, including the ill-fated court-packing scheme, could be felt. The political machinations of Chicago Mayor Edward Kelly, a Roosevelt supporter, added to the disillusionment. A continual roaring shout of "We want Roosevelt" turned out to be the amplified voice of a single man concealed in the cellar, a carnival barker's trick orchestrated by the mayor. The delegates still voted resoundingly for Roosevelt, but they did so with distaste. More than a dozen vice presidential candidates were dangling, each wondering if he might be the president's choice.[14]

Frances called the president to tell him that she believed he needed to show up to counteract the gloom. He needed to mobilize the troops for the campaign ahead. FDR told her he had resolved not to go, but he wondered aloud if Eleanor's presence would help. He suggested Frances call and ask her. " 'Don't let Eleanor know that I am putting any pressure on her,' " he told Frances.[15]

Then Roosevelt turned to the last major issue before the convention. He asked Frances again if she thought Wallace would be a good choice for vice president. "Well, you know I've thought for a long time that Wallace would be the best possible man if you want him," Frances said.[16]

"You know, he's got lots of qualities that would be very good," Roosevelt told her. "In the first place, he's an honorable upright man. We know that. We know also that he's not going to cut under you. He's not going to let you down. He's a man of a great deal of ability."

"Yes, I think he is a man of a great deal of ability," she echoed.

"Well, I think he could be a great help to the President. Don't you?"

"Yes," she said.

"Well, I think he'd be very good. Don't you think he'd be good, Frances?"

"I think he'd be very good," she said. She reviewed with him the other candidates, but they kept returning to Wallace. Finally he made up his mind and told her to tell Harry Hopkins.

Frances hung up the phone, grabbed her hat, and rushed over to Hopkins's hotel suite. On the way, she concocted a cover story for reporters if they asked her what she was doing there. Only one reporter questioned her, and her ruse worked. She told him she wanted to discuss an aspect of the Equal Rights Amendment and started to describe it. Bored, he quickly departed, unaware that she had led him away from a major scoop. With the coast clear, Frances tracked down Hopkins and spoke to him privately.

"I've just talked to the president on the telephone," she said. "He says that he has made up his mind that he wants Wallace for Vice President."[17]

Hopkins confirmed it with the president. Then he told Wallace. Frances turned to the task of asking Eleanor to sooth the ruffled feathers in Chicago and to ease the way for Wallace. She called her.

"Things look black here; the temper of the convention is very ugly," Eleanor later recalled Frances telling her. Frances called Eleanor again to tell her the president wouldn't make an appearance. Would she, please?[18]

Eleanor said she wouldn't come unless she received an invitation from Farley—a steep precondition because Farley felt betrayed by the president because he thought they had had an understanding that Farley would run for president in 1940. Then Eleanor called Franklin, who told her it would be "nice" if she were to go but that she shouldn't consider it mandatory. So she waited. After a complex choreography of calls and much ego-soothing by Frances, Eleanor finally flew to Chicago. She was met at the airport by Farley and escorted to the convention floor, where she gave a speech that turned the mood around.

Henry Wallace was named vice president, though unenthusiastically. Wallace wasn't completely aware of Frances's efforts on his behalf. "I think she was working for me, although there wasn't any formal relationship of any sort," he said later.[19]

But the president knew that Frances had played a key role in ensuring a successful convention. Soon afterward he wrote her: "This is just a very personal note to tell you how much I appreciate all that you did at the Convention. I know that you must feel very happy about your part. All of our friends have told me how grand you were and you know, without me telling you, how happy that makes me."[20]

In Wallace, Frances helped select a vice president who changed the role of the office, enhancing its broader domestic and international aspects. Frances's nominee stood by FDR's side as the country entered World War II and stayed with the president almost until its conclusion.

But the handsome Iowan wasn't a perfect choice. It soon emerged that Wallace brought with him some political liabilities. Within a few months of the convention, an incident occurred that haunted the rest of his career. Wallace was a religious man who enjoyed exploring many philosophical concepts. He was corresponding with Nicholas Roerich, a Russian-born scholar of mysticism and religion who had a museum in New York City, and he eventually became an enthusiastic proponent of Roerich's peace-making campaign. Frances had known of Roerich's work for years. During the campaign, a packet of letters between Wallace and Roerich came to light, in which the two men discussed religion, history, and current events. Wallace addressed the man with the traditional honorific of "guru," or "master." The letters puzzled the back-slapping, beer-drinking politicos who represented a large part of the Democratic Party machine, and they came to view Wallace with suspicion. The letters also betrayed a naive idealism in Wallace that Roerich may have exploited to his advantage. The vice president appeared easily deluded by people claiming superior spiritual insight.[21]

Roosevelt also found the correspondence curious. Shaking his head, he'd laugh about a controversy that involved religion instead of sex. "Oh, my God, isn't it something?" he asked. "Letters are always cropping up in campaigns, but in this case there's no girl. What a pity!"[22]

The Republicans nominated Wendell Willkie, who Frances considered one of their best candidates in decades. Even the Republican Party platform gave her a great sense of accomplishment. It sounded largely like a continuation of Democratic Party programs.

"Well, now I think we can sleep quietly and peacefully," she said to another Labor Department official. "The Republicans have adopted our platform, and that means that our program is permanent."[23]

But Wilkie soon made some missteps. Talking to a labor audience in Pittsburgh, Willkie bombastically pledged to the union members that his labor secretary would be an appointee from labor's ranks. Willkie took it another step. "And it won't be a woman either!"[24]

Frances and the president shared a laugh about it later, viewing the comment as a political faux pas. It was a "needless mistake" that won him applause at the expense of alienating many votes. Many women, including Republicans, cabled him to protest.

"My God, couldn't he see what he did?" FDR said to Frances. "He had it. It was all coming to him if he had just stopped right there."

Despite her earlier misgivings about a third term, Frances campaigned hard for Roosevelt that fall. Her specialty was addressing a bipartisan audience, often speaking in polite opposition to a Republican. She delighted in bringing new supporters to the Democrats and viewed it as a waste of time to preach to those who were already in the party choir.

Roosevelt garnered 55 percent of the vote, partially because of his pledge to stay out of the war—even as he prepared to enter it. Willkie tried in vain to expose the deception, but FDR once again rode a tide of popularity to victory.

Frances planned to leave office at the start of the third term. Her work was shifting to a back burner as the country focused on war. Her role running interference between Roosevelt and people he had offended, including his wife, had grown tiresome. Frances also believed she had accomplished as much as she could, and that the Republican Party platform had secured her successes. "It seemed to me that our program was now bipartisan. Nobody would ever abandon Social Security. Nobody would ever abandon the regulation of hours and wages, the prohibition of child labor, and all that kind of thing. That was done. I had accomplished what I had come to do," she said.[25]

She had also grown weary of wielding power. "The more authority you have, the more impossible situations you are going to be up against, and the more your conscience is going to be boiling all the time and keeping you awake nights," she said.

Frances asked Roosevelt's permission to step down. She had a few attractive job offers. But Roosevelt wouldn't say yes or no. He needed time to think about it.

She accepted the delay because she felt protective of him. Seeking a third term had cost him much popularity, and her departure would add to his problems. Weeks passed, and still the president hadn't decided. Finally Frances asked Eleanor for help.

"Now, see here, you see the president more often than I do," Frances said to her. ". . . Will you kindly find out just when he's going to act on my resignation?"[26]

"Oh, but I don't get a chance to talk to him," Eleanor said.

"All right, but you can make a chance," Perkins said.

Eleanor hesitated, then agreed. "I don't always get a chance to talk to him about anything serious," she said. "It's sometimes as much as a week before I get in a word about anything that is purely business and not just personal matters such as 'Have you paid that bill?' "

In about a week, Eleanor's answer arrived in a note. "I have talked to him about it and the answer is no, absolutely no."

Frances called Eleanor to ask what it meant.

"That's it," she said. "He says that he can't be bothered with it. He can't have another problem on his hands. Everything's going all right so far as he's concerned. He's absolutely unwilling to make any change now."

"That doesn't mean forever, does it?"

"Oh, I suppose not, but that's what he feels for the present at any rate."

A few days later, at a Cabinet meeting, Frances approached the president on another matter. "Did you hear from my missus?" he asked.

"Yes, it's bright of you to communicate with me like that," she told the president.

"I meant to tell you myself, but the more I thought of it, the more I didn't see how I was going to do it," he said. "It's personal, I suppose. I know who you are, what you'll do, what you won't do. You know me. You see lots of things that most people don't see. You keep me guarded against a lot of things that no new man here would protect me from."

She decided then that she would "drop dead in her traces" rather than abandon him, particularly in the face of war.

But after the 1940 campaign, Frances found herself slipping into the background. The president was preoccupied with war preparations. He viewed her as a pacifist, partly out of sexism and partly because of her affiliation with the women of Hull House, who had led antiwar movements for decades. Roosevelt became reluctant to share plans with her when he thought she would disagree. This grated on Frances because she believed that America should do everything it could to help the British, even going directly to England's defense. She endorsed the idea of giving armaments and old warships to the British in the Lend-Lease program, a Roosevelt idea that allowed the United States to label ships "obsolete," outmaneuvering congressional opponents of foreign aid.

"I regard the British—I did then, I do now—as the defenders of civilization, to whom we are deeply indebted for the protection of our own civilization, not only for its birth, breeding, and infant protection, but for all the basic political protections like the Magna Charta, the Bill of Rights, and all that sort of thing. They sprang out of English experience and English genius, and we inherited these things and took them over almost without a thought. There . . . is a deep sympathy between our two cultures. It's impossible to overlook it." [27]

No matter what she said, however, Roosevelt continued to view Frances as a pacifist, and said irritating things about it to her in cabinet meetings.

"Well, Frances, you know a battleship isn't the worst thing in the world," he would say. Franklin's view of her as a political partner changed as testosterone levels rose in preparation for the war.[28]

Much of official Washington continued to be mystified by the relationship between Roosevelt and Frances. Platonic friendships between men and women are common enough in reality but are usually not acknowledged. Frances's relationship with the president was a troubling anomaly. No European or American woman before Frances had ever played such a high-profile role in public life, unless within a hereditary aristocracy or because of a sexual liaison. Only one woman was permitted to hold a position of high respect in 1940s Washington—and that was the president's wife, who occupied a time-honored position.

Some Washington insiders, however, knew the truth. An article in *Colliers* in August 1944 titled "The Woman Nobody Knows," squarely identified the New Deal as a Frances Perkins creation.

An accompanying cartoon underscored the nation's discomfort with women in authority. It showed two uniformed soldiers on a beach, deliberating over whether to approach a statuesque blonde in a bathing suit. "We better approach her carefully," one says to the other. "She might be a superior officer."[29]

Chapter 30

MADNESS, MISALLIANCES, AND A NUDE BISEXUAL WATER SPRITE

The bright spot in Frances's life during these otherwise-gloomy years was the successful life Susanna had launched with her husband, David.

Having no money worries, David and Susie Hare traveled around the country, flying from coast to coast. They had an apartment in New York City but also spent much time in the Southwest because they were interested in Native American art. David's mother, Betty, was an art collector who had been a supporter of the Armory Show in 1913, and later became an important financial contributor to the American Museum of Natural History. In 1940, the museum gave David a commission to document the Pueblo Indians using cutting-edge photography techniques.

When they returned to New York, David had an exhibit of his work in a solo show at a prestigious New York gallery, and he opened a commercial photography studio. The young couple moved to Roxbury, Connecticut, which was becoming an artists' colony of some renown, where they were surrounded by a circle of interesting friends. For two young art enthusiasts, life seemed a paradise.[1]

But there's always a serpent in Eden.

Hare's greatest interest was in surrealism, an innovative art form then sweeping Europe. Hare and his mother were well connected in the international art scene, and his cousin Kay Sage, a painter living in Paris, was romantically involved with another painter, Yves Tanguy, whom she married in 1940. The Hares and their friends began to hear disturbing stories about what was happening to avant-garde artists in Europe as the Nazi movement spread, and the French surrealists seemed at particular risk once France fell to the Germans.

David's mother and Susanna together prevailed on Frances to save members of the surrealist movement by helping get them admitted as refugees. Frances needed little convincing that some individuals were in peril; she had been pressing for an expansion of immigration from Europe since 1933. Frances also provided assistance to Varian Fry's American Rescue Committee, which brought many other experimental artists to safety in the United States.

Frances provided this help at some risk to herself, since she had recently faced impeachment charges and was losing control of the immigration department. Many European artists seeking admission had fallen out of favor with the Nazis because of their socialist and communist views, opinions equally unwelcome in the United States.

Once they arrived, many of the artist refugees moved to western Connecticut, in and around Roxbury. It was a fast set, unconventional, scornful of tradition. A picture taken of Susanna showed her lounging on the grass on a summer day, part of a pack of famous artists that included Alexander Calder, the American sculptor known for his mobiles; French surrealist painter André Masson; and Teeny Matisse, the wife of Pierre Matisse and the former and future wife of painter Marcel Duchamp.[2]

The group also included André Breton, a Frenchman and author of the *Surrealist Manifesto*. He came to New York with his beautiful wife, Jacqueline Lamba, a talented artist who performed as a nude water sprite at a Montmartre dance hall in Paris around the time he met her. Breton chronicled their romance in his book *Mad Love*. Both had been members of the Communist Party in France, and Lamba worked with the Greek Communist Party before moving to Paris. Art patroness Peggy Guggenheim paid their passage to the United States; Susanna wrote an affidavit supporting their entry.[3]

Once they arrived, Breton, Marcel Duchamp, and Max Ernst established a new surrealist journal called *VVV* to bring together artists in exile. Originally, they hoped that Robert Motherwell would edit it, but instead they selected David Hare. Hare, with his poor writing skills, was an incongruous choice. Perhaps they were looking for a financial patron more than a wordsmith. Jacqueline Lamba, who spoke English, translated. She communicated for Breton, who spoke no English and didn't care to learn it.[4]

Hare fell "head-over-heels" in love with Lamba. Lamba was restless and irritated with her narcissistic husband, and she quickly warmed to David instead. Soon Hare and Lamba began a flagrant affair in which they were seen walking nude on the beaches of Long Island Sound, along a shoreline where some of Frances's friends had beach cottages. They left their spouses and shared an apartment where they raised Lamba's daughter by Breton. Nudity was a hallmark of their homemaking. Lamba and Hare paraded nude in front of Breton, now middle-aged and too modest to appear in a bathing suit, when he visited his daughter.[5]

Susanna was crushed. Still in love with David, she tried pathetically to keep him, but he was bewitched by the feline Frenchwoman. Lamba couldn't decide if she preferred her husband or her lover, so she decided to take some time away and visit longtime friends in Mexico City, Communists Diego Rivera and his wife, Frida Kahlo, both unconventional artists. They were friends of Russian Communist Leon Trotsky, who had fled Russia and was living in Mexico City. Trotsky actually lived with Rivera for a time. In 1939, the year Frances faced impeachment, Trotsky volunteered to testify about Communism before the House Committee on Un-American Affairs, the same committee that had been probing Frances's failure to deport Bridges, but Trotsky's trip was canceled.

When Lamba got to Mexico City, she had an affair with Kahlo. Returning to the United States, she was detained at the border for reasons unknown. Intrusive immigration officers questioned Lamba closely about her sexual life before readmitting her to the country. No doubt her Communism and her ties to Trotsky, Rivera, and Kahlo offered reason for some federal scrutiny, but Lamba's friends suspected that Frances was behind it all. Certainly by this time Frances would have had much reason to keep Lamba away from her daughter's husband.

Susanna now regretted the affidavit she had written on Lamba's behalf, commenting wryly that Lamba "had not been among those worth saving."

On March 2, 1945, after seven stormy years, Susanna and Hare divorced. He sued first, alleging desertion. Susanna entered a cross-complaint charging mental cruelty. Susanna moved into a small apartment in New York City; Lamba and Hare, who had the resources to live anywhere, moved to Roxbury, where David and Susanna had once lived together. They decorated their home in a Southwestern motif that won the admiration of their friend Simone de Beauvoir when she came to visit. But Hare couldn't remain faithful to Lamba either. Lamba left him and returned to France after a party at which Hare introduced her as his wife and the guest blurted out, "Which one?"[6]

Newspaper articles about Susanna and David's divorce highlighted their connection to Frances Perkins. The articles were brief and contained none of these lurid details, but the announcements must have been intensely uncomfortable for Frances, who hated scandal or any attention to her personal life and who opposed divorce on religious grounds.[7]

Frances nonetheless arranged the financial settlement between Susanna and David, which included a trust fund to give Susanna financial security. Frances negotiated the arrangement with David's mother, Betty.

For several years Susanna received financial support in this way. But when the pair later learned that Hare was not legally bound by the agreement, Susanna released him from it. The end of the settlement, of course, put responsibility for Susanna back on Frances's shoulders.[8]

It took Susanna several years to recover from the divorce. She sunk into a deep depression. Her mental health problems reappeared.

Frances had raised questions about the match, but it had turned out worse than she ever could have imagined. Undoubtedly she found it difficult to discover that her daughter had been involved with adulterers, surrealists, uncloseted lesbians, and Trotskyites, people who could jeopardize her own political future, particularly as she had just narrowly survived an impeachment attempt. Fortunately for Frances, Susanna's misadventures did not become public knowledge, but Frances dealt with the sorrows in her life by becoming more deeply religious.

During this period, Frances retreated even more into prayer, and her visits to the All Saints Convent sustained her. "I don't see how people who don't believe in God can go on in this world as it is today," she once said.[9]

Over the next decade, Frances prepared herself carefully for her confession sessions with an Episcopal priest, making notes of her failures to live up to her Christian values and excoriating herself for disappointing her loved ones. Around Christmas 1944, for example, she had castigated herself for feeling "self-pity" about Susanna's problems and admitted that at times she felt "despair" verging on a death wish.

She also prayed that she could overcome the "residue of bitterness and anger" that she had toward her son-in-law. She felt "fear of him," probably because of his negative influence on Susanna. Moreover, she wrote, she had committed the sin of "anger" by being "cross and impatient at daughter, who is trying but [deserves] sympathy." And last, she said, she resented the "authentic lack of helping hands from others whom I have often helped."[10]

She devoutly practiced penitence and abstinence during religious seasons, such as Lent. She pledged to go to Mass every Sunday, to go to church at least three other times each week, to say the Rosary and the Stations of the Cross once a week, and to pray each morning and night. During Lent, she restricted her diet to six hundred calories a day, nine hundred on Sunday, and cut out sugar, butter, milk, ice cream, cake, bread, bacon, dessert, rolls, cocktails, whiskey, and candy.[11]

Frances worried about Susanna's proclivity for sexual adventurism and risky behavior, fretting that her daughter could cause herself real damage. Susanna developed intense infatuations with people Frances considered inappropriate, including lower-class people who were impressed by her association with the Roosevelts. She also behaved obsessively about some older men, such as the Romanian sculptor Constantin Brancusi, who was living in Paris. Susanna had developed a "fixation" on him, Frances wrote.

"It is like the temptations of the saints—she gives in," Frances wrote to herself.[12]

Susanna's illnesses followed the same pattern that she had exhibited earlier, with symptoms notably similar to Paul's. Susanna would turn from a normal and pleasant person who dressed appropriately into an arrogant, loud woman, careless in appearance, drinking to excess, lacking self-control. Then she turned "vicious." Susanna made grandiose plans, then found them impossible to carry out. She crashed in disappointment.

Frances agonized over whether she was somehow to blame for the mental illness suffered by both her daughter and husband, even though the biochemical evidence was obvious, and the ailment was hereditary. "I have given way to morbid superstition that I am the cause of others' nervous collapse, my husband, my daughter.... [It] frightens and oppresses me," she observed.

Sexism then was so deep-rooted that even some of Frances's closest friends assumed her elevation in public life had contributed to her husband's mental illness. "Apparently at one time he'd held a very good position," Henry Wallace said in his oral history. "Then when she began to become more noted than he, it preyed on his mind and produced a strange situation."[13]

Some who had witnessed Paul's collapse, who had seen his excessive drinking, long before she went into government employment, forgot that he was ill before Frances joined FDR's Cabinet. "A belief was emerging among her friends that he was the sacrifice on the altar of her career," wrote George Martin.[14]

Religion wasn't Frances's only consolation. She liked the taste of liquor, and during the late 1930s, as her problems mounted, she often drank to excess. "Give me one that's got some bite," she would tell friends. She preferred hard liquor to sherries or other beverages that older women often enjoy, and she expected people to match her drink for drink.

Horace M. Albright, a mining industry executive who had been an Interior Department official during the Hoover administration, recalled a malicious joke he and some colleagues played on Frances at a crowded cocktail party.

"It seems that Mrs. Perkins likes a cocktail, but she didn't want to go over and get it," he said, still chuckling years later. "Our friend just brought her drinks fast enough, and other people talked to her a little bit, until she had her transfixed against the door. She didn't dare leave it. She just stood there all evening. I don't know who broke her loose and took her to her official car."[15]

In more ways than one, Frances stood alone in a doorway. She realized she would need to provide for Susanna after her own death. She wrote to Wyzanski, by then a federal judge in Boston, asking for advice about establishing a family trust, which could be used for "dependents [who] were not likely to be able to look after themselves and each other reliably, effectively and sensibly." She said she had only "a very small sum to leave," but wanted it "safeguarded, so that it will really take care of Susanna and my husband, who although considerably older than I am, may easily outlive me and who is, as you know, not entirely competent."

Frances needed Wyzanski's help drafting the document because she preferred to discuss it with him rather than her relatives. "I don't like to talk to my own relatives about it," she wrote. "You know how shy I am about personal matters. I would rather discuss them with a bus conductor than with a relative. As a matter of fact, it has been my only grip on independence all my life."[16]

Chapter 31

THE WAR COMES

*O*n a Sunday morning in early December 1941, Frances was hard at work on a report in her room at New York City's Cosmopolitan Club. She'd gone home to speak to Latin American officials on ways to forge better ties with the United States. Frances rose early to attend church, and by early afternoon she had settled in with a stenographer. She ordered room service—soup and sandwiches for two—so they could work without interruption. Frances dictated, and the stenographer pounded away on a typewriter. Later, Frances packed to return to Washington while the secretary finished the manuscript.

Then the telephone rang. Delaney, her Labor Department chauffeur, asked when he should pick her up. Frances said this wasn't necessary. She would take the overnight train and go to the office by cab.

"Miss Perkins, they say on the radio that the Cabinet's been called in for tonight," he said.[1]

"No, Delaney," she said.

"I was at the ballpark, and I heard them say it," he insisted. Frances said she seldom believed what she heard on the radio, but she would call back when she learned more. She hung up, and almost immediately the phone rang again. This time it was the White House, asking her to get to Washington immediately for an 8 p.m. meeting.

"What's the trouble?" Frances asked. "The war," the operator said tersely.

"Something has gone wrong," Frances told the stenographer. She asked the woman to secure a seat on the next plane to Washington while she finished packing. The women flagged a taxi, and Frances dictated as they rushed to the airport. The city streets appeared normal, with no newsboys hawking papers and crying "EXTRA," as they normally did when a big story broke.

At the airport, other taxis disgorged Vice President Wallace and Postmaster General Frank Walker. They, too, had received the urgent White House call but knew no more than Frances about the emergency. Perhaps Churchill had been killed, or London had been seized by the enemy. No one mentioned the Japanese, although Frances recalled a vague report at a recent Cabinet meeting. She asked herself, "What became of the Japanese fleet that was at sea Friday?"

Knowing little, the officials resorted to mundane chitchat. Frances told herself not to be alarmed. They boarded a special charter plane and enjoyed an uneventful flight. Delaney met the plane and drove the trio to the White House, filling them in on additional details.

"It said on the radio that the Japs were shooting at us," he said.

"The Japs?" they said.

"That the Japs were shooting at American ships. They've been dropping bombs on them," he said, adding that it happened in Honolulu.

"That's impossible," said the three officials.

They found Roosevelt at his desk in the Blue Room, an oval room on the second floor over the White House south portico. Maps covered the walls, and people bustled in and out. Roosevelt, a cigarette hanging from his mouth, didn't notice them at first. He was surrounded by military aides who were showing him papers and pointing to the maps.

Frank Knox was agitated; Henry Stimson darted about in an adjacent room; Cordell Hull seemed preternaturally calm, his fingers laced together to form a temple. Francis Biddle, now attorney general, rushed in, his eyes wide.

"For God's sake, what has happened?" he burst out.[2]

A naval aide approached and told the Cabinet officials that a Japanese fleet that morning bombed Pearl Harbor, "which is the great naval installation in Hawaii," he explained. Many died and many ships were lost. Little else was known.[3]

White House press officer Steve Early strode into the room to declare that more information had come in. "Things are worse than were reported earlier," he said.[4]

Frances felt a creeping horror. The U.S. Navy had been vulnerable to attack. Was the Pacific Coast similarly vulnerable? Only days earlier, Cabinet officers had deliberated over whether to send aid to the British. Now, she wondered if the British would have to come to the aid of Americans.

The Cabinet officers composed themselves, then sat down and waited. Around 9 p.m., the president finally looked up and noticed them. His face and lips were pulled down; his skin looked gray. To Frances, it looked as if he hadn't slept the previous night, though she had no idea why. FDR couldn't possibly have known the night before that something was amiss in Hawaii. What she thought looked like sleeplessness was probably just strain, she decided.

Roosevelt spoke slowly, filling in the details. Damage was much more severe than previously reported, he told them gravely. His pride in the U.S. Navy was so great from his days as assistant secretary that he almost choked up as he described how badly prepared the navy had been at Pearl Harbor, how officers had taken the night off and left subordinates in control, how bombs had dropped on ships that were tied up and couldn't be moved quickly.

"Find out, for God's sake, why the ships were tied up in rows," he told Knox twice. "That's the way they berth them," Knox replied.[5]

Then Roosevelt presented a declaration of war he was preparing. He didn't encourage discussion but simply wanted their reaction to the wording. No one questioned the decision to declare war. It seemed the correct response to a sneak attack.

Sometime during that evening, Roosevelt's strange demeanor caught Frances's attention. She found herself studying the president, unnerved by his body language and careful wording. His expression was peculiar, one Frances had seen many times before when he was displeased but didn't intend to reveal details.

"Sometimes I've seen it on his face when he was carrying through a plan which not everybody in the room approved of and about which he didn't intend to tell too much," she said later. ". . . It was the sort of expression that he sometimes used when people were making recommendations to him and he was saying, 'Oh, yes, oh, yes, oh, yes,' without the slightest intention of doing anything about it. . . . In other words, there have been times when I associated that expression with a certain kind of evasiveness."[6]

Frances felt strongly that "something was wrong" in Roosevelt's behavior. When she got home that night, she jotted her observations in pencil on White House stationery. She recorded her thoughts so that she could recall them should it ever prove necessary. She did not want to admit that she thought FDR might have played a "false role" that day, that he had prior knowledge of the situation in Hawaii, or that he had information that might have saved lives. But she was convinced that "his surprise was not as great as the surprise of the rest of us."[7]

She also thought that Roosevelt was secretly glad the waiting was over, that at last he could take action. She wasn't the only one who thought so. As the White House meeting broke up, Walker approached Frances and whispered, "You know, I think the boss must have a great sense of relief that this has happened. . . . This is a great load off his mind. I thought the load on his mind was just going to kill him, going to break him down . . . At least we know what to do now."[8]

"Yes, I think so," Frances replied.

For more than a year, it had been clear that war in the Pacific was inevitable. Japan was dominated by fierce, militaristic nationalists, and their forces were expanding across Asia in the same predatory way that the Germans were consuming Europe. Both the United States and Japan had been infected with a racism that allowed each to underestimate the strength of the other.

The war drumbeat intensified in November. On November 7, Hull told the full Cabinet that the Japanese were likely to attack at any time. On November 30, General Hideki Tojo of Japan gave a speech in Tokyo calling for the nation to establish an East Asian "co-Prosperity sphere," urging East Asian people to "purge" Anglo-Americans. The Japanese amassed 175,000 soldiers in Indonesia, far more than needed to subdue that nation, suggesting the Japanese planned to use Indonesia as a base for further expansion. The Roosevelt administration warned American forces in the Pacific to brace for attack but theorized the assault would come at Guam, the Philippines, or Wake Island, not at Pearl Harbor, the heart of America's Pacific defenses. The United States decoded Japanese cables between Tokyo and its embassy in Washington, learning in the previous twenty-four hours that an attack somewhere was imminent.

Within days of the assault on Hawaii, the Japanese went on to Guam, the Philippines, Wake Island, and Hong Kong.

Perkins wondered what Roosevelt was hiding.

At the very least, it is clear that Pearl Harbor was not the kind of complete surprise that many people in the general public believed. The Japanese needed vast preparations to execute the coordinated assault, and rumors of some attack had circulated in Tokyo for months. In early

1941, a Peruvian diplomat reported to the U.S. Embassy that he had heard about Japanese preparations. The account was dismissed when the information's source was traced to an embassy cook. But clearly, some threat had been predicted by many observers.[9]

It is possible that FDR not only knew that an attack was imminent somewhere in the Pacific, but also had made a deliberate decision not to try to head off that attack. There are reasons to believe Roosevelt secretly welcomed the prospect of at least a small and peripheral attack someplace—not just to end uncertainty, but for reasons of policy. The Germans and Japanese were murderous bullies on a global rampage, and at some point they would have to be restrained. A galvanizing event was certain to mobilize public support. Frances knew FDR had keen intuitions about unfolding events, almost like premonitions. Roosevelt, confident of American naval prowess, may have assumed that the warning to the Pacific fleet was sufficient to ensure any damage would be kept limited.

On the other hand, FDR was desperately worried at the prospect of fighting a two-front war. On December 6, he had secretly written to Emperor Hirohito pleading for peace in the Pacific, and the attack proved his appeal had been summarily rejected by the Japanese. For that reason, he must have felt doubly humiliated to learn how poorly prepared the American forces had been for an attack, even after the command had been placed on alert. FDR, who had led a charmed life in many ways, must have been chagrined at this military failure. The expression Frances saw on his face may have reflected FDR's efforts to remain stoic as he wrestled with rage, anguish, and a sense of personal responsibility.

As events played out, the damage was devastating. About twenty-four hundred American servicemen died. Almost two hundred aircraft were destroyed, and four battleships were demolished or badly damaged. The greatest death toll came on the USS *Arizona,* which suffered a direct hit in a magazine, the compartment where explosives are stored. Roosevelt had been assistant secretary of the navy when the vessel was launched.

The most horrific accounts involved sailors stationed on the battleships *West Virginia* and *Utah,* which sank quickly with scores of sailors trapped inside. Over the next few days, the sailors slowly smothered to death. No tools were available to cut into the ships' steel hulls. The sailors tapped desperate messages, until finally the tapping died away. The

American public fumed as well over reports of Japanese pilots intentionally strafing civilians, even children, in their attack on the port city.[10]

On December 8, Frances went to Congress to hear the president make the case for war. There was a "terrible tenseness" in the hall. She noted to herself the "absolute lack of the usual loose-mouthed jollity that goes on whenever Congress meets in full session." Cabinet officers assembled in the speaker's room, then marched to assigned places on the floor. The president's arrival was greeted by thunderous applause. The attack had swept away political divisions and gave the country a unified fighting front.[11]

Filled with anger and determination, FDR's speech galvanized the nation. "Yesterday, December 7, 1941—a date which will live in infamy— the United States of America was suddenly and deliberately" attacked, he said. His call for a declaration of war on Japan passed almost unanimously in both the House and Senate. The only dissent came from Congresswoman Jeannette Rankin of Montana, a committed pacifist.[12]

On December 11, Germany and Italy declared war on the United States. The world was now at war, and things changed quickly.

Pearl Harbor marked an important life transition for Frances in several other important ways. It was certainly the end of an era. Roosevelt's call to arms forced the New Deal into the background. Winning the war was paramount, and war was a male preserve. As admirals, generals, and hawks on the Hill and within the administration gathered around Roosevelt, there was suddenly less room for a woman. FDR created special new wartime agencies that dealt with labor and economic questions, and he pointedly excluded Frances from their leadership. Roosevelt administration official Bernard Gladieux said that Frances was a "political liability" when Roosevelt sought congressional consensus on defense matters.[13]

During the run-up to war, she had already found herself pushed from the inner circle. Now, during the war itself, she spent her time handling sideshow skirmishes between the battling AFL and CIO, and grappling with hungry bureaucrats hoping to expand their empires. Her desire to oppose these forces diminished. She worked long hours but she had lost her verve. She seemed dispirited in some profound way after December 7.

Roosevelt stripped offices from her as he had done with the immigration service, moving agencies from one place to another. In Washington, where power is often measured by the extent of the dominion, not the quality of accomplishments, Frances appeared increasingly weak, but this development allowed Roosevelt to achieve his political goals. Roosevelt did the same thing to other agencies, too, most notably the Department of Agriculture—each time to gain some small advantage—but Frances's enemies took glee in highlighting anything that injured her standing.

Political pragmatism trumped concern for Frances's feelings. Her ally Isador Lubin, who later worked in the White House, said Roosevelt was merely being practical when he had withheld the Social Security agency from Frances.

In 1939, the Employment Service, which Frances had developed into an effective national program, also had been removed from her domain. It was moved to the newly created Federal Security Administration, where Social Security, with its state unemployment insurance functions, was housed, as part of a sweeping congressional reorganization plan. Frances was furious. She later said they "burglarized" the service, stealing it from her department.[14]

Social Security Board officials, including people Frances had recruited and promoted, engineered the effort. They believed they were in the right. Social Security, which operated the unemployment insurance system, had ended up financially supporting the network of job-hunting offices. It was natural that Social Security officials wanted more control over an organization they were bankrolling, and they claimed that program administration was duplicative. Frances had argued that the transfer meant that the bureaucrats primarily trained to dispense unemployment compensation checks now would also be helping discouraged job-seekers think innovatively about finding good-paying jobs. The skills were different. To many in the administration, the transfer had made sense, but for Frances, shifting the department elsewhere was a bad decision—but also a personal assault and a blow to her agency's prestige.[15]

Only a handful of people criticized the decision to move the employment service. One was Sophonisba Breckinridge, an old friend from the Hull House crowd who worked in the school of public welfare at the University of Chicago. She was one of the few remaining activists there, since many of the original Hull House women and suffrage leaders were now old and feeble or had died. In a letter to FDR, Breckinridge called the decision to transfer the employment service not just a poor choice but also a disloyal one.

"There is another and deeper source of regret and that is at the moment when the Secretary of Labor has showed herself a public official of the highest ability, the greatest devotion and unflinching courage, she seems to receive at the hands of a friend a kind of blow that must be a very great satisfaction to those who attack her, not for her weaknesses, if she has any, but because of her strength and because of her sex," Breckinridge wrote.

She sent Eleanor a copy, perhaps assuming that the president's wife would stand up for her longtime friend.[16]

But the First Lady also was working against Frances. Vacationing in the spring of 1939 at her pastoral Val-Kill estate, Eleanor had issued orders in a letter to Mary Dewson, Frances's former National Consumers League ally who had become a Democratic Party official. "Dear Molly," she wrote. "Under the reorganization, the Employment Service and the Unemployment Compensation are to be put under the Federal Security Agency. There is some fear that Frances Perkins will oppose it. I think if you speak to her, it will have more weight than if I were to do it. Much love, ER."[17]

The Labor Department staff shriveled as one agency after another was removed from it. In fiscal year 1940, the department had 7,301 employees; one year later, it was down to 3,696.[18]

Frances's authority eroded on other fronts. The wartime labor boom increased strikes and other labor actions, as workers who had lost economic ground during the Depression demanded their share of wartime prosperity. The NLRB, the agency created by Senator Wagner, fell into disfavor with the press and Congress. Even among liberals, it was increasingly viewed as a case of idealism run amok. Indeed, some Communists had worked themselves into key positions and were more interested in promoting chaos than in relieving labor strife. Frances had been denied power over the NLRB, making it impossible for her to address its problems. Yet many mistakenly believed the NLRB was under her dominion. To some, she appeared to be failing at running an organization over which she actually had no legal power whatsoever.

Labor unions compounded their problems with vicious infighting. The warring factions were so eager to steal members from one another that they caused economic chaos, shutting down even those businesses whose owners were trying hard to work with their unions. "Very little labor statesmanship, I may say, was being exhibited, but labor competition was very vigorous," Frances recalled sourly.[19]

Instead of defending the Labor Department, labor union officials instead frequently attacked Frances personally. When she sought to negotiate peace between the AFL and the CIO, suggesting that they try to solve "snarly little problems such as who is to be president of what," Green lashed out at her.

"The cause of peace would be promoted and advanced if Secretary Perkins would keep her mouth shut," Green told reporters.[20]

The Labor Department's Conciliation Service tried to settle strikes, but since it lacked power to force settlements, more people believed that stronger action was needed. New government boards appeared to deal with defense-related employment and economic problems. Roosevelt generally asked Frances to sit on the boards, but he gave her no policy authority. Instead citizens with no agency experience assumed equal positions on the boards. Their egos ballooned, and some compounded problems by holding public hearings that deteriorated into grandstanding. The labor unionists on the boards, often the most aggressive members, usually dominated them, leading to more public criticism of their disruptive tactics.

Each board sought to steal resources from government agencies. Frances again defended her domain, fighting against one such new board, the War Manpower Commission, "tooth and nail," as she put it. Her efforts were ineffectual. The Employment Service, already removed from her agency, was moved once again, from the Social Security Administration and to this new wartime commission.[21]

Frances began to think of herself as an unappreciated mother. She imagined the agencies she had created as her children, thinking about them as a woman thinks about her success in her own family . . . "you don't have the prestige and you don't ask for that. But what you thought ought to be done, got done by one device or another."[22]

She did not air her grievances publicly, but she raged about them in private. When NLRB member William Leiserson gave a speech in February 1943 about wartime labor relations, Frances obtained a copy and fiercely annotated it for her records. Leiserson described the Office of Production Management, another new labor board creation, as "double-headed management," confused and disorderly. In her note, Frances caustically wrote that the office was created that way "against advice of FP." Her notes documented her silent fury.[23]

On one front she succeeded, however. From the beginning, she fought efforts to draft American women. During World War I, she had been secretary of the New York City Council of Women for War Work, a vast effort to gather data on potential female workers, their skills and readiness for duty, to prepare them for mobilization. They found that many women handled responsibilities for the young and aged and that recruiting them would require finding others to replace them on the home front. Frances thought that drafting women was inefficient and possibly injurious to families. She worried if young women were conscripted and died on the front, they would leave behind orphaned children.

Frances's position on female conscription placed her at odds with Roosevelt, whose other advisers frequently commented on the approximately 10 million women who could be "potential" war workers. Eleanor supported a female draft as "only fair."[24]

Instead, Frances urged that the country encourage women to take wartime work if they wished to do so, with the enticement of good wages. This would bring women into wartime factory work just as effectively as a draft, but without the coercion and bureaucracy. Posters and advertisements urged women to step up to jobs in defense industries. Working women were cheered on with vigor, gaining popular currency in the artist's rendition of "Rosie the Riveter," a young woman wearing a red bandanna and flexing her arm to show muscle. By 1942, some 4 million women worked in war industries; by the end of the war the number had risen to 7 million.[25]

Both male and female workers flocked to the new defense industries. Frances's cook in Maine went to Bath Iron Works to earn $48 a week, getting a hefty pay hike. A blueberry picker went on Bath's payroll at $25 a week for sweeping up. Teachers left schools to work at airplane factories, and farmers headed to the factories. For the first time, large numbers of women found profitable employment outside the home.

Married women, hounded out of the workforce during the Depression, suddenly were considered unpatriotic if they did not work. A Labor Department chart in 1943 dramatically illustrated the percentage of homemakers who were absent from the workplace, calling them "estimated additions to the labor force."[26]

The war consumed all their lives. The children of the elite served their country too. The president's four sons went off to war; Frances's nephews took up arms. Hopkins's son died in combat, and Winant's son was imprisoned behind enemy lines.

The war took over the national agenda, but Frances never stopped trying to complete the initial list of items she had presented to Roosevelt when she took the job. Health insurance had been omitted from the Social Security Act because of opposition by the American Medical Association, but Frances kept the issue alive. As early as November 1935, just three months after passage of the Social Security Act, she wrote to FDR and asked for further study. In November 1940, she drafted a letter to be signed by Roosevelt that requested her to keep pursuing the issue. The letter, written as an official request from the president to the secretary of labor, asked her to create a committee to study "health security and other gaps in the program." In 1943, a department press release quoted Frances saying that a "detailed plan" was being prepared for an expanded Social Security benefit that would cover illness, nonindustrial accidents, maternity care, and hospitalization. She expected to pay for this with a payroll tax.[27]

Nothing came of her efforts. FDR lost interest in spending political capital for domestic programs. The nation's mood had changed, and FDR recognized it. People were less inclined to seek government aid than they were in 1934. The past decade's hardships seemed like faded memories as the economy cranked up with war mobilization. In December 1940, 7.4 million people were unemployed; in December 1943, only 1 million workers were jobless. About 1.5 million people worked in the defense industry in 1940; 20 million did so by December 1943. Meanwhile, some 9 million Americans joined the armed forces, a tenfold increase from four years earlier.[28]

Government aid for health insurance seemed less necessary than it had been in the past. Employment growth meant a rapid expansion in the number of people with health insurance, and fewer lived in fear of becoming sick. The law of unintended consequences played a role. Hoping to reduce inflation, the federal government imposed wage caps, so employers came up with new ways to entice workers. Some offered health insurance, which was affordable for employers because the workforce was young and medical care was still relatively simple. In effect, the government increased private health insurance, even though it had been politically impossible to implement public health insurance.

Gaps remained, however. Sick people who lost their jobs, or old people who became unemployable, still found themselves without insurance. Private programs typically provided coverage only to those healthy enough to be employed.

By 1943, as a war victory seemed assured, Roosevelt turned his attention to the postwar era and his hopes for a new international alliance to be called the United Nations. He wanted to pave the way for a lasting peace before the war was over. Frances wanted to see the International Labor Organization survive as well. The organization continued to operate in Montreal.

The war, in which vast populations were forced into slave labor by the Nazis and Japanese, convinced Frances once again of the ILO's importance. She hoped to see the ILO set basic labor standards that would improve workers' lives across the globe. She realized that poor and underdeveloped countries would likely have weaker regulations, but she felt they needed at least minimum protections. She raised this issue with the president and others.

The English and other Europeans seemed likely to support the ILO, but State Department officials suggested that Frances enlist the other great power, the Soviet Union. She arranged for Cordell Hull to raise the issue in talks, but the Russians were noncommittal. Hull suggested that Frances approach the Russian ambassador in Washington.

She obtained an interview with a diplomat, Andrei Gromyko, at the Russian embassy on Sixteenth Street, after clearing it first with the State Department. She and another department official arrived to a chilly reception. Frances sought to flatter, complimenting Gromyko on some small thing he had done, but the technique, which often worked on American men, dropped like a lead weight. She explained the ILO and asked for his support in keeping it alive. Gromyko spoke no English and listened impassively to the translator, offering little more than "yes" or "I say" at the appropriate places.

Frances visited again, with much the same results. She got no indication of Gromyko's opinion. Then one day Gromyko showed up alone at Frances's office, smiling and chatty. No longer observed by other Russians, he spoke in fluent English. He sat down and explained why ILO participation presented a challenge for the Russians. In Russia, he said, trade union officials were appointed by the government. It was their job to ensure that workers had good wages and labor conditions, but they also had responsibility for achieving maximum production.

Frances laughed and explained that in America laborers picked their own union leaders, who worked with employers to establish fair working hours and wages. Sometimes, she said, American workers go on strike to achieve those goals. "What would you do if there should be a strike?" she asked.

"Oh, that is unthinkable, unthinkable," Gromyko replied. "They could not strike, of course. In no properly conducted country would there ever be a strike."[29]

The two engaged in an animated give-and-take about government's proper role in labor relations. In Russia, the government controlled employers and unions, while in Western-style democracies the three groups operated independently. The ILO, Frances explained, followed the Western model, and the three groups were separately represented there. Gromyko finally conceded that while Russia wouldn't oppose the ILO, it was unlikely to become an active member. Yet even that was important information. Frances informed the State Department that other nations could push ahead to reestablish the ILO because no major power would object.

Frances soon learned that part of the reason Gromyko opened up was that the Soviet government had issued new directives for embassy staff to be friendlier. Later she watched with interest as Gromyko behaved bearishly as a United Nations ambassador. She viewed him as a man who believed in Russia's communist ideals and was willing to do the bidding of his superiors. The dutiful apparatchik eventually became president of the Soviet Union.

Frances then had to solidify U.S. and English backing for the ILO as part of the postwar world order. She felt confident that Roosevelt supported it in principle, but she decided to seal the two commitments in one meeting, when Winston Churchill was scheduled to visit Washington. "Now while the PM is here, we must now sew this up—sew this ILO stuff up," she told Roosevelt. "Because if the Prime Minister and you agree to this, it will be done."[30]

Roosevelt suggested she come to dinner and talk to Churchill, and she joined them for a meal a few days after his arrival. But the gathering turned out to be too big for private talk, and the president was tired.

"No good," Frances whispered to Roosevelt. "We haven't had a minute to talk about the ILO."

Roosevelt admitted he had forgotten. "I'm nearly dead," he said. "I have to talk to the PM all night and he gets bright ideas in the middle of the night and comes pattering down the hall to my bedroom in his bare feet."

Roosevelt asked her back the next night, at a family dinner with few other guests. Roosevelt seated her next to Churchill, but she had difficulty getting his attention because he was so preoccupied with the food. He ate one plate of food voraciously, and then another. Finally, Perkins decided to try.

"I want to describe to you the International Labor Organization, and I want to get your assent to putting it into the charter," she told him. "The President, I think, wants it done. At least he's aware of it."

She described the ILO's history and mission, and its survival after the flight to Canada, which she believed indicative of its strong inner spirit. Churchill grunted his assent, then asked if she knew what the Russians would do. Frances told him they would not oppose it. Again he grunted. Frances pressed for a more definitive response as they concluded dinner.

"Now Mr. Churchill, have I got your promise—have I absolutely got a go-ahead sign from you—that this is all right?"

Churchill pointed his thumb at Roosevelt. "It's up to the Boss," he said. "Whatever he says, goes."

"All right, let's take it up with him right now, hmmm?" she said.

The president was being wheeled out of the dining room to watch a film on the second floor. Frances urged Churchill to walk alongside Roosevelt's wheelchair while she took the other side. She told Roosevelt that she and Churchill had discussed the ILO, and he feigned surprise, asking Churchill what he thought of the idea.

"Up to you, up to you," Churchill said.

"Well, I think it's a good idea, what do you say?" Roosevelt said. "I think it's a good idea, don't you Winston?"

"All right. If you want it, it's good," Churchill said.

"Well, don't you think it's a good idea?"

"Oh, yes, yes, I do," Churchill said.

The trio entered the second-floor hall where movies were shown.

"Now all I want is an assurance that I may say to all hands, and be supported in this, that the President and the Prime Minister have promised me that this will be on the agenda and that this is the position that we will both take," Frances said. The men nodded. And it was done. As the film began, Frances collapsed into her seat, utterly exhausted.

The ILO survived the war. Its Philadelphia Declaration, adopted in 1943, contained some famous words: "Poverty anywhere constitutes a danger to prosperity everywhere." It called on nations to examine their foreign and domestic economic policies to determine how they affected human beings.

Labor, it said, is not simply a commodity like steel or grain; all humans have a right to pursue their material well-being. It endorsed unionization as a way for workers to improve their financial situation. The declaration also called for the development of increased trade among nations as a basis for world peace, and for wealthier nations to help poorer countries develop economically. It advocated full employment and increased standards of living for workers. It foreshadowed the Marshall Plan, under which America helped boost the economies of its former allies and enemies in the belief that increased global trade would mean better opportunities for all.

At its heart, the Philadelphia Declaration encapsulated Frances's New Deal ideals, calling for social security programs for the poor and aged, protection of workers' health and safety, the provision of child welfare and maternity protection, and the assurance of equal educational and vocational opportunity. Frances had helped make her dream become a worldwide vision.

Chapter 32

LAST DAYS OF THE ROOSEVELT ADMINISTRATION

By 1944, Roosevelt had been president for more than a decade. It was a foregone conclusion that he would run for president once again, and his election seemed assured, with the country deep in war and unwilling to shift leaders. Wallace had been a loyal and dependable ally to the president, and he assumed he would be the president's running mate once again.

But a coterie of new Roosevelt advisers, men Frances didn't like or trust, was growing in power around Roosevelt, and she was watching them with increasing suspicion. Two men in particular, Robert Hannegan, chairman of the Democratic National Committee, and James Byrnes, by now a key aide to Roosevelt, deeply disliked Wallace, a liberal, and wanted to remove him from the vice presidency.

But Wallace, oblivious to the danger, chose this moment to blithely embark on a trip to China, in May and June of 1944. The United States was close to its Asian allies, China and Russia, and many top officials had seized the opportunity to make fact-finding trips to the two nations. Many intellectuals were eager to make a visit to countries that had been difficult to visit for many years, but which were known to be exotic and interesting. They wanted to take an opportunity that might not come again.

Frances couldn't believe it when she heard Wallace was going.

"Oh, Henry, why are you going there?" she asked him. "Everybody else is going, why do you join the procession of citizens going to have a look-see on the government?"[1]

"Well, I think it's important that I go," he said. Over the next days, as the secret opposition to Wallace escalated, Frances sensed it, and her concerns about Wallace's trip also grew. She knew he was increasingly vulnerable to attacks by the manipulative Byrnes and Hannegan.

"I want to speak to you seriously," Frances said. "I don't think you ought to go away at this time. I don't think you ought to go out of the country . . . Henry, I think somebody will sell you down the river while your back's turned."

Wallace reassured her that he had gotten Roosevelt's okay. Frances reminded him that people who are out of sight slip out of mind. Wallace just laughed, saying he would risk it.

Within the next few months, Frances's fears materialized. Byrnes planted suspicions about Wallace, hoping to be the vice presidential candidate himself. What Byrnes didn't know, however, was that other people were telling FDR they considered Byrnes unelectable because he had been born Roman Catholic and converted to Protestantism. FDR asked Frances's opinion, based on experience with Al Smith.

"Yes, I know that's so," she said. ". . . Any man who's ever been anywhere near the Roman Church has got the devil's mark on him."[2]

Two important candidates emerged. One was Supreme Court Justice William O. Douglas, who chaired the Securities and Exchange Commission. The other was Harry Truman, the young man who first saw Frances campaigning for Al Smith in Independence, when she was hounded by KKK sympathizers. Truman, who had gotten his first federal job through Frances's intervention, was now a U.S. senator from Missouri.

Frances believed Roosevelt wanted to keep Wallace, but the president was weary, ailing, preoccupied by the war, and worn down by Wallace's critics. Buckling under the pressure, Roosevelt let Hannegan sway him. As the convention began in Chicago, Roosevelt felt pressure to name his vice presidential choice. He said Wallace was his *personal* favorite, but he would allow delegates to the convention to decide. Hannegan told reporters that FDR preferred Truman, though Hannegan knew that FDR had been equivocal about who the vice presidential candidate should be.

Frances went to the convention convinced that Wallace was the vice presidential nominee, but she learned that Democratic insiders had finagled the outcome "in some sort of slightly irregular way" so that Truman emerged as the leading contender.[3] He eventually won the nomination, a surprising turn of events. Truman's work chairing a committee that investigated war expenditures had gotten good publicity, but he was little known by party regulars.

Wallace said little after returning from the convention, demonstrating his stoicism in the face of what Perkins considered a "very crushing blow." He accepted the situation, and the president, who felt somewhat ashamed over what had happened, began casting about for another post for him.[4]

Around Christmas, Roosevelt called Frances to his office and told her to ask Wallace what Cabinet job he wanted. "Henry can have anything he really wants except State [Department]," the president told her.[5] Of course, Wallace wanted State, and the only other posting he fancied was Commerce, then held by Texas businessman Jesse Jones. By now, Wallace, too, had gotten bitten by the presidential bug, and he reasoned that the Commerce post would give him greater contact with American businessmen and boost his eventual shot at the presidency.

Since Jones had fallen out of favor with Roosevelt, and the president felt guilty about Wallace, FDR decided to give Jones's post to Wallace. Frances urged the president to tell Jones diplomatically, but the president was ill and busily preparing for a trip. He gave the task to Hopkins, his loyal assistant, who was in declining health as well. Hopkins terminated Jones in a curt telephone call, and Jones responded furiously with an angry letter that he prepared to make public.

"Oh, Harry, that's terrible," Frances told Hopkins when she learned what he had done. "You've hurt the old man's feelings and made an enemy."[6]

She rushed over to Jones's hotel to try to block the letter from reaching the press and found Jones upset and his wife verging on tears.

"Oh, Mr. Jones, I am so sorry," Frances told him. "I don't think the president wanted you to be offended in this way, and I think it's a brutal thing to have done."

Jones listed a litany of grievances against Roosevelt, and Frances listened sympathetically. But it was too late. Jones had already given the critical letter to newspaper reporters, and the public split meant the men parted ways with animosity. Wallace was confirmed secretary of commerce a few months later.

By December 1944, Frances wanted out, too. Four years had passed since she had pressed Roosevelt for her release from office. She was weary from more than a decade of stress and abuse at the hands of reporters and congressmen. She saw her old friend Rose Schneiderman and confided her plans.

"I had quite a talk with Frances and I believe she is definitely leaving the department," Schneiderman wrote their mutual friend, Mary Dreier.

ABOVE: At Eleanor Roosevelt's request, Frances regularly attended luncheon gatherings for the wives of Cabinet officers. *(Frances Perkins Papers, Rare Book & Manuscript Library, Columbia University)*

RIGHT: Washington housemate and close ally, the heiress Mary Harriman Rumsey, who founded the Junior League, was an avid horsewoman. *(Courtesy of David Mortimer)*

Caroline Love O'Day, U.S. congresswoman from New York and longtime friend. *(Courtesy of the Department of Labor)*

Longshoreman and labor leader Harry Bridges (second from right) leads a picket parade in San Francisco seeking important concessions for maritime workers, 1934. *(The Bancroft Library, University of California, Berkeley)*

Frances inspects the Border Patrol, a branch of the U.S. Immigration Service, which she oversees as secretary of labor. *(Frances Perkins Papers, Rare Book & Manuscript Library, Columbia University)*

ABOVE: President Franklin Delano Roosevelt signs into law the Social Security Act, one of Frances Perkins's primary policy initiatives; Perkins is standing behind him; man in dark suit to president's right is Senator Robert F. Wagner. August 14, 1935. *(Franklin D. Roosevelt Presidential Library)*

RIGHT: Susanna Wilson weds David Hare, 1938. *(David Hare Papers, The Young-Mallin Archive)*

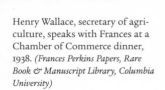

Henry Wallace, secretary of agriculture, speaks with Frances at a Chamber of Commerce dinner, 1938. *(Frances Perkins Papers, Rare Book & Manuscript Library, Columbia University)*

Frances Perkins, on left, and Molly Dewson, member of the Social Security Board, 1938. *(Frances Perkins Papers, Rare Book & Manuscript Library, Columbia University)*

Frances prepares to descend into a mine shaft to take a look at working conditions underground, 1940. *(Frances Perkins Papers, Rare Book & Manuscript Library, Columbia University)*

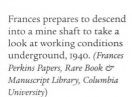

Frances looks on as a female defense manufacturing worker—Rosie the Riveter—demonstrates how she does her job, 1943. *(Frances Perkins Papers, Rare Book & Manuscript Library, Columbia University)*

LEFT: Susanna and Paul sitting together on the stairs outside the family home in Newcastle, Thanksgiving 1944. *(Courtesy of Tomlin Coggeshall)*

BELOW: Frances Perkins leaves the White House in an official car soon after learning of FDR's death, April 12, 1945. *(Harry S. Truman Library/ National Archives)*

Harry S. Truman taking the oath of office for president, Frances Perkins to the far left, April 12, 1945. *(National Park Service, Abbie Rowe, Courtesy of Harry S. Truman Library)*

President Truman and Ambassador Averell Harriman, August 1945. *(U.S. Army Signal Corps, Courtesy of Harry S. Truman Library)*

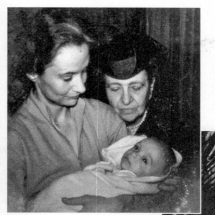

Susanna holds newborn
son, Tomlin Coggeshall, as
her mother looks on, 1954.
(Courtesy of Tomlin Coggeshall)

President John F. Kennedy
confers with Frances
after she gives a speech in
Washington, D.C. *(Frances
Perkins Papers, Rare Book &
Manuscript Library, Columbia
University)*

Jacqueline Kennedy, wife of Democratic presidential candidate John F. Kennedy, convened a meeting of Democratic women to discuss issues of political and civic concern;
Frances Perkins, who appears at her left, was an honored guest, 1960. *(© Bettmann/Corbis)*

Frances Perkins and Eleanor Roosevelt, allies for a lifetime, share some memories at a ceremony in New York City. *(Kheel Center, Cornell University/ILGWU Archives)*

"Twelve years of sniping on the part of the newspapers has had its effect on her, I think. She is just kind of tired of it all . . . I do hope the president makes some place for her because she really must work in order to meet her obligations to her husband."[7]

Frances, in fact, already had written a five-page resignation letter. She asked to be relieved of duty on inauguration day. She outlined her accomplishments over twelve years, which she noted represented a "turning point in our national life—a turning from careless neglect of human values and toward an order (voluntarily established by the people through representative government) of mutual and practical benevolence within a free competitive industrial economy."

She reminded FDR of her role in the Civilian Conservation Corps, the Public Works Program, and the labor aspects of the National Industrial Recovery Act. She reminded him that he had entrusted her with the research, legislative program, popularization, and establishment of unemployment insurance, old-age pensions, and the welfare program. She described how she had reduced child labor in America, minimized workplace accidents, and converted the Bureau of Labor Statistics into a "trusted" source of information. The Fair Labor Standards Act brought about the minimum wage, the concept of the forty-hour workweek, and paying for overtime. She greatly expanded the U.S. Conciliation Service in dealing with strikes. She dealt with many labor questions during the war, when skilled manpower was vital and women moved into formerly male jobs.

"I have recited all these items in the hope that the recollection of them will convey to you the reason for my deep appreciation for your vision and leadership and for the opportunity which you have given me to share in this service to the people of our country," she wrote. "With one major exception all the items we discussed as 'among the practical possibilities' before you took office have been accomplished or begun," she wrote. The one thing left undone was health care assistance for the ill and jobless.

She ended the letter, saying: "I hope this will be upon your agenda for the near future."[8]

Official Washington knew Frances intended to go. On January 25, 1945, Harold Ickes wrote to FDR suggesting Justice William Douglas, the man who had been considered as a potential vice president, as a strong candidate for her job. But FDR already had responded to Frances.

In January 1945 FDR wrote, complimenting Frances on the letter, calling it "tremendously interesting." It showed "concisely and clearly all that you have accomplished in the Department of Labor," he wrote. He again turned down her resignation.

"There are many other things to do—matters with which you are familiar—and as I told you Friday, your resignation is not one of them. It is hereby declined. Indeed, it is rejected and refused. I will see you as soon as I get back. As ever yours, FDR."[9]

In private, however, he had begged her to stay, she told a few close friends. He clasped her shoulder, crying, and asked her not to leave. Once again, she decided to stay a bit longer. It was only one of several emotional exchanges she had with the president in 1944 and 1945.[10]

FDR, now sixty-three, was no longer the energetic soul he had been. His health was slipping. He had fainting spells and sometimes felt he did not have the strength to go on. Frances told Tom Eliot that around the time Roosevelt took office for the fourth time, she had spoken privately with him. "Frances, I can't do it," he told her, to which she replied, "Mr. President, you must."[11]

The inauguration day activities started, as had become customary, with a religious service in the mid-morning attended by the president's closest advisers, friends, and relatives. Princess Martha of Norway and her children, who were visiting as diplomatic guests, attended. The war made it unsafe for the president to attend services at St. John's Church, so they held the ceremony in the East Room of the White House, with part of the choir from St. John's singing from the grand parlor's edges.

The president appeared, looking weak and thinner, but his eyes were bright as he sat in the front row. He couldn't kneel, but he bent over in prayer reverently. Finally, after the service ended, Roosevelt sat up and shook himself. Mrs. Roosevelt rose, the clergy left, and the others filed out.

Frances watched the president from across the room. She was aware of the mounting pressures, that he had important work to do but was finding it hard to muster the strength. She knew he was planning to go away. Nobody would reveal where, but she and the others assumed he was bound somewhere to negotiate the shape of the postwar world with the Russians and Churchill.

"This is the cross the Lord has laid upon him, and he's got to expend every ounce of energy he's got to pull this thing through," Frances thought. "He's got to do it."[12]

Her instinct, she said later, was to shelter him in some way, but she realized he couldn't be protected. "This is the place he's called to, and he's got to do it," she said to herself. "You have to do it because you are there, and you have the responsibility. And there was no earthly way of saying, 'This man can't go because he is sick.' "

Frances stopped by to say a word to him as the service ended, and Roosevelt squeezed her hand. "Remember, I'll pray for you every day of my life, while you're gone," she told him.[13]

"For God's sake, do, Frances, I need it," he answered.

The inauguration was held at noon at the White House. Although only two hours had passed, the president looked considerably sicker. His eyes were glassy, and his cheeks were drawn. He seemed to have lost control of the muscles around his jaw, and his mouth looked slack. His hands were weak and trembling. Frances watched him with concern.

He managed to stand throughout the inaugural address, but as he stepped down from the lectern, he leaned heavily on an aide. His wheelchair stood by the podium, and he sat down in it quickly.

Frances was invited to the White House for a luncheon, where guests were being escorted one at a time to the Red Room to speak briefly with the president. Eleanor asked Frances if she wanted to see him, but she said no, and Eleanor nodded appreciatively. But Belle Roosevelt, the wife of Teddy Roosevelt's son Kermit, went in and exited the room a few minutes later, horrified at FDR's appearance. The doctor had just given him a good bill of health, Frances reassured her.

Edith Wilson, Woodrow Wilson's widow, was similarly shocked at FDR's appearance and unable to conceal her reaction.

"Oh, Miss Perkins, did you get a good look at the president?" she said. "Oh, it frightened me. He looks exactly as my husband looked when he went into his decline."[14]

Her comment frightened Frances, but she put her fingers to her lips. "Don't say that to another soul," she told Edith.

"I guess you're right," Edith said.

"He has a great and terrible job to do," Frances told her. "Don't say a word. He's got to do it, even if it kills him. He's got to do it."

The Frankfurters also thought Roosevelt's health was failing.

"He has the look of a doomed man," Marion Frankfurter told her husband, Felix, on inauguration day.[15]

Roosevelt was conscious enough of his deteriorating health that he made some contingency plans for the administration. At a Cabinet meeting before he left for the Yalta Conference, he gave instructions on what should happen if he were to be stricken with illness. Pointing to Edward Stettinius, who had replaced Cordell Hull as secretary of state, Roosevelt said he should call a meeting of the Cabinet and "take necessary decisions." Frankfurter said the president wanted to ensure that his wife did not end up running the government, as Edith Wilson had after Woodrow Wilson's health broke.[16]

FDR still had some very good days. In the early spring of 1945, after his return from Yalta, Frances met with Roosevelt and found him joyful at the prospect of heading off for Warm Springs in a day or so. She made an appointment with him to discuss the ILO. As she often did, she also had a short list of items to present for approval.

FDR had some exciting news to tell her: "Frances, I'll tell you something," he said. "Eleanor and I are going to England!"

Frances recoiled. "It's terribly dangerous," she burst out. "The Germans will get after you."[17]

He hastened to reassure her. Though they were alone in the room, FDR put his hand to the side of his mouth and whispered his next words to her. "It isn't going to be until May; we're going in May," he said. "Frances, the war will be over by then."

She saw that he was completely confident. "Are you sure?" she said. Yes, he told her.

He leaned back in his chair and grew expansive. He had decided on a new plan, to be launched once the war was over and the United Nations was operating. He would go to Saudi Arabia with a team of engineers and figure out how to irrigate the desert, to relieve some of the terrible poverty he had seen in the Mideast.

"We could do wonders," he mused aloud.[18]

Chapter 33

HARRY TRUMAN

At 5:50 p.m. on a spring afternoon in April 1945, Frances got a call from the White House summoning her to an emergency Cabinet meeting ten minutes later. What could it be, she wondered. A much-awaited surrender? Frances put on her hat and rushed to the White House. An aide greeted her but no one else spoke as she entered the corridor. Frances caught a glimpse of Anna, Roosevelt's daughter, and gave her a friendly wave.

Frances entered the Cabinet room and found Truman and Fred Vinson, director of the Office of Emergency Stabilization, standing solemnly.

"The President is dead," Truman said.[1]

Frances looked away quickly to try to absorb the crushing news. She made the sign of the cross. Her last conversation with Roosevelt—when he had excitedly discussed his plans for economic development in the Middle East—left her ill prepared for his death.

The men filled her in as best they could, but they knew only sketchy details. Eleanor, they said, had learned that the president had a fatal stroke in Warm Springs, Georgia.

The Cabinet members slowly filtered into the White House. Truman rose to make a more formal announcement of FDR's death and to ask for the Cabinet's support. Frances thought Truman looked frightened at inheriting a task he had not sought. His words struck Frances as characteristic of the down-to-earth and modest man. He told them he did not feel worthy or strong enough to carry this load, but that "with the help of God" he would do it, and would do it as well as he could.[2]

Truman would not have been Frances's choice for president. He came from a middle-class background and had not been raised to rule, as Roosevelt had. His political connections were of the small-town variety, and his only Washington experience was as a one-term senator. Roosevelt's endorsement of him as vice president had been lukewarm. During the eighty-one days Truman served as vice president, Roosevelt had hardly acknowledged him.

But as soon as she learned of FDR's death, Frances sensed that Truman would work out all right. She had, after all, known Truman for years and thought him to be competent, resourceful, inventive, and intelligent. Frances thought to herself, "He'll make out all right, because he has the type of mind and spirit to be humble, to begin at the beginning and not to think he knows everything."[3]

Bess Truman stood by, her eyes red and swollen from crying, as Chief Justice Harlan Stone swore in Truman as president. During the ceremony, Frances prayed for FDR, and for Truman as well.

Afterward, the group milled about. Frances's friend Isador Lubin wept and buried his face in her shoulder, a scene captured by a photographer. This shot was published the next day with the caption, "Secretary Perkins gives way to grief." This irritated the always-stoic Frances, who resented the implication that she was the one who had broken down in public.

Since his inauguration for a fourth term, Roosevelt's health had fluctuated. Some days he appeared to be expiring before people's eyes, but at other times his ebullient charm shone through. In February the president made his unannounced trip to Yalta to meet with Churchill and Stalin. They discussed plans for governing Europe after defeat of the now-disintegrating Axis nations and for forming an international framework that would become the United Nations. Already Churchill and Roosevelt shared a growing concern about the plans of the duplicitous and expansionist Russian leader, whose onetime pact with Hitler had led to the dismemberment of Poland.

The pace and rigor of the negotiations had taken its toll. After four years of round-the-clock duty managing a global war, several of the Americans found their health faltering. Roosevelt appeared drawn and wan; Harry Hopkins, lean to the point of emaciation, was rushed away to recuperate in Marrakech; and General Edwin "Pa" Watson, Roosevelt's loyal pal, had a stroke and died on the voyage home to the United States. Roosevelt himself was weak on his return. When he addressed

Congress about the events in Yalta, for the first time he had to speak to them seated because he could no longer stand. Roosevelt decided to go to Warm Springs, ever his fountain of youth, for renewal. Eleanor offered to come along, but he gently dissuaded her.

Roosevelt seemed to be recovering in those early days of April. He regained his appetite, and the color returned to his skin. Roosevelt's daughter, Anna, had invited Lucy Mercer Rutherford, Roosevelt's one-time paramour, who had been banished years before when Eleanor became aware of FDR's infidelity, to visit him in Warm Springs. Roosevelt spent several peaceful days in the company of two women who loved him: Lucy and his cousin, Margaret Suckley. He was sitting for a portrait one afternoon when he suddenly complained of a "terrific pain" in his head and lapsed into unconsciousness. While Lucy applied camphor to his nostrils and Margaret held his hand, the president slipped away. He suffered a cerebral hemorrhage and died at 3:35 that afternoon.

At the first sign of the president's distress, Roosevelt aide Marvin McIntyre called Eleanor to tell her that the president had fainted. She asked if she should head to Warm Springs immediately, which would mean disappointing the crowd at the Sulgrave Club in Washington, where she was expected. McIntyre told her to stick to her schedule. After a while, another aide, Steve Early, called and urged her to return to the White House. She listened to the rest of the program and only then slipped back to the White House. There, she learned that the president had died. She calmly donned a black dress, sent the news to her children, and phoned for Vice President Truman, who was drinking with his Capitol Hill cronies.[4]

Truman was ushered up to Mrs. Roosevelt's second-floor study, where she waited for him. She placed her arm around his shoulder. "Harry, the President is dead," she said quietly. He stood speechless, then asked if there was anything he could do to help her. She looked at him compassionately. "Is there anything we can do for you?" she responded. "For you are the one in trouble now."[5]

The transfer of power began in minutes.

Frances's friend Gertrude Ely, who had helped care for Susanna at Bryn Mawr, was in Washington that day, and she went to Frances's office to wait for her while she was at the White House. Frances asked Ely to stay with her that night, and the two disconsolate women attended a short service at St. James' Church. After a meal, they walked back to the White House, where they joined a crowd gathering outside. People milled about the street, seeking the company of strangers to share their shock.

Frances found herself beside a soldier, who spoke to her without looking in her direction. "I felt as if I knew him," he said.[6]

"Yes," Frances said. The young man paused.

"I felt as if he knew me, and I felt as if he liked me," he said.

The women went home to Frances's house and stayed up for hours, talking about Roosevelt. Over the next few days, Frances learned details of his death, including Eleanor's betrayal by her own daughter, who arranged for the rendezvous between Roosevelt and Lucy Mercer. Frances was incensed. Henry Morgenthau, too, had apparently accepted the situation, having dined with Lucy and Franklin in Warm Springs while his own wife, one of Eleanor's closest friends, was hospitalized in Florida.[7]

FDR's body arrived in Washington by train the next day. Eleanor decided that Roosevelt's funeral should be private and held at the White House. She said she had an agreement with the president about his funeral ceremony. Frances secretly disagreed. Because of the depth of mourning, she thought people should have the chance to attend the ceremony. Frances thought it could have been held at the National Cathedral.

Instead, the funeral service was held in the East Room at the White House. The mourners sang hymns that FDR had selected for his mother's funeral: "Faith of Our Fathers" and "Oh, God, Our Help in Ages Past."

Eleanor's comportment earned Frances's admiration. She presided over the ceremony with dignity, grace, and composure. The mourners left by train for Hyde Park, where the president was to be laid to rest. As the train wound its way up the Atlantic Coast, thousands lined the route.

In Hyde Park, the procession drove up the hill to the president's house, to the Rose Garden where he would be buried. Frances knew that was where the president wanted to be laid to rest. He had told her so before, when they toured the grounds. She laughed at him for being morose enough to plan his own funeral. He told her all he wanted at the grave was a white marble slab engraved with his name.

It had been a warm day then, with hedges in bloom, but on the day they buried Roosevelt, it was "cold and raw, much colder than it had been in Washington, and the wind was blowing," she recalled later.[8]

Father Anthony, the priest at St. James' Episcopal Church in Hyde Park, where FDR was senior warden, led the formal prayers. Then he moved into the Office of the Invitatory, an ancient rite that was part of the Sarum Book of Hours. "Let his holy angels take charge of thee," he intoned.

The service made no reference to FDR's presidency, to his honors or earthly power. Instead, it called him as a lamb back to God. The service comforted Frances—but also left her immensely sad.

Frances, Wallace, and Ickes—the three Cabinet members who had worked together and battled each other through twelve years of Roosevelt's administration—stood side by side at FDR's grave, as they had sat each week at the Cabinet table. As the ceremony ended, the flag was given to Eleanor Roosevelt. The family walked out of the cemetery, with the Cabinet members following. Making the sign of the cross, Frances said the same five words she said at the graves of all her loved ones— her mother, her father, her closest friends. "May God rest his soul," she said.[9]

Overhearing her, Wallace noticed that her inflection suggested that she believed FDR had a particularly restless soul. Both had been devoted friends to FDR, and both had suffered at his hands.

As they left the cemetery, she recalled later, the sun broke through the clouds. She noticed bits of green appearing on the branches and bushes. "The little leaves, just the bare signals of spring [were] on the trees," Frances thought.

The mourners boarded the train for the return to Washington. Eleanor had a private stateroom, and one by one people went to express their condolences, Mrs. Truman among them. Eleanor told Bess that she would help prepare her for her first press conference and introduce her to the newspaperwomen. Frances, however, privately advised Bess that she was not obligated to hold press conferences as Eleanor had done— and Bess looked relieved.

In those next few weeks, a few people wrote to Frances to express their understanding of her own grief. Her longtime friend Mary Dreier wrote her an affectionate letter. Frances wrote back saying the condolence had been comforting.

"You are quite right that people throughout the world trusted him to somehow lead them to the actual accomplishment of freedom and righteousness. There was a great sympathy between him and the people in the mass, as well as between him and individuals. This quality of his, as you know, came to him after his illness. That sympathy between him and the world and people was something he acquired out of suffering—not consciously, but just a result of it."[10]

To Margaret Bondfield, Frances wrote, "Thank you for your sympathy. It has been a very hard blow to accept . . . I felt badly that he had to die. He did not want to; he wasn't through by any means in his own mind. He wanted to have a hand in the peace and in the construction of the new world; he was full of ideas, not all of them technically perfect but all of them alert to the general conception that all human beings long for a better world and that we must begin to work for it and build for it constructively."[11]

Frances shared another letter with Eleanor Roosevelt, from her friend Charles Culp Burlingham. The letter spoke to FDR's optimism in overcoming obstacles. To Frances, it was the one tribute that most characterized him. "FDR was never disappointed; if things went wrong he took another tack," Burlingham wrote. Frances and Eleanor read the letter together sitting in the White House the day before Eleanor moved out for good.

"She was able to appear at leisure, although the bare walls and bookcases and the loaded desks and the black-bordered paper bore mute testimony to her work," Frances wrote to her friend. "There were other people there, but we went out in the hall and sat on a bench like two schoolgirls, and talked about FD[R]. You will be glad to know that she can cry, and it is in an honest, natural, healthy fashion, not for publication. She is a great person really. Everything she has said and done, even to the last word, 'The story is over,' is almost perfect."[12]

🔺

*F*ollowing in the footsteps of such impressive personalities, Truman faced a daunting task. FDR thought him so insignificant that he never bothered to share the details about the war or foreign affairs with him. Now Truman was assuming responsibility for the world's largest military force, facing the most far-flung war in history. In those first few days he did little to inspire confidence. He fervently asked a group of reporters to pray for him, telling them he felt like a "load of hay" had fallen on his head. When one responded by saying, "Good luck, Mr. President," Truman told him: "I wish you didn't have to call me that."[13]

For the first month Truman kept FDR's Cabinet intact, relying on the members' expertise to keep government running. But almost immediately Frances sensed the cabinet dissolving, in the way a family breaks up when a beloved father dies.

Frances noticed that Truman was recovering his nerve. She had seen him begin to get a grip on himself on the return from the funeral. Certainly he would need all his strength: The Germans were on the verge of surrender, and Truman faced a momentous decision about using a powerful new weapon, the atomic bomb, to end the conflict with Japan. The magnitude of the horrors inflicted by the Nazis was just coming to light.

Three weeks after Roosevelt's death, Hitler committed suicide. On May 7, the Germans surrendered, and on May 8, Truman announced the end of the war in Europe. The Japanese fought on. At Truman's orders and at the urging of James Byrnes, then a top Truman adviser, the war-fatigued U.S. military dropped an atomic bomb on the Japanese city of Hiroshima on August 6, killing eighty thousand people, most of them civilians, and three days later, another on Nagasaki, killing an additional seventy thousand. Emperor Hirohito surrendered on August 15.

Frances was not there for these final actions of the war. She was the first Cabinet member to tell Truman she would step down, and she immediately prepared for her departure. In a meeting with Truman, Frances suggested he might want a "great, strong man" in the Labor Department to present the image of a muscular government settling labor disturbances. Truman laughed and said it was true, but that he still didn't want her to resign.[14]

In fact, he had asked his closest friends whether men could ever be "comfortable" if a woman were present. "A great lady," he called her in his private notes, but added that she knew "nothing about politics."[15]

He also came under pressure from the men in the Cabinet, all of whom preferred that she be removed, according to Mathew J. Connelly, Truman's executive assistant and then appointments secretary. Which Cabinet members felt this way, Connelly was asked. "I would say practically all of them," Connelly replied. In the Cabinet around that time were Ickes, Wallace, Morgenthau, Stimson, Biddle, Walker, Vinson, Forrestal, Hannegan, and George C. Marshall. Insiders said the men, many of whom also privately admired Frances, said they would need to restrain their comments if a lady were present, and that she would inhibit their deliberations.[16]

Finally Truman conceded, and once he made the decision, she was told to step down quickly. She wrote a resignation letter, sent it over by messenger, and quietly packed her belongings.

Outside observers thought Truman was eager to get rid of her. "As everybody knows, Miss Perkins was hoisted out of her job as soon as decently possible by Truman," wrote Doris Fleeson in the *Washington Star,* noting that Frances had suffered a "record of congressional attacks, considering that no question was ever raised about her motives or her integrity."[17]

What appeared to be a public rebuff masked a markedly more congenial personal relationship, however. Truman knew that Frances had provided his entrée into federal service in 1933 when she approved him for the director of the Federal Reemployment Service in Missouri. Over the years, he came to "understand and appreciate" her "ability and stature." During his Senate years, they dined regularly and discussed government problems. "As the years went by I learned what a fine human being she was," he wrote.[18]

Labor Department Administrative Assistant James E. Dodson, who helped Frances manage the departmental budgets, recalled that Truman regarded her with respect. Once while Truman was a senator, for example, the department had a problem with its appropriation, and Dodson suggested that he and Frances visit Truman. They made an appointment and headed up to Capitol Hill. Truman greeted them genially.

"Why Miss Perkins," he said, "you didn't have to come up to see me. If you had given me a call I would gladly have come down to your office."[19]

As she had done with all her supervisors, she spent the few months before she left office studying Truman's management style and personality type, to better understand him. She noted, for example, that Truman preferred to receive memos that were brief, with specific recommendations for action.

Frances parted on good terms with Truman, unlike many others in the carryover administration. Truman later said he had never heard a "word or a criticism" from Frances, and considered her a friend.[20]

Even after she submitted her resignation letter, Truman agreed to let her attend the ILO conference in Paris in 1945, as she had planned to do with the support of Churchill and Roosevelt.

Truman told her that he wanted to bring her back in some other post and asked her to consider what she would like to do. She told him she wanted to be head of the Social Security program, which she "had fathered" and that she hoped to guide to be "sensible and practical and liberal." She didn't want to push out Federal Security Administrator Paul McNutt, but if he were to resign, she would eagerly take over. Truman said he would consider it.[21]

Her last day was July 1, 1945, a time of Cabinet transition. Robert Hannegan, who maneuvered Truman into the vice presidency under Roosevelt, became postmaster general. Byrnes became secretary of state. The conservative Democrats surrounding Truman "were not the Perkins type," said Isador Lubin, who had moved from BLS into Roosevelt's inner circle. Now people like Frances and Lubin were seen as out of step. "There won't be any place in this administration for people like you," Byrnes told Lubin. Byrnes felt the New Deal "had come to an end," Lubin recalled.[22]

One of the few Roosevelt insiders to remain was Henry Wallace, who Truman asked to continue as commerce secretary. The two rivals for the vice presidency met frequently, and Wallace spoke to Frances warmly about Truman.

Some people acknowledged the magnitude of what she had achieved in her post. Supreme Court justice Felix Frankfurter wrote lauding her accomplishments and regretting how they had been little appreciated, especially by the news media. He added that her tenure also had been overshadowed by the war, which created an impossible situation for her; her gender hadn't helped either. "In view of the persistence of obstinate prejudices in public affairs, this is still a man's world (although some men are now attempting the constitutional elimination of the sexes!) and any woman Secretary would have been imprisoned by the internecine strife within Labor."[23]

Frances wrote back to Frankfurter: "I had, as you know, a program in mind," she wrote.

You know all about it because I talked with you about most of it and asked your advice on most of it. . . . The program is almost accomplished. Everything except health insurance, dear Felix, that I had on my original list and some things which weren't on the original list we have been able to do because the climate was right for social change.[24]

Hundreds of people swarmed to a recognition dinner in her honor, and people who publicly blasted her now clamored to toast her. The menu featured diamondback terrapin soup and breast of capon. Dessert was frozen eggnog and raspberry sherbet, accompanied by a chocolate cupcake. Serving generous plaudits from the podium was Eric Johnston, president of the U.S. Chamber of Commerce, whose members had once tried to unseat Frances as labor secretary. Two other men, cohosting the event as equal vice chairs, were William Green of the AFL and Philip Murray of the CIO. Eleanor was busy elsewhere and didn't attend, but sent a nice telegram.[25]

Truman named in Frances's place his Senate crony Lewis Schwellenbach, who had gained fame with Truman when they were labeled two of the "Four Horsemen" as junior senators. Frances contacted him immediately to offer support and assistance. Schwellenbach, who had dined in Frances's home in 1940 at a dinner honoring actress Helen Gahagan, responded churlishly, treating her with contempt. He had left the Senate to accept a judgeship in eastern Washington State, and he came to believe negative reports about her handling of the department. He thought he would be cleaning house. Schwellenbach wrote back to Frances a terse letter declining her offer to find him a hotel in Washington. Even so, Frances met Schwellenbach and his wife at the train station. He seemed uninterested in hearing details about the agency, instead lavishing his attention on his small dog, a Pekingese.

Frances was set on her heels.

"We talked about the little dog, and I talked about the state of the government," she recalled.[26]

Schwellenbach arranged for his own swearing-in to be conducted by a friend in the Senate. This turned out later to be invalid because senators were not legally authorized to administer oaths. Later a department official swore him in properly.

Schwellenbach did everything he could to distance himself from Frances. Then he showed up in her office and took over her desk, unconcerned about her schedule of last-minute items. Frances moved to another office to wrap things up. "It was a day of perfect hell," she said later.[27]

In the following weeks, Frances started to mentally detach from the Labor Department. Schwellenbach performed badly in office, as she had expected, and became viewed as one of the agency's most incompetent secretaries. He knew little about labor, and then grew ill and wasn't able to handle a worsening situation. Truman called to Washington John R. Steelman, the man Frances had chosen as director of the conciliation service, to assist him.

Ickes, now retired and penning a newspaper column, wrote that he realized what a good job Frances had done. "When Miss Perkins was Secretary of Labor, she was hounded and harassed with sadistic delight. There was a consistent demand that President Roosevelt replace her by a strong he-man," Ickes wrote. "Well we have two strong he-men—John Steelman and Lewis Schwellenbach—running the labor policies of the Government. . . . I wonder if our labor affairs would not be in more competent hands if only Secretary Perkins was back on the job."

Steelman agreed, telling an interviewer: "Well, of course I wished many times for Miss Perkins myself!"[28]

Out of the hot seat, Frances couldn't restrain herself from gloating privately when Schwellenbach faltered. The war was over, and American companies emerged triumphant, so labor unions could afford to increase their demands. "Every time I would read in the paper that there was another strike, I would laugh and laugh and laugh," she said.[29]

She avoided chuckling when department employees came to her with outrage over Schwellenbach's performance. She couldn't resist hearing stories about his beloved dog. He brought the pooch to the office each day, asking the secretary to prepare its special meals. Messengers were assigned to take the dog for walks, and the chauffeur was assigned to drive the pet back and forth between Schwellenbach's office and home.

"I mean, that sort of thing was just comic, you know, and I used to wonder how in the world does he get away with it?" she said. "But that comes from being a big, strong man."[30]

Chapter 34

THE TRUMAN
ADMINISTRATION

Saddened and weary, Frances was not sorry to leave behind official life in Washington. Truman held out the possibility of a new job, but at that moment, in July 1945, with the war in the Pacific not quite over, Frances felt eager to get away. Her only definite plan was to attend the summer ILO conference in Paris.

Shortly before leaving office, however, she was contacted by literary agent George Bye, who suggested that she write a book about Roosevelt. She laughed off the idea. Bye persisted. Frances said she couldn't afford to do it. He said he would arrange an advance against royalties with Viking Press.

The prospect terrified Frances. "Why, how do I know I will be able to do it?" she asked. "I don't dare take the money. You mustn't say that, George, because if I take the money and don't deliver, what happens?" [1]

When she heard about the offer, Susanna pressured her mother to accept. Many Roosevelt insiders, including Eleanor, earned large sums by writing their stories. "Oh, do it Mother, don't be so stupid," Susanna chided. Finally, Frances agreed. She signed the contract in London and then tried to forget about it.

She continued to tie up loose ends from her old job. In July 1945 the British public showed its traditional ingratitude to its great men and refused to reelect Prime Minister Churchill. Frances wrote to offer some consolation:

> Many are telling you what you have done for England. May
> I thank you for the service you have rendered for the United
> States and its people—for moral leadership, for opening many
> eyes so that they could see what was the true question before the
> civilized world and for having and using the personal qualities

which could make Americans as well as British trust you and understand you, in this great crisis of our times. . . . In one of the last interviews I had with President Roosevelt, after relating a trifling incident of your recent meeting in the Crimea, he said with that friendly and recollecting look he sometimes has and with a chuckle, "The P.M. is a great feller; you know I love the old cuss."[2]

*T*here is no record of Churchill's response to Frances. It is possible that he did not write back, which seems unlikely, but such a letter—Winston Churchill reminiscing about Roosevelt—would have been valuable to any number of people.

*F*rances's trip to the ILO conference went well, and she was greeted with cheers by the delegates from other nations, who gave her a standing ovation. They knew she had helped the organization to survive. On her return to the United States, she moved back to the New York City apartment that had been her home base since the 1920s and reluctantly turned back to the book project. She promptly panicked. Frances at first dictated to a secretary, then realized she needed a research assistant and then another stenographer. She spoke into a Dictaphone, working mostly from 10 p.m. to 3 a.m., when the house was quiet. When the secretaries arrived in the morning, they transcribed Frances's dictation. Soon Frances had an enormous amount of material drafted, but it was poorly organized, so she hired a young *New York Times* reporter, Howard Taubman, to put the book together. In the final weeks, Frances employed Taubman, a researcher, and five stenographers, frantically trying to meet the due date of May 15, 1946.

Frances, the longtime proponent of a forty-hour workweek, laughingly called it "slave labor," with the women coming early and staying late, during an unusually early and hot summer.

Taubman pushed Frances to include many personal details, but as usual, she was guarded. When she wrote about adding artists' work to the Civil Works Project, she noted that the suggestion had reached FDR's ear through the insistence of a "young girl who was a member of the family of a Cabinet member." She declined to mention Susanna by name.

Taubman elicited some items about Roosevelt and his relationship with Eleanor, such as Frances's recollection of how FDR admired Eleanor's hair. But Frances wouldn't go beyond these safely neutral comments, saying that some of what she knew was "privileged communication." Even so, her descriptions worked their way into dozens of later books about Roosevelt, including some that mentioned Frances's role in his administration only in passing.

Frances, ever loyal to FDR, purposely omitted details that might have made Roosevelt seem more human. For example, in a section about FDR's flirtation with Madame Chiang Kai-shek, who flattered FDR by calling him "sophisticated," Frances noted that the exchange illustrated Roosevelt's "simple human vanity" because "he would not have liked to be thought unsophisticated." In her personal copy of the book, Frances wrote a notation into the margin: "But he was." She was already looking for ways to give future biographers clues to what she could not bring herself to say directly.[3]

As Roosevelt's closest friend for decades, Frances had insights into the man unsurpassed by anyone except his wife. Even with its omissions, Frances's book, *The Roosevelt I Knew,* was the first definitive biography of the president. It chronicled their time together from their first meeting in 1910 and over the thirty-five subsequent years. The book was published in November 1946. The reviews were positive, and the book quickly hit number one on the best-seller list, and stayed there for more than ten weeks.

Frances's book might have sold better if she had promoted it, but the notoriously publicity-shy woman rebuffed most attempts to circulate it through the cocktail party and news-interview circuit. She acknowledged that she was a "very, very difficult" author to handle because she considered even a limited press tour to be "agony." As soon as the book was launched, she disappeared to the Maine family homestead.[4]

Her observations about FDR and her recollections were viewed as factually reliable, even by the former president's staunchest critics. John T. Flynn, author of *The Roosevelt Myth,* a 1948 book excoriating FDR and most of his lieutenants, cited Frances and her book twenty-one times, at one point referring to one of her accounts as incontrovertible because she is "truthful."[5]

In late August 1946, Paul Fitzpatrick, chairman of the New York State Democratic committee, called Frances in Maine to say Truman wished to appoint her to a government post. "There's going to be a vacancy . . . in a particular situation," he told her with great delicacy. Frances responded that she had told Truman of her wish to serve on the Social Security Board.

Fitzpatrick told her that particular job wasn't available because a Democratic party official, Oscar Ewing, wanted it. Instead, Fitzpatrick said, they wanted to name her to the Civil Service Commission, to replace another woman, Lucille Foster McMillin, whose stroke a year earlier had left her what he called "almost non compos mentis." Frances would be one of three commissioners charged with administering federal employment law.

Less than thrilled, Frances repeated that she had been hoping for the Social Security post. The next day, Truman called personally and told Frances he needed her as a civil service commissioner.

"That's very good of you," Frances said, but "is it absolutely out of the question to consider me for Social Security?"[6]

"Well, I know you'd like that, and I see why," he said. "It's right up your line and you were responsible for the Act entirely . . . But we're in a kind of a jam, you know. We have to take care of many people and many things, and Oscar Ewing wants it. He's been a great supporter of the Democratic Party and a great contributor."

Frances stalled, saying she might take the civil service job but wanted to talk about it in person. Truman agreed to meet a few days later. She went to Washington and was there when Truman abruptly fired Frances's old friend Henry Wallace from his post as secretary of commerce. Both men gave her their own accounts of what had happened—and the two perspectives provided a chilling reminder of how fast careers rise and fall in Washington, and how quickly insiders abandon those who are pushed out.

Wallace, long interested in foreign diplomacy, had called for a sweeping peace initiative with the Soviet Union: "If modern war can cost us $400 billion, we should be willing and happy to pay much more for peace," he said in a speech.

Wallace had discussed it with Truman, who gave the idea his enthusiastic approval. James Byrnes, now secretary of state, and long an enemy and rival of Wallace's, hit the ceiling and told Truman he would resign if Wallace could not be prevented from discussing foreign affairs. He began pressing for his dismissal. Within a week, on Friday, Truman fired Wallace, or more precisely, required him to resign. Truman took this step in typical fashion, Frances noted: "He always did act very promptly."[7]

Soon afterward, Wallace's well-liked daughter, Jean, married investment banker Leslie Douglas in a lavish wedding at St. Alban's Episcopal Church in Washington. All of official Washington had been invited, and acceptances had poured in. Now, however, attendance was notably sparse, and the atmosphere was tense and joyless. Betty Beale, society reporter for the *Washington Star,* bustled about with cynical glee. "Oh gee, this is a juicy story," she told Frances. "All the people accepted and nobody here!"[8]

But life goes on, and despite her friendship with the Wallaces, Frances was sixty-six and still had an ailing husband to support. She accepted the post with the Civil Service Commission and was sworn into office in October 1946. This time she took her new office and she was greeted with open arms. Harry Mitchell, the chairman and a Democrat, shared many of Frances's views, and the other member, Arthur Flemming, a Republican, was congenial and energetic. She found the work interesting, since it dealt with the full range of staffing and personnel issues in the federal government.

The commission's primary goal was removing partisan political considerations from hiring and firing decisions, a challenge because each incoming administration wants to reward its supporters. The commission conducted civil service examinations, rated candidates, and listened to the appeals of fired government workers. It also implemented policies set by Congress, such as rules giving hiring preference to veterans. The commissioners stumbled through the thorny terrain of determining whether one worker was unfairly favored over another.

These tasks brought the commissioners into contact with the inner workings of every government agency. "I don't know of any spot in the government that gives you a better bird's-eye view of the entire government than the Civil Service Commission other than the Bureau of the Budget," Flemming recalled later. "You see, Theodore Roosevelt spent six years on the U.S. Civil Service Commission, and I know that he is quoted as having said that it was possibly the most valuable training he had for the presidency."[9]

Frances was a wonderful addition, he said, because she had the unique ability to take in "the biggest picture imaginable."

In 1946, the commission was dealing with downsizing. The government payroll had swelled to 3 million people during the war but needed to be reduced to fewer than 2 million. Many workers had created comfortable lives in secure government jobs, with good salaries and reasonable work hours. Meanwhile, returning veterans were reclaiming their positions, and their substitutes were laid off.

Federal personnel managers had enhanced power, and some now began to apply new moral criteria to federal employees. They made inquiries into the personal lives of workers, ferreting out those they deemed unworthy. While Frances endorsed raising ethical standards and agreed that employees should be expected to behave "in a manner befitting ladies and gentlemen," she also worried that the government was intruding on its employees' civil liberties.

"What difference does it make to us if a man entertains ladies in his room?" she asked. "How is this going to reflect on his ability to do his job?"

The inquiries often had the effect of precluding from government employment people who were merely broad-minded. Tom Eliot, now in a private law practice in Boston, told Frances he had been asked to provide a reference for a longtime government employee, and the investigator asked him if the man had ever expressed any liberal views. "We've got to know who is disloyal, you know," the woman told Eliot. Others were turned down because they had entertained blacks or Jews in their homes, Eliot told Frances.[10]

Frances opposed the background checks that became part of the hiring process, calling them "snooping" into personal lives. She also differed with her colleagues, particularly Flemming, over preemployment medical screening, which she opposed as an invasion of privacy.[11]

One reason she might not have liked such investigations into people's lives was that she now had yet another secret to hide. She had turned seventy in 1950, and by law should have been forced to retire, or at least to admit the error to Truman, who could have made an exception in her case. That would have required her to acknowledge she was older than she claimed to be, however. She had voted for the removal of other employees who misrepresented their ages at the time they were hired into federal government. Frances actually ended up working illegally for the federal government, having long ago misstated her own age.

Meanwhile, the old Democratic Party unity, which had shown cracks during the Roosevelt administration, now permanently fractured. Tensions with the Soviet Union were escalating, and could easily lead to a new war. The progressive and conservative factions of the party grew further apart as racial tensions rose. Domestic problems set aside during the war now erupted, and Truman was buffeted in every direction. He had to walk a careful line to avoid inflaming public opinion.

Frances still worked diligently, but unlike in the 1930s, she receded from public view. She provided quiet counsel to those in the administration and had come to love the president.[12]

In these years, Paul, at last partially recovered, came to live with Frances in Washington in a house at 2127 Leroy Place in the District. She had purchased it after Caroline O'Day left Washington in 1941. Paul was a shadowy figure who spoke little when they entertained. Susanna remained problematic. Financially dependent on Frances after her divorce from David Hare, she often exhibited the same stormy behavior and childish rebellions that she had shown as a teenager.

Frances's old friend Sinclair Lewis died in 1951, destroyed by alcoholism. She had witnessed the arc of his life, and had recognized his brilliance when he was just a gawky and failing newspaperman. Frances wrote his former wife, Dorothy Thompson, a letter and received one in return describing Lewis's last days: "His end, Frances, was like a Greek tragedy . . . His death brings me great pain. Above all the pain that he never knew my solitary tears. We are all too stiff-necked—we of puritan [heritage], which was his, too."[13]

An earlier death, however, had dealt a particularly painful blow. John Winant, the man Frances had drawn into Roosevelt's sphere and championed to head the ILO, committed suicide. He had been cast aside by the Republican Party when he allied himself with Roosevelt, and after the war he returned to an uncertain future in the United States. His son John, an American soldier captured by the Nazis and imprisoned in Germany, returned from the war deeply traumatized. He received particularly cruel treatment because of his father's high position in the Roosevelt administration as ambassador to Great Britain. Winant was in financial straits and disappointed in a book he was writing. On November 3, 1947, Winant climbed the stairs to his son's bedroom, took out a revolver, and shot himself.[14]

Again, Frances placed a wall around her emotions. Other mourners traveling with her on the train to Winant's funeral recalled Frances as rigid, almost unresponsive, as she dressed for the service. Winant had been an unusually attractive man, and Frances had clearly felt affection for him. Her letters to Winant during the war enclosed vitamin tablets and urged him to take care of himself. Deeply self-critical, Frances undoubtedly worried whether she had encouraged Winant to take a path that might have injured him. Certainly his life would have been easier if he had remained within the Republican fold and simply found a corporate job, as Al Smith had done. Instead, Winant's life of global public service had alienated him from the Republican Party, jeopardized his relationship with his family, caused specific hurt to his son, and left Winant facing impoverishment. Winant unfortunately died without knowing that Frances and her friends had arranged for him to be named to a position with the newly formed United Nations.

As the 1948 presidential election approached, Truman's prospects for reelection against Republican Thomas E. Dewey appeared increasingly grim. Gamblers placed Dewey ahead by 15 to 1; some said 30 to 1. Most major newspapers endorsed Dewey. For months, Truman's allies had pressed Eleanor Roosevelt, who viewed the former haberdasher with disdain, to endorse him. Her refusal was a blow, since Eleanor commanded intense loyalty among Democrats. Eleanor said coyly that she had removed herself from political life.

Privately, however, Eleanor wrote in June 1948 to Truman's political adviser Robert Hannegan, making it clear that she had never forgiven Truman for removing Frances from the Cabinet without replacing her with another woman. Eleanor acknowledged that Frances "was not particularly popular during the last few years as Secretary of Labor." She noted acerbically that Truman had found no other women to replace her in the Cabinet, and that Truman had made "no suggestion so far of any woman or women in comparably important positions."[15]

By October, Truman's reelection campaign hung by a thread, and Dewey appeared poised for victory, partially because Henry Wallace was running a splinter campaign for the presidency himself. Eleanor Roosevelt was in Paris, leading the American delegation to the United Nations and staying at the Hôtel de Crillon, when the telephone rang. It was Frances, telling her that newspaper columnist Drew Pearson was reporting that Eleanor's refusal to explicitly endorse Truman meant that she favored Dewey. Frances told Eleanor that for the good of the Democratic Party, she needed to reconsider her decision.

Under this pressure, Eleanor sent Truman a letter saying she was "unqualifiedly" for him as the presidential candidate. She also urged Democrats and Independents to vote the Democratic ticket. Her experience as a United Nations delegate had underscored to her the importance of maintaining continuity in American policies while a new and stable Europe struggled to emerge from the wreckage of the war.

Eleanor sent a copy of her letter to Frances as proof of her efforts, but she added a note explaining her reservations more thoroughly. She hesitated to endorse Truman because he was, in her opinion, "a weak and vacillating person" who had chosen Cabinet officials poorly.

"Nevertheless, since you asked me to send you the enclosed letter, I am doing so because you are quite right, if we are going down to defeat, we probably should go down having done what we could for the candidate and we should try for a good vote," she wrote.[16]

It's unclear how much effect Eleanor's endorsement had on Truman's campaign. His biographers say he connected to his audiences in a new, more energetic way in the last month of the campaign. But Eleanor's endorsement so soon before the vote also inspired Roosevelt-era Democrats to get to the polls to protect the party and the New Deal legacy. And Frances's role in persuading her to give it was pivotal.

Truman's loss had seemed so certain that the *Chicago Tribune,* anticipating an easy Dewey win, printed and circulated the paper with its famous "Dewey Defeats Truman" headline, thereafter finding itself a laughingstock.

Frances was considerably less surprised. She had campaigned actively for Truman in upstate New York and Pennsylvania, even though Wallace was running against him. She had been Wallace's champion, but somewhere along the way she lost faith in him as a potential president. Despite their shared liberalism, they now saw communism in starkly different ways. Frances had come to believe that Communists posed a threat, but Wallace was still more sympathetic to them. Some of his campaign workers were Communists. Frances's long experience on the campaign trail had honed her instincts, and she was pretty sure that Truman would be reelected. She had seen that Henry Wallace's chances were far more remote. "I mean, nobody expected to vote for him," she said.[17]

The mainstream Democratic Party, however, was so discouraged that it didn't book the grand ballroom at the Mayflower for a victory party, something it ordinarily did. Frances made sure Truman knew she was rooting for him, counting ballots when other party activists had given up and gone home. At 2 a.m., she sent a telegram of congratulations to the Excelsior Springs spa in Missouri, where he was staying. In his cheerful response, he noted she was one of the first to reach him with the news.[18]

After squeaking to victory, Truman was secure in the job of president once again. And with a new term approaching, Frances's political agenda had another shot. Truman presented to Congress a twenty-one-point program, proposing the expansion of Social Security, a full-employment program, a permanent Fair Employment Practices Act, and public housing and slum clearance—all items that Frances had endorsed for years. The program became known as the Fair Deal. Truman didn't have as much success as Roosevelt had had in getting his agenda enacted, but still he made some significant advances.

The postwar planning in which Frances had participated also bore fruit. Instead of deindustrializing Germany, as Morgenthau had urged, Truman enacted the Marshall Plan, named for his secretary of state George Marshall, which stimulated economic recovery in war-ravaged Europe, including Germany. The strategy represented the vision Roosevelt and Frances had shared about how to handle postwar international economic development.

Chapter 35

COMMUNISM

$\mathcal{D}$uring these Truman years, Frances was quietly dealing with a problem that could have destroyed the Democratic Party.

As soon as the war ended, the Soviet Union appeared intent on installing puppet regimes throughout Eastern Europe, further widening the gap that ideological differences had already created. The Soviet Union aggressively moved to create its own atomic bomb, building on U.S. technology and using espionage to speed its progress. In 1948, the Russians exploded their own bomb.

The Americans and British long had been skeptical about Soviet intentions. As a result, between 1942 and 1945, the United States and Great Britain engaged in the Venona Project, intercepting encrypted cables between Russian intelligence agencies and Soviet spies based in America. They began successfully decrypting these messages in 1946. National security officials kept the information secret, but released some facts through the FBI, and through that agency to Truman. The deciphered messages exposed several hundred Americans, including some government officials, as communist spies.[1]

The FBI learned that the Soviet spying effort was amazingly successful, with people reporting back to Russia on developments in radar, sonar, and munitions technology, as well as diplomatic initiatives and troop movements. The FBI first learned of the Manhattan Project when it saw it mentioned in materials obtained through Soviet espionage.[2]

By 1947, Truman was informed of these internal concerns, and he worried about other ways federal government employees might be aiding the Soviets. He sent the Civil Service Commission a top-secret memo saying that some government employees might be Soviet sympathizers. Soon rumors flew in Washington. Names of likely spies circulated. Conservatives believed a conspiracy was afoot and that Russians were securing inside secrets that would allow them to destroy the country. Leftists, however, saw the cases as baseless attacks on liberals who were not given enough information to defend themselves or confront their nameless accusers.

And some were still more cynical. Some free-market capitalists in America equated progressive liberalism and the regulatory structures imposed during the New Deal with the worst excesses of Stalinism. They accused American progressives of consorting with murderers and spies. Seeking to recapture the White House with an unpopular domestic agenda, they tried to blacken the Democratic Party's reputation by suggesting that liberal Democrats were not just opponents but also traitors.

Frances knew the issue demanded careful handling. When the three commissioners met to discuss who to send to a meeting called at the White House, she saw that Chairman Harry Mitchell, who was nearly seventy, wanted to hand the matter over to the commission's director or counsel rather than go himself. Flemming, the young, ambitious Republican on the commission, clearly sought the opportunity. Frances thought this could be harmful to the Democratic Party. She considered volunteering, and decided it wouldn't be wise for her to participate. Informants against Communists often brought forward some accusation of sexual peccadillo, and she realized it made the men uncomfortable discussing such cases with a woman present. She also knew of the Truman administration's basic discomfort with women. She decided she would be more effective working behind the scenes, she recalled.

Flemming opened his mouth to offer to attend the White House meeting, so she hastened to speak up first. "Mr. Mitchell, you must go yourself," she told him. "Nobody else must go . . . It may be a destructive thing or it may be a constructive thing, but you must do it yourself."[3]

Mitchell reluctantly agreed. When he returned from the meeting, he called Frances into his office and closed the door. "Oh, my, this one's terrible!" Mitchell said. "The information that the president has got is shocking."

Frances found it hard to believe, but as she listened, she became more convinced it might be true. The Justice Department had discovered that many government workers, possibly hundreds, were leading double lives, publicly as government officials, while privately joining radical political organizations, including communist and fascist groups. Over a lifetime, Frances had learned to suspect claims of subversive activities, so she questioned Mitchell closely.

"What radical ideas, Mr. Mitchell? . . . Because what's a radical idea? . . . Some of those things would be very good. What's the matter with it? Is it a question really of any of them betraying their country?"[4]

In many cases, Mitchell said, they had proof of the memberships or other compelling evidence. Now Mitchell and Frances wrestled with their fundamental belief that people have a right to their own political views, weighed against the risk posed by Machiavellian Soviet spymasters angling for advantage by placing secret Communists in key government posts.

Mitchell was "greatly disturbed," Frances recalled, over the idea that just being a Communist Party member or having been a member was sufficient to strip a man of his government job. But Frances countered that Justice Oliver Wendell Holmes, whom she had long revered, said that although a person may have a constitutional right to his beliefs, he has no constitutional right to be a government official. In other words, with so many people wanting federal jobs, why accept or employ people who might prove problematic?

Frances turned the issue over in her mind. During the war, many federal employees were hired without normal scrutiny. Some, she knew, had done some suspicious things. And some may have joined the Communist Party at some point in their lives. Over the years, she had suspected several people of being Communist, and potentially dangerous, and she believed that the facts, in time, had proved her right.

Mitchell and Frances felt they should find ways to rid the government of potential traitors. They decided that the best tack was to investigate whether the person had, in fact, committed perjury by denying Communist Party membership at the time he or she was hired and took the oath of office. They reasoned that this deliberate deception by an applicant increased the likelihood that he had some sinister intent. It also made it easier to take action, since the misrepresentation was similar to claiming to have a college degree when he or she did not.

The next problem was determining what specific action to take when problems surfaced. Some White House committee members wanted these workers turned over to the FBI for possible prosecution, but Mitchell, at Frances's urging, argued that the cases should remain within the Civil Service Commission, which would treat them more humanely.

Given the intense emotions brewing over these questions, Frances wanted to insulate the commission from political pressure. She proposed that a committee of government employees first assess the cases. Its decisions could be appealed to an outside loyalty review board, composed of respected citizens who were not government employees. The review board would issue final rulings. Frances and Mitchell took the plan to Truman, and he liked it immediately.

"He saw at once that any decision we made would right away be kicked around in politics: 'Oh, the Civil Service Commission is protecting that skunk, so Harry Truman's to blame for that,' or 'The Civil Service Commission is jumping on this man when they shouldn't do it, and Harry Truman is to blame,' " Frances recalled.[5]

Frances told the men she thought the president of the loyalty review board should be a Republican—one of her favorite strategies to derail opposition. Mitchell disliked this idea because of his own partisanship, but Frances explained it would deflect political fallout. Truman agreed, and Frances then considered who would be best for the role. She asked, and was rejected by, John Lord O'Brian, a prominent constitutional lawyer, and Owen J. Roberts, the former Supreme Court justice who famously switched his position, permitting the New Deal legislation to survive.

Finally, Seth Richardson, a Montana Republican who served as Justice Department solicitor under Hoover, accepted. Tall and raw-boned, with a booming voice, he was the kind of broad-minded liberal Republican Frances liked so well.

"I can't think of anybody I would rather have," Truman told Frances. "I think Seth Richardson's just fine. I think he's a number one man, I think he's very good."[6]

Truman unveiled the plan on March 21, 1947, issuing Executive Order 9835, which created the nation's first peacetime loyalty program. It called for background investigations of all federal employees and job seekers. The Civil Service Commission would oversee the process, although several departments formed their own inquiry panels. The executive order also created the Loyalty Review Board, as proposed by Frances, to give employees an avenue for appeals.[7]

Frances thought the breadth of the inquiry program was in some ways "absurd," but universal application seemed the only way to ensure a fair process. The only aspect that Frances resisted was fingerprinting, which she considered an invasion of privacy.

Frances assumed the difficult role of assembling the review board. Some key members included Harry Connery, former president of the American Legion; New York lawyer George W. Alger; legal scholars Harry A. Bigelow and Paul M. Hebert; Meta Glass, the former president of Sweet Briar College; and Henry L. Shattuck, a member of the Massachusetts House of Representatives. Many people ducked the request to serve, as Shattuck did when Flemming first called.

"Besides," Shattuck dryly told Flemming, "witchhunting does not appeal to me."[8]

"That is just the reason we asked you," Flemming responded, and so Shattuck agreed to serve.

The board convened on November 4, 1947, and over the next few years officials examined the records of about 4.8 million individuals. About twelve hundred of these quietly left government or withdrew their applications, and about 560 were affirmatively removed from office or denied employment. About 212 federal employees were dismissed on grounds that they were potentially disloyal or security risks.[9]

The board was attacked from both left and right. People on the right feared the effort was a whitewash; people on the left thought that Truman yielded to the partisan conservative attacks on liberals. At one board hearing, Professors Thomas I. Emerson and Fowler V. Harper of Yale Law School urged Truman to revoke the executive order and dissolve the loyalty board. Shattuck responded that they may have been "ideologically right," but that if they were interested in the practical "protection of the employees," they should leave the board alone. Shattuck had come to believe that if moderates did not deal with potentially problematic employees, then others with much more hard-line attitudes would take on the job. Frances approached Shattuck after the hearing had ended.

"I am glad you said that," she said. "You were entirely right."[10]

Many cases came to the board backed only by flimsy FBI evidence, in some cases the word of former Communist spies Elizabeth Bentley and Whittaker Chambers, both of whom had renounced communism and were eager to expose their former associates. The reasons for this sketchiness only later became apparent. Many specific details were gleaned from the top-secret Venona cables and remained confidential. Investigations therefore had to proceed with very limited information.

It was hard for the service board to know how much to rely on this evidence. It was difficult to ascertain whether informants were truthful, and whether it was safe for them to even try to tell the truth. The Russians had exploited the idealism of many of their American enthusiasts. Once enticed into the movement, the Americans could be blackmailed into helping the party because exposure of their membership could ruin them. And if the Russians thought recruits had turned on them, they might be murdered. Walter Krivitsky, a KGB officer who defected to the West, wrote a book on his espionage activities, and two years later he was found shot dead in a Washington hotel room. Some Americans suspected of disloyalty were called to Moscow and disappeared.[11]

Among the most controversial cases the Loyalty Review Board faced was that of John S. Service, a State Department officer who was a China specialist. The son of American Christian missionaries, he was fluent in the local Chinese dialect by age eleven and spent his teenage years in Shanghai. He became a key State Department diplomat in China during World War II. At the time, China was splintering into warring factions, with Communist insurgents pitted against the controlling Nationalist Chinese, also known as the Kuomintang. Service came to believe the Nationalist Chinese, led by Chiang Kai-shek, were corrupt and that the Communists would emerge victorious.

Service was sent back to the United States in disgrace. Frustrated and angry, Service gave State Department documents to journalists, including some who were covert Communists. Service and five people with whom he had shared documents were arrested in June 1945 and charged with conspiracy to commit espionage. The charges were dismissed by year's end, although some of those charged paid small fines. Service returned to work at the State Department.[12]

In early 1950, Senator Joseph McCarthy of Wisconsin, whose reelection campaign had been flagging, made Communism his signature issue. He had seen the tactic work for Dies of Texas, as well as for a young congressman from California, Richard Nixon. McCarthy even considered Dies a pioneer in the new movement. At a speech in West Virginia, McCarthy stated emphatically that he had a list of 205 communists in the State Department. He was unable to provide it to reporters because, he said, it was stored with his luggage. McCarthy soon developed a pattern of making inflammatory charges, then misplacing the supporting documents.[13]

As a result of McCarthy's allegations, Service's name reemerged, and he was pegged as a likely Communist. This time, the newly created Loyalty Review Board investigated the matter, and through that proceeding, Service was dismissed from his job. Shattuck, who served on his review panel, said that they could not prove that Service was pro-Communist, but it was clear that he had showed poor judgment in sharing confidential documents, including troop dispositions and military plans. On these grounds alone, Shattuck said, Service deserved dismissal, and the State Department fired him in 1951. Service appealed all the way to the U.S. Supreme Court, which ruled in his favor, and he was reinstated. He could no longer get a security clearance, however, and finally resigned in frustration.[14]

Frances knew personally some of the people whose cases were referred to the commission. One young man, who had worked for the U.S. Information Service, where he had broadcast the American point of view to French towns during the Resistance, interviewed Frances in Paris in 1945. Before the war, as a college student, he had been a member of the Young Communist League, even carrying a flag around campus and going to Alaska to organize communist cells. Upon graduation, he'd left that all behind and had been working in government for about five years. The government review turned up this history. The man, now a husband and father, came to Frances and begged for her help. He admitted the charge of communism against him was true:

> I came out of college in the midst of the Depression, and I
> thought it was terrible, and I thought the Communists had the
> answer, and I was hotheaded and I thought this was all that
> could be done, and everybody else was so foul and deceiving,
> and they were covering up trouble, and trying to make out
> that things were all right when they weren't all right, and I
> was disgusted and th[ey] probably had the answer. I joined the
> Communist Youth Movement. I never formed any cells among
> the workers on these boats to Alaska, but I did agitate a little
> and tell 'em how everything was wrong.
>
> Then I got back, and by this time I was settling down and
> I had to earn a living, and I forgot about it. Then came the

Roosevelt Administration, which seemed to be really intending to do something for people. . . . And then came the War, and I wanted to turn my talents to the defense of my country, and so I volunteered my services and I was accepted, and nobody said anything to me about Communism.[15]

"But you took the oath of office, didn't you?" Frances asked. "Well, you know you said you were not a Communist."

The young man said he did not realize what was written on the little card he signed when he took the oath. He did not read it. In other words, Frances gently explained, he perjured himself by not reading the card carefully before taking the oath. She urged him to resign to avoid perjury charges. He moved to Southern California and founded a small newspaper. Frances kept apprised of his whereabouts through his annual Christmas cards.

The two Communists-turned-whistleblowers, Chambers and Bentley, identified dozens as Communists. Many people did not take them seriously. But they both gained wide audience when they testified before the House Un-American Affairs Committee.

Bentley, dubbed the "Blonde Spy Queen" by the *New York Herald Tribune,* was a Vassar graduate who had fallen in love with Jacob Golos, a Russian who had been part of the Bolshevik movement during the Russian Revolution. Golos moved to the United States and owned a company associated with Intourist, the Soviet travel agency. This business disguised his real occupation as a Soviet Union spymaster. After he died, however, Bentley became disenchanted with the Russians, and decided to share her information with the FBI.

Bentley identified William Remington, an affable and intelligent Commerce Department official who had been an economist with the War Production Board. Remington vehemently denied the allegations. The Loyalty Review Board initially found in his favor, and he was restored to duty. Then his wife, who had divorced him in the meantime, testified before a grand jury that Remington had belonged to the Communist Party when he was a Dartmouth College student. Bentley alleged that Remington mimeographed press releases and gave them to her at a cigar store. Even Bentley had considered his contributions insignificant. To Frances, Remington's actions seemed more "silly and naïve" than wicked, but because he denied his Communist link, he was sent to prison on a perjury conviction. There he was attacked and killed by two fellow inmates. Washington-area liberals considered Remington's death an unnecessary martyrdom.[16]

Chambers, a former *Time* magazine editor, had been drawn to communism in his youth, but when Hitler and Stalin signed their nonaggression pact and carved up Europe, Chambers feared that Stalin would receive U.S. military secrets from American collaborators and share them with Hitler. He identified as Communist agents several State Department employees, including Laurence Duggan and economist Lauchlin Currie, a special assistant to Roosevelt. He said that Soviet spies had gained plans for two battleships and sketches of weapon prototypes. Chambers gained a receptive ear with Richard Nixon.[17]

The most important alleged spy that Chambers identified was Alger Hiss, a State Department official who had accompanied Roosevelt to Yalta. News from inside the American camp could have helped Stalin know how aggressively he could push for a dominant role in Eastern Europe. But Chambers seemed unusually obsessed with the svelte, urbane, Harvard-educated Hiss. Chambers showed a memory for specific details about Hiss that struck some observers as indicative of thwarted love. Hiss was a bird-watcher and Chambers talked of Hiss's enthusiasm when he spotted a rare prothonotary warbler. Hiss inadvertently confirmed Chambers's story when questioners mentioned the bird, and Hiss described his thrill at seeing the creature.

Hiss proclaimed his innocence, and many friends had trouble believing he could betray the American government. Wyzanski, for example, who was politically conservative in many ways, had known Hiss since their days at Harvard Law School. Hiss had been a law clerk for Oliver Wendell Holmes. Wyzanski had dined with Hiss and his wife, Priscilla, and he liked them both. So when Hiss was accused of being a Communist, Wyzanski staunchly defended him, endangering his own reputation. Hiss himself was oddly reticent about presenting evidence that would have proved his innocence.[18]

Another of Chambers's allegations was that Alger's brother, Donald, a Labor Department lawyer, was also a Communist and had sought to handle the Bridges deportation case on the government's behalf. As it happened, Chambers added, Donald Hiss was instead directed by the Communist Party to transfer to the State Department's Philippines section, so that he could give Russia diplomatic information about developments in Asia. This charge, involving an important Labor Department case, would, if proven, have made Frances seem to be a fool, or worse yet, complicit.[19]

And, apparently, there was some truth behind the charges. Labor Department officials did, in fact, intend to have Donald Hiss preside over Bridges's trial. In a letter to immigration officials in San Francisco, James L. Houghteling, Immigration Commissioner, had written that Hiss, formerly assistant solicitor of labor, and now on the legal staff of the State Department, would serve as acting immigration inspector so that he could manage the trial. Houghteling had expected Hiss to return from the State Department to perform the task.[20]

Frances herself had asked a State Department official to make Hiss available so that he could preside over the trial. "As you know," she wrote, "his transfer to the State Department was a source of serious concern to the legal staff here as he was the only member fully cognizant of the various aspects of this important immigration case."[21]

The Bridges case might have come down to one alleged Russian agent prosecuting another alleged Russian agent. Donald Hiss, too, said he was not a Communist. According to Chambers, Donald Hiss dropped his effort to handle the Bridges case after the Russians decided Bridges was expendable because the chance of getting classified State Department information from Asia was more valuable.

Later Frances said not a word about the incident, and it got no public attention, but she noted that she had read Whittaker Chambers's book in 1952. It made her, she said, "sort of ill," in fact, almost "nauseated," but she added little additional detail.[22]

Cases confronting the Civil Service Commission posed many thorny civil liberties questions. Evidence was presented anonymously by unnamed individuals known under such FBI codes as agent T-25, "known to be a reliable reporter," or T-32, who is of "doubtful" validity. FBI officials refused to disclose the sources' identity.

Some who seemed implausible spies were accused. But not all of them were innocent, Frances came to believe. The conservative Council of Jewish Women approached Frances to help a young woman they were sure was not a Communist. Frances met her and considered her a "plain Jane" who couldn't possibly be a spy, so she contacted the FBI to demand more information. She discovered that on three occasions the woman had been examined and then immediately called her communist contact to report that she believed she had been cleared. The FBI heard these conversations because they were tapping the telephone of her contact.[23]

At some point, as efforts to expose Communist agents expanded, the process did in fact disintegrate, as Shattuck had feared, into a witchhunt. Frances blamed the press for covering the redbaiting by self-serving politicians. McCarthy, Dies, and Nixon had learned they could earn headlines with accusations of communism. If the charges later proved groundless, the press would largely ignore it.

Some allegations and counterallegations became laughable. Walt Disney, a leading Hollywood conservative and militantly antiunion, believed the cartoonists drawing Mickey Mouse and Minnie Mouse were Communists because they were trying to unionize. He accused the League of Women Voters of being a Communist-front organization because he erroneously thought it issued a statement supporting the cartoonists. The statement actually came from the League of Women Shoppers. Disney apologized after the League of Women Voters threatened to boycott Disney movies.[24]

Targets didn't find these accusations all that funny. Many people subjected to withering allegations simply collapsed under the strain. Author Alvah Bessie counted seventeen people who had heart attacks or committed suicide while facing treason changes. But some may indeed have been Communists who gave secrets to the Russians. Harry Dexter White, assistant to the treasury secretary, was later shown to have communicated with the Soviets. He died soon after he was accused.

Frances believed she had done the right thing in helping ease many Communists and former Communists out of the government: "Communism is a strange doctrine ... and it does—and there's no question about this—it does put a question of double loyalty to the most conscientious man who is ever appointed to office," she said later.[25]

The allegations of Communist influence gave new ammunition to labor union opponents. As Frances feared, the NLRB's creation and its handling of controversial cases provoked a backlash. In 1947, Congress had imposed new restrictions on trade unions that limited their future growth. Republicans successfully included in this measure a requirement that all union leaders swear that they did not believe in communism or associate with Communists. Some Communists willingly signed the oaths, not concerned about making false statements, but the new requirements chilled potential new leadership. It placed union leaders at risk of perjury charges if they were ever investigated. It also forced many effective organizers out of the movement. Such requirements had never been imposed on any group of private citizens.[26]

In 1948, an employee of the attorney general's office called the FBI to ask if Frances herself had ever been investigated and if so, what conclusions had been reached. Four years later, in 1952, Donald S. Dawson, a Truman administration official, asked for a specific check of Frances's records. The FBI informed Truman administration officials that no troublesome material surfaced. Her own loyalty form of February 21, 1949, had received the FBI's stamp of approval: "No Disloyal Data FBI files," it reported.[27]

By the time McCarthy's barrage of unfounded accusations began, Frances and the Civil Service Commission already had counseled the most problematic people out of government and dismissed a few hundred others who refused to go voluntarily. McCarthy's efforts to attack former officials made him look foolish, particularly on television, and his abusive tactics turned liberals, and eventually many conservatives as well, against him. By cleaning house before McCarthy and Nixon came into power, Frances performed yet another valuable service to the Democratic Party—but it won her few admirers among the liberals who were longtime friends.

The allegations against men like Alger Hiss and William Remington were never substantiated in their lifetimes, and until their deaths they continued to assert their innocence. More facts became clear in some cases only after the publication of the Venona cables in 1995 and the opening of Kremlin files, according to some Cold War scholars. In Hiss's case, Hungarian documents found in the Budapest Interior Ministry in 1993 recounted his secret undercover work, and the State Department revealed that Hiss had obtained unauthorized access to reports on atomic energy and military intelligence. Hiss also turned out to be mentioned in the Venona cables. These discoveries have given Whittaker Chambers's allegations about Alger and Donald Hiss additional credibility.

Chapter 36

END OF THE
TRUMAN ERA

*F*rances accepted with more grace and kindness than other Roosevelt insiders the differences between FDR and his successor. One night in particular placed the contrasts in sharp relief.

It was a dinner on December 4, 1952. The Republican Dwight Eisenhower had just been elected, and Truman gave a farewell dinner in honor of his Cabinet, which he generously interpreted as everyone who had served under him, including Roosevelt appointees whom he had inherited. Adlai Stevenson, the recent presidential candidate who had just been defeated, and his sister and brother-in-law were invited as well.

More than seventy people attended, including Francis Biddle, Henry Wallace, and Henry Morgenthau, Jr., who came with his new wife, a Frenchwoman. Many of FDR's other appointees had died, including Harold Ickes and Henry Stimson.

The Truman appointees were gawky and awkward, partly because they were unfamiliar with the formal protocol. Truman had apparently discontinued these dinners, and Frances assumed that this was at Mrs. Truman's behest, because she did not much care for formal events. Such dinners, a valuable networking tool, had been a standard part of White House social life during the Roosevelt years.

The Trumans received their guests cordially, and the conversation was pleasant. There had been stormy exchanges in the past between many of the guests, but here at the reunion, everyone spoke amiably. Frances was seated between Wallace and Dan A. Kimball, secretary of the navy, who escorted her into the hall.

"It's fun to look around this room and see all these people," Kimball said to Frances confidentially. "My, when I look them all over and when I think of the things that everybody in this room has said about everybody else, it's a wonder that the room holds us. The number of hatchets that must have been buried to get into this room are fantastic."[1]

Frances thought of the fireworks between Truman and Wallace, who had been rivals for the vice presidency and then for the presidency, and how Ickes "had left in a blaze" when he accused Truman of selling out taxpayers with the appointment of a California oilman, Edwin Pauley, to be undersecretary of the navy.

The women played an important role in the dinner, Frances recalled. "They made the party go on the social side, just as they would in any other party," she said. "If you've been out in Washington society at all, you're accustomed to dining and being very, very pleasant to people you don't like at all who are plotting against you in your work or in your husband's. It's your business to make everything very pleasant."

The president circulated, making a point to chat privately with everyone present. "Thank you for what you have done for me," he told Frances. "Thank you for standing by. I remember how you stood by when things were so difficult. What you did in that terrible transition period. It was a great relief to know you were there."

Though pleasant, the dinner lacked polish and fell flat, Frances observed. She thought Truman suffered from the absence of the kind of staff who could help him handle things graciously. She remembered what the women used to do for Roosevelt, how Missy LeHand, Eleanor, and Frances were always thinking ahead about what he would need and preparing speaking notes for him. Without loyal and loving support, Truman's comments came out sounding undistinguished. The president stood up and spoke, then sat down, without being given a proper introduction by a senior official. Then he forgot to turn the floor over to Adlai Stevenson, the popular Illinois governor who had just been defeated for the presidency. Stevenson had entered the race at Truman's urging.

Later somebody asked Truman why he hadn't given Stevenson a chance to speak. He said he forgot, and that Bess "gave him hell for forgetting him too . . . but she was too far away from me to kick under the table."

The dinner symbolized, in Frances's mind, a key difference between Roosevelt and Truman. It was a question of social grace. At a culminating moment in his administration, when Truman had the chance to say something that would allow his colleagues to savor their contributions during twenty years of Democratic rule, Truman failed to note the significance of that special evening.

After Truman sat down, there was uncomfortable silence. Vinson, now a Supreme Court justice, the man who as a congressman had reduced the welfare payments to mothers during the Social Security debate, rose and made some inconsequential remarks about the great job Truman had done. Then he sat down. Somebody nudged him. "Oh, yes, I forgot," he said. "I want to propose a toast to the President of the United States."

Frances wanted to excuse the Trumans' lack of savoir faire. She realized they were under personal stress, that Bess's mother was ill upstairs and they were concerned about her failing health. She knew Truman could be shy, reluctant to seize center stage. But she found herself disappointed that the end of the epoch was marked so haphazardly.

"The occasion just dribbled away without recognizing itself as an era which had finished. . . . There was no, 'What we have implanted in the minds of the American people goes on forever.' When you think of the tremendous social evolution and change, plus the meeting of the challenge of an impossible war, the arming of America intellectually, spiritually and physically in record time to fight and win that war on a world basis, then the combination of decisions and accidents which have brought America into a position of world leadership, however reluctantly, yet gathering ourselves together and accepting it, you have to realize that these were the people who did it. All those people took some part in one or the other of those three terrific projects which are the events of this twenty year period which we are now ending because the people want somebody else to do it. Pray God that they will do as well as we have done. I thought of things like that to say then. I thought of a thousand speeches as I listened. I thought to myself, Why didn't I realize this? Why didn't I butt in and write somebody's little remarks for them the way I used to?"

Instead, after Vinson's small toast, Truman thanked him, offering his arm to the lady on his right as they exited the room. The dinner was over. The moment was gone.[2]

Chapter 37

MANY TRANSITIONS

$\mathcal{S}$everal important chapters of Frances Perkins's life closed in the last months of 1952. Her husband Paul died, and the twenty-year Democratic reign came to an end. But, as they always did for Frances, other doors opened.

In forty years of marriage, Paul had worked for only short periods, including those first few happy years when he was a trusted mayoral adviser. He had lived for long stretches of time in expensive sanatoriums, where he played bridge and tennis on good days and received comfort on bad ones. During periods of recovery he lived in boarding homes in pastoral settings, cared for by a manservant, or at the family home in Maine.

He needed to be carefully monitored, as he suffered recurrent breakdowns and was also an alcoholic. He could enjoy some minor hobbies and interests as long as no stress was placed on him.

Frances frequently visited him on weekends during all those years, but he was never well enough that Frances could be confident that he wouldn't create a scene of some kind in a public place. Even after the spotlight had shifted away from her, she worried about what he might do. She told Henry Wallace and others that she would liked to have had the job as American representative to the ILO in Switzerland, but her family responsibilities had not permitted it. Now, however, with the less-demanding job at the Civil Service Commission, and with a cook and a maid to help her run the household and manage Paul, she was for the first time in years able to keep him at home with her.

But Paul's new presence in Washington made entertaining difficult. She invited only trusted friends for dinner. The tone was quite different from the lively work luncheons she shared with colleagues or the easy gaiety she shared with Mary Rumsey. Paul was often sullen or silent.

In October 1952, Paul suffered a stroke. He needed constant attendance during his last weeks because he would abruptly get out of bed and fall down, risking additional injury. Paul went into a final decline between Christmas and New Year's, and Frances arranged for him to receive the last rites. He spoke only occasionally. He suffered a final devastating stroke on December 31, fell unconscious, and died. He was seventy-six. Paul's years of incapacitation made death almost a relief, but it was a melancholy departure all the same.

Paul was laid to rest in the Perkins family burial ground in Newcastle, above and overlooking the Damariscotta River, with another burial plot left vacant beside it, waiting for Frances's arrival.

The Newcastle clan found some levity in noting that Paul, an excellent tennis player, was buried close to a tennis court. "Makes it possible for Paul to supervise our playing even now," one of the children told Frances.[1]

As she often did in times of adversity, Frances found solace in her religion: "Thank you so much for your kind and sympathetic words about Paul's death," Frances wrote a Mount Holyoke friend. "These things are truly past man's understanding, but it is and has always been a comfort to me to know that in the midst of all the troubles he has had, he had remained a true believer. He died in the faith of the Church, received the Last Sacraments and was buried with all the warmth and hope with which the Church surrounds us at the time of our great transition, greeted by the Saints, the Prophets and the Patriarchs, escorted by the Angels of the Guardians, surely we go to our Paradise in love and mercy."[2]

Frances's friends spread the news of Paul's death. "Paul Wilson, as you know, died during the holidays," wrote Arthur Altmeyer of the Social Security Administration to Dewson. "It, of course, was a sad ending to an unhappy life. However, Frances Perkins can feel that she did everything humanly possible to ease his path through life, and therefore I am glad that her sadness is assuaged somewhat by the fact that she can have no self-reproach."[3]

After a lifetime of providing for Paul, Frances felt untethered. She had maintained the pretense that she could consult with him on important questions, and his death was "very unsettling," she wrote a friend, the Englishwoman Ethel Salter:

> One couldn't wish him to go on living in the condition he was in. He was paralyzed and nearly speechless. One knows it is a blessing, particularly when one thinks of the long sicknesses one can go through in that kind of tortured life. Still the human memory is so made that it easily turns back to the days when youth, health, hope and success all seemed to give promise of a long and interesting life together.[4]

Frances always found refuge from her personal problems in her work, but now that avenue was closing as well. Republican Dwight Eisenhower, the five-star general who had served as Supreme Commander of the Allies Forces in Europe, had swept to victory on November 4, 1952. Adlai Stevenson's defeat meant that the Democrats were out and the Republicans were headed to town. Senior government officers traditionally offer their resignations. Frances cleared her desk the day after Eisenhower's election, then waited a few months to receive confirmation that her resignation had been accepted. Eventually it was.

Frances's stately redbrick townhouse, with six bedrooms and a large drawing room, was put up for sale, but remained on the market for three months without a single serious bid. Many new administration officials had yet to arrive in the city.

"I have been tempted to take a berth on the *Queen Mary* and come over to England and probably should have done so if my resignation had been promptly accepted and my house promptly sold," she told Salter. "Neither one has happened. They would accept my resignation very promptly I expected but they have had some difficulty getting replacements. That is not my problem. That is a matter for the White House. I feel a strange irresponsibility about it somehow. That is what comes over you when another party takes over—irresponsibility for government."

At last the house sold, and Frances prepared to leave Washington on April 10, her seventy-third birthday, not wanting to be "hanging around there like a Peri at the Gates of Paradise," she wrote her friend Charles Burlingham. The phrase referenced a lyric poem in which a young genie laments her exclusion from heaven.

"Also, I thought it much better for my temper and blood pressure not to be where I heard the verbatim accounts of all the little episodes in which the major idea seems to be to destroy or get rid of everything that had been done by the Democrats in twenty years," she wrote.[5]

Frances embarked on an uncertain life. She had accepted a six-week lecturing position at the University of Illinois in rural Bloomington. As she packed her belongings, Frances felt low, disoriented, and fearful. "It was sort of a shock. I'd had a good many shocks in the course of one year, as a matter of fact. I had quite a few that year."[6]

Her relationship with her daughter was no longer a consolation. Susanna suffered repeated emotional breakdowns. Her manic-depressive symptoms mirrored her father's, but she refused to believe she had an illness, and so instead she blamed her mother for her problems. Almost twenty years of talk therapy had convinced her that her mother's failures at parenting were to blame for her difficulties.

Then, in 1953, the year after Paul's death, Susanna's life took a turn for the better when she remarried, this time to a talented artist named Calvert Coggeshall. Coggeshall had been left with three children when his wife deserted him. Susanna became stepmother to a boy and two girls. She went to live with them in Stonington, Connecticut.

Frances was enthusiastic about the match, especially after Susanna gave birth to a son, Tomlin, in September 1954. Frances adored the blue-eyed baby who from birth shared Paul's good looks. Susanna's marriage was "this time to a grown up man who seems responsible, kind and considerate," Frances wrote. "I take it there is no fortune there, but he is creative and earns a good deal as he goes along. And as perhaps you know, Suzanna [sic] has a beautiful young son, now a year old, who seems to be a model of quiet nerves and amiable disposition. Pray God it will last."[7]

Nevertheless Frances spent these years engaged in deep self-examination. She agonized about losing her mental grip. Frances derided herself for her "sin of pride." She missed being seen as an important person, and she felt ashamed for feeling such an unworthy emotion.

Frances also castigated herself for being a poor mother, blaming herself for trying to control her daughter financially. "I want her to look to me," she wrote in an intensely self-critical note intended for her own eyes only. "I impoverish myself to give to her—if I approve. I don't love her."[8]

She worried that she had become greedy. Frances knew she needed to economize but said she went too far and was "tense with figuring and scheming" about money. She blamed herself for what she called "general sloth," such as failing to offer hospitality, or withdrawing from people, or in allowing herself to be "too much alone." She chided herself for other perceived character defects, questioning her racial attitudes. She excoriated herself on almost every front, and then she tried to offer herself comfort.

One scrap of paper in her desk contained these words: "Remember . . . we are only day laborers in the vineyard of the Lord—we are not the architect—the planner—God is that. We are to do our daily stint faithfully and then leave it to the architect God—Lay our course of bricks and not to question or worry about the total structure—that is God's business. Also Remember that Christ did his greatest work of redemption when he hung helpless on the CROSS."

But at some point, as she had at other junctures in her life, when Paul first became ill, when Mary Harriman died, and when Roosevelt had asked her not to resign, Frances again squared her shoulders and moved ahead. She was guided in this by a family story. A wealthy relative had been named an ambassador overseas, and the family discussed this appointment with some amusement. Her redoubtable grandmother said, "In America, one must be prepared either to go up suddenly or to come down suddenly, and one has to do either with grace." When Frances recalled that story, she decided to accept the change in her own circumstances with greater serenity.[9]

One challenge was finding employment. Her teaching stint in Illinois was successful but temporary. She had been at the center of power for two decades, she possessed a still-rare graduate degree, and funding for higher education was surging as college enrollments boomed as a result of the GI Bill. She was offered short-term posts at a university in Salzburg and at the University of Wisconsin but, oddly, not a single university offered permanent employment. She had passed up the deanships at major universities, but now even these women's colleges, including Radcliffe, which once had courted her, now declined to make offers, even of one-year teaching slots. Frances had developed a reputation for radicalism that made many university presidents afraid to hire her. But she needed a regular income. She was coming to realize that her dreamy and artistic son-in-law, though gifted, was unable to fully support his family, particularly in the style to which Susanna was accustomed. Susanna, meanwhile, either couldn't or wouldn't work. Their comfort, and Tomlin's education, depended on Frances. At seventy-seven, she needed a full-time job—and finally one came calling.[10]

In 1957 a young labor-relations professor named Maurice Neufeld heard Frances talk about the New Deal at a conference of historians. Neufeld and his wife, Hinda, were spellbound by Frances's charm, wisdom, and experience. After her lecture, Neufeld approached her about joining Cornell University's fledgling new Industrial and Labor Relations School, a state-funded program. Her reputation and historical importance seemed to make his question almost impertinent. Neufeld asked if she would consider coming to teach at Cornell.

"Well, why don't you ask me and see?" she asked impishly.[11]

The offer was made, and soon Frances was there to teach U.S. labor history and the New Deal legacy. When Frances joined the faculty, the School of Industrial and Labor Relations occupied what its professors called the "academic slums" of the famously scenic campus. It was located in temporary wooden buildings that had been put up as military barracks; its library was housed in a Quonset hut. Like an unwanted stepchild, it occupied these inauspicious quarters until, at long last, the veterinary school moved to new space, and the ILR moved into its buildings.

Frances was not hired as a full professor but as a visiting lecturer, with a smaller income. At first she lived in residential hotels and entertained in restaurants.

Frances's year-round living arrangements were precarious. She soon turned over to Susanna's family her rent-controlled Manhattan apartment, the spacious four-bedroom flat at 1239 Madison Avenue that she had first rented in 1929. It was the only way they could afford to live in New York City, where Calvert needed to work. Her generosity left Frances without her own home in the city. When Molly Dewson wrote her in 1958 and asked where she was living, Frances admitted she had no home.[12]

"I am sorry I can't give you a firm address," she wrote to Dewson. "The Cosmopolitan Club, New York City, is the very best one I've got. As you know, I don't live anywhere, except here for a couple of months in the summer. I have been at the University of Illinois, Europe, Wisconsin, or Cornell University every year since 1954. The result is no permanent fixed abode, and I am going back to Cornell this coming year. So continue to bother the Cosmopolitan Club! It's the best address I know."[13]

But soon, as in the past, a friend came through for her. Margaret Poole, the widow of novelist Ernest Poole, the woman who had helped her purchase a wardrobe for Washington back in 1933, invited her to stay with her in Manhattan whenever she came to New York. It was a spectacular apartment—decorated in white, with rich Chinese carpets and exquisite carved Chinese screens. Margaret was the matriarch of the Poole family, and Frances became almost a part of the family, routinely spending Christmas Eve with the Pooles rather than with Susanna's family.[14]

Frances spent much of the regular school year in Ithaca teaching her popular and well-attended classes. Students found her lectures eye-opening, particularly when she described how haphazard was the original concoction that became the New Deal. She entered campus life with gusto. Her memory for people amazed Neufeld. She retained her knack for memorizing names and faces, and could find a friend in almost any crowd.[15]

Frances made a point of taking the faculty wives under her wing. At that time, it was rare for women to be hired as university professors. The wives of young professors who met their husbands in college or graduate school frequently accompanied them on their first academic postings, and found themselves thrust into homemaker roles many found confining and demeaning. Roslyn Blum, wife of a young Cornell scholar, recalled that Frances invited the wives to academic events and included them in dinner parties. "She was an incredible woman," Blum said. "If not for her, I might have lost my mind like a lot of other faculty wives."[16]

Many people on campus found her little idiosyncrasies endearing. When Frances arrived at the Administration Building to have her photograph taken, the photographer suggested she remove her hat. She responded with spirit: "I was born with my hat on." Frances was invited to join an elite, all-male luncheon group that met on Thursdays. A friend asked her if it was true that the group was now accepting women. "No, it is not true," she said. "Only men are admitted."[17]

Soon she joined another all-male society. Not long after arriving at Cornell, Frances visited Telluride House, an unusual campus organization. It had been founded in 1911 by a mining and electricity magnate who had the idea of bringing together high-minded students, living and learning together, in beautiful surroundings. The house was a comfortable and spacious Arts and Crafts–style mansion, with wooden plank floors and high ceilings, eclectically furnished with valuable Stickley furniture. Large windows overlooked sloping lawns. In a distant echo of Jane Addams's Chicago Hull House, visiting scholars were invited to join the Telluride House residents over dinner to discuss popular culture, history, civic life, or scientific advances.

The environment was charming, prestigious, and free, and the students invited to live there generally accepted with pride. Only men received the prized invitations.

But times were changing. The young president of Telluride House, Christopher Breiseth, conceived the idea that the first woman to live at Telluride should be the most important career woman the United States had produced—Frances Perkins. Breiseth approached Neufeld and asked if he thought Frances would enjoy living with the students. Neufeld thought she might. Breiseth began securing the approvals. Then one night the young men invited Frances and the Neufelds to the house for dinner.

The Neufelds were in on the secret, so Maurice and Hinda arranged to drive Frances to Telluride so the young men could "pop the question." Later the Neufelds drove her home. She asked them inside, and then shared her good news.

"Do you know what those boys have done?" she asked with delight. "I feel like a bride on her wedding night!"[18]

Soon Frances moved to Telluride House, where she lived in a small room upstairs, painted yellow, in a large house filled with boisterous young men. She enjoyed the students enormously, cultivating the students who she thought demonstrated the most promise. She became close friends with a young scholar named Allan Bloom; she was devoted to Breiseth; she spent time with another young student named Paul Wolfowitz. They all enjoyed her deadpan humor, keen insights, and dry wit.

"She was so unassuming and unpretentious that it was easy to underestimate her," Wolfowitz recalled. "It took a while to realize how astute she was, how sharp she was."[19]

She used her appearance as a cover, Bloom told others. She sought to look "boring, unthreatening," for it masked her piercing intellect and gave her more privacy. Frances and Bloom were decades apart in age, but the affection between them was real. "She made my heart jump," Bloom told an interviewer later. "Leaping with joy."[20]

Frances forged tight bonds with many of the young men, balancing the roles of mother, mentor, friend, and camp counselor. The high-decibel level in a house packed with twenty-year-old boys would have proved irritating to many women entering their twilight years, but Frances took the tumult in stride. "One advantage was that her hearing had gotten so bad it didn't bother her, living with thirty noisy boys," recalled Abe Shulsky, another resident.[21]

Frances entered their life diplomatically, faithfully attending Monday night house meetings. Telluride House was an exercise in self-government. When the boys voted to give up the houseman to save money, she expressed some doubts but did not oppose it, merely noting in the next weeks that the house was notably dirty by Sunday night. When the cook asked for a wage increase, and the boys wanted to turn her down, she warned: "You only find out how valuable a competent servant is after he has left."[22]

In one area she did raise a concern. She disapproved of the tendency at Telluride to select for admission only the boys with the highest academic grades, noting that it is often the C student with strong leadership skills and a good personality who makes a greater mark on the world. "Franklin Roosevelt would never be admitted to a first-class college today," she said.

Frances took her own responsibilities at the house seriously. Telluride House's garden had been left untended, and soon Frances made its revitalization her cause. She especially loved heirloom flowers and would watch to see when elegant old houses, viewed as past their prime, were scheduled for demolition. She assigned the boys to fetch cuttings from the oldest flowering bushes on the properties. The garden "wasn't neglected for long after Frances Perkins got there," Neufeld recalled. "She got them working on it and it became a beautiful garden."[23]

As gifts, she gave the students copies of *Gracian's Manual: A Truthtelling Manual and the Art of Worldly Wisdom,* a Machiavellian compendium of the teachings of a Spanish Jesuit priest named Baltasar Gracián, who commented acerbically on the nature of power when Spain was at the zenith of its empire in the mid-1600s. Gracián's book is a survival road map for the person of integrity in a world where the unworthy often rise to the most powerful posts. Speaking truth to power is often a hazardous line of work, as Gracián found: At the end of his life, he was silenced by clerical officials, stripped of his university post, exiled, and imprisoned.

In her personal copy of *Gracian's Manual,* Frances marked some passages as particularly astute, including this one on the use of human motivations:

> Discover each man's thumbscrew. It is the way to move his
> will, more skill than force being required to know how to get
> at the heart of anyone; there is no will without its leanings,
> which differ as desires differ. All men are idolators, some of
> honor, others of greed, and the most of pleasure: the trick lies
> in knowing these idols that are so powerful, thus knowing
> the impulse that moves every man: it is like having the key to
> another man's will, with which to get at the spring within, by no
> means always his best, but more frequently, his worst, for there
> are more unholy men in this world than holy; divine the ruling
> passion of a man, excite him with a word, and then attack him
> through his pet weakness, that invariably checkmates his free
> will.

Another dealt with character:

> Be gracious: for those who govern it is the grand manner
> through which to please; it is the halo of the mighty by which
> they gain the good will of a populace. This is the single advantage of power, that it enables the holder to do more good; those
> are friends who make friends.[24]

Although some people couldn't see her uniqueness, something that had haunted Frances all her life, others appreciated her almost immediately. Both Neufeld and Breiseth found Frances so fascinating that they kept diaries, taking note of things she said and did, and particularly what she remembered of her Roosevelt years.

They also had a window into Frances's interior life that few people had ever had. In 1958, for example, during a lighthearted dinner party at which people talked about the old New England customs, Frances shared an interesting bit of folk wisdom from Maine that suggested the family strains she had faced as a child. She noted that volcanic emotions rest under the surface of the seemingly reserved inhabitants of the state. For that reason, she said, there is a saying in Maine that people should never go hunting with relatives. Relatives know you too well, she related, so it is better to hunt with strangers. She said people in Maine had long noticed that relatives who go hunting together are more likely to turn up dead.[25]

In 1963, Frances told Bloom that she always kept her distance and never allowed anyone to get too close. Why, Bloom asked. "I am afraid of being hurt," she said.[26]

Frances reveled in youthful Telluride House because other aspects of her life had taken on a funereal cast. She was increasingly called on to attend her friends' services as they grew ill and died. One friend, for example, lapsed in and out of consciousness as she succumbed during the heat of a New York City summer. The woman had only one child, an invalid daughter, and Frances and another friend shared the death-watch.[27]

Attending funerals in distant towns often posed transportation problems. Frances, now eighty-three, never liked loud machines, and she refused to fly in a plane. The railroad line to Ithaca shut down soon after her arrival, and she didn't drive, so she traveled to and from the remote college town by bus. This often required four or five bus transfers each way. But she refused to stop attending funerals, feeling that each of her old comrades deserved a final salute. Bloom tried to keep an eye on her comings and goings.[28]

A steady flow of famous people came to meet with her at Cornell, including labor leaders Walter Reuther and Jimmy Hoffa and politicians Henry Wallace and James Farley. Farley, ever the ward boss, also asked to visit an ailing Democratic activist who was hospitalized, and young Paul Wolfowitz drove him there. The man visibly rallied because Farley had made the effort to see him.

At another function, former president Truman warmly greeted Frances with a kiss, explaining that she was the only woman he kissed except for his wife and daughter.[29]

In due course, the Kennedy family consulted with her as they entered the White House. Frances actually preferred Lyndon Johnson, John Kennedy's vice president, whom she considered a brilliant politician. But she was charmed by JFK at a meeting in Washington in March 1963, when he unexpectedly appeared early at a speech at which she was giving the opening remarks. He had come ahead of schedule to hear Frances speak. She quickly offered him her chair, then regaled him with stories of the early days of the Roosevelt administration, when the buildings were so dilapidated. She spread her fingers wide to demonstrate how large the cockroaches in the Labor Department had been.[30]

Frances had always predicted a politician's likely success by taking measure of his wife. Frances quickly noted Jackie's intelligence and wit. The students at Telluride were thrilled when a beautiful bouquet of flowers arrived at the front hall, addressed to Miss Perkins, with warm regards from Jacqueline Kennedy.[31]

Jackie was thanking Frances for attending and serving as spokeswoman for a group of prominent Democratic women who convened at the Kennedy home on N Street in Georgetown to discuss public affairs, including issues affecting education, medical care for the aged, and the high cost of living. The event must have had some bittersweet moments for Frances, who had left Washington almost a decade earlier. Jackie's home backed up to the house Frances had shared with Mary Rumsey, where Frances had finalized the details in the Social Security plan.

Frances told the young faculty wives at Cornell how impressed she had been by the president's wife. "That woman speaks softly, but listen to every word," she told them.[32]

Although now largely outside the public limelight, Frances still remained secretive about her life. Over lunch at the university with several professors, including Neufeld, Frances was asked by one of the group, a scholar of American history, whether she would one day write a book about herself.

"I shall not," she replied.

"Well, that will make it all the more difficult for your own biographer to deal with your career," her friend Neufeld interjected.

"I have already seen to it that it will be indeed very difficult for him to write my biography," Frances said. "I have had all my private papers and letters destroyed."

The young scholar was aghast. "Have you no sense of history?"

"No, none at all," Frances said.[33]

In reality, Frances had saved many letters, and she wrote notes that she placed in her records at Columbia University and elsewhere, elaborating on at least selected points for the benefit of the future biographer she publicly spurned.

Then she told the lunchtime group that she had also refused to answer many questions for the census. Someone assured her that she should not fear the government, because census records are maintained confidentially.

"They say they do," Frances said. "But I had to fight more than one battle to keep documents which were confidential out of the hands of the FBI when the Immigration Service was under the Secretary of Labor. Government has grown and grown and invades more and more areas of our lives. We have to put a stop to that growth somewhere."

She was also worried that the program she had created—Social Security—was being used as a way to place numbers on people and track their activities for commercial purposes, said Peter Poole. "She never would have approved" a program established to provide old-age pensions being used to make sure people paid their bills.[34]

But she remained enormously proud of what she had done for the American people. At a meeting to celebrate the twenty-fifth anniversary of Social Security, Frances said: "One thing I know: Social Security is so firmly embedded in the American psychology today that no politician, no political party, no political group could possibly destroy this Act and still maintain our democratic system," she told them. "It is safe. It is safe forever, and for the everlasting benefit of the people of the United States."[35]

But while Social Security survived, Frances's friends continued dropping away. In late 1962, Eleanor Roosevelt was dying. Frances wrote to her, and Eleanor's daughter, Anna, wrote back.

"Mother continues to slip away slowly," Anna wrote to Frances. "She does not know much of what goes on around her most of the time. It is very sad to watch."[36]

Frances had a curiously ambivalent relationship with Eleanor. Yet the two women also loved each other, as only comrades-in-arms can do. A photographer captured their closeness at a ceremony marking the fiftieth anniversary of the Triangle fire. Wrinkled and bent with age, they sat closely, smiling fondly at what they had achieved in improving working conditions.

But at the end Eleanor Roosevelt got the adulation and luxurious life that Frances must have felt she deserved. While Frances was teaching at a poorly funded state program, living on a small income, Eleanor Roosevelt, enriched by her self-promotion, lucrative speaking engagements, and well-paid advertising endorsements during her husband's presidency, lived comfortably in New York City, surrounded by admirers. Eleanor had earned at least $1.2 million during the first seven years of her husband's presidency alone, when Frances was working long hours and scrambling to support her family on a government salary. Eleanor remained a popular public figure, becoming a delegate to the United Nations. She was Franklin's living legacy; Frances was becoming forgotten. Frances grieved when Eleanor died in November 1962 but expressed impatience to her Cornell friends about the fuss the press was making. Some commentators suggested that Mrs. Roosevelt was actually the moving figure behind the Roosevelt administration, a galling interpretation to the woman who had drafted the laws, helped enact them, and then administered them.[37]

Some even viewed Eleanor as a religious icon. Frances recalled meeting an Italian immigrant who told her that at night, when he prayed to the Madonna, it was Eleanor Roosevelt's face that he saw. "In the next few days we are going to hear a great deal about how much Mrs. R did for mankind," she told Breiseth. "But the striking fact about Eleanor Roosevelt to those of us who knew her for many years was how much she did for herself."[38]

But Frances returned from the funeral trip to Hyde Park with a new appreciation for Eleanor, having been greatly moved by the emotional outpouring from hordes of average Americans, including some who were young and knew Eleanor only when her White House days were over. Eleanor's benevolence, humanitarianism, even her gawky appearance, endeared her to people around the world. Her simple language reached more hearts than Frances's intellectualism and rationality.

Frances, too, was starting to falter. She struggled to write her long-planned book about Al Smith. Suffering from a heart condition, she found that the effort seemed more than she could bear. She tried to find someone to help her write it and turned to a promising young sociologist, Daniel Patrick Moynihan, who had worked with Averell Harriman in New York before becoming assistant secretary of labor. Moynihan wanted to do it but didn't have the time.[39]

Frances grew frail. She had dizzy spells and was increasingly fatigued, hard of hearing, and occasionally incontinent. She had trouble climbing stairs and clung to the railing, always loathe to ask for help. It became more difficult for her to give classroom talks extemporaneously, and she became more dependent on written notes.

She lost her vision dramatically, going blind in one eye when a blood vessel burst while she was delivering a lecture. She gamely continued with the talk. But the damage was permanent, and Frances retained only partial vision in the other eye. She later compared it to being "struck blind" as Saint Paul had been.[40]

From then on, Frances identified people approaching her by their general physical shape and their voices. Sometimes she mistook someone and then tried to cover up her error by blaming poor lighting.[41]

On other occasions, she covered up her fragility by offering to help others. When Benjamin Aaron, an academic from California, came to visit Ithaca, Frances invited him out to lunch. Crossing an icy street, they quickly realized the pavement was treacherous. Frances turned to Aaron, four decades her junior, and said, "Mr. Aaron, let me take your arm. I don't want you to fall." With Frances gripping his arm, the two safely crossed.[42]

It might have been time for her to retire, but she couldn't afford to do so because she depended on the $10,000 a year she earned as a university instructor. Her lifetime earnings as a public servant had gone mostly to support her husband and daughter. In fact, Susanna had another nervous breakdown in 1964, requiring additional mental care.[43]

In addition to her teaching pay, Frances also continued to receive royalties on sales of *The Roosevelt I Knew*. She typically received payments twice a year, $700 twice yearly in 1955, for example. These payments were earmarked, in Frances's mind, for Susanna's family. Frances quietly set aside a trust fund for them, setting conditions to ensure the money would be doled out slowly.[44]

Frances mentioned her family rarely, and Susanna seemed to know equally little about her mother's life in Ithaca. Though her mother was virtually blind, living in a remote area in New York, traveling back and forth to New York City by bus, Susanna seemed uninterested. When Neufeld called her once to see how her mother was faring, Susanna wasn't sure who Maurice Neufeld was—though he was the man who had helped Frances secure her employment at Cornell.

Frances felt great anguish, not at Susanna's failures, but at her own. Frances had trouble accepting that many of her daughter's problems were psychological and on some level she kept believing that Susanna could better manage her life if she simply exhibited the same kind of "self-control" that Frances herself did. Susanna drank heavily and had emotional outbursts. She depended on her mother but also resented her for it.[45]

By 1965, the estrangement between mother and daughter was almost complete. Frances was no longer invited to share Thanksgiving or Christmas dinners with the family at the apartment she had given over to them. Susanna had barred Frances from visiting Tomlin, a selfish action that hurt Frances deeply.

None of the children were ever told about Frances's benevolence while Susanna was alive. In fact, they recalled, Susanna generally ridiculed her mother, as she did many people who worked for a living. Frances had spent her life laboring on behalf of America's workers and had produced a child of the leisure class, more ornamental than useful, who felt contempt for people who worked for a living.[46]

Frances dealt with the family tensions as she did any other unpleasant aspect of her life. Abe Shulsky, who lived at Telluride House, almost never heard her speak of Susanna. "I knew there was a daughter, and I knew there was a problem," Shulsky said. She similarly said little to her fellow parishioners at St. John's Episcopal Church in Ithaca. Louise Rideout, who also attended regularly, spoke to Frances frequently but knew little about her personal life. "I never even knew she had a daughter or that she had been married."[47]

With Susanna distant both emotionally and geographically, there was no one to care for Frances. Neufeld and Bloom monitored Frances's health and shared information about her condition, because she was reluctant to let anyone know of her increasing infirmity.

"Our society and culture provide no way for us to take care, with dignity, of queens when they grow old," Bloom told Neufeld. He spent many hours with Frances, talking about American life and culture, sharing a love of great literature.[48]

Frances also worried about the growing secularization of America, which she viewed as the antithesis of what made the country great. The country had prospered, she thought, because it encouraged faith-based utopian visions that brought communal thinking, planning for the good of the majority, to people who would otherwise revert to a selfish individualism. She deeply resented what she called the "ranting" of "third-rate minds," people who wanted all traces of religion removed from popular culture and public life. She thought people banning the Lord's Prayer and Bible reading from the school represented only a small percentage of a population with deeply religious roots, and should not have been allowed to reshape public discourse.

"What they have done is bring about the glorification of secularization, which I think is terrible," she said. "The founding fathers of this country founded it under God. 'In God We Trust' they put on the coinage. They began their Declaration and their Constitution with references to Almighty God. They jolly well knew they served God and not man, and that they had no hope of success with any nation so conceived if they didn't do it under the will and under the rule of God."

It was incomprehensible to Frances to think of excluding religion from public life altogether, for it was her religious motivation—to do what Jesus would want one to do—that drove her and fueled all that she had done.[49]

Chapter 38

LAST DAYS

*I*n the spring of 1965, Frances told friends she planned to visit one of her Telluride students in Barcelona. At eighty-five, the product of a long-lived family, she considered herself invincible.

Her energy was inspirational. Christopher Breiseth, now a Cornell graduate teaching history at Williams College, told Frances she inspired him to conquer his own fatigue to accomplish more.

"You're wrong to do that," she replied. "The young must rest for they must conserve their energy for the many things they have to do. The old have nothing to rest for. If they do not keep pushing they will give up."[1]

The previous fall, Frances commuted between rural New Jersey and rural New York to teach two seminars on the New Deal at Princeton University. Then she traveled to Washington to attend LBJ's inauguration, catching a bad cold. She wasn't feeling well when she returned to New York and was running a high fever, but she still insisted on having lunch with her son-in-law, Calvert Coggeshall. Calvert's life with Susanna was not easy, and Frances didn't want to disappoint him. After lunch, she returned to Margaret Poole's apartment, climbed into bed, and piled covers high to ward off a chill. She shivered for hours before a doctor was called. Admitted to the hospital, she was diagnosed with pneumonia. Frances fought it off, but she left the hospital with a racking cough that lasted months. For a while, she told no one at Cornell about the illness, and then she mentioned it to her colleague Neufeld while visiting his office. He expressed concern, but she shrugged it off.[2]

"I can still run faster than the Grim Reaper!" she told him. Her grandmother had lived to 101 and Frances, too, expected as much.[3]

With that sense of fortitude, in late April 1965, Frances journeyed to Johns Hopkins Hospital in Baltimore to see an eye specialist. She stayed again at her beloved All Saints Convent, where the sisters were shocked by her physical deterioration. Her eyesight was mostly gone, and she was hard of hearing. When the bell rang for early mass, Frances didn't hear it and missed the Sunday morning service.[4]

Finally leaving Catonsville, Frances came back through New York City and stopped to stay once more with Margaret Poole. Despite her fatigue, she attended the ballet one night, but she could no longer see the stars, Margot Fonteyn and Rudolph Nureyev. Frances's main reason for visiting was to address a lung ailment, possibly a complication from the pneumonia. The doctors recommended a short hospital stay. She called a Cornell secretary to convey details, first swearing her to secrecy. She expected to return on May 1 and was scheduled to address graduating seniors the next day at Syracuse University.[5]

Frances checked into Midtown Hospital, under the care of her doctor and friend Margaret Janeway. The doctor called Cornell a few days later to report that Frances was not yet well enough to return. Frances fretted about the work she was missing, and was dressing to go home when she suffered a stroke, and then, in the next days, several more. Semiconscious, Frances needed intravenous feeding and seemed to have lost the use of one of her hands. She recognized Susanna, who must have been notified by the doctor, and tried to speak with her, but could not make intelligible sounds. Her health deteriorated further over the next week.

Susanna called the Cornell secretary, asking if people at the school knew how ill her mother was. Susanna pressed the secretary about the whereabouts of Frances's manuscript on Al Smith's life. Frances had received a publisher's advance but the book was still unfinished, and Susanna was eager to find the manuscript and get the rest of the money due to Frances upon its completion. The secretary informed Neufeld about Frances, but, respecting Frances's penchant for secrecy, the two of them decided to keep the information on her latest illness to themselves.[6]

Hearing nothing from New York, Allan Bloom and other Telluride students became anxious. Bloom called Neufeld, who offered few details. Bloom then decided to call Margaret Poole directly, and only then learned the bad news. By May 12, the *New York Times* also learned that Frances was fading and contacted Susanna for obituary details. At Susanna's request, and because she seemed unaware of the details of her mother's life, Neufeld drafted a chronology. Susanna asked whether the obituary should mention the incomplete Al Smith biography, which she assumed was nearly written. Frances's book on Roosevelt made money that Susanna would inherit, and her daughter was eager to see another book completed.[7]

As it turned out, however, Frances had been too ill to write much of the book, and she found herself stymied in trying to characterize the bitter split between Smith and Roosevelt, as she loved and felt loyal to both men. It was a rare failure for her. Only fragments of her manuscript were ever published, in a book written by Matthew and Hannah Josephson.

Frances lapsed into a coma and died at the hospital on May 14, 1965, at the age of eighty-five. It seems likely that Frances, who had so often traveled to inconvenient locations to bid her friends farewell and pray with them as they passed away, was alone when she died. None of Susanna's friends, Tomlin, or her stepchildren ever heard Susanna discuss her mother's passing. Susanna did not seem particularly saddened at her mother's death, but Calvert cried.

And at Cornell Frances was truly mourned. At a memorial service, Maurice Neufeld led with a tribute to Frances, who "appeared among us out of history." He said she had lived by the creed of her grandmother: "When in doubt, do what is right."[8]

A requiem mass was held at the Church of the Resurrection in New York City. In lieu of flowers, Susanna asked friends to contribute to the Miles Memorial Hospital in Newcastle, Maine, or to the Retreat House of the Redeemer, an Episcopal retreat in New York City. Frances's closest Cornell friends flew to New York on the university plane; the Telluride boys drove down by car.

Planned years earlier by Frances, the service was strictly liturgical, as FDR's had been. It was hot and the thick smell of incense overpowered the little church. The service began with readings from Psalms 23, 91, and 123: "The Lord Is My Shepherd," "You Who Live in the Shelter of the Most High," and "To You I Lift Up My Eyes." Frances chose the verses to sum up her life's meaning.[9]

Isador Lubin was there, with his new wife, Carol Riegelman, the plucky secretary who had helped lead ILO officials to safety at the outbreak of World War II. The adherence to formula disturbed them. "We were sort of horrified at the formality of it," Riegelman said later. But to those in Perkins's own High Church tradition, those rituals were familiar and comforting.

Susanna suggested that the Telluride boys serve as pallbearers, including Wolfowitz, who would later become deputy secretary of defense and president of the World Bank. Also in attendance was Breiseth, who would make the New Deal his life work, first as a scholar and then as director of the Franklin and Eleanor Roosevelt Institute at Hyde Park.

"To the strains of 'Oh, God, Our Help in Ages Past,' Frances's casket was carried from the church by eight young Telluride students," Breiseth wrote, noting that none had been born before 1940, when Frances's monumental work was almost completed. "Few faces showed greater grief than theirs," he said.[10]

Many of Frances's friends said good-bye, including James Farley, Bessie Hillman, Francis Biddle, and former New York governor Charles Poletti. Neufeld noted in his diary, that "most of Frances Perkins' other friends and associates during the New Deal have already disappeared from earth."[11]

But they hadn't really. The New Dealers had passed the torch to the next generation. In a lecture at Cornell's Catherwood Library, Frances had recalled the funeral of a fellow New Dealer. She saw a congregation full of young faces, all inspired to improve the world.

"I realized that we had done something for this country when we started the New Deal because it started a whole generation of people then just young and pouring out of colleges and universities, it had started them on careers which were forwarding some part of the New Deal and in which they had almost without exception continued . . ." she told the audience.[12]

The secret of Frances's success was that she had done what she did selflessly, without hope of personal gain or public recognition, for those who would come afterward. It was a perpetuation of the Hull House tradition of the old teaching the young how to advocate for the yet-unborn.

It is a great historic irony that Frances is now virtually unknown. Factory and office occupancy codes, fire escapes and other fire-prevention mechanisms are her legacy. About 44 million people collect Social Security checks each month; millions receive unemployment and worker's compensation or the minimum wage; others get to go home after an eight-hour day because of the Fair Labor Standards Act. Very few know the name of the woman responsible for their benefits.

As she had once told Felix Frankfurter, as she stepped down from office:

"I came to work for God, FDR and the millions of forgotten, plain, common working men. The last conversation . . . I had with F.D.[R.] was of such a nature that I could say with the Psalmist, 'My cup runneth over and surely goodness and mercy shall follow me.' "[13]

NOTES

PROLOGUE

1. "Nothing like this . . .": Reminiscences of Frances Perkins, part 3, pp. 606–07 (1951–1955, Columbia University Oral History Research Office Collection (hereafter CUOHROC); Frances Perkins, *The Roosevelt I Knew* (New York: Viking, 1946), pp. 150–52.

CHAPTER I: CHILDHOOD AND YOUTH

1. "There my dear . . .": Reminiscences of Frances Perkins, part 3, pp. 652–53, 1951–1955, CUOHROC.
2. "High Points in the History of the Newcastle-Damariscotta area," p. 32; author interviews with Tomlin Coggeshall; "History of Ancient Sheepscott," pp. 180–81.
3. Ruth Backes papers, Mount Holyoke College Archives and Special Collections; George Martin, *Madam Secretary* (Boston: Houghton Mifflin, 1976); Frances Perkins family papers, Butler Library, Columbia University.
4. David McCullough, *John Adams* (New York: Simon & Schuster, 2001), pp. 44, 49, 62, 132–33, citing "Diary and Autobiography of John Adams," L. H. Butterfield, ed.
5. Author interview with Susanna Coggeshall; Oliver Otis papers, George J. Mitchell Department of Special Collections and Archives, Bowdoin College.
6. "Newcastle and 'Scotta Folk Know Roosevelt's Cabinet Secretary of Labor by Girlhood Name of 'Fannie Perkins,' " *Lewiston Journal,* Aug. 24, 1935, p. 1; Winifred Wandersee, *Be Ye Stedfast: Frances Perkins to Mid-Life* (unpublished manuscript), pp. 4–6.
7. "magnificent . . .": Reminiscences of Frances Perkins, part 1, pp. 175–76, 1951–1955, CUOHROC.
8. *Worcester Evening Telegram,* Mar. 1, 1933, p. 1.
9. "vicarious physical agony . . .": Reminiscences of Frances Perkins, part I, p. 185, 1951–1955, CUOHROC.
10. "New world . . .": Reminiscences of Frances Perkins, part 1, p. 183, 1951–1955, CUOHROC.
11. Jacob A. Riis, *How the Other Half Lives* (New York: Dover, 1971) (reprint of 1901 edition), pp. 129–30.
12. "time of complacency . . .": Frederick Lewis Allen, *The Big Change: America Transforms Itself* (New York: Perennial Library, 1952), pp. 8–9.
13. Ruth Owen Jones, *Frances Perkins: Her Years at Mount Holyoke,* Mount Holyoke College Archives (1898–1902), pp. 1–2; Mount Holyoke College Web site.
14. Jones, p. 6.
15. "Miss Perkins Won Mount Holyoke Honor," *Boston Globe,* Feb. 27, 1933; Jones, p. 20;

Bill Severn, *Frances Perkins, A Member of the Cabinet* (New York: Hawthorn Books, 1976), p. 17.

16. "Miss Perkins Active When at Mount Holyoke," *Springfield Republican*, Mar. 1, 1933; Anna Mary Wells, *Miss Marks and Miss Woolley* (Boston: Houghton Mifflin, 1978), pp. 47–48, 53, 65, 67, 76; "Secretary Perkins as a Mount Holyoke Student," *Boston Globe*, Mar. 4, 1933.

17. Wandersee, *Be Ye Stedfast*, p. 12; Florence Kelley biographical materials, Frances Perkins papers, Rare Book and Manuscript Library, Columbia University (hereafter FP papers, RBML, Columbia); Editorial, *Lexington Herald*, FP papers, Columbia; *Municipal Platform*, Socialist Party (Ann Arbor, MI: March 6, 1901); Martin, *Madam Secretary*, p. 51; Josephine Goldmark, *Impatient Crusader: Florence Kelley's Life Story* (Urbana: University of Illinois Press, 1953), pp. 36–47.

18. Martin, p. 49.

19. "den of iniquity . . .": Reminiscences of Frances Perkins, part 1, p. 23, 1951–1955, CUOHROC.

20. "Well, that's very interesting . . .": Reminiscences of Frances Perkins, part 1, pp. 5–6, 1951–1955, CUOHROC.

21. "Well, nothing seemed to turn up . . .": Class letter, 1902, biographical file, Perkins, box 1 of 2, folder 10 (Mount Holyoke Trustees), as cited in Wandersee.

22. *Worcester Evening Gazette*, Mar. 1, 1933, p. 1.

23. Class letter, as cited by Wandersee, p. 23.

24. *Worcester Telegram*, May 1965, T-15.

CHAPTER 2: BECOMING FRANCES PERKINS

1. Author interview with Arthur Miller, archivist at Lake Forest College; *The 1907 Forester*, Lake Forest Archives; Ferry Hall catalogues (1904–1907), Lake Forest Archives.

2. Raelene Lyons Bowman and Anne Morgan De Acetis, *The Church of the Holy Spirit: The First 100 Years* (Lake Forest, IL.: Church of the Holy Spirit, 2002).

3. Consuelo Vanderbilt Balsan, *The Glitter and the Gold* (Maidstone, Kent: George Mann Books, 1973).

4. Jane Addams, *Twenty Years at Hull House* (Boston: St. Martin's, 1999), p. 80.

5. Upton Sinclair, *The Jungle* (New York: Doubleday Page, 1906); U.S. Census Bureau, Population of 100 Biggest Urban Areas (by decade).

6. Alice Hamilton, *Exploring the Dangerous Trades* (Boston: Little Brown, 1943), p. 83; Milton Mayer, "Charlotte Carr: Settlement Lady," cited in *100 Years at Hull House*, Mary Lynn McCree Bryan and Allen F. Davis, editors (Bloomington: Indiana University Press, 1969), pp. 225–26.

7. "The only answer . . .": Reminiscences of Frances Perkins, part I, pp. 12–13, 1951–1955, CUOHROC.

8. "an evil to be avoided . . .": Reminiscences of Frances Perkins, part 1, p. 9, 1951–1955, CUOHROC.

9. Semi-annual Statement of the Philadelphia Research and Protective Association (1909 or 1910), Philadelphia folder, FP papers, RBML, Columbia.

10. "really evil . . .": Reminiscences of Frances Perkins, part 1, pp. 30–32, 1951–1955, CUOHROC.

11. University of Pennsylvania Archives, Alumnae Records Collection, Box 2065; Wharton School History, University of Pennsylvania; Reminiscences of Frances Perkins, part 1, p. 65, 1951–1955, CUOHROC.

12. George N. Caylor papers, New York Public Library, "Brother Joe," pp. 132–38, "Frances Perkins Memoir," pp. 1, 4, 7, 8.

CHAPTER 3: THE YOUNG ACTIVIST HITS NEW YORK

1. Christine Stansell, *American Moderns: Bohemian New York and the Creation of a New Century* (New York: Henry Holt, 2000), p. 3.
2. Reminiscences of Frances Perkins, part 1, p. 299, 1951–1955, CUOHROC.
3. "sparks . . .": Reminiscences of Frances Perkins, part 1, pp. 236, 1951–1955, CUOHROC.
4. Robert Caro, *The Power Broker: Robert Moses and the Fall of New York* (New York: Knopf, 1974), pp. 65–67.
5. Mark Schorer, *Sinclair Lewis: An American Life* (New York: McGraw-Hill, 1961), p. 191; FP to Mark Schorer, Feb. 4, 1959, Schorer papers, Bancroft Library, University of California; Will Irwin, *The Making of a Reporter* (New York: Putnam, 1942), pp. 198–99.
6. "Talk on Feminism Draws Great Crowd," *New York Times*, Feb. 18, 1914, p. 2.
7. Letter to Mount Holyoke Alumni (1909), pp. 59–60, Mount Holyoke College Archives and Special Collections, South Hadley, MA.
8. Meryl Nader, "The Pittsburgh Survey," Iona College, BPD Update, fall 2003, Association of Baccalaureate Social Work Program Directors.
9. FP to Helen Phelps Stokes, Apr. 20, 1910, FP papers, Coggeshall addition, RBML, Columbia. A salary of $1,000 per year was equivalent to $22,800 per year in 2007, adjusted for inflation.
10. "training of the conscience . . .": Frances Perkins address, "The Living Spirit of Florence Kelley," Dec. 8, 1939, FP papers, Coggeshall addition, RBML, Columbia; National Consumers League papers, Library of Congress.
11. Penny Colman, *A Woman Unafraid: The Achievements of Frances Perkins* (New York: Atheneum, 1993), pp. 27–28.
12. Florence Kelley memorial service, Apr. 8, 1932, Florence Kelley papers, Schlesinger Library, Radcliffe Institute for Advanced Study, Harvard University; interview with Mrs. Smith, Kelley's secretary, National Consumers League papers, Library of Congress; "Living Spirit of Florence Kelley"; "Hours of Expressmen," *New York Times*, Nov. 11, 1910, p. 8.
13. "I'd much rather get . . .": Reminiscences of Frances Perkins, part 1, p. 58, 1951–1955, CUOHROC.
14. "My dear Miss Perkins . . .": Theodore Roosevelt papers, Library of Congress, Reel 364, Series 3A, Jan. 31, 1911.
15. "You'd better keep . . .": Reminiscences of Frances Perkins, part 1, p. 237, 1951–1955, CUOHROC.

CHAPTER 4: THE TRIANGLE SHIRTWAIST FIRE

1. Gerald W. McFarland, *Inside Greenwich Village* (Amherst: University of Massachusetts Press, 2001), pp. 78–91, 112–16.
2. "One by one . . .": Reminiscences of Frances Perkins, part 1, p. 126, 1951–1955, CUOHROC; David Von Drehle, *Triangle: The Fire That Changed America* (New York: Atlantic Monthly Press, 2003); FP lecture at Cornell University's School of Industrial and Labor Relations, Sept. 30, 1964, Kheel Center, Martin P. Catherwood Library, Cornell University.
3. Leon Stein, *The Triangle Fire* (Ithaca, NY: Cornell University Press, 2001) pp. 18–19.
4. "a true example . . .": Reminiscences of Frances Perkins, part 1, p. 48, 1951–1955, CUOHROC.

5. Stein, p. 167.
6. Stein, pp. 143–44.
7. Winifred Wandersee, *Be Ye Stedfast: Frances Perkins to Mid-Life* (unpublished manuscript), pp. 13–14; Will Irwin, *The Making of a Reporter* (New York: Putnam, 1942), p. 113.

CHAPTER 5: FINDING ALLIES IN TAMMANY HALL

1. "Fix it up . . .": Reminiscences of Frances Perkins, part 1, pp. 85–88, 1951–1955, CUOHROC.
2. George Martin, *Madam Secretary* (Boston: Houghton Mifflin, 1976), p. 80.
3. "Al Smith had . . .": Reminiscences of Frances Perkins, part 1, p. 105, 1951–1955, CUOHROC.
4. "They don't mean . . .": Reminiscences of Frances Perkins, part 1, p. 108, 1951–1955, CUOHROC; Martin, pp. 91–97.
5. "How many women . . .": Reminiscences of Frances Perkins, part 1, p. 109, 1951–1955, CUOHROC.
6. "Me sister was a poor girl . . .": Reminiscences of Frances Perkins, part 1, p. 110, 1951–1955, CUOHROC.
7. "Pauline . . .": Reminiscences of Frances Perkins, part 1, p. 112, 1951–1955, CUOHROC.
8. 1912 Consumers League Report, National Consumers League papers, Library of Congress, Box A6, 1912 annual folder.
9. Martin, pp. 91–99.
10. "All I know is this . . .": Reminiscences of Frances Perkins, part 1, pp. 213–14, 1951–1955, CUOHROC.
11. Original draft of *The Roosevelt I Knew*, chapter 1, p. 5, FP papers, RBML, Columbia; Reminiscences of Frances Perkins, part 1, p. 231, 1951–1955, CUOHROC.

CHAPTER 6: TEDDY ROOSEVELT AND FRANCES PERKINS

1. "Delighted to see you . . .": John A. Kingsbury papers, unpublished manuscript, part III, box 16; Kingsbury to Alfred E. Smith, Dec. 13, 1932, part II, box 20, Kingsbury papers, Library of Congress; Kathleen Dalton, *Theodore Roosevelt: A Strenuous Life* (New York: Vintage Books, 2002), pp. 362–403.
2. Scott Nearing to FP, Jan. 29, 1912, FP papers, Coggeshall addition, RBML, Columbia.
3. "The Consumer's League is the only . . .": Reminiscences of Frances Perkins, part 1, p. 135, 1951–1955, CUOHROC, box 42, folder 1912, notes for Committee on Safety, FP papers, RBML, Columbia.
4. Preliminary Report of the Factory Investigating Commission, State of New York, 1912, vol. 1, p. 18.
5. It became more apparent that legislation was needed after Isaac Harris and Max Blanck, proprietors of the Triangle Company, with the help of a clever attorney, were acquitted in December 1911 of responsibility in the 146 deaths, despite testimony that they had locked doors and had barred the workers' escape. Judge Thomas C. T. Crain, a former government official who had been accused several years earlier of weak enforcement of safety-code laws in tenements after a fire that killed twenty, who were also trapped behind locked doors, presided over the trial. Judge Crain had instructed the jury that, to convict, they needed to know that the men were specifically aware that the doors were locked at the time. His jury instructions made a guilty verdict a near impossibility. This story is masterfully told in David Von Drehle, *Triangle: The Fire That Changed America* (New York: Atlantic Monthly Press, 2003).
6. Casey Cavanaugh Grant, P.E., "Triangle Fire Stirs Outrage and Reform," *NFPA Journal*,

May/June 1993, pp. 73–82; David Von Drehle, *Triangle: The Fire That Changed America;* Martin, pp. 103–121; Preliminary Report.

7. Martin, p. 108.

8. Frances Perkins sought to drive points home emotionally and vividly. A series of drawings illustrated panicked workers trying to flee a burning building, hanging from ledges, and perched on flimsy fire escapes. She engaged Lewis Hines, a famous photographer, to take pictures of unsanitary and dangerous working conditions. Dozens of such pictures and drawings appear throughout the Factory Investigating Commission's official reports. One photo, for example, showed a dirty kitten playing on a bread board in a bakery while the baker drank from a whiskey bottle; many others depicted tired mothers with their children shelling nuts or sewing beads onto ball gowns in their tenement apartments.

9. Reminiscences of Frances Perkins, part 1, pp. 170–73, 1951–1955, CUOHROC; Factory Investigating Commission, Second and Third Reports.

10. Frances Perkins's keynote address, National Fire Protection Association proceedings, May 13–15, 1913, National Fire Protection Association Archives, Quincy, Massachusetts; author interview with Casey Grant, chief systems and applications engineer and historian, NFPA.

11. A3027-77 Factory Investigating Commission, FIC folder, New York State Archives, Albany, New York; Reminiscences of Frances Perkins, part 1, p. 168, 1951–1955, CUOHROC; Fourth Report of Factory Investigating Commission, 1915, volume 1, pp. 77–79.

CHAPTER 7: A GOOD MATCH

1. Author interview with Susanna Coggeshall.

2. Carol Callahan, *Prairie Avenue Cookbook* (Chicago: Chicago Architecture Foundation, 1993), pp. 2–7.

3. Catherine Bruck, archivist, Illinois Institute of Technology, March 26, 2001, regarding Paul Wilson yearbook item 1899; Illinois Institute of Technology Web site.

4. Correspondence with Ben Stone, University of Chicago library, Mar. 19, 2001.

5. Robert Caro, *The Power Broker: Robert Moses and the Fall of New York* (New York: Knopf, 1974), p. 60.

6. PCW to FP, Restricted Box 118A, family correspondence, FP papers, Coggeshall addition, RBML, Columbia.

7. FP to PCW, Dec. 24, year unknown, Restricted Box 118A, family correspondence, FP papers, Coggeshall addition, RBML, Columbia.

8. George Martin, *Madam Secretary* (Boston: Houghton Mifflin, 1976), pp. 122–29, citing FP papers, RBML, Columbia.

9. "To think I write to you like this . . . ," "I feel you and your perfect love . . . ," "They do get on my nerves . . .": FP to PCW, Restricted Box 118A, family correspondence, FP papers, Coggeshall addition, RBML, Columbia.

10. Lately Thomas, *The Mayor Who Mastered New York* (New York: William Morrow, 1969), pp. 494–95.

11. "I would have liked . . .": Frederick Perkins to FP, Sept. 28, 1913, Restricted Box 118B, family correspondence, FP papers, Coggeshall addition, RBML, Columbia.

12. "I'm so glad . . .": FP to Mrs. Marshall Wilson, family correspondence, FP papers, Coggeshall addition, RBML, Columbia.

13. "as we summon the courage . . .": Martin, p. 124, citing FP papers, RBML, Columbia.

14. "Dear Old France . . .": Sinclair Lewis to FP, Friday, date unknown, 1913, Sinclair Lewis Collection, Macalester College, St. Paul, MN.

15. John A. Kingsbury to FP, Oct. 1, 1913, Kingsbury papers, Library of Congress.

16. Handwritten note by FP, box 42, folder 1909–58, circa 1910–12, on New York School of Philanthropy letterhead stationery, FP papers, RBML, Columbia.

17. The Triangle fire, sadly enough, reverberated on their wedding day. Frances was alone in her Waverly Place apartment dressing for the wedding when the telephone rang. Max Blanck, proprietor of the Triangle Company, had been arrested once again for locking workplace doors, this time at his new apparel factory. He had been found guilty and was awaiting sentencing. His wife and mother were on the line, begging Frances to urge clemency. Frances was sympathetic but decided not to intervene. Blanck was given a $20 fine, the minimum punishment possible, and the judge apologized for having to fine him at all. Reminiscences of Frances Perkins, part 1, pp. 275–79, 1951–1955, CUOHROC; David Von Drehle, *Triangle: The Fire That Changed America* (New York: Atlantic Monthly Press, 2003).

CHAPTER 8: MARRIED LIFE

1. "Lots of fun!" Fourth letter of the Class of 1902, Mount Holyoke College, Special Collections, South Hadley, MA.

2. "Mrs. is understood . . .": Reminiscences of Frances Perkins, part 1, pp. 244–47, 1951–1955, CUOHROC.

3. Fourth letter.

4. Lately Thomas, *The Mayor Who Mastered New York* (New York: William Morrow, 1969), p. 201.

5. "full story of why . . .": Reminiscences of Frances Perkins, part 1, pp. 275–76, 1951–1955, CUOHROC. "I've always been amused at myself," she added.

6. John Purroy Mitchel papers, box 56 scrapbooks, Library of Congress.

7. "He was acute . . .": "John Purroy Mitchel," *Outlook,* 24 July, pp. 479–81, Mitchel papers, Library of Congress.

8. "too intense . . .": Reminiscences of Frances Perkins, part 1, pp. 286–88, 1951–1955, CUOHROC.

9. *New York World,* May 3, 1914.

10. *New York World,* May 5, 1914, Mitchel papers, Library of Congress.

11. Penny Colman, *A Woman Unafraid: The Achievements of Frances Perkins* (New York: Atheneum, 1993), p. 31.

12. *New York World,* Oct. 15, 1915; *New York Times,* Oct. 10, 1915; *New York American,* undated, Mitchel papers, Library of Congress.

13. Colman, p. 32.

14. FP to PCW, 1915, no exact date, Restricted Box 118A, family correspondence, FP papers, Coggeshall addition, RBML, Columbia.

CHAPTER 9: MOTHERHOOD

1. Author interview with Susanna Coggeshall.

2. FP to PCW, Dec. 24, Restricted Box 118A, family correspondence, FP papers, Coggeshall addition, RBML, Columbia.

3. Author interview with Susanna Coggeshall.

4. George Martin, *Madam Secretary* (Boston: Houghton Mifflin, 1976), p. 129.

5. PCW to FP, Sept. 19, 1917, FP papers, RBML, Columbia, cited in Martin, p. 129.

6. "most successful piece of social work . . .": Reminiscences of Frances Perkins, part 1, p. 403, 1951–1955, CUOHROC.

7. "Preliminary Report to Club Members on the Maternity Center, Sept. 15, 1917 to Oct. 1, 1918," Women's City Club of New York.

8. "Report of the Work of the Maternity Center Association, Apr. 1918–Dec. 31, 1921," Maternity Center Association, New York.

9. Maternity Center Association records.

10. "very smart woman . . .": Reminiscences of Hazel Corbin, pp. 13–14, 1970, CUOHROC; Elizabeth Cohen Arnold oral history, Radcliffe Institute, Schlesinger Library, Harvard University; Maternity Center Association records.

11. PCW to John Purroy Mitchel, Dec. 31, 1917; Mitchel to PCW, Dec. 31, 1917, Mitchel papers, box 20, Library of Congress.

12. Mitchel papers, Library of Congress.

13. Henry Bruere to FP, Mar. 28, 1918, box 106, FP papers, RBML, Columbia.

14. Author interviews with Susanna and Tomlin Coggeshall.

15. "It was always . . .": Reminiscences of Frances Perkins, part 3, p. 640, 1951–1955, CUOHROC.

16. Alumni Archives, Dartmouth College, Class of 1900, Nov. 22, 1923; Nov. 9, 1946.

17. Notes for lectures, Oct. 1911, box 42, FP papers, RBML, Columbia.

18. Author interviews with Susanna Coggeshall.

19. "had to hustle . . .": Reminiscences of Frances Perkins, part 3, pp. 641–42, 1951–1955, CUOHROC; Martin, pp. 135–37.

20. "While I could hope . . .": Reminiscences of Frances Perkins, part 3, pp. 641–42, 1951–1955, CUOHROC.

21. Author interview with Alison Bruere Carnahan.

CHAPTER 10: THE INDOMITABLE AL SMITH

1. "I want to be the first . . .": Reminiscences of Frances Perkins, part 1, pp. 432–34, CUOHROC.

2. Elizabeth Israels Perry, *Belle Moskowitz: Feminine Politics and the Exercise of Power in the Age of Alfred E. Smith* (New York: Oxford University Press, 1987), pp. 116–19.

3. "We'll talk about that later . . .": Reminiscences of Frances Perkins, part 1, pp. 438–40, 1951–1955, CUOHROC.

4. "If you girls . . .": Reminiscences of Frances Perkins, part 1, pp. 443–44, 1951–1955, CUOHROC.

5. *New York Times,* cited in Bill Severn, *Frances Perkins: A Member of the Cabinet* (New York: Hawthorn Books, 1976), p. 60.

6. "Smith Again Acts on Milk Situation," *New York Times,* Jan. 17, 1919, p. 13.

7. Severn, p. 61.

8. George Martin, *Madam Secretary* (Boston: Houghton Mifflin, 1976), p. 144.

9. "There were to be . . .": Reminiscences of Frances Perkins, part 2, pp. 215–16, CUOHROC.

10. Matthew Josephson, *Al Smith: Hero of the Cities, A Political Portrait Drawing on the Papers of Frances Perkins* (Boston: Houghton Mifflin, 1969), p. 219.

11. Martin, p. 147.

12. Reminiscences of Frances Perkins, part 2, p. 97, 1951–1955, CUOHROC.

13. "All the dirt was hauled . . .": Reminiscences of Frances Perkins, part 2, pp. 15–16, 1951–1955, CUOHROC.

14. "little more blonde . . .": Reminiscences of Frances Perkins, part 2, p. 113, 1951–1955, CUOHROC.

15. Alfred E. Smith, *Up to Now: An Autobiography* (New York: Viking, 1929), pp. 177–78.

16. "My plan of action . . .": Reminiscences of Frances Perkins, part 2, p. 133, 1951–1955, CUOHROC.

17. "Do us a favor . . .": Smith, pp. 177–78.

18. "intimate friend . . .": Reminiscences of Frances Perkins, part 2, p. 148, 1951–1955, CUOHROC.

19. "John Mitchell Dies of Pneumonia," *New York Times,* Sept. 10, 1919, p. 8; Reminiscences of Frances Perkins, part 2, pp. 180–86, 1951–1955, CUOHROC.

20. "tragic grief . . .": Reminiscences of Frances Perkins, part 2, p. 157, 1951–1955, CUOHROC.

21. "Jimmy, this is Al Smith . . .": Reminiscences of Frances Perkins, part 2, p. 347–48, 1951–1955, CUOHROC.

22. "Jimmy, that's all right . . .": Reminiscences of Frances Perkins, part 2, p. 348, 1951–1955, CUOHROC.

23. "You do your duty . . .": Reminiscences of Frances Perkins, part 2, p. 349, 1951–1955, CUOHROC.

CHAPTER 11: FDR AND AL SMITH

1. Gene Fowler, *The Life and Times of Jimmy Walker: Beau James* (New York: Viking, 1949), pp. 262–63.

2. "considerably disappointed . . .": Reminiscences of Frances Perkins, part 1, pp. 206, 239–40, 1951–1955, CUOHROC; Conrad Black, *Franklin Delano Roosevelt: Champion of Freedom* (New York: Public Affairs, 2003), p. 59.

3. "I do remember . . .": Reminiscences of Frances Perkins, part 2, p. 68, 1951–1955, CUOHROC.

4. "I would like to think . . .": Reminiscences of Frances Perkins, part 2, p. 78, 1951–1955, CUOHROC.

5. Reminiscences of Frances Perkins, part 2, pp. 557–59, 1951–1955, CUOHROC; Perkins, *The Roosevelt I Knew* (New York: Viking, 1946), pp. 41–43.

6. Author interview with Susanna Coggeshall; FP papers, RBML, Columbia.

7. "I have never known . . .": FP to Mrs. Mogielnicki, Sept. 30, 1963, Mogielnicki family papers.

8. "rough, East side . . .": Reminiscences of Frances Perkins, part 2, pp. 303–11, 1951–1955, CUOHROC; Matthew Josephson, *Al Smith: Hero of the Cities, A Political Portrait Drawing on the Papers of Frances Perkins* (Boston: Houghton Mifflin, 1969).

9. "When the Republicans . . .": Reminiscences of Frances Perkins, part 2, p. 337, 1951–1955, CUOHROC.

10. Gerard D. Reilly, interview of Oct. 22, 1965, p. 2: interviews about FP by James R. Anderson with Department of Labor staff, #5812, box 1, Kheel Center, Martin P. Catherwood Library, Cornell University.

11. "The problem was to keep . . .": Reminiscences of Frances Perkins, part 2, pp. 579–96, 604, 1951–1955, CUOHROC.

12. "It was perfectly clear . . .": Reminiscences of Frances Perkins, part 2, pp. 579–80, 1951–1955, CUOHROC.

13. "wrought up . . .": Reminiscences of Frances Perkins, part 2, pp. 661–76, 1951–1955, CUOHROC; George Martin, *Madam Secretary* (Boston: Houghton Mifflin, 1976), pp. 519–20.

14. Reminiscences of Frances Perkins, part 2, pp. 675, 1951–1955, CUOHROC; David McCullough, *Truman* (New York: Simon & Schuster, 1992), Alonzo Hamby, *Man of the People: A Life of Harry S. Truman* (New York: Oxford University Press, 1995).

15. Reminiscences of Frances Perkins, part 2, pp. 575–77, 1951–1955, CUOHROC.

16. Josephson, p. 403.

17. "I'll stay with you . . .": Reminiscences of Frances Perkins, part 2, pp. 695–97, 1951–1955, CUOHROC.

CHAPTER 12: WITH THE ROOSEVELTS IN ALBANY

1. George Martin, *Madam Secretary* (Boston: Houghton Mifflin, 1976), p. 206; Reminiscences of Frances Perkins, part 2, p. 726, 1951–1955, CUOHROC; Kenneth S. Davis, *FDR: The New York Years, 1908–1933* (New York: Random House, 1994).

2. "one of the reasons . . .": Reminiscences of Frances Perkins, part 2, p. 720, 1951–1955, CUOHROC. Moskowitz was crushed. She died soon after, at fifty-five, a "broken woman . . . who never recovered from her disappointment," wrote U.S. congresswoman Mary Norton in the unpublished manuscript "Madame Congresswoman," box 17, Mary T. Norton folder, Lorena Hickok papers, Franklin D. Roosevelt Library, Hyde Park, N.Y.

3. "You have to decide . . .": Reminiscences of Frances Perkins, part 3, pp. 14, 1951–1955, CUOHROC.

4. "You're not going to ask me . . .": Reminiscences of Frances Perkins, part 3, pp. 23–24, 1951–1955, CUOHROC.

5. "To tell you the truth . . .": Reminiscences of Frances Perkins, part 2, pp. 698–99, 1951–1955, CUOHROC.

6. "Eddie, I could cry . . .": Reminiscences of Edward Duryea Dowling, p. 113, 1963, CUOHROC.

7. "I've never known a person . . .": Reminiscences of Frances Perkins, part 3, p. 36, 1951–1955, CUOHROC.

8. Frances Perkins, *The Roosevelt I Knew* (New York: Viking, 1946), p. 53.

9. "It was like a constant house party . . .": Reminiscences of Frances Perkins, part 3, pp. 288–89, 1951–1955, CUOHROC.

10. "How To Save in Big Homes," *New York Times,* July 17, 1917, p. 3.

11. "Then we moved up . . .": Reminiscences of Frances Perkins, part 3, p. 538, 1951–1955, CUOHROC; Blanche Wiesen Cook, *Eleanor Roosevelt,* vol. 1 (New York: Penguin, 1993).

12. "A newspaper person's fiction . . .": Reminiscences of Frances Perkins, part 3, p. 529, 1951–1955, CUOHROC.

13. "I suppose it was partly then . . .": Reminiscences of Frances Perkins, part 3, pp. 214–16, 1951–1955, CUOHROC.

14. Bill Severn, *Frances Perkins: A Member of the Cabinet* (New York: Hawthorn Books, 1976), pp. 86–88; Frances Perkins speech, Industrial Commissioner, 1929, as cited by the Social Security Administration.

CHAPTER 13: FDR BECOMES PRESIDENT

1. John Kenneth Galbraith, *The Great Crash of 1929* (New York: Time, 1954); Maury Klein, *Rainbow's End: The Crash of 1929* (New York: Oxford University Press, 2001); William Leach, *Land of Desire* (New York: Pantheon Books, 1993).

2. Gail Radford, *Modern Housing for America: Policy Struggles in the New Deal Era* (Chicago: University of Chicago Press, 1996), pp. 10–22.

3. "Everybody was enjoying himself . . .": Reminiscences of Frances Perkins, part 3, pp. 411–12, 1951–1955, CUOHROC.

4. Studs Terkel, *Hard Times* (New York: New Press, 1970, 1986); Irving Bernstein, *The Lean Years* (Boston: Houghton Mifflin, 1960); *The Great Depression,* David A. Shannon, ed. (Englewood Cliffs, NJ: Prentice Hall, 1960); Frances Perkins, *The Roosevelt I Knew*, pp. 90–108.

5. C. Lowell Harris, *History and Policies of the Home Owners' Loan Corporation* (Washington, DC: National Bureau of Economic Research, 1951), p. 2; Julian Zimmerman, *The FHA Story in Summary* (Washington: Federal Housing Administration, 1959).

6. "All sorts of amateurs . . .": Frances Perkins, *The Roosevelt I Knew* (New York: Viking, 1946), p. 94.
7. FP to Governor Franklin Roosevelt, Oct. 23, 1931, folder 864, FP papers, RBML, Columbia; Women's Rights Collection, Schlesinger Library, Radcliffe Institute, Harvard University.
8. Kenneth S. Davis, *FDR: The New York Years, 1908–1933* (New York: Random House, 1994), pp. 158–59, 164–66, 269–70.
9. "The President of the United States has deceived . . .": Reminiscences of Frances Perkins, p. 3, pp. 454, 1951–1955, CUOHROC; Edgar Weinberg, "BLS and the Economy: A Centennial Timetable," *Monthly Labor Review*, Nov. 1984.
10. "I have done something . . .": Reminiscences of Frances Perkins, part 3, pp. 455–57, 1951–1955, CUOHROC.
11. "We kept him on the run . . .": Reminiscence of Frances Perkins, part 3, p. 457, 1951–1955, CUOHROC.
12. Isador Lubin Oral History, U.S. Labor Department, Catherwood Library, Kheel Center, Cornell University, p. 1.
13. Telegram, FP to FDR, Mar. 4, 1932; Telegram, FDR to FP, Mar. 4, 1932, FDR Library.

CHAPTER 14: FRANCES BECOMES SECRETARY OF LABOR

1. Clara Beyer to FP, Dec. 5, 1932, box 3, Clara Beyer papers, Schlesinger Library, Radcliffe Institute, Harvard University.
2. "scribbling away . . .": Reminiscences of Frances Perkins, part 3, p. 512, 1951–1955, CUOHROC.
3. FP to Clara Beyer, Oct. 7, 1932, Clara Beyer papers, box 3, Schlesinger Library, Radcliffe Institute, Harvard University.
4. Mary Dewson, *An Aid to the End,* unpublished manuscript, FDR Library; Susan Ware, *Partner and I: Molly Dewson, Feminism, and New Deal Politics* (New Haven: Yale University Press, 1989).
5. Democratic National Committee papers, box 458, FDR Library: Jane Addams to FDR, Dec. 8, 1932; Lincoln Filene to FDR, Nov. 15, 1932; Ethelbert Stewart to FDR.
6. Clara Beyer to Mary Dewson, Nov. 14, 1932, Democratic National Committee papers, FDR Library.
7. Charles E. Wyzanski to Richard Neustadt, recounting story told to him by Brandeis associate Paul Freund, Sept. 24, 1984, p. 3, Charles E. Wyzanski papers, Massachusetts Historical Society (hereafter MHS).
8. George Martin, *Madam Secretary* (Boston: Houghton Mifflin, 1976), pp. 229–30.
9. "there will be less death . . .": Florence Kelley to FP; FP to Florence Kelley, box 6A, National Consumers League papers, Library of Congress.
10. "horrified . . .": Reminiscences of Frances Perkins, part 3, p. 560, 1951–1955, CUOHROC.
11. Margaret Bondfield to FP, Dec. 15, 1931, Margaret Grace Bondfield papers, Archives & Special Collections Library, Vassar College Libraries, Poughkeepsie, N.Y.
12. "Why, certainly I know . . .": Reminiscences of Frances Perkins, part 3, p. 568, 1951–1955, CUOHROC.
13. "grave personal difficulties . . .": Reminiscences of Frances Perkins, part 3, p. 519, 1951–1955, CUOHROC.
14. "Sure, I know . . .": Reminiscences of Frances Perkins, part 3, p. 570, 1951–1955, CUOHROC.
15. *Adkins v. Children's Hospital,* 261 U.S. 525 (1923); *Hammer v. Dagenhart,* 247 U.S. 251 (1918); *Lochner v. New York,* 198 U.S. 45 (1905).

16. "You don't know anything . . .": Reminiscences of Frances Perkins, part 3, p. 572, 1951–1955, CUOHROC; "Nobody knew, least of all the President-elect . . .": Reminiscences of Frances Perkins, part 3, p. 573, 1951–1955, CUOHROC.

17. "Good evening . . .": Reminiscences of Frances Perkins, part 3, p. 580, 1951–1955, CUOHROC; Wickersham Report, National Commission on Law Observance and Enforcement, 1931; Martin, pp. 236–42.

18. "He looks like an American . . .": The account on the following pages is condensed from the Reminiscences of Frances Perkins, part 3, pp. 580–608, 1951–1955, CUOHROC, describing in detail the meeting between Perkins and FDR.

19. Testimonial dinner to Frances Perkins, Mar. 24, 1933, box 46, FP papers, RBML, Columbia.

CHAPTER 15: THE PIONEER

1. "Green Hits Choice of Miss Perkins," Associated Press, *Washington Star,* Mar. 1, 1933, Martin Luther King Library, Washington, D.C.

2. Lavinia Engle to Mary Dewson, box 3, Mary W. Dewson papers, FDR Library.

3. Clara Beyer, March 15, 1933, Clara Beyer papers, Schlesinger Library, Radcliffe Institute, Harvard University; Penny Colman, *A Woman Unafraid* (New York: Atheneum, 1993), p. 3, citing editorial in the *Baltimore Sun.*

4. "man of great integrity . . .": George Martin, *Madam Secretary* (Boston: Houghton Mifflin, 1976), pp. 3–4.

5. "bitter, sour, mean . . .": Reminiscences of Frances Perkins, part 4, p. 3, 1951–1955, CUOHROC.

6. "perfect bedlam . . .": Reminiscences of Frances Perkins, part 4, p. 9, 1951–1955, CUOHROC; Martin, pp. 4–9.

7. "You're Miss Perkins . . .": The following account is condensed from the Reminiscences of Frances Perkins, part 4, pp. 19–24, 1951–1955, CUOHROC.

8. FDR Inaugural Address, Mar. 4, 1933.

9. "It was a revival of faith . . .": Reminiscences of Frances Perkins, part 4, pp. 28–30, 1951–1955, CUOHROC.

10. "rather slight and feminine . . .": Reminiscences of Katharine Lenroot, 1965, pp. 64a, 64b, CUOHROC.

11. Bess Furman, *Washington Byline* (New York: Knopf, 1949), pp. 61–69.

12. "I knew intuitively . . .": Reminiscences of Frances Perkins, part 4, pp. 67–69, 1951–1955, CUOHROC.

13. "I hope you don't mind . . .": Reminiscences of Frances Perkins, part 4, p. 66, 1951–1955, CUOHROC.

14. "delighted . . .": William Woodin to FP, Mar. 12, 1933, Department of the Treasury file, Labor Department Records, National Archives.

15. "determined pout . . .": Reminiscences of Frances Perkins, part 4, pp. 82–83, 1951–1955, CUOHROC.

16. James MacGregor Burns, *Roosevelt: The Lion and the Fox* (San Diego, CA: Harcourt Brace Jovanovich, 1956), p. 150.

17. "I could see . . .": Reminiscences of Frances Perkins, part 4, pp. 178–81, 1951–1955, CUOHROC.

18. "I hadn't known him . . .": Reminiscences of Frances Perkins, part 4, p. 197, 1951–1955, CUOHROC; Martin, pp. 16–17.

CHAPTER 16: SKELETONS IN THE LABOR DEPARTMENT CLOSET

1. "Well, we might as well . . .": Reminiscences of Frances Perkins, part 4, p. 97, 1951–1955, CUOHROC.
2. "Wickersham didn't find a quarter of it . . .": Reminiscences of Frances Perkins, part 4, p. 119, 1951–1955, CUOHROC.
3. "They're low-lived people . . .": Reminiscences of Frances Perkins, part 4, pp. 133–34, 1951–1955, CUOHROC.
4. "Feathers are beginning to fly . . .": Clara Beyer to Elizabeth Brandeis, Mar. 15, 1933, Clara Beyer papers, Schlesinger Library, Radcliffe Institute, Harvard University.
5. "If you're going to do . . .": Reminiscences of Frances Perkins, part 4, pp. 212–13, 1951–1955, CUOHROC.
6. "quite a rich man . . .": Reminiscences of Frances Perkins, part 4, pp. 210–11, 1951–1955, CUOHROC.
7. "What are you doing here . . .": Reminiscences of Frances Perkins, part 4, pp. 229–33, 1951–1955, CUOHROC.
8. "Salary of $9,000 Year Man Is Sifted;" "55 Out as Federal Shakeup Is Started by Miss Perkins," *Washington Post*, Jan. 22, 1933, p. 2; ibid., Jan. 25, 1949, p. 1.
9. George Martin, *Madam Secretary* (Boston: Houghton Mifflin, 1976), pp. 292–93.
10. "Yes, I'll take it . . .": Isador Lubin, interview of April 4, 1966: interviews about FP by James R. Anderson with Department of Labor, #5812, box 1, Kheel Center, Martin P. Catherwood Library, Cornell University.
11. Edgar Weinberg, "BLS and the Economy: A Centennial Timetable," *Monthly Labor Review*, Nov. 1984, pp. 29–37.
12. Henry R. Guzda, "The U.S. Employment Service at 50," *Monthly Labor Review*, June 1983, p. 17.
13. "Both of those girls . . .": Reminiscences of Frances Perkins, part 4, p. 129, 1951–1955, CUOHROC.
14. "Although he was very much . . .": Reminiscences of Frances Perkins, part 4, p. 342, 1951–1955, CUOHROC.
15. "Call me Madam . . .": Reminiscences of Frances Perkins, part 4, p. 373, 1951–1955, CUOHROC.
16. Bess Furman, *Washington Byline* (New York: Knopf, 1949), p. 164.
17. Louis Stark private family papers, courtesy of Laura Stark Steele.

CHAPTER 17: JUMP-STARTING THE ECONOMY

1. "We had been seeing . . .": Reminiscences of Frances Perkins, part 4, pp. 500–01, 1951–1955, CUOHROC.
2. "Well, Mr. President, what are they going to do . . .": The following account is condensed from the Reminiscences of Frances Perkins, part 4, pp. 480–86, 1951–1955, CUOHROC; Perkins, *The Roosevelt I Knew*, pp. 177–81.
3. "Sovietism . . .": Arthur Schlesinger, *The Coming of the New Deal* (Boston: Houghton Mifflin, 1959), p. 337.
4. "The remark in that hearing room . . .": Reminiscences of Frances Perkins, part 4, pp. 491–93, 1951–1955, CUOHROC.
5. Civilian Conservation Corps, Labor Department Records, National Archives.
6. CCC Records, Labor Department, 1938 folder, National Archives.
7. Schlesinger, *Coming of the New Deal*, pp. 338–39.
8. CCC, Labor Department Records, box 26, National Archives.
9. Nancy Woloch, *Women and the American Experience* (New York: Knopf, 1984), p. 431.

10. CCC, Labor Department Records, box 26, National Archives.

11. A. F. Hinriches to FP, Nov. 9, 1935, box 34, FP papers, RBML, Columbia.

12. W. Frank Persons to FP, May 9, 1935, FP papers, RBML, Columbia.

13. Confidential memo from Persons to FP, Aug. 6, 1935, box 37, FP papers, RBML, Columbia.

14. "Well, Bill and I have decided . . .": Reminiscences of Frances Perkins, part 4, pp. 471–79, 1951–1955, CUOHROC; Schlesinger, *Coming of the New Deal,* pp. 264–66.

15. Schlesinger, *Coming of the New Deal,* pp. 266–75.

16. "I guess I prefer Hopkins . . .": Reminiscences of Frances Perkins, part 4, p. 479, 1951–1955, CUOHROC.

17. Alonzo L. Hamby, *Man of the People: A Life of Harry S. Truman* (New York: Oxford University Press, 1995), pp. 184–85.

18. "unemployed businessman . . .": Reminiscences of Frances Perkins, part 5, p. 461, 1951–1955, CUOHROC.

19. FDR, State of the Union Address, Jan. 4, 1935, as cited by Karenna Gore Schiff, *Lighting the Way: Nine Women Who Changed Modern America* (New York: Miramax Books, 2005), p. 175.

20. "She annoyed me so with it . . .": Reminiscences of Frances Perkins, part 4, pp. 512–14, 1951–1955, CUOHROC.

21. Henry R. Guzda, "The U.S. Employment Service at 50," *Monthly Labor Review,* June 1983, p. 18.

22. T. H. Watkins, *Righteous Pilgrim: The Life and Times of Harold L. Ickes* (New York: Henry Holt, 1990), p. 347.

23. C. Lowell Harris, *History and Policies of the Home Owners' Loan Corporation* (Washington: National Bureau of Economic Research, 1951), pp. 1–13.

24. Gail Radford, *Modern Housing for America: Policy Struggles in the New Deal Era* (Chicago: University of Chicago Press, 1996), pp. 49–51.

25. Julian Zimmerman, *The FHA Story in Summary* (Washington: Federal Housing Administration, 1959).

26. "narrow escape . . .": Reminiscences of Frances Perkins, part 3, pp. 458–59.

CHAPTER 18: AT HOME WITH MARY HARRIMAN

1. "Frances Perkins, Crusader," *Washington Star,* Feb. 1933, p. 3.

2. Sir R. C. Lindsay to Sir John Simon, Jan. 23, 1935, ref #FO 37118760, British National Archives.

3. Charles E. Wyzanski to Maude Wyzanski, Apr. 21, 1933, Charles E. Wyzanski papers, MHS.

4. "Capital Has a Rigid Calling Card Code," *Washington Post,* Dec. 24, 1933, p. SM5.

5. Reminiscences of Frances Perkins, part 2, pp. 86–87, 1951–1955, CUOHROC.

6. Marjory Potts, "Averell Harriman Remembers Mary," *Junior League Review,* Fall 1983.

7. *Time* magazine, profile of Averell Harriman, Nov. 14, 1955, pp. 31–35.

8. *Washington Post,* Aug. 11, 1933, p. 8. Also Nov. 10, 1934, p. 13.

9. CEW to MW, May 28, 1933, box 22, Charles E. Wyzanski papers, MHS.

10. "Mrs. Longworth Gives View of New Deal Fetes," *Washington Post,* Nov. 10, 1934, p. 13.

11. Winifred Wandersee interview with Susanna Coggeshall, June 27, 1990, Wandersee papers, Kheel Center, Cornell University. CEW to MW, Aug. 16, 1933, Charles E. Wyzanski papers, MHS.

12. "warm, outgoing . . .": Reminiscences of Katharine Lenroot, 1965, pp. 63–64, CUOHROC.

13. Frances Perkins, *The Roosevelt I Knew* (New York: Viking, 1946), pp. 222–23.

14. "Washington itself, particularly in 1933 . . .": Frances Perkins, *The Roosevelt I Knew* (New York: Viking, 1946), p. 21.

15. CEW to MW, May 28, 1933, box 22, Charles E. Wyzanski papers, MHS.

16. "I felt we had a major . . .": Reminiscences of Frances Perkins, part 5, p. 464, 1951–1955, CUOHROC.

17. "All God's Chillun' . . .": Reminiscences of Frances Perkins, part 5, pp. 473-74, 1951–1955, CUOHROC.

18. "ornate . . .": Reminiscences of Frances Perkins, part 4, pp. 152-53, 1951–1955, CUOHROC.

19. "Actual Expense of Running Washington House," H. F. Evers to Mr. Pemberton, Dec. 27, 1934, settling Mary's estate. Averell Harriman papers, box 5, Library of Congress. Adjusted for inflation, Rumsey spent $13,187 in 1933 or $198,454 in 2007 terms; Perkins contributed $450 or $6,772. In 1934, Rumsey spent $22,081, or $350,159 in 2007 terms, and Perkins offered $800, or $12,686.

20. "News of Society," p. 16, newspaper identification missing. Rumsey folder, Washingtoniana room, Martin Luther King Library, Washington, D.C.

21. Reminiscences of Frances Perkins, part 2, pp. 86-87, 1951–1955, CUOHROC; Grace Brownell Daniels to FP, Dec. 25, 1934, FP papers, RBML, Columbia.

22. Susan Ware, *Partner and I: Molly Dewson, Feminism and New Deal Politics* (New Haven: Yale University Press, 1987), pp. 56-57. Lillian Faderman, *To Believe in Women* (Boston: Houghton Mifflin, 1999) and *Surpassing the Love of Men* (New York: HarperCollins, 1981). Anna Mary Wells, *Miss Marks and Miss Woolley* (Boston: Houghton Mifflin, 1978).

23. "empty-headed . . .": author interview with Alison Bruere Carnahan.

24. "was worldly enough to want to launch Susanna . . .": author interview with Jane Gunther.

25. "very flowery . . .": author interview with Susanna Coggeshall.

26. Jewell Fenzi and Allida Black, *Democratic Women: An Oral History of the Women's National Democratic Club*, Women's National Democratic Club records.

27. "Susanna Wilson Honored by Dinner," *New York Times*, Dec. 23, 1934, p. N6.

28. Raymond Robins to Margaret Dreier Robins, Apr. 8, 1933, Papers of the Women's Trade Union League and its Principal Leaders, microfilm, Research Publications, Woodbridge, CT, 1981.

29. Author interviews with Kathleen Mortimer, David Mortimer.

30. "dark, surprisingly large and eager . . .": Sinclair Lewis, *Ann Vickers* (New York: Doubleday, Doran, 1933).

31. Sally E. Parry, "The Changing Fictional Faces of Sinclair Lewis' Wives," *Studies in American Fiction*, Spring 1989, 17.1, p. 65-78.

32. FP to Sinclair Lewis, Nov. 12, 1930, Frances Perkins folder, box 23, Dorothy Thompson Collection, Syracuse University; Michael Lewis to FP, Feb. 12, 1951, FP papers, RBML, Columbia.

CHAPTER 19: BLUE EAGLE: A FIRST TRY AT "CIVILIZING CAPITALISM"

1. Landon Storrs, *Civilizing Capitalism* (Chapel Hill: University of North Carolina Press, 2000).

2. "very brilliant scheme . . .": Reminiscences of Frances Perkins, part 5, p. 1, 1951–1955, CUOHROC.

3. "delicate, detailed thinking-out . . .": Reminiscences of Frances Perkins, part 5, p. 16, 1951–1955, CUOHROC.

4. "curiously restless, uncontrolled . . .": Reminiscences of Frances Perkins, part 5, pp. 18-21, 1951–1955, CUOHROC.

5. Sir R. C. Lindsay to the Right Honorable Anthony Eden, Jan. 6, 1938, ref# F O371/21541, British National Archives.

6. "full of jealousy and animosity . . .": Reminiscences of Frances Perkins, part 5, p. 22, 1951–1955, CUOHROC.

7. "somewhat exotic . . .": Reminiscences of Frances Perkins, part 5, p. 29, 1951–1955, CUOHROC.

8. William G. Van Meter, "A History of the Chamber of Commerce of the United States, 1912–1975," unpublished manuscript, Nov. 1989, pp. 100–15. Copy provided to author.

9. "great mind . . .": Reminiscences of Frances Perkins, part 5, p. 31, 1951–1955, CUOHROC.

10. Slater Mill Web site, Pawtucket, RI.

11. Alfred D. Chandler Jr., Thomas K. McCraw, and Richard S. Tedlow, *Management Past and Present: A Casebook on the History of American Business* (Cincinnati: South-Western College Publishing, 2000), pp. 1–79 to 1–80.

12. "Children Freed," *Time* magazine, July 10, 1933, p. 11.

13. "set of lunatics and grafters . . .": Reminiscences of Frances Perkins, part 5, pp. 54–55, 1951–1955, CUOHROC.

14. "almost an accident . . .": Reminiscences of Frances Perkins, part 5, pp. 68–69, 1951–1955, CUOHROC; Leon Keyserling, Mar. 19, 1969, Kheel Center for Labor-Management Documentation and Archives Oral Histories, #6058 OH, box 6, Kheel Center, Martin P. Catherwood Library, Cornell University.

15. "Well, of course, that won't mean anything . . .": Reminiscences of Frances Perkins, part 5, pp. 61–62, 1951–1955, CUOHROC.

16. "Well, now, do you want . . .": Reminiscences of Frances Perkins, part 5, p. 72, 1951–1955, CUOHROC.

17. "You've got to decide it . . .": Reminiscences of Frances Perkins, part 5, p. 80, 1951–1955, CUOHROC.

18. "Wouldn't it be all right . . .": Reminiscences of Frances Perkins, part 5, p. 82, 1951–1955, CUOHROC.

19. "streaks of genius . . .": Reminiscences of Frances Perkins, part 5, p. 93, 1951–1955, CUOHROC.

20. "You'd better interpose . . .": Reminiscences of Frances Perkins, part 5, p. 95, 1951–1955, CUOHROC.

21. "The hell he is . . .": Reminiscences of Frances Perkins, part 5, p. 156, 1951–1955, CUOHROC.

22. "Stick with him, Frances . . .": Reminiscences of Frances Perkins, part 5, pp. 160–64, 1951–1955, CUOHROC.

23. James MacGregor Burns, *Roosevelt: The Lion and the Fox* (San Diego, CA: Harcourt Brace Jovanovich, 1956), volume 1, p. 192.

24. Van Meter, pp. 100–15.

25. Reminiscences of Frances Perkins, part 5, pp. 486–87, 1951–1955, CUOHROC.

26. Approved Code Industry File, Cotton Textile, box 1812, RG9, NRA, National Archives.

27. Records of Advisory Bodies, Labor Advisory Board, Correspondence of Leo Wolman, A-C, box 8174, RG9, NRA, National Archives.

28. Records of Advisory Bodies, NRA, J. B. Butler to William Green, Apr. 11, 1934, National Archives.

29. Approved Code Industry File, Cotton Textile labor, box 1815, RG9, NRA, National Archives.

30. "nobody gave a tinker's damn . . .": Reminiscences of Frances Perkins, part 5, p. 368, 1951–1955, CUOHROC.

31. Lillian Holmen Mohr, *Frances Perkins: "That Woman in FDR's Cabinet!"* (Croton-on-Hudson, NY: North River Press, 1979), p. 149.

32. "best man in the Cabinet . . .": FPOH, part 5, pp. 482–83; Ellis W. Hawley, *The New Deal and the Problem of Monopoly* (New York: Fordham University Press, 1966), p. 82.

33. "big boys in the industry . . .": Reminiscences of Frances Perkins, part 5, p. 489, 1951–1955, CUOHROC.

34. *Washington Post,* Aug. 19, 1934, p. M1; ibid., Aug. 24, 1934, p. 1.

35. "very red in the face . . .": Reminiscences of Frances Perkins, part 5, pp. 562–69, 1951–1955, CUOHROC.

36. "Do not agree with Cummings . . .": Reminiscences of Frances Perkins, part 7, p. 54, 1951–1955, CUOHROC.

37. "very glad to be rid . . .": The following account is condensed from the Reminiscences of Frances Perkins, part 7, pp. 61–69, 1951–1955, CUOHROC.

CHAPTER 20: REFUGEES AND REGULATIONS

1. "absolutely silent, stricken . . .": Reminiscences of Frances Perkins, part 7, pp. 322–23, 1951–1955, CUOHROC.

2. Robert Jackson, Opening Address for the United States, Nuremberg Trials, *Nazi Conspiracy and Aggression,* volume I, chapter VII, Office of the United States Counsel for Prosecution of Axis Criminality (Washington: Government Printing Office, 1946), p. 129; Timothy W. Mason, *Social Policy in the Third Reich* (Providence: Berg Publishers, 1993), p. 22; Ian Kershaw, *Hitler: 1889–1936: Hubris* (New York: Norton, 2000), pp. 475–77.

3. "Says Nazis Killed Group of Socialists," *New York Times,* July 29, 1933, p. 5.

4. "Text of William Green's Speech Urging German Boycott," *New York Times,* Oct. 14, 1933, p. 2.

5. Opening Address, p. 130.

6. "Labor Here Attacks Reich Ban on Unions," *New York Times,* May 5, 1933, p. 9; "Labor and the Holocaust: An Introduction to the Jewish Labor Committee," a history prepared by Arieh Lebowitz, JLC Collection, Wagner Labor Archives, New York University.

7. William E. Dodd, *Ambassador Dodd's Diary,* edited by William E. Dodd Jr. and Martha Dodd (New York: Harcourt Brace, 1941), p. 5.

8. "100,000 Jews Face Ruin in Germany," *New York Times,* Aug. 21, 1933, p. 2.

9. CEW to MW, Jan. 12, 1934, Charles E. Wyzanski papers, MHS.

10. Felix Frankfurter to FP, Apr. 27, 1933, box 4, FP papers, RBML, Columbia.

11. Marian L. Smith, "Overview of INS History," originally published in *A Historical Guide to the U.S. Government* (New York: Oxford University Press, 1998).

12. *22nd Annual Report of the Secretary of Labor* (Washington: Government Printing Office, 1934).

13. *23rd Annual Report of the Secretary of Labor* (Washington: Government Printing Office, 1936), p. 78.

14. Charles E. Wyzanski papers, Harvard Law School Library, box 3, folder 13.

15. Wyzanski papers, ibid.

16. CEW to MW, Oct. 25, 1933, Oct. 28, 1933, Charles E. Wyzanski papers, MHS.

17. Dodd, p. 409.

18. CEW to MW, Jan 12, 1934, Charles E. Wyzanski papers, MHS.

19. Bat-Ami Zucker, "Frances Perkins and the German-Jewish Refugees, 1933–1940," *American Jewish History* 89 (2001), p. 15.

20. Charles E. Wyzanski papers, cartons 27 and 33, MHS.

21. Felix Frankfurter to FP, Dec. 21, 1933, FP papers, RBML, Columbia.

22. Zucker, pp. 4, 5; Dodd, pp. 92–93.

23. Zucker, p. 27, citing *Washington Herald* article of Dec. 4, 1934; also citing minutes of the German-Jewish Children's Aid Board, Feb. 14, 1935, citing Joseph P. Chamberlain papers, folder 249, YIVO Archives, New York City.

24. Zucker, p. 30.

25. Mary Anderson to FP, Jan. 20, 1934, Carol Lubin papers, International Labor Organization, Schlesinger Library, Radcliffe Institute, Harvard University.
26. CEW to MW, Jan. 24, 1934, Charles E. Wyzanski papers, MHS.
27. George Martin, *Madam Secretary* (Boston: Houghton Mifflin, 1976), pp. 427-28.
28. Telegram, Harold Butler to FP, Aug. 21, 1934, ILO, Frances Perkins papers, Women's Rights Collection, Schlesinger Library, Radcliffe Institute, Harvard University.
29. Memoranda, CEW to FP, Sept. 10, 1934; State Department to FP, July 3, 1935, Frances Perkins papers, Women's Rights Collection, Schlesinger Library, Radcliffe Institute, Harvard University.

CHAPTER 21: REBUILDING THE HOUSE OF LABOR

1. Frances Perkins, "Eight Years as Madame Secretary," *Fortune* magazine, July 1941.
2. *Worcester Evening Gazette,* Mar. 1, 1933, p. 1; John P. Frey oral history, Columbia University, p. 555.
3. "deep, lower endocrine excitement . . .": Reminiscences of Frances Perkins, part 4, p. 298, 1951-1955, CUOHROC.
4. Irving Bernstein, *The Lean Years* (Boston: Houghton Mifflin, 1960), pp. 111-17.
5. Maurice Neufeld diary, May 14, 16, 1962, Library of Congress, cited by Wandersee. Melvyn Dubovsky and Warren Van Tine, *John L. Lewis: A Biography* (Champaign, IL: University of Illinois Press, 1986).
6. Irving Bernstein, *The Turbulent Years* (Boston: Houghton Mifflin, 1970), pp. 66-75; Bernstein, *The Lean Years;* Matthew Josephson, *Sidney Hillman: Statesman of American Labor* (Garden City, NY: Doubleday, 1952).
7. Reminiscences of Cyrus Ching, 1965-1967, p. 412, CUOHROC; Bernstein, *The Lean Years,* pp. 95-96.
8. "labor proposals . . .": Reminiscences of Frances Perkins, part 4, pp. 312-21, 1951-1955, CUOHROC.
9. "They didn't care about . . .": Reminiscences of Frances Perkins, part 1, p. 59, 1951-1955, CUOHROC.
10. "The AF of L didn't know . . .": Reminiscences of Frances Perkins, part 2, pp. 490-91, 1951-1955, CUOHROC.
11. Bernstein, *The Turbulent Years,* pp. 160-68.
12. Conciliation, Imperial Valley, May 8, 1934, Labor Department Record Group, National Archives.
13. "courage and vim and vigor . . .": Reminiscences of Frances Perkins, part 4, p. 490, 1951-1955, CUOHROC.
14. S. J. Wooff, *New York Times,* Aug. 5, 1934.
15. "I was a red hot labor man . . .": Reminiscences of Frances Perkins, part 2, pp. 165-66, 1951-1955, CUOHROC.
16. Photograph of Hugh Johnson with labor leaders on advisory panel, June 22, 1933, Rose Schneiderman papers, New York University.
17. "You can't do that . . .": Reminiscences of Frances Perkins, part 5, pp. 341-42, 1951-1955, CUOHROC.
18. "I have come to the conclusion . . .": Reminiscences of Frances Perkins, part 5, p. 347, 1951-1955, CUOHROC. "Mayor of Homestead Routs Miss Perkins and 'Radicals'," *Washington Post,* Aug. 1, 1933, p. 3.
19. Charles E. Wyzanski papers, June 20, 1934, box 22, MHS.
20. Author interview with John Dunlop, former secretary of labor, university professor, Harvard University; Isador Lubin oral history, April 4, 1966, pp. 9-13, Kheel Center, Cornell University.

CHAPTER 22: LABOR SHAKES OFF ITS SLUMBER

1. Irving Bernstein *The Turbulent Years* (Boston: Houghton Mifflin, 1970), pp. 40–45; Frances Jurkowitz to FP, July 15, 1933, Conciliation Strike, Coal Misc., Labor Department Records Group, National Archives.

2. "It was the most remarkable thing . . .": Reminiscences of Frances Perkins, part 5, p. 232, 1951–1955, CUOHROC.

3. "You have to cook . . .": Reminiscences of Frances Perkins, part 5, p. 228, 1951–1955, CUOHROC.

4. Labor Unions, Consolidated Approved Code Industry File/Hosiery, NRA RG6, box 2767, NRA, National Archives.

5. "Each side was scared to death . . .": Reminiscences of Mary Heaton Vorse, Spring 1937, p. 40, CUOHROC.

6. CEW to MW, Aug. 1, 1933, Charles E. Wyzanski papers, MHS; Department of Labor, *Annual Reports,* 1933 and 1934.

7. "It is pretty encouraging . . .": FDR, Nov. 8, 1933, *Roosevelt Presidential Press Conferences,* vol. 2, pp. 431–33, FDR Library.

8. "The companies had a positive rule . . .": Reminiscences of Frances Perkins, part 6, pp. 28–29, 1951–1955, CUOHROC; Bernstein, pp. 499–501; 545–52.

9. Philip Taft, *Organized Labor in American History* (New York: Harper & Row, 1964), pp. 484–503.

10. "Anybody who would say . . .": Reminiscences of Joseph Curran, 1964, pp. 52–54, CUOHROC.

11. Reminiscences of M. Headley Stone, oral history, pp. 71–72, 1969, CUOHROC.

12. Author interview with Leslie O'Rear, president of the Illinois Labor History Society, Feb. 7, 2001.

13. Bernstein, *The Turbulent Years,* p. 263.

14. Ibid, pp. 252–98.

15. Conciliation—Longshore, May 14, 1934, Labor Department Records Group, National Archives.

16. Charles P. Larrowe, *Harry Bridges: The Rise and Fall of Radical Labor in the United States* (New York: Lawrence Hill & Co., 1972); Bernstein, pp. 252–91.

17. CEW to MW, July 18, 1934, Charles E. Wyzanski papers, MHS.

18. "Yes, it's unfortunate . . .": The following account is condensed from Reminiscences of Frances Perkins, part 6, pp. 293–99, 1951–1955, CUOHROC.

19. Conrad Black, *Franklin Delano Roosevelt: Champion of Freedom* (New York: Public Affairs, 2003), pp. 323–24.

20. Bernstein, *The Turbulent Years,* pp. 297–98.

21. "A more active and intensified . . .": Strikes, Records of Advisory Bodies, Records of Labor Advisory Board, Subject Files, Feb. 1934–July 1935, Sec-W, RG9, NRA, National Archives.

22. "a quiet, orderly man . . .": Reminiscences of Frances Perkins, part 6, pp. 325–26, 1951–1955, CUOHROC.

23. "He was just an inexplicable man . . .": Reminiscences of Frances Perkins, part 6, pp. 340–41, 1951–1955, CUOHROC.

CHAPTER 23: THE UNION MOVEMENT REVITALIZES AND SPLITS APART

1. Philip Taft, *Organized Labor in American History* (New York: Harper & Row, 1964), pp. 445–48.

2. Leon Keyserling, Mar. 19, 1969, pp. 3–4, Kheel Center for Labor-Management

Documentation and Archives Oral Histories, #6058 OH, box 5, Kheel Center, Martin P. Catherwood Library, Cornell University.

3. National Recovery Administration Release 2876, Jan. 23, 1934, Approved Code Industry File, Cotton Textile, Labor, box 1815, Record Group 9, NRA, National Archives.

4. "This is an educational process . . .": Reminiscences of Frances Perkins, part 5, pp. 240–41, 1951–1955, CUOHROC.

5. Irving Bernstein, *The Turbulent Years* (Boston: Houghton Mifflin, 1970), p. 186.

6. "Why don't we agree . . .": Reminiscences of Frances Perkins, part 5, pp. 246–58, 1951–1955, CUOHROC.

7. "hazardous . . .": Reminiscences of Frances Perkins, part 5, pp. 508–09, 1951–1955, CUOHROC.

8. CEW to MW, Feb. 28, 1934, Charles E. Wyzanski papers, MHS.

9. "He never lifted a finger . . .": Reminiscences of Frances Perkins, part 7, p. 147, 1951–1955, CUOHROC.

10. "I did all that I could . . .": Reminiscences of Frances Perkins, part 5, p. 510, 1951–1955, CUOHROC.

11. "almost uncanny ability . . .": William Hammatt Davis oral history, pp. 54–55, 1954, CUOHROC.

12. CEW to Joseph L. Rauh, Jan. 5, 1983, Charles E. Wyzanski papers, MHS.

13. CEW to MW, May 3, 1935, Charles E. Wyzanski papers, MHS.

14. Robert F. Wagner papers, Georgetown University.

15. "keep very close . . .": Reminiscences of Frances Perkins, part 7, p. 150, 1951–1955, CUOHROC.

16. Joseph Warren Madden, Oct. 29, 1968, Kheel Center for Labor-Management Documentation and Archives Oral Histories, #6058 OH, box 5, Kheel Center, Martin P. Catherwood Library, Cornell University.

17. "thankless . . .": Reminiscences of Frances Perkins, part 7, pp. 152–56, 1951–1955, CUOHROC; CEW to MW, July 13, 1935; July 19, 1935; July 29, 1935, Charles E. Wyzanski papers, MHS.

18. Bernstein, pp. 386–431.

19. "Three unions could . . .": Reminiscences of James B. Carey, p. 67, 1958, CUOHROC.

20. Reminiscences of James B. Carey, p. 73, 1958, CUOHROC.

21. Bernstein, *The Turbulent Years,* pp. 400–01.

22. Frances Perkins, "Eight Years as Madame Secretary," *Fortune* magazine, July 1941.

23. Stanley V. White, Works Progress Administration, to FP, Mar. 29, 1937, FP papers, RBML, Columbia.

24. Madden, pp. 88–89.

25. "You can't do the kind of work . . .": Reminiscences of Frances Perkins, part 7, pp. 206–07, 1951–1955, CUOHROC.

26. Paul Herzog, Jan. 6, 1972, Kheel Center for Labor-Management Documentation and Archives Oral Histories, #6058 OH, box 6, Kheel Center, Martin P. Catherwood Library, Cornell University.

27. FDR to FP, July 25, 1941, President's Secretary's File, box 57, FDR Library.

28. Lloyd K. Garrison to Charles Culp Burlingham, July 1, 1940, Charles C. Burlingham papers, Harvard Law School Library, box 6, folder 5.

29. "The leadership took it . . .": Reminiscences of Robert Houghwout Jackson, pp. 533, 535, 1952, CUOHROC.

30. J. R. Steelman to FP, July 13, 1939, box 333, ER papers, FDR Library.

CHAPTER 24: SOCIAL SECURITY

1. Preliminary Recommendations on Old Age Security, Committee on Economic Security, Nov. 27, 1934, Frances Perkins papers, Women's Rights Collection, Schlesinger Library, Radcliffe Institute, Harvard University.

2. "I want all the neighbors . . .": cited in Irving Bernstein, *A Caring Society: The New Deal, the Worker and the Great Depression* (Boston: Houghton Mifflin, 1985), p. 63.

3. "It is probably . . .": George Martin, *Madam Secretary* (Boston: Houghton Mifflin, 1976), p. 341, citing James Russell Anderson's thesis, "The New Deal Career of Frances Perkins," Western Reserve University, 1968.

4. "big laugh from the audience . . .": Thomas H. Eliot, *Recollections of the New Deal* (Boston: Northeastern University Press, 1992), p. 73.

5. Edwin Witte, *The Development of the Social Security Act* (Madison: University of Wisconsin Press, 1962), pp. 3–4.

6. Martin, p. 342.

7. "That man, that man!" Eliot, p. 85.

8. "Remember, Papa wants to know . . .": Reminiscences of Frances Perkins, part 7, p. 861, 1951–1955, CUOHROC.

9. Witte, pp. 5–6.

10. Witte, pp. 36–37.

11. Frances Perkins speech, "The Roots of Social Security," Oct. 23, 1962, Social Security Administration Web site.

12. Eliot, p. 95.

13. CEW to MW, Jan. 24, 1934, Charles E. Wyzanski papers, MHS.

14. Perkins, "Roots of Social Security" speech.

15. "The whole economic security thing is a fiasco . . .": Louis Stark to Stark family, Nov. 15, 1934, private family papers of Laura Steele Stark.

16. Arthur Krock, *New York Times,* Nov. 20, 1934, p. 20; Raymond Clapper, *Washington Post,* Nov. 16, 1934, p. 2.

17. Witte, pp. 44–47.

18. Author interview with Maurice Neufeld.

19. Witte, pp. 187–88; Louis Stark, *New York Times,* Jan. 20, 1935.

20. Eliot, p. 102.

21. "Wagner Social Security Plan Attacked by Experts as Hazy," by Louis Stark, Jan. 20, 1935, p. E8.

22. Eliot, p. 120.

23. Witte, pp. 81–82.

24. Economic Security hearings, Jan.–Feb. 1935, box 12, FP papers, Schlesinger Library, Radcliffe Institute.

25. "ultimate socialistic control . . .": Eliot, p. xiv.

26. Witte, pp. 88–89.

27. Louis Stark, "Hopes Are Fading for Social Security Bill," *New York Times,* Mar. 30, 1935, p. 4.

28. Bernstein, *A Caring Society,* p. 69.

29. "sin . . .": Reminiscences of Maurine Mulliner, p. 26, 1967, CUOHROC.

30. Witte, pp. 162–65.

31. Linda Gordon, *Pitied But Not Entitled* (Cambridge, MA: Harvard University Press, 1994), pp. 21, 191.

32. Martha May Eliot oral history, p. 364, Schlesinger Library, Radcliffe Institute, Harvard University.

33. Witte, pp. 190–92.

34. FP to Mary Ross, Dec. 12, 1934, Frances Perkins papers, Women's Rights Collection,

Schlesinger Library, Radcliffe Institute, Harvard University; Kingsbury, regarding talk with Hopkins, Jan. 16, 1935, part II, box 12, Kingsbury papers, Library of Congress.

35. "Doctors on Debate on Social Medicine," *New York Times,* Jan. 3, 1934.
36. Reminiscences of D. Isidore Falk, pp. 124–29, 73–87, 1968, CUOHROC.
37. "Roosevelt Signs Security Bill to Benefit 30 Million Citizens," *Washington Post,* Aug. 15, 1935, p. 1.
38. "The one person . . .": Reminiscences of Maurine Mulliner, p. 42, 1967, CUOHROC.
39. "She virtually forced . . .": Charles E. Wyzanski to Henry W. Bragdon, Nov. 5, 1974, Charles E. Wyzanski papers, MHS.
40. "Roots of Social Security," p. 4.
41. "Miss Perkins Praises Social Bill Passage," *New York Times,* Aug. 11, 1935, p. 12.
42. Eliot, p. 147.
43. Martin, p. 356.

CHAPTER 25: FAMILY PROBLEMS

1. Susanna Winslow Perkins Wilson school records, Record Group 4R, Bryn Mawr College Archives; author interview with Alison Bruere Carnahan.
2. William Astor to FP, May 15, 1934, box 1, FP papers, RBML, Columbia.
3. Author interviews and/or correspondence with Susanna's Bryn Mawr classmates Ann Keay Beneduce, Virginia H. Proctor, Sister Catherine Louise, Society of St. Margaret, Boston, and others.
4. Bryn Mawr records.
5. Dr. Charles Lambert to Harlow S. Wilson, Sept. 21, 1934, Harlow S. Wilson to FP, Sept. 23, 1934, Perkins private family papers, restricted box 163, FP papers, Coggeshall addition, RBML, Columbia.
6. *Washington Star,* Nov. 18, 1934, p. 1, Martin Luther King Library, Washington, D.C.
7. W. Averell Harriman papers, Library of Congress.
8. Author interview with Susanna Coggeshall; Winifred Wandersee interview with Susanna Coggeshall; CEW to MW, Dec. 19, 1934, Charles E. Wyzanski papers, MHS.
9. *Washington Star,* Dec. 19, 1934, Martin Luther King Library, Washington, D.C.
10. Elizabeth (no last name) to FP, unidentified correspondence, Dec. 24, 1934, Frances Perkins papers, Coggeshall addition, RBML, Columbia, cited in Wandersee papers, Cornell University.
11. Mary Dreier to FP, Dec. 19, 1934, box 106, FP papers, Coggeshall addition, RBML, Columbia.
12. Averell Harriman papers, Library of Congress; author interview with Susanna Coggeshall.
13. Paul DeForest Hicks, "Caroline O'Day: The Gentlewoman from New York" (published by New York State Historical Association in 2007); Marion Dickerman entry on O'Day in *Notable American Women,* vol. 2 (Cambridge, MA: 1971), pp. 648–50; author interview with Daniel O'Day, Caroline's grandson.
14. CEW to MW, Jan. 28, 1935, box 22, Charles E. Wyzanski papers, MHS; *Washington Post,* Mar. 13, 1935, p. 14.
15. "New Dealers Lease House," *Washington Post,* July 26, 1935, p. 13; "charming red brick house . . .": *Washington Star,* Feb. 1936, Martin Luther King Library, Washington, D.C.
16. Bryn Mawr records.
17. Bryn Mawr records.
18. Private Perkins family papers.
19. George Martin, *Madam Secretary* (Boston: Houghton Mifflin, 1976), p. 472, based on his interview with Susanna Coggeshall.
20. Author interviews with Jane Gunther.

21. Martin, p. 471.
22. Author interview with psychiatrist Candida Fink; Judith Lederman and Candida Fink, *The Ups and Downs of Raising a Bipolar Child* (New York: Fireside, 2003).
23. Author interview with Stephen Robeson-Miller; Maternity Center Association records and newspaper clippings.
24. "It is neither senility...": David Hare to Stephen Robeson-Miller, Oct. 1988, Miller private papers, Cambridge, Massachusetts.
25. Author interviews with Peter Poole, Jane Gunther.
26. "not a solid citizen...": author interview with Susanna Coggeshall.
27. Carol Riegelman Lubin interviews with author; Interview with Ruth Backes, Mount Holyoke Archives.
28. FP to Miss Sarah McDonald, July 17, 1937, FP papers, RBML, Columbia.
29. *Washington Post*, Jan. 12, 1937, p. 13.
30. *Washington Post*, June 7, 1936, p. X8; June 12, 1937, p. 13; Feb. 27, 1937, p. 10; Apr. 16, 1937, p. 19; May 16, 1937, p. S9.
31. "Secretary Perkins' Daughter Becomes Bride of DM Hare," *Washington Star*, Mar. 13, 1938, Martin Luther King Library, Washington, D.C.
32. Author interview with Jane Gunther; *Washington Post*, July 15, 1935.

CHAPTER 26: COURT-PACKING, WAGES, AND HOURS

1. CEW to MW, July 9, 1935, Charles E. Wyzanski papers, MHS.
2. Harold Ickes, *The Secret Diary of Harold Ickes*, Sunday, May 26, 1940.
3. Ickes diaries, Sunday, May 23, 1937.
4. Ickes diaries, pp. 2376–78, Sept.–Oct. 1937.
5. Charles E. Wyzanski letters, MHS.
6. Felix Frankfurter to CEW, Apr. 9, 1937, Charles E. Wyzanski papers, 1937–1942, MHS.
7. "Never mind, I have something...": Frances Perkins, *The Roosevelt I Knew* (New York: Viking Press, 1946), pp. 248–50.
8. Felix Frankfurter to CEW, April 9, 1937, Charles E. Wyzanski papers, Harvard Law School Library, box 1, folder 11.
9. Ickes diaries, as cited in George Martin, *Madam Secretary* (Boston: Houghton Mifflin, 1976), p. 388.
10. Peter Diamond, "Charles E. Wyzanski, Jr.: A Biography" (draft manuscript).
11. "Miss Perkins Cites Wage Law Needs," *Washington Post*, July 24, 1937, p. 11.
12. Seth D. Harris, "Conceptions of Fairness and the Fair Labor Standards Act," *Hofstra Labor & Employment Law Journal*, fall 2000.
13. "really very satisfactory...": Reminiscences of Frances Perkins, part 7, pp. 3–5, 1951–1955, CUOHROC.
14. "States Have Made 1937 a Banner Year for Hour and Wage Laws," Clara Beyer papers, Schlesinger Library, Radcliffe Institute, Harvard University.
15. "breaking up the Supreme Court...": Reminiscences of Frances Perkins, account condensed from part 7, pp. 87–90, 1951–1955, CUOHROC.
16. "author, instigator and persuader...": Reminiscences of Frances Perkins, part 7, p. 104, 1951–1955, CUOHROC.
17. "I have never been one...": Reminiscences of Frances Perkins, part 7, pp. 105–06, 1951–1955, CUOHROC.
18. "wasn't a good lawyer...": Reminiscences of Frances Perkins, part 7, p. 108, 1951–1955, CUOHROC.
19. "historic event...": Reminiscences of Frances Perkins, account condensed from part 7, pp. 71–76, 1951–1955, CUOHROC.

20. "I think that the court . . .": Reminiscences of Robert Houghwoot Jackson, pp. 485–86, 1952, CUOHROC.

21. "most virtuoso performance . . .": Elinor Morehouse Herrick to Charles Culp Burlingham, Jan. 24, 1958, Charles Culp Burlingham papers, Harvard Law School Library, box 8, folder 5.

22. "let it ride a while . . .": Reminiscences of Frances Perkins, account condensed from part 7, pp. 79–82, 1951–1955, CUOHROC.

23. "Attempts to Have Plan Recommitted," *Washington Post,* Nov. 23, 1937, p. 1.

24. 81 Cong. Rec. 57797, July 28, 1937, statement of Senator William Borah.

25. "Senate Decides to Act Quickly on Wages Bill," *Washington Post,* July 31, 1937, p. 1.

26. Oral history of Gerard Reilly, U.S. Labor Department, Oct. 22, 1965, pp. 4, 9.

27. "Power to Fix Wages Taken from Board," *Washington Post,* July 9, 1937, p. 1; Martin, pp. 388–92.

28. Rose Schneiderman to Clara Beyer, Nov. 27, 1937, Clara Beyer papers, Schlesinger Library, Radcliffe Institute, Harvard University.

29. Author interview with Harry Kelber.

CHAPTER 27: IMPEACHMENT

1. "militant and effective . . .": Reminiscences of Frances Perkins, part 6, p. 449, 1951–1955, CUOHROC.

2. "merely because they had been active . . .": Reminiscences of Frances Perkins, part 6, p. 443, 1951–1955, CUOHROC.

3. "trifling . . .": Reminiscences of Frances Perkins, part 6, pp. 392–93, 1951–1955, CUOHROC.

4. CEW to MW, Jan. 2, 1934, Charles E. Wyzanski papers, MHS.

5. "Personally she detested him . . .": Wyzanski, life overview, p. 21, Charles E. Wyzanski papers, Harvard Law School Library, Perkins materials.

6. Gerard Reilly to FP, Oct. 4, 1937; Reilly to James L. Houghteling, Oct. 6, 1937; Reilly to FP, Oct. 13, 1937, box 38, FP papers, RBML, Columbia; Charles P. Larrowe, *Harry Bridges: The Rise and Fall of Radical Labor in the United States* (New York: Lawrence Hill, 1972), pp. 139–40.

7. Frances Perkins, *The Roosevelt I Knew* (New York: Viking, 1946), pp. 317–18.

8. T. H. Watkins, *Righteous Pilgrim: The Life and Times of Harold L. Ickes* (New York: Henry Holt, 1990), pp. 632–35.

9. "proved that I was a Jew . . .": Reminiscences of Frances Perkins, part 6, p. 416, 1951–1955, CUOHROC.

10. "All of the people were Protestant Christians . . .": FP to Mrs. W. MacMillan, April 1, 1936, Lowell Mellet papers, FDR Library.

11. "Oh they can't impeach you . . .": Reminiscences of Frances Perkins, part 6, pp. 499–500, 1951–1955, CUOHROC.

12. "My American Diary," Nov. 21, 1938, Margaret Grace Bondfield papers, Archives and Special Collections Library, Vassar College Libraries, Poughkeepsie, NY.

13. Bondfield papers, Vassar College Libraries.

14. "Many Democrats as well . . .": See "Resolution Suggesting Perkins' Impeachment Introduced in House," Associated Press, *Washington Star,* Jan. 24, 1939.

15. "sat in unusual silence . . .": *Washington Post,* Jan. 25, 1939, p. 1.

16. Mary LaDame folder, box 35, FP papers, RBML, Columbia.

17. "Miss Perkins is not a Communist . . .": FBI Report, Subject: Frances Perkins, Memorandum from FBI director to U.S. Attorney General, Aug. 13, 1948, citing *Saturday Evening Post,* July 27, 1940.

18. "The Congress was full . . .": Reminiscences of Frances Perkins, part 6, p. 482, 1951–1955, CUOHROC.

19. "without substance . . .": Reminiscences of Thomas Irwin Emerson, 1953, CUOHROC.
20. "a sympathetic word . . .": Reminiscences of Frances Perkins, part 6, p. 494, 1951–1955, CUOHROC.
21. *Roosevelt Presidential Press Conferences*, vol. 13, Jan. 24, 1939, pp. 86–88; Review of 1939 press conferences, FDR Library.
22. "Of course, if I had wept . . .": Reminiscences of Frances Perkins, part 6, pp. 486–87, 1951–1955, CUOHROC.
23. Author interview with Mother Virginia, Oct. 2001, All Saints Convent, Catonsville, Maryland.
24. "I came to realize . . .": Reminiscences of Frances Perkins, part 6, pp. 506–508, 1951–1955, CUOHROC.
25. "it seemed like hours . . .": Reminiscences of Frances Perkins, account condensed from part 6, pp. 506–28, 1951–1955, CUOHROC.
26. Charles E. Wyzanski's personal draft of FP's statement in response to impeachment challenge, written Jan. 27, 1939. Wyzanski family papers.
27. "sharpening their knives . . .": Reminiscences of Frances Perkins, part 6, pp. 519–20, 1951–1955, CUOHROC.
28. "nobody ever repeats . . .": Reminiscences of Frances Perkins, part 6, p. 514, 1951–1955, CUOHROC.
29. "It's just like being tried for any crime . . .": Reminiscences of Frances Perkins, part 6, pp. 527–28, 1951–1955, CUOHROC.
30. George Martin, *Madam Secretary* (Boston: Houghton Mifflin, 1976), pp. 415–16.
31. Radio address of U.S. Representative Parnell Thomas, delivered via NBC, 7:15 p.m., Wednesday, Mar. 29, 1939, box 40, FP papers, RBML, Columbia.
32. "Besides, it will be nice and cool . . .": Reminiscences of Frances Perkins, part 6, p. 542, 1951–1955, CUOHROC.
33. Reminiscences of James M. Landis, pp. 54–64, 1964, CUOHROC.
34. Author interview with John Earl Haynes, archivist at Library of Congress, author of *Venona: Decoding Soviet Espionage in America.*

CHAPTER 28: WAR CLOUDS AND REFUGEES

1. Robert Dallek, *Franklin Delano Roosevelt and American Foreign Policy* (New York: Oxford University Press, 1979), p. 101.
2. "We are definitely opposed . . .": R. J. Hooffstetter to FP, May 11, 1941; Mrs. J. Maloney to FP, May 23, 1941; "A Mother" to FP, received Jan. 19, 1942, Labor Department Records, box 105, National Archives.
3. Author interview with Daniel O'Day.
4. Bat-Ami Zucker, "Frances Perkins and the German-Jewish Refugees, 1933–1940," *American Jewish History* 89 (2001), p. 35, citing "Franklin D. Roosevelt and Foreign Affairs," Sept.–Nov., 1938, vol. 7, edited by Donald B. Schewe (New York: Garland Publishing, 1979); Roosevelt press conference, Nov. 18, 1938.
5. Conrad Black, *Franklin Delano Roosevelt: Champion of Freedom* (New York: Public Affairs, 2003), pp. 490–93.
6. "Do you think . . .": Unpublished portion of 623-page draft of *The Roosevelt I Knew,* chapter on the war years, pp. 4–5, FP papers, RBML, Columbia.
7. "Up until that time . . .": Reminiscences of Frances Perkins, part 7, p. 340, 1951–1955, CUOHROC.
8. "I never can believe . . .": Reminiscences of Frances Perkins, part 7, p. 371, 1951–1955, CUOHROC.
9. "Pfui! Pfui!" Reminiscences of Frances Perkins, part 7, p. 359, 1951–1955, CUOHROC.

10. "They talk about the French . . .": Reminiscences of Frances Perkins, part 7, pp. 353–55, 1951–1955, CUOHROC.

11. "Frankly, Bill . . .": Reminiscences of Frances Perkins, part 7, p. 361, 1951–1955, CUOHROC.

12. "very great cruelty . . .": Reminiscences of Frances Perkins, part 7, p. 362, 1951–1955, CUOHROC.

13. "Hmmm. Hmmm.": Reminiscences of Frances Perkins, part 7, 374–75, 1951–1955, CUOHROC.

14. Dallek, pp. 196–98.

15. "That isn't possible . . .": Reminiscences of Frances Perkins, part 7, pp. 334–36, 1951–1955, CUOHROC.

16. "God gave them reason . . .": Reminiscences of Frances Perkins, part 7, p. 342, 1951–1955, CUOHROC.

17. Doris Kearns Goodwin, *No Ordinary Time* (New York: Simon & Schuster, 1994), p. 23.

18. Malcolm Hill, *Churchill: His Radical Decade* (London: Othila Press, 1999).

19. "What's he like . . . ?" Reminiscences of Frances Perkins, account condensed from part 8, pp. 17–23, 1951–1955, CUOHROC.

20. "These are very difficult days . . .": Reminiscences of Frances Perkins, part 7, p. 639–42, 1951–1955, CUOHROC.

21. "the elements of disintegration . . .": Reminiscences of Frances Perkins, part 7, p. 376, 1951–1955, CUOHROC.

22. "Why, Bob, you're the only man . . .": Reminiscences of Robert Houghwout Jackson, pp. 998–1001, 1952, CUOHROC.

23. "turned to his soup . . .": Reminiscences of Robert Houghwout Jackson, pp. 1006–08, 1952, CUOHROC.

24. "Today the situation has changed . . .": *Roosevelt Presidential Press Conferences,* number 645, May 21, 1940, volume 15, pp. 352–53, FDR Library.

25. "Thank God!": Reminiscences of Henry Wallace, p. 1142, June 6, 1940, CUOHROC.

26. Zucker, p. 40.

27. "I assume that you know . . .": Charles Culp Burlingham to Felix Frankfurter, June 4, 1940, Charles C. Burlingham papers, Harvard Law School Library, box 5, folder 20.

28. Martin, pp. 442–443.

29. FDR to FP, March 4, 1935, folder 875, box 5, FP papers, Women's Rights Collection, Schlesinger Library, Radcliffe Institute, Harvard University; Bernard Bellush interview with Edward J. Phelan, July 21, 1951, Bellush papers, FDR Library.

30. "because their presence . . .": Isador Lubin to FP, Apr. 18, 1939, box 5, folder 877, FP papers, Schlesinger Library, Radcliffe Institute, Harvard University.

31. 1941 ILO conference transcript, FP papers, Schlesinger Library, Radcliffe Institute, Harvard University; ibid., statement of Polish delegate Mr. Stanszyk.

32. "The welfare of labor . . .": Isador Lubin to Mary LaDame, Nov. 13, 1939, folder 879, box 5, Frances Perkins papers, Schlesinger Library, Radcliffe Institute, Harvard University.

33. "We'll all be slaughtered . . .": author interview with Carol Riegelman Lubin.

34. Draft text for confidential report, Carol Lubin papers; FP papers, folder 880, Schlesinger Library, Radcliffe Institute, Harvard University.

35. Henry I. Harriman to FP, folder 880; Hull telegram to Winant, July 1, 1940, folder 880, FP papers, Schlesinger Library, Radcliffe Institute, Harvard University.

36. "explain fully to you . . .": Sumner Welles to FP, July 3, 1940, folder 880, FP papers, Schlesinger Library, Radcliffe Institute, Harvard University.

37. "Decision may be liquidation . . .": John Winant to FP, folder 880, box 5, FP papers, Schlesinger Library, Radcliffe Institute, Harvard University.

38. Author interviews with Carol Riegelman Lubin, March 23–25, 2001; Frances Perkins, *The Roosevelt I Knew* (New York: Viking, 1946), p. 344.

39. Author interview with Carol Riegelman Lubin.

40. "He typified to the British . . .": interview of Sir Arthur Salter by Bernard Bellush, July 9, 1951, Bellush papers, FDR Library.

41. Reminiscences of Frances Perkins, part 8, p. 626, 1951–1955, CUOHROC; ILO papers, Schlesinger Library, Radcliffe Institute, Harvard University.

42. Correspondence on ILO, 1941, folder 906, box 8, FP papers, Schlesinger Library, Radcliffe Institute, Harvard University.

43. "They were just horrible sights . . .": Reminiscences of Frances Perkins, part 8, p. 833, 1951–1955, CUOHROC.

44. "In those days, the ILO . . .": Statement by President Franklin D. Roosevelt, Nov. 6, 1941, FP papers, Schlesinger Library, Radcliffe Institute, Harvard University.

45. "I was immensely affected . . .": Caroline O'Day to Mary Dreier, Sept. 28, 1939, Mary Dreier papers, Schlesinger Library, Radcliffe Institute, Harvard University.

46. *Washington Star,* June 19, 1941; author interview with Daniel O'Day.

CHAPTER 29: FRANCES AND FRANKLIN

1. Christopher Breiseth, *The Frances Perkins I Knew* (Worcester, MA: FDR American Heritage Center Museum, 1966), pp. 11–12.

2. "Franklin Roosevelt's relations . . .": Arthur Krock, cited by Irving Bernstein, *Turbulent Years* (Boston: Houghton Mifflin, 1970), p. 10.

3. "Well, Mr. President . . .": CEW to MW, April 25, 1934, Charles E. Wyzanski papers, MHS.

4. "After all these years . . .": FDR to FP, July 16, 1940, President's Secretary's Files/Labor, FDR Library.

5. "He got a lot of fun . . .": Cyrus Ching, Oct. 12, 1966, p. 386, Kheel Center for Labor-Management Documentation and Archives Oral Histories, #6058 OH, box 6, Kheel Center, Martin P. Catherwood Library, Cornell University.

6. "close personal friendship . . .": Reminiscences of Claude Wickard, pp. 3282, 3528, 1619, 3181, 1953, CUOHROC.

7. "Oh, I have been reading . . .": *Roosevelt Presidential Press Conferences,* number 655, June 25, 1940, volume 15, pp. 594–96.

8. "How little the critics know!" Note for inclusion in Frances Perkins file, Charles E. Wyzanski papers, MHS.

9. "presidential timbre . . .": Reminiscences of Frances Perkins, part 7, pp. 378–81, 1951–1955, CUOHROC.

10. "Why do you think he wants it?" Reminiscences of Frances Perkins, part 7, p. 392, 1951–1955, CUOHROC.

11. "Well, how do you know . . .": Reminiscences of Frances Perkins, part 7, p. 379, 1951–1955, CUOHROC.

12. "Wallace, if he comes . . .": Reminiscences of Frances Perkins, part 7, p. 412, 1951–1955, CUOHROC.

13. "fit to be the wife . . .": Reminiscences of Frances Perkins, part 7, p. 435, 1951–1955, CUOHROC.

14. George Martin, *Madam Secretary* (Boston: Houghton Mifflin, 1976), pp. 341–42.

15. "Don't let Eleanor know . . .": Reminiscences of Frances Perkins, part 7, pp. 460–61, 1951–1955, CUOHROC.

16. "Well, you know I've thought . . .": Reminiscences of Frances Perkins, part 7, pp. 461–64, 1951–1955, CUOHROC.

17. "I've just talked . . .": Reminiscences of Frances Perkins, part 7, p. 465, 1951–1955, CUOHROC.

18. "Things look black here . . .": Eleanor Roosevelt, *This I Remember* (New York: Harper & Brothers, 1949), p. 214; James Farley, *Jim Farley's Story* (New York: McGraw-Hill,

1948), pp. 277–83; Reminiscences of Frances Perkins, part 7, pp. 450–75, 1951–1955, CUOHROC.

19. "I think she was working . . .": Reminiscences of Henry A. Wallace, pp. 1239–40, 1953, CUOHROC.

20. "This is just a very personal note . . .": FDR to FP, Aug. 3, 1940, FDR Library.

21. John Culver and John Hyde, *American Dreamer: Life and Times of Henry Wallace* (New York: Norton, 2000), pp. 130–46.

22. "Oh, my God, isn't it something . . .": Reminiscences of Frances Perkins, part 7, p. 413, 1951–1955, CUOHROC.

23. "Well, now I think . . .": Reminiscences of Frances Perkins, part 7, p. 698, 1951–1955, CUOHROC.

24. "And it won't be a woman . . .": Reminiscences of Frances Perkins, part 7, pp. 698–700, 1951–1955, CUOHROC.

25. "It seemed to me . . .": Reminiscences of Frances Perkins, part 7, p. 824, 1951–1955, CUOHROC.

26. "Now, see here, you see the President . . .": Reminiscences of Frances Perkins, account condensed from part 7, pp. 824-31, 1951–1955, CUOHROC.

27. "I regard the British . . .": Reminiscences of Frances Perkins, part 7, pp. 835-36, 841, 1951–1955, CUOHROC.

28. "Well, Frances, you know . . .": Reminiscences of Frances Perkins, part 7, p. 845, 1951–1955, CUOHROC.

29. Jerry Kluttz and Herbert Asbury, "The Woman Nobody Knows," *Collier's* magazine, Aug. 5, 1944; cartoon by Louis Priscilla.

CHAPTER 30: MADNESS, MISALLIANCES, AND A NUDE BISEXUAL WATER SPRITE

1. Author interviews with Susanna Coggeshall, Stephen Robeson Miller, Salomon Grimberg, and Ellen Russotto.

2. Salomon Grimberg, "Jacqueline Lamba: In Spite of Everything, Spring," catalogue for art exhibit at Stony Brook State University of New York, 2001–2002.

3. Grimberg; Miller.

4. Grimberg.

5. Grimberg.

6. Grimberg; also Grimberg interviews with Susanna Coggeshall.

7. "David M. Hare Divorced," *New York Times,* Mar. 3, 1945, p. 13.

8. Winifred Wandersee interview with Susanna Coggeshall, June 27, 1990, Kheel Center, Martin P. Catherwood Library, Cornell University.

9. "I don't see how . . .": "Frances Perkins, the First Woman in Cabinet, Is Dead," *New York Times,* May 15, 1965, p. 1.

10. Religious notes, Christmas 1944, Frances Perkins private family papers, restricted box 163, family correspondence, FP papers, Coggeshall addition, RBML, Columbia.

11. Cosmopolitan Club envelope, marked "Lent," restricted box 163, family correspondence, FP papers, Coggeshall addition, RBML, Columbia.

12. Perkins private family papers, restricted box 163, family correspondence, FP papers, Coggeshall addition, RBML, Columbia.

13. "Apparently at one time . . .": Reminiscences of Henry A. Wallace, p. 1680, 1953, CUOHROC.

14. "A belief was emerging . . .": George Martin, *Madam Secretary* (Boston: Houghton Mifflin, 1976), p. 170.

15. "It seems that Mrs. Perkins . . .": Reminiscences of Horace M. Albright, pp. 775–76, 1957 and 1960, CUOHROC.

16. Frances Perkins to Charles E. Wyzanski, July 14, 1949, Charles E. Wyzanski papers, Harvard Law School Library, box 2, folder 24.

CHAPTER 31: THE WAR COMES

1. "Miss Perkins, they say on the radio . . .": Reminiscences of Frances Perkins, part 8, p. 54 (following account is condensed from pages 51–62), 1951–1955, CUOHROC.
2. "For God's sake, what has happened?": Reminiscences of Frances Perkins, part 8, p. 65, 1951–1955, CUOHROC.
3. "which is the great naval installation . . .": Reminiscences of Frances Perkins, part 8, p. 65, 1951–1955, CUOHROC.
4. "Things are worse . . .": Reminiscences of Frances Perkins, part 8, p. 66, 1951–1955, CUOHROC.
5. "Find out, for God's sake . . .": Reminiscences of Frances Perkins, part 8, pp. 69–70, 1951–1955, CUOHROC.
6. "Sometimes I've seen it on his face . . .": Reminiscences of Frances Perkins, part 8, p. 84, 1951–1955, CUOHROC.
7. "something was wrong . . .": Reminiscences of Frances Perkins, part 8, p. 86, 1951–1955, CUOHROC.
8. "You know, I think the boss . . .": Reminiscences of Frances Perkins, part 8, p. 88, 1951–1955, CUOHROC.
9. Gordon W. Prange, *At Dawn We Slept: The Untold Story of Pearl Harbor* (New York: McGraw-Hill, 1981), pp. 30–31.
10. Prange, pp. 687–88.
11. "absolute lack of the usually loose-mouthed jollity . . .": Reminiscences of Frances Perkins, part 8, p. 94, 1951–1955, CUOHROC.
12. Conrad Black, *Franklin Delano Roosevelt: Champion of Freedom* (New York: Public Affairs, 2003), pp. 602–03.
13. "political liability . . .": Reminiscences of Bernard Gladieux, pp. 141, 348–50, 1951, CUOHROC.
14. "burglarized . . .": Reminiscences of Frances Perkins, part 8, p. 143, 1951–1955, CUOHROC.
15. "Reorganization of the Labor Department," thesis presented at the University of Minnesota by Francis Edward Rourke, Nov. 1951, pp. 216–21.
16. Sophonisba Breckinridge to FDR and Eleanor Roosevelt, May 9, 1939, FP papers, Coggeshall addition, box 106, RBML, Columbia.
17. Eleanor Roosevelt to Mary Dewson, April 30, 1939, Dewson papers, box 3, folder 2, FDR Library.
18. Rourke thesis, pp. 225–26.
19. "Very little labor statesmanship . . .": Reminiscences of Frances Perkins, part 8, p. 204, 1951–1955, CUOHROC.
20. "The cause of peace would be promoted . . .": See "Green Advises Miss Perkins to Keep Silent," Associated Press, *Washington Star,* June 23, 1939.
21. "tooth and nail . . .": Reminiscences of Frances Perkins, part 7, p. 615, 1951–1955, CUOHROC.
22. "you don't have the prestige . . .": Reminiscences of Frances Perkins, part 7, p. 880, 1951–1955, CUOHROC.
23. "Labor Relations and the War," speech by William M. Leiserson, New York, Feb. 18, 1942, FP papers, RBML, Columbia.
24. "only fair . . .": Reminiscences of Frances Perkins, part 8, p. 107, 1951–1955, CUOHROC.

25. Penny Colman, *A Woman Unafraid: The Achievements of Frances Perkins* (New York: Atheneum, 1993), pp. 100–01.

26. "Women in the Labor Force and Estimated Additions to the Labor Force," Frances Perkins papers, Columbia University.

27. Letter of Transmittal, FP to FDR, Nov. 6, 1935; proposed letter from FDR to FP, Nov. 19, 1940; Department of Labor press release, Feb. 14, 1943 (not clear if circulated), Frances Perkins papers, Schlesinger Library, Radcliffe Institute, Harvard University.

28. "War Shifts in Labor Force," U.S. Department of Labor, Women's Rights Collection, Part II, Schlesinger Library, Radcliffe Institute, Harvard University.

29. "Oh, that is unthinkable . . .": Reminiscences of Frances Perkins, part 8, p. 616, 1951–1955, CUOHROC.

30. "Now while the PM is here . . .": Reminiscences of Frances Perkins, part 8, p. 639, and following account condensed from pp. 639–45, 1951–1955, CUOHROC.

CHAPTER 32: LAST DAYS OF THE ROOSEVELT ADMINISTRATION

1. "Oh, Henry, why are you going there?" Reminiscences of Frances Perkins, part 8, pp. 503–04, 1951–1955, CUOHROC.

2. "Yes, I know that's so . . .": Reminiscences of Frances Perkins, part 8, p. 519, 1951–1955, CUOHROC.

3. "in some sort of slightly irregular way . . .": Reminiscences of Frances Perkins, part 8, p. 539, 1951–1955, CUOHROC.

4. "very crushing blow . . .": Reminiscences of Frances Perkins, part 8, pp. 539–40, 1951–1955, CUOHROC.

5. "Henry can have anything he really wants . . .": Reminiscences of Frances Perkins, part 8, pp. 543–44, 1951–1955, CUOHROC.

6. "Oh, Harry, that's terrible . . .": Reminiscences of Frances Perkins, part 8, p. 551, 1951–1955, CUOHROC.

7. Rose Schneiderman to Mary Dreier, Dec. 19, 1944, Mary Dreier papers, Schlesinger Library, Radcliffe Institute, Harvard University.

8. FP to FDR, Dec. 1, 1944, FDR Library.

9. FDR to FP, Jan. 22, 1945, President's Secretary's Files/Labor, FDR Library.

10. Wyzanski papers; Thomas H. Eliot, *Recollections of the New Deal* (Boston: Northeastern University Press, 1992).

11. "Frances, I can't do it . . .": Author interview with Lois Eliot.

12. "This is the cross . . .": Reminiscences of Frances Perkins, part 8, pp. 279–80, 1951–1955, CUOHROC.

13. "Remember, I'll pray for you . . .": Reminiscences of Frances Perkins, part 8, pp. 279–80, 1951–1955, CUOHROC.

14. "Oh, Miss Perkins, did you get a good look . . .": Reminiscences of Frances Perkins, part 8, pp. 286–87, 1951–1955, CUOHROC.

15. "He has the look of a doomed man . . .": Felix Frankfurter to Charles Culp Burlingham, April 24, 1945, Charles Culp Burlingham papers, Harvard Law School Library, box 5, folder 6.

16. Frankfurter to Burlingham, ibid.

17. "Frances, I'll tell you something . . .": Frances Perkins, *The Roosevelt I Knew* (New York: Viking, 1946), p. 396.

18. "We could do wonders . . .": Reminiscences of Frances Perkins, part 8, p. 762, 1951–1955, CUOHROC.

CHAPTER 33: HARRY TRUMAN

1. "The president is dead . . .": Reminiscences of Frances Perkins, part 7, p. 711, 1951–1955, CUOHROC.
2. "with the help of God . . .": Reminiscences of Frances Perkins, part 8, p. 780, 1951–1955, CUOHROC.
3. "He'll make out all right . . .": Reminiscences of Frances Perkins, part 8, pp. 779–81, 1951–1955, CUOHROC.
4. Conrad Black, *Franklin Delano Roosevelt: Champion of Freedom* (New York: Public Affairs, 2003), pp. 1107–12.
5. "Harry the president is dead . . .": Harry S. Truman, *Memoirs,* vol. 1: *Year of Decisions* (Garden City, NY: Doubleday, 1955), pp. 4–5.
6. "I felt as if I knew him . . .": Reminiscences of Frances Perkins, part 8, p. 790, 1951–1955, CUOHROC.
7. Black, pp. 1110–11.
8. "cold and raw . . .": Reminiscences of Frances Perkins, part 8, p. 800, and following account condensed from pp. 800–07, 1951–1955, CUOHROC.
9. "May God rest his soul . . .": Reminiscences of Henry A. Wallace, p. 3693, 1953, CUOHROC; Christopher Breiseth, *The Frances Perkins I Knew* (Worcester, MA: FDR American Heritage Center Museum, 1966).
10. "You are quite right . . .": FP to Mary Dreier, Mary Dreier papers, Schlesinger Library, Radcliffe Institute, Harvard University.
11. "Thank you for your sympathy . . .": FP to Margaret Bondfield, May 11, 1945, Bondfield papers, box 2.29, Vassar College.
12. "She was able to appear at leisure . . .": FP to Charles Culp Burlingham, May 7, 1945, Charles Culp Burlingham papers, Harvard Law School, box 14, folder 4.
13. "Good luck, Mr. President . . .": Truman, p. 19.
14. "great, strong man . . .": Reminiscences of Frances Perkins, part 8, p. 842, 1951–1955, CUOHROC.
15. Alonzo L. Hamby, *Man of the People: A Life of Harry S. Truman* (New York: Oxford University Press, 1995), citing Truman to Jonathan Daniels, Feb. 26, 1950, unsent, President's Secretary's Files, Harry S. Truman Library, also citing Eben Ayers diary, pp. 306–07.
16. "I would say . . .": Mathew J. Connelly oral history, p. 15, Aug. 21, 1968, Harry S. Truman Library.
17. "As everybody knows . . .": Doris Fleeson, "Miss Perkins Finds Men Have Trouble 'Handling Labor' Too," *Washington Star,* Jan. 18, 1949, Washingtoniana Room, Martin Luther King Library, Washington, D.C.
18. "As the years went by . . .": Truman, p. 96.
19. "Why Miss Perkins . . .": James E. Dodson oral history, pp. 30–31, conducted by U.S. Department of Labor, Labor Department Archives.
20. "word or a criticism . . .": Reminiscences of Frances Perkins, part 8, p. 850, 1951–1955, CUOHROC.
21. "had fathered . . .": Reminiscences of Frances Perkins, part 8, p. 848, 1951–1955, CUOHROC.
22. "There won't be any place . . .": Reminiscences of Isador Lubin, pp. 84–85, 94, 1957, CUOHROC.
23. "In view of the persistence . . .": Felix Frankfurter to FP, FP papers, RBML, Columbia.
24. FP to Felix Frankfurter, June 7, 1945, FP papers, box 4, RBML, Columbia.
25. Perkins recognition dinner menu and program, June 1945, box 707, folder 283, Robert F. Wagner papers, Georgetown University Special Collections.

26. "We talked about the little dog . . .": Reminiscences of Frances Perkins, part 8, p. 858, 1951–1955, CUOHROC.

27. "It was a day of perfect hell . . .": Reminiscences of Frances Perkins, part 8, p. 866, 1951–1955, CUOHROC.

28. "Well, of course . . .": Reminiscences of John Roy Steelman, pp. 122, 356, 1957, 1968, CUOHROC, citing Ickes editorial.

29. "Every time I would read . . .": Reminiscences of Frances Perkins, part 8, p. 869, 1951–1955, CUOHROC.

30. "I mean, that sort of thing . . .": Reminiscences of Frances Perkins, part 8, p. 872, 1951–1955, CUOHROC.

CHAPTER 34: THE TRUMAN ADMINISTRATION

1. "Why, how do I know . . .": Reminiscences of Frances Perkins, part 9, pp. 5–6, 1951–1955, CUOHROC.

2. FP to Winston Churchill, Aug. 2, 1945, Churchill Archives Center, Churchill College, Cambridge, England.

3. Notations in FP's personal copy of *The Roosevelt I Knew,* kept in family home library in Damariscotta, ME.

4. "very, very difficult . . .": Reminiscences of Frances Perkins, part 9, p. 25, 1951–1955, CUOHROC.

5. John T. Flynn, *The Roosevelt Myth* (Garden City, NY: Garden City Publishing, 1948), pp. 223, 405.

6. "That's very good of you . . .": Reminiscences of Frances Perkins, part 8, pp. 571–73, 1951–1955, CUOHROC.

7. "He always did act very promptly . . .": Reminiscences of Frances Perkins, part 8, p. 578, 1951–1955, CUOHROC.

8. "Oh gee, this is a juicy story . . .": Reminiscences of Frances Perkins, part 8, pp. 579–82, 1951–1955, CUOHROC.

9. "I don't know . . .": Reminiscences of Arthur Flemming, pp. 21–22, 1964, CUOHROC.

10. Tom Eliot to FP, April 23, 1947, FP papers, RBML, Columbia.

11. "Miss Perkins Opposes Flemming on Issue of Personal Freedom for U.S. Employees," *Washington Star,* Nov. 17, 1946, Martin Luther King Library, Washington, DC.

12. Author interview with Philip Kaiser, fall 2001.

13. Dorothy Thompson to FP, Feb. 9, 1951, Sinclair Lewis letters, Macalester College.

14. Author interview with Carol Riegelman Lubin.

15. Eleanor Roosevelt to Robert Hannegan, June 3, 1945, Eleanor Roosevelt papers, no. 005240, George Washington University.

16. Eleanor Roosevelt to FP, Oct. 4, 1948, Eleanor Roosevelt papers, no. 007876, George Washington University.

17. "I mean, nobody expected to vote for him." Reminiscences of Frances Perkins, part 9, pp. 171–72, 1951–1955, CUOHROC.

18. Reminiscences of Frances Perkins, part 9, p. 168, 1951–1955, CUOHROC.

CHAPTER 35: COMMUNISM

1. John Earl Haynes and Harvey Klehr, *Venona: Decoding Soviet Espionage in America* (New Haven: Yale University Press, 1999), cited in John Earl Haynes and Harvey Klehr, *In Denial: Historians, Communism & Espionage* (San Francisco: Encounter Books, 2003), p. 6.

2. John Earl Haynes and Harvey Klehr, *Early Cold War Spies: The Espionage Trials That Shaped American Politics* (New York: Cambridge University Press, 2006), p. 24.

3. "Mr. Mitchell, you must go yourself . . .": Reminiscences of Frances Perkins, part 9, pp. 44-45, 1951-1955, CUOHROC.

4. "What radical ideas . . .": Reminiscences of Frances Perkins, part 9, p. 46, and following account condensed from pp. 44-60, 1951-1955, CUOHROC.

5. "He saw at once . . .": Reminiscences of Frances Perkins, part 9, p. 79, 1951-1955, CUOHROC.

6. "I can't think of anybody . . .": Reminiscences of Frances Perkins, part 9, p. 84, 1951-1955, CUOHROC.

7. William K. Klingaman, *Encyclopedia of the McCarthy Era* (New York: Facts on File, 1996), pp. 239-40.

8. Henry L. Shattuck, "The Loyalty Review Board of the U.S. Civil Service Commission, 1947-1953," Proceedings of the Massachusetts Historical Society, Jan.-Dec. 1966, pp. 63-67.

9. Shattuck, pp. 79-80; Klingaman, p. 240.

10. Shattuck, p. 67.

11. Haynes, *Early Cold War Spies,* p. 24.

12. Haynes, *Early Cold War Spies,* pp. 33-37.

13. Klingaman, p. 256.

14. Shattuck, pp. 77-79; Haynes, p. 43.

15. "I came out of college . . .": Reminiscences of Frances Perkins, part 9, pp. 62-65, 1951-1955, CUOHROC.

16. Haynes, pp. 73-79.

17. Sam Tanenhaus, *Whittaker Chambers: A Biography* (New York: Random House, 1997), pp. 159-63.

18. CEW to MW, March 3, 1934, Charles E. Wyzanski papers, MHS; Alger Hiss, *Alger Hiss: Recollections of a Life* (New York: Arcade Publishing, 1988), pp. 202-07.

19. Testimony of Whittaker Chambers Before the House Committee on Un-American Activities, Aug. 7, 1948.

20. James L. Houghteling to Edward A. Cahill, Apr. 15, 1938, RG 174, James P. Mitchell files, box 201, National Archives.

21. FP to Francis B. Sayre, Apr. 22, 1938, RG 174, James P. Mitchell files, box 291, National Archives.

22. "sort of ill . . .": Reminiscences of Frances Perkins, part 4, p. 466, 1951-1955, CUOHROC.

23. "plain Jane . . .": Reminiscences of Frances Perkins, part 9, pp. 107-08, 1951-1955, CUOHROC.

24. Klingaman, pp. 237-38.

25. "Communism is a strange doctrine . . .": Reminiscences of Frances Perkins, part 9, pp. 93-94, 1951-1955, CUOHROC.

26. Klingaman, pp. 361-62.

27. FBI report on Frances Perkins, A. H. Belmont to D. M. Ladd, Apr. 26, 1952.

CHAPTER 36: END OF THE TRUMAN ERA

1. "It's fun to look around . . .": Reminiscences of Frances Perkins, part 7, p. 718, and following account condensed from pp. 714-37, 1951-1955, CUOHROC; Alonzo Hamby, *Man of the People: A Life of Harry S. Truman* (New York: Oxford University Press, 1995), pp. 306-09.

2. "The occasion just dribbled away . . .": Reminiscences of Frances Perkins, part 7, p. 731, 1951-1955, CUOHROC.

CHAPTER 37: MANY TRANSITIONS

1. "Makes it possible . . .": FP to Molly Shanklin, Jan. 15, 1953, FP papers, Coggeshall addition, RBML, Columbia.
2. "Thank you so much . . .": FP to Mrs. Florence Polk Holding (Mrs. Archibold Holding), March 9, 1953, Mount Holyoke College Archives and Special Collections.
3. "Paul Wilson, as you know, died . . .": Arthur Altmeyer to Mary Dewson, Feb. 24, 1953, container 1, Mary Dewson papers, FDR Library.
4. FP to Ethyl Salter, Feb. 25, 1953, FP papers, Coggeshall addition, RBML, Columbia.
5. "Also, I thought it much better . . .": FP to Charles Culp Burlingham, May 8, 1953, Charles Culp Burlingham papers, Harvard Law School Library, box 14, folder 4.
6. "It was sort of a shock . . .": Reminiscences of Frances Perkins, part 9, p. 188, 1951–1955, CUOHROC.
7. FP to Mrs. Stoneborough, Jan. 14, 1956, FP papers, Coggeshall addition, RBML, Columbia.
8. "I want her to look to me . . .": FP notes for confessional, Maurice Neufeld papers, Library of Congress.
9. "In America, one must be prepared . . .": Maurice Neufeld diary, Oct. 8, 1958, Maurice Neufeld papers, Library of Congress.
10. George Martin, *Madam Secretary* (Boston: Houghton Mifflin, 1976), p. 483.
11. Author interview with Maurice Neufeld.
12. Ruth Backes interview with Tomlin Coggeshall, Backes papers, Mount Holyoke Archives.
13. "I am sorry I can't give you a firm address . . .": FP to Mary Dewson, July 28, 1958, FDR Library.
14. Ruth Backes interview with Margaret Van Dyne, transcribed Apr. 18, 1994, Mount Holyoke College Archives.
15. "The ILR School at 50: Voices of the Faculty, Alumni & Friends" (Ithaca, NY: Cornell University, 1996), pp. 51–52.
16. "She was an incredible woman . . .": Author interview with Roslyn Blum.
17. "I was born . . .": Feb. 6, 1960, diary of Maurice Neufeld, Maurice Neufeld papers, Library of Congress; "No, it is not true," June 18, 1966, Neufeld diary.
18. Christopher Breiseth, *The Frances Perkins I Knew* (Worcester, MA: FDR American Heritage Center Museum, 1966); author interviews with Breiseth and Neufeld.
19. Author interview with Paul Wolfowitz.
20. Barbara Brasch Rey interview with Allan Bloom, Feb. 8, 1992, Ruth Backes papers, Mount Holyoke College Archives and Special Collections.
21. Author interview with Abe Shulsky.
22. "You only find out . . .": Author interview with Christopher Breiseth.
23. "wasn't neglected for long . . .": Neufeld diary, June 3, 1958, Library of Congress.
24. Citations from *Gracian's Manual*, maxims number 21, 26, and 32, originally published in Spanish in 1653, revised edition published by Charles C. Thomas, Springfield, IL, 1945; maxims marked in Perkins's personal copy of book.
25. Account of a conversation from June 3, 1958, recounted in diary of Maurice Neufeld, July 19, 1958, Maurice Neufeld papers, Library of Congress.
26. Maurice Neufeld diary, September 1963, Maurice Neufeld papers, Library of Congress.
27. FP to Frances White, July 26, 1964, Kheel Center, Martin P. Catherwood Library, Cornell University.
28. Brasch Rey interview with Bloom.
29. Author interviews with Breiseth and Wolfowitz; Martin, p. 486.
30. Author interview with Dan Lazorchick.

31. Breiseth, pp. 15-16.
32. Author interview with Roslyn Blum.
33. Maurice Neufeld diary, Dec. 26, 1957, Maurice Neufeld papers, Library of Congress.
34. Author interview with Peter Poole.
35. Frances Perkins speech, "The Roots of Social Security," Oct. 23, 1962, Social Security Administration Web site.
36. "Mother continues to slip away . . .": Anna Roosevelt Boettiger to FP, Nov. 7, 1962, FP papers, Coggeshall addition, box 106, RBML, Columbia.
37. John T. Flynn, *The Roosevelt Myth* (Garden City, NY: Garden City Publishing, 1948), p. 423; author interviews with Neufeld and Breiseth.
38. Neufeld diary, Nov. 13, 1964; Nov. 27 notation; Breiseth, pp. 20-21.
39. Daniel Patrick Moynihan to FP, Sept. 17, 1963, Maurice Neufeld papers, Library of Congress.
40. Author interviews with Neufeld and Susanna Coggeshall.
41. Breiseth, pp. 18-19.
42. "Mr. Aaron let me take your arm . . .": Author interview with Benjamin Aaron.
43. Author interview with Neufeld.
44. Author interview with Neufeld.
45. Author interview with Neufeld.
46. Author interviews with Kate Coggeshall Hammatt, John Coggeshall, and David Plowden.
47. Author interviews with Abe Shulsky and Louise Rideout.
48. Maurice Neufeld diary, May 30, 1964, recounting conversation of May 22, 1964, Maurice Neufeld papers, Library of Congress.
49. "What they have done . . .": Reminiscences of Frances Perkins, part 2, pp. 240-48, 1951-1955, CUOHROC.

CHAPTER 38: LAST DAYS

1. Christopher Breiseth, *The Frances Perkins I Knew* (Worcester, MA: FDR American Heritage Center Museum, 1966), pp. 21-22.
2. Lillian Holmen Mohr, *Frances Perkins: "That Woman in FDR's Cabinet!"* (Croton-on-Hudson, NY: North River Press, 1979), p. 295; interview with Maurice Neufeld.
3. "I can still run faster . . .": Maurice Neufeld diary, pp. 6-7, spring 1965, Maurice Neufeld papers, Library of Congress.
4. Author interview with Mother Virginia, All Saints Convent, Catonsville, Maryland.
5. Martin, p. 488; Mohr, p. 295.
6. Author interview with Maurice Neufeld; Neufeld diary, May 1965, Maurice Neufeld papers, Library of Congress.
7. Author interview with Neufeld.
8. Requiem mass, Episcopal Church at Cornell University, May 18, 1965, Christopher Breiseth private papers.
9. Backes interview with Carol Riegelman Lubin.
10. Breiseth, pp. 21-22.
11. Neufeld diary, May 23, 1965, Library of Congress.
12. "I realized . . .": Frances Perkins lecture at Cornell, Sept. 22, 1964, Kheel Center, Martin P. Catherwood Library, Cornell University.
13. FP to Felix Frankfurter, June 7, 1945, FP papers, RBML, Columbia.

BIBLIOGRAPHY

Abramson, Rudy. *Spanning the Century: The Life of W. Averell Harriman.* New York: William Morrow, 1992.

Addams, Jane. *Twenty Years at Hull House.* Boston: St. Martin's, 1999.

Addams, Jane, and Emily G. Balch and Alice Hamilton. *Women at the Hague: The International Conference of Women and Its Results.* New York: Garland Publishing, 1971 (with new introduction by Mercedes M. Randall).

Albino, Donna. *Mount Holyoke College.* Charleston, South Carolina: Arcadia Publishing, 2000.

Alcock, Antony. *History of the ILO.* London: Macmillan, 1971.

Allen, Frederick Lewis. *The Big Change—1900 to 1950.* New York: Harper & Row, 1952.

Allen, Robert S., and William V. Shannon. *The Truman Merry-Go-Round.* New York: Vanguard Press, 1950.

Alsop, Joseph. *FDR.* New York: Gramercy Books, 1982.

Altmeyer, Arthur J. *The Formative Years of Social Security.* Madison: University of Wisconsin Press, 1966.

Amberg, Edna, and William H. Allen. *Civic Lessons from Mitchel's Defeat.* New York: Institute for Public Service, April 1921.

American Institute of Architects. *Guide to Chicago.* San Diego: Harcourt Brace, 1993.

Andrews, Bert. *Washington Witch Hunt.* New York: Random House, 1948.

Appella, Giuseppe, and Ellen Russotto, *David Hare: Opere del 1940 al 1992.* Roma: Edizioni della Cometa, 2005.

Baker, Leonard. *Brandeis and Frankfurter.* New York: New York University Press, 1986.

Baker, Liva. *Felix Frankfurter.* New York: Coward-McCann, 1969.

Balsan, Consuelo Vanderbilt. *The Glitter and the Gold.* Maidstone, Kent: George Mann Books, 1973.

Bartoletti, Susan Campbell. *Kids on Strike.* Boston: Houghton Mifflin, 1999.

Beam, Alex. *Gracefully Insane: The Rise and Fall of America's Premier Mental Hospital.* New York: Public Affairs, 2001.

Beard, Rick, and Leslie Cohen Berlowitz. *Greenwich Village.* New Brunswick, NJ: Rutgers University Press, 1993.

Bellush, Bernard. *He Walked Alone: A Biography of John Gilbert Winant.* The Hague: Mouton & Co., 1968.

Bernays, Edward. *Biography of an Idea: Memoirs of Public Relations Counsel Edward L. Bernays.* New York: Simon & Schuster, 1965.

Bernstein, Irving. *A Caring Society: The New Deal, the Worker and the Great Depression.* Boston: Houghton Mifflin, 1985.

Bernstein, Irving. *The Lean Years.* Boston: Houghton Mifflin, 1960.

Bernstein, Irving. *The Turbulent Years.* Boston: Houghton Mifflin, 1970.

Biddle, Francis. *In Brief Authority.* Garden City, NY: Doubleday, 1962.

Black, Allida M. *Casting Her Own Shadow: Eleanor Roosevelt and the Shaping of Postwar Liberalism.* New York: Columbia University Press, 1996.

Black, Conrad. *Franklin Delano Roosevelt: Champion of Freedom.* New York: Public Affairs, 2003.

Blair, Emily Newell. *Bridging Two Eras.* Columbia: University of Missouri Press, 1999.

Bloom, Vera. *There's No Place Like Washington.* New York: Putnam, 1944.

Blumberg, Dorothy Rose. *Florence Kelley: The Making of a Social Pioneer.* New York: Augustus M. Kelley, 1966.

Blumenthal, Sue. *Clara Mortenson Beyer: A Life of Clear Direction.* Privately printed, 1990.

Bondfield, Margaret. *A Life's Work.* London: Hutchinson & Co., 1948.

Bowman, Raelene Lyons, and Anne Morgan DeAcetis. *The Church of the Holy Spirit: The First 100 Years.* Lake Forest, IL: Church of Holy Spirit, 2002.

Boyer, Richard O., and Herbert M. Morais. *Labor's Untold Story.* New York: United Electrical, Radio & Machine Workers of America, 1955.

Breiseth, Christopher. *The Frances Perkins I Knew.* Worcester, MA: The FDR American Heritage Center Museum (originally written 1966).

Breitman, Richard, Barbara McDonald Stewart, and Severin Hochberg, ed. *Advocate for the Doomed: The Diaries and Papers of James G. McDonald 1932–1935.* Bloomington: Indiana University Press, 2007.

Brinkley, Alan. *The End of Reform.* New York. Vintage Books, 1995.

Brinkley, Alan. *Voices of Protest.* New York: Vintage Books, 1983.

Brody, David. *The Butcher Workmen: A Study of Unionization.* Cambridge: Harvard University Press, 1964.

Bryan, Mary Lynn McKree, and Allen F. Davis. *100 Years at Hull House.* Bloomington: Indiana University Press, 1969.

Burgoyne, Arthur G. The *Homestead Strike of 1892.* Pittsburgh: University of Pittsburgh Press, 1979, reprint of 1893 account.

Burns, James MacGregor. *Roosevelt: The Lion and the Fox.* San Diego: Harcourt Brace Jovanovich, 1956.

Caldwell, George S. *Wit and Wisdom of Harry S. Truman.* New York: Stein and Day, 1973.

Callahan, Carol. *Prairie Avenue Cookbook.* Carbondale: Southern Illinois University Press, 1993.

Campbell, Persia. *Mary Williamson Harriman.* New York: Columbia University Press, 1960.

Caro, Robert. The *Power Broker: Robert Moses and the Fall of New York.* New York: Alfred A. Knopf, 1974.

Chandler, Alfred D., Thomas K. McCraw, and Richard S. Tedlow. *Management, Past and Present: A Casebook on the History of American Business.* Cincinnati: South-Western College Publishing, 2000.

Chen, Constance M. *The Sex Side of Life.* New York: The New Press, 1996.

Chernow, Ron. *Titan: The Life of John D. Rockefeller, Sr.* New York: Random House, 1998.

Childs, Marquis W. *I Write from Washington.* New York: Harper & Row, 1942.

Churchill, Winston. *Triumph and Tragedy.* Boston: Houghton Mifflin, 1953.

Clapper, Olive Ewing. *Washington Tapestry.* New York: McGraw-Hill, 1946.

Cohen, Lizabeth. *Making a New Deal.* Cambridge, England: Cambridge University Press, 1990.

Colman, Penny. *A Woman Unafraid.* New York: Atheneum, 1993.

Colman, Penny. *Strike!* Brookfield, CT: Millbrook Press, 1995.

Cook, Alice. *A Lifetime of Labor.* New York: The Feminist Press at City University of New York, 1998.

Cook, Blanche Wiesen. *Eleanor Roosevelt,* vols. 1 & 2. New York: Penguin Books, 1993 and 2000.

Crunden, Robert M. *Ministers of Reform: The Progressives' Achievement in American Civilization, 1889–1920.* New York: Basic Books, 1982.

Culver, John, and John Hyde. *American Dreamer: Life and Times of Henry Wallace.* New York: Norton, 2000.

Cushman, David Quimby. *The History of Ancient Sheepscot and Newcastle.* Bath, Maine: E. Upton & Sons, Printers, 1882.

Dallek, Robert. *Franklin Delano Roosevelt and American Foreign Policy.* New York: Oxford University Press, 1995.

Dalton, Kathleen. *Theodore Roosevelt: A Strenuous Life.* New York: Vintage Books, 2002.

Davis, Kenneth S. *Invincible Summer: An Intimate Portrait of the Roosevelts, Based on the Recollections of Marion Dickerman.* New York: Atheneum, 1974.

Davis, Kenneth S. *FDR: The New York Years, 1928–1933.* New York: Random House, 1994.

Dewson, Mary. *An Aid to the End.* Unpublished manuscript.

Diamond, Peter. *Charles E. Wyzanski Jr., The New Deal, and the Constitutional Revolution of 1937.* Provided to the author in draft manuscript.

Dodd, William. *Ambassador Dodd's Diary.* New York: Harcourt Brace, 1941.

Dolnick, Edward. *Madness on the Couch.* New York: Simon & Schuster, 1998.

Dreier, Mary. *Margaret Dreier Robins.* New York: Island Press Cooperative, 1950.

Dubinsky, David, with A. H. Raskin. *David Dubinsky: A Life with Labor.* New York: Simon & Schuster, 1977.

Dubois, Ellen Carol. *Harriot Stanton Blatch and the Winning of Women's Suffrage.* New Haven: Yale University Press, 1997.

Dubois, Ellen Carol. "Working Women, Class Relations and Suffrage Militance." *Journal of American History* 74 (1987).

Dunlop, M.H. *Gilded City: Scandal and Sensation in Turn of the Century New York.* New York: HarperCollins, 2000.

Dye, Nancy Schrom. *As Equals and As Sisters: Feminism, the Labor Movement, and the Women's Trade Union League of New York.* Columbia: University of Missouri Press, 1980.

Economic Security, Committee on. *Social Security in America: The Factual Background of the Social Security Act as Summarized from Staff Reports to the Committee on Economic Security.* Washington: Social Security Board, 1937.

Eliot, Thomas H. *Recollections of the New Deal.* Boston: Northeastern University Press, 1992.

Elshtain, Jean Bethke. *Jane Addams and the Dream of American Democracy.* New York: Basic Books, 2002.

Enright, Dominique. *The Wicked Wit of Winston Churchill.* London: Michael O'Mara Books, 2001.

Faber, Doris. *Life of Lorena Hickok.* New York: William Morrow, 1980.

Faderman, Lillian. *To Believe in Women.* Boston: Houghton Mifflin: 1999.

Faderman, Lillian. *Surpassing the Love of Men.* New York: HarperCollins, 1981.

Farley, James. *Jim Farley's Story.* New York: McGraw-Hill, 1948.

Federal Bureau of Investigation, Subject Study: Frances Perkins. Investigation Requested by Donald S. Dawson, Administrative Assistant to President Truman, seeking subversive derogatory information on Perkins, 1952.

Felder, Deborah. *The 100 Most Influential Women of all Time.* Secaucus, NJ: Carol Publishing, 1996.

Ferrell, Robert H. *Off the Record: The Private Papers of Harry S. Truman.* New York: Harper & Row, 1980.

Ferrell, Robert H. *Harry S. Truman: A Life.* Columbia, MO: University of Missouri Press, 1994.

Finan, Christopher M. *Alfred E. Smith: The Happy Warrior.* New York: Farrar, Straus and Giroux, 2002.

Flexnor, Eleanor, and Ellen Fitzpatrick. *Century of Struggle.* Cambridge: Harvard University Press, 1959.

Flynn, Elizabeth Gurley. *The Rebel Girl.* New York: International Publishers, 1955.

Flynn, John T. *The Roosevelt Myth.* Garden City, NY: Garden City Publishing, 1948.

Foner, Nancy. *From Ellis Island to JFK.* New Haven: Yale University Press, 2000.

Fowler, Gene. *Beau James: The Life and Times of Jimmy Walker.* New York: Viking, 1949.

Fox, James. *Five Sisters: The Langhornes of Virginia.* New York: Simon & Schuster, 2000.

Franck, Dan. *Bohemian Paris.* New York: Grove Press, 1998.

Fraser, Steven. *Labor Will Rule.* Ithaca: Cornell University Press, 1991.

Fraser, Steve, and Gary Gerstle. *The Rise and Fall of the New Deal Order.* Princeton: Princeton University Press, 1989.

Furman, Bess. *Washington By-line.* New York: Knopf, 1949.

Galbraith, John Kenneth. *The Great Crash of 1929.* New York: Time, Inc., 1954.

Gall, Gilbert J. *Pursuing Justice: Lee Pressman, the New Deal and the CIO.* Albany: State University of New York Press, 1999.

Gannon, Thomas. *Newport Mansions in the Gilded Age.* Little Compton, RI: Fort Church Publishers, 1996.

Geary, Dick. *European Labor Protest, 1848–1939.* London: Croom Helm Ltd., 1981.

Gerber, Robin. *Leadership the Eleanor Roosevelt Way.* New York: Prentiss Hall, 2002.

Gilman, Charlotte Perkins. *The Charlotte Perkins Gilman Reader.* New York: Pantheon, 1980.

Gluck, Sherna. *From Parlor to Prison: Five Suffragists Talk.* New York: Vintage Books, 1976.

Goldberg, Joseph P., and William T. Moye. *The First 100 Years of the Bureau of Labor Statistics.* Washington, D.C.: BLS, 1985.

Goldmark, Josephine. *Impatient Crusader: Florence Kelley's Life Story.* Urbana: University of Illinois Press, 1953.

Goodwin, Doris Kearns. *No Ordinary Time.* New York: Simon & Schuster, 1994.

Goodwyn, Lawrence. *The Populist Moment.* New York: Oxford University Press, 1978.

Gordon, Linda. *Pitied But Not Entitled.* Cambridge: Harvard University Press, 1994.

Gormley, Ken. *Archibald Cox, Conscience of a Nation.* Reading, MA: Addison-Wesley, 1997.

Gracián, Baltasar. *The Art of Worldly Wisdom ("Gracian's Manual").* Translated by Martin Fischer. Springfield, IL: Charles C. Thomas, 1934, 1939, 1945.

Graham, Katharine, *Katharine Graham's Washington.* New York: Knopf, 2002.

Greenwald, Richard A. *The Triangle Fire, the Protocols of Peace, and Industrial Democracy.* Philadelphia: Temple University Press, 2005.

Gregory, James N. *American Exodus.* New York: Oxford University Press, 1989.

Grimberg, Salomon. *Frida Kahlo: The Little Deer.* Essay and Catalog. Oxford, OH: Miami University, 1997.

Grimberg, Salomon. "Jacqueline Lamba: From Darkness, With Light," *Woman's Art Journal* 22 (Spring/Summer, 2001).

Grimberg, Salomon. "Jacqueline Lamba: In Spite of Everything, Spring." Stony Brook, NY: Pollock-Krasner House, 2001.

Gusfield, Joseph R. *Symbolic Crusade.* Urbana: University of Illinois Press, 1986.

Haller, Mark H. *Eugenics.* New Brunswick, NJ: Rutgers University Press, 1963.

Hamby, Alonzo L. *Man of the People: A Life of Harry S. Truman.* New York: Oxford University Press, 1995.

Hamilton, Alice. *Exploring the Dangerous Trades.* Boston: Little Brown, 1943.

Hamilton, Cicely. *Diana of Dobson's.* Peterborough, Canada: Broadview Press, 2003.

Hamilton, Edith. *The Greek Way.* New York: Norton, 1930.

Hamilton, Mary Agnes. *Margaret Bondfield.* New York: Thomas Seltzer, 1925.

Hapgood, Norman, and Henry Moskowitz. *Up From the City Streets: Alfred E. Smith.* New York: Harcourt, Brace, 1927.

Hareven, Tamara K. *Eleanor Roosevelt, An American Conscience.* Chicago: Quadrangle Books, 1968.

Harris, C. Lowell. *History and Policies of the Home Owners' Loan Corp.* Washington, D.C.: National Bureau of Economic Research, 1951.

Harris, Seth. "Conceptions of Fairness and the Fair Labor Standards Act." *Hofstra Labor & Employment Law Journal* 18 (Fall 2000): 19.

Hawley, Ellis W. *The New Deal and the Problem of Monopoly.* New York: Fordham University Press, 1966.

Hawley, Ellis W., Murry N. Rothbard, Robert F. Himmelberg, and Gerald D. Nash. *Herbert Hoover and the Crisis of American Capitalism.* Rochester, VT: Schenkman Books, 1973.

Haynes, John Earl, and Harvey Klehr. *Early Cold War Spies: The Espionage Trials That Shaped American Politics.* New York: Cambridge University Press, 2006.

Haynes, John Earl, and Harvey Klehr. *In Denial: Historians, Communism & Espionage.* San Francisco: Encounter Books, 2003.

Haynes, John Earl, and Harvey Klehr. *Venona: Decoding Soviet Espionage in America.* New Haven: Yale University Press, 1999.

Hicks, Paul. "Caroline O'Day: The Gentlewoman from New York." Unpublished manuscript.

Hill, Malcolm. *Churchill: His Radical Decade.* London: Othila Press, 1999.

Hiss, Alger. *Recollections of a Life.* Boston: Little, Brown, 1989.

Huthmacher, Robert M. *Senator Robert Wagner and the Rise of Urban Liberalism.* New York: Atheneum, 1968.

Ickes, Harold. *The Secret Diary of Harold Ickes.* New York: Simon & Schuster, 1953.

Ickes, Harold. *The Secret Diary of Harold Ickes.* Full unedited version, on microfiche at Harvard University Library.

Ickes, Harold. *Back to Work: The Story of the PWA.* New York: Macmillan, 1935.

Irwin, Will. *The Making of a Reporter.* New York: Putnam, 1942.

Jenkins, Roy. *Churchill.* London: Macmillan, 2001.

Johnson, Hugh S. *The Blue Eagle from Egg to Earth.* New York: Greenwood Press, 1968.

Josephson, Matthew. *Al Smith: Hero of the Cities, A Political Portrait Drawing on the Papers of Frances Perkins.* Boston: Houghton Mifflin, 1969.

Josephson, Matthew. *Sidney Hillman: Statesman of American Labor.* Garden City, NY: Doubleday, 1952.

Josephson, Matthew. *The Robber Barons.* New York: Harcourt Brace & World, 1934.

Kamp, Barton. *Worcester,* vols. I and II. Charleston, SC: Arcadia Publishing, 1998.

Kehoe, Elisabeth. *The Titled Americans.* New York: Atlantic Monthly Press, 2004.

Kelley, Robin D.G. *Hammer and Hoe.* Chapel Hill: University of North Carolina Press, 1990.

Kenneally, James J. *Women and the American Trade Unions.* St. Albans, VT: Eden Press Women's Publications, 1978.

Kershaw, Ian. *Hitler, 1889–1936: Hubris.* New York, Norton, 2000.

Klein, Maury. *Rainbow's End: The Crash of 1929.* New York: Oxford University Press, 2001.

Klingaman, William K. *Encyclopedia of the McCarthy Era.* New York: Facts on File, 1996.

Kurth, Peter. *American Cassandra: The Life of Dorothy Thompson.* Boston: Little, Brown, 1990.

Labor, Department of. *Annual Reports,* 1933 to 1945. Washington, D.C.: Government Printing Office.

Larrowe, Charles P. *Harry Bridges: The Rise and Fall of Radical Labor in the United States.* New York: Lawrence Hill & Co., 1972.

Lash, Joseph P. *Eleanor and Franklin.* New York: Norton, 1971.

Leach, William. *Land of Desire.* New York: Pantheon Books, 1993.

Leavitt, Judith Walzer. *Brought to Bed: Childbearing in America, 1750 to 1950.* New York: Oxford University Press, 1988.

Leavitt, Judith Walzer. *Typhoid Mary.* Boston: Beacon Press, 1996.

Lederman, Judith, and Candida Fink. *The Ups and Downs of Raising a Bipolar Child.* New York: Simon & Schuster, 2003.

Leuchtenburg, William E. *Franklin D. Roosevelt and the New Deal.* New York: Harper & Row, 1963.

Lewinson, Edwin R. *John Purroy Mitchel: Boy Mayor of New York.* New York: Astra Books, 1965.

Lewis, Sinclair. *Ann Vickers.* New York: Dell, 1932.

Litwack, Leon. *The American Labor Movement.* Englewood Cliffs, NJ: Prentice-Hall, 1962.

Lombard, Helen. *Washington Waltz.* New York: Knopf, 1941.

Lowi, Theodore. *At the Pleasure of the Mayor.* New York: Free Press of Glencoe, 1964.

Lubin, Carol Riegelman. *Social Justice for Women.* Durham: Duke University Press, 1990.

Lucas, J. Anthony. *Big Trouble.* New York: Simon & Schuster, 1997.

MacLaury, Judson, *To Advance Their Opportunities: Federal Policies Toward African American Workers From World War II to the Civil Rights Act of 1964.* Knoxville, TN.: Newfound Press, 2008.

Marcuse, Maxwell. *This Was New York!* New York: LIM Press, 1969.

Martin, George. *Madam Secretary.* Boston: Houghton Mifflin, 1976.

Martin, Ralph. *Jennie: The Life of Lady Randolph Churchill,* vols. 1 and 2. Englewood Cliffs, NJ: Prentice-Hall, 1969, 1971.

Marx, Karl, and Friedrich Engels. *The Communist Manifesto and Other Writings.* First published in 1848, reprinted by Barnes & Noble Classics, 2005.

Mason, Tim. *Social Policy in the Third Reich.* Providence: Burg Publishers, 1993.

Maternity Center. *The Maternity Center Association Report, 1918–1921.* New York.

McCraw, Thomas K. *American Business, 1920–2000: How It Worked.* Wheeling, IL: Harlan Davidson Inc., 2000.

McCullough, David. *John Adams.* New York: Simon & Schuster, 2001.

McCullough, David. *Truman.* New York: Simon & Schuster, 1992.

McFarland, Gerald W. *Inside Greenwich Village.* Amherst: University of Massachusetts Press, 2001.

McJimsey, George. *Harry Hopkins.* Cambridge: Harvard University Press, 1987.

McKersie, Robert B., J. Gormley Miller, Robert L. Aronson, and Robert R. Julian. *The ILR School at Fifty.* Ithaca, NY: School of Industrial and Labor Relations, Cornell University, 1996.

McPherson, Stephanie Sammartino. *Peace and Bread: The Story of Jane Addams.* Minneapolis: Carolrhoda Books, 1993.

Meachem, Jon. *Franklin and Winston: An Intimate Portrait of an Epic Friendship.* New York: Random House, 2003.

Meyer, Agnes. *Out of These Roots.* Boston: Little, Brown, 1953.

Miller, Merle. *Plain Speaking: An Oral Biography of Harry S. Truman.* New York: Putnam, 1974.

Miller, Stephen Robeson, "Comprehensive Biography of Kay Sage and Illustrated Catalogue Raisonne of Her Surrealist Work," Archives of American Art, Smithsonian Institution, Washington, D.C., 1983 (microfilm reel numbers 2886–2888).

Minton, Bruce, and John Stuart. *Men Who Lead Labor.* New York: Modern Age Books, 1937.

Mohr, Lillian Holmen. *Frances Perkins: "That Woman in FDR's Cabinet!"* Croton-on-Hudson, NY: North River Press, 1979.

Morgenthau, Henry. *Morgenthau Diaries, Years of Crisis,* edited by John Morton Blum. Boston: Houghton Mifflin, 1959.

Morris, Edmund. *Theodore Rex.* New York: The Modern Library, 2001.

Moscow, Warren. *What Have You Done for Me Lately? The Ins and Outs of New York City Politics.* Englewood Cliffs, NJ: Prentice-Hall, 1967.

Murphy, Bruce Allen. *The Brandeis/Frankfurter Connection.* New York: Oxford University Press, 1982.

Mushabac, Jane, and Angela Wigan. *A Short and Remarkable History of New York.* New York: Fordham University Press, 1999.

Nash, Gerald, Noel Pugach, and Richard F. Tomasson. *Social Security: The First Half Century.* Albuquerque: University of New Mexico Press, 1988.

Nevins, Allan. *Herbert H. Lehman and His Era.* New York: Scribner's, 1963.

Newcastle-Damariscotta Women's Club. *High Points in the History of the Newcastle-Damariscotta Area.* Women's Club, 1976.

New York State. *Preliminary Report of the Factory Investigating Commission.* New York: The Argus Co., 1912.

New York State. *Second Report of the Factory Investigating Commission,* vols. 1 and 2. New York: The Argus Co., 1913.

New York State. *Third Report of the Factory Investigating Commission.* New York: The Argus Co., 1914.

New York State. *Fourth Report of the Factory Investigating Commission.* New York: The Argus Co., 1915.

Norton, Mary. *Madame Congresswoman.* Unpublished manuscript.

Parker, Richard. *John Kenneth Galbraith.* New York: Farrar, Straus & Giroux, 2005.

Parrish, Michael E. *Felix Frankfurter and His Times.* New York: Free Press, 1982.

Patterson, Jerry E. *The First 400: Mrs. Astor's New York in the Gilded Age.* New York: Rizzoli, 2000.

Payne, Elizabeth Anne. *Reform, Labor, and Feminism: Margaret Dreier Robins and the Women's Trade Union League.* Urbana: University of Illinois Press, 1988.

Pearson, Drew. *Drew Pearson's Diaries.* New York: Holt, Rinehart & Winston, 1974.

Perkins, Frances. *The Roosevelt I Knew.* New York: Viking Press, 1946.

Perkins, Frances. *People at Work.* New York: John Day Co., 1934.

Perry, Elisabeth Israels. *Belle Moskowitz: Feminine Politics and the Exercise of Power in the Age of Alfred E. Smith.* New York: Oxford University Press, 1987.

Persico, Joseph H. *Edward R. Murrow.* New York: McGraw-Hill, 1989.

Phelan, Edward. "The International Labor Organization: Its Ideals and Results." *Studies, An Irish Quarterly Review* (Dec. 1925): 611–22.

Phelan, Edward. "Some Reminiscences of the ILO." *Studies, An Irish Quarterly Review* (Aug. 1954): 241–69.

Phelan, Edward. "The ILO Sets Up Its Wartime Centre in Canada." *Studies, An Irish Quarterly Review* (Summer 1955): 151–70.

Phelan, Edward. "The ILO Turns the Corner." *Studies, An Irish Quarterly Review* (Summer 1956): 160–86.

Phelan, Edward. "After Pearl Harbor: ILO Problems." *Studies, An Irish Quarterly Review* (Summer 1957): 193–206.

Phillips, Kevin. *Wealth and Democracy.* New York: Random House, 2002.

Prange, Gordon W. *At Dawn We Slept: The Untold Story of Pearl Harbor.* New York: McGraw-Hill, 1981.

Radford, Gail. *Modern Housing for America: Policy Struggles in the New Deal Era.* Chicago: University of Chicago Press, 1996.

Reilly, Philip R. *The Surgical Solution.* Baltimore: Johns Hopkins University Press, 1991.

Riis, Jacob A. *How the Other Half Lives.* New York: Dover Publications, 1971 (reprint of 1890 and 1901 editions).

Riordan, William. *Plunkett of Tammany Hall.* New York: E. P. Dutton, 1963.

Roosevelt, Eleanor. *This I Remember.* New York: Harper & Brothers, 1949.

Roosevelt, Eleanor. *This Is My Story.* New York: Harper & Brothers, 1937.

Roosevelt, Elliott, and James Brough. *The Roosevelts of Hyde Park: An Untold Story.* New York: Putnam, 1973.

Rourke, Edward. *Reorganization of the Labor Department.* Thesis, University of Minnesota, 1951.

Sanders, Ronald. *The Lower East Side*. New York: Dover Publications, 1979, 1994.

Sante, Luc. *Low Life*. New York: Vintage Departures, 1991.

Schiff, Karenna Gore. *Lighting the Way: Nine Women Who Changed Modern America*. New York: Miramax Books, 2005.

Schlesinger, Arthur M. Jr. *The Politics of Upheaval*. Boston: Houghton Mifflin, 1960.

Schlesinger, Arthur M. Jr. *The Coming of the New Deal*. Boston: Houghton Mifflin, 1959.

Schlesinger, Arthur M. Jr. *The Crisis of the Old World Order*. Boston: Houghton Mifflin, 1957.

Schneiderman, Rose. *All for One*. New York: Paul S. Eriksson, 1967.

Schneirov, Richard, and Thomas J. Suhrbur. *Union Brotherhood, Union Town*. Carbondale, IL: Southern Illinois University Press, 1988.

Schorer, Mark. *Sinclair Lewis: An American Life*. New York: McGraw-Hill, 1961.

Selvin, David F. *A Terrible Anger: The 1934 Waterfront and General Strikes in San Francisco*. Detroit: Wayne State University Press, 1996.

Severn, Bill. *Frances Perkins: A Member of the Cabinet*. New York: Hawthorn Books, 1976.

Shannon, David A. *The Great Depression*. Englewood Cliffs, NJ: Prentice-Hall, 1960.

Shaw, Frederick. *The History of the New York City Legislature*. New York: Columbia University Press, 1954.

Shearon, Marjorie. "Economic Security in Old Age: Social and Economic Factors Contributing to Old-Age Dependency." Social Security Board Bureau of Research and Statistics. Washington, D.C.: U.S. Government Printing Office, 1937.

Sheean, Vincent. *Dorothy and Red*. Boston: Houghton Mifflin, 1963.

Shorter, Edward. *A History of Psychiatry: From the Era of the Asylum to the Age of Prozac*. New York: John Wiley, 1997.

Skocpol, Theda. "Political Response to Capitalist Crisis: Neo-Marxist Theories of the State and the Case of the New Deal," based on a paper delivered to American Sociological Association, Boston, 1979.

Sloan, Alfred P. *My Years with General Motors*. Garden City, NY: Doubleday, 1963.

Smiley, Gene. *Rethinking the Great Depression*. Chicago: Ivan R. Dee, 2002.

Smith, Alfred E. *Up to Now: An Autobiography*. New York: Viking, 1929.

Stansell, Christine. *American Moderns*. New York: Henry Holt & Co., 2000.

Stein, Leon. *The Triangle Fire*. Ithaca: Cornell University Press, 2001.

Steinbeck, James. *The Grapes of Wrath*. New York: Penguin Books, 1976.

Storrs, Landon R. Y. *Civilizing Capitalism*. Chapel Hill: University of North Carolina Press, 2000.

Stuart, Sarah Payne. *My First Cousin Once Removed: Money, Madness, and the Family of Robert Lowell*. New York: HarperCollins, 1998.

Taft, Philip. *Organized Labor in American History*. New York: Harper & Row, 1964.

Tanenhaus, Sam. *Whittaker Chambers: A Biography*. New York: Modern Library, 1998.

Tarnow, Fritz. "Labor and Trade Unionism in Germany." *Annals of the American Academy of Political and Social Science* 260 (1948): 90–98.

Tentler, Leslie Woodcock. *Wage-Earning Women: Industrial Work and Family Life in the United States, 1900–1930*. New York: Oxford University Press, 1979.

Terkel, Studs. *Hard Times*. New York: The New Press, 1970, 1986.

Thomas, Lately. *The Mayor Who Mastered New York: The Life and Opinions of William J. Gaynor*. New York: William Morrow, 1969.

Truman, Harry S. *Memoirs*, vols. 1 and 2. Garden City, NY: Doubleday, 1955 and 1956.

Truman, Harry S. *Where the Buck Stops*. New York: Warner Books, 1989.

Truman, Harry S. *Letters Home by Harry Truman*, edited by Monte M. Poen. New York: Putnam, 1984.

Truman, Harry S. *Strictly Personal and Confidential: The Letters Harry Truman Never Mailed*, edited by Monte M. Poen. Boston: Little, Brown, 1982.

Truman, Margaret. *Harry S. Truman*. New York: William Morrow, 1973.

Unofficial Observer. *The New Dealers.* New York: Simon & Schuster, 1934.

Van Meter, William G. *A History of the Chamber of Commerce of the United States.* Unpublished manuscript, 1989.

Von Drehle, David. *Triangle: The Fire That Changed America.* New York: Atlantic Monthly Press, 2003.

Wandersee, Winifred D. *Be Ye Stedfast: Frances Perkins to Mid-Life.* Unpublished manuscript, estate of Winifred D. Wandersee, 1994.

Ware, Susan. *Beyond Suffrage: Women of the New Deal.* Cambridge: Harvard University Press. 1981.

Ware, Susan. *Partner and I: Molly Dewson, Feminism, and New Deal Politics.* New Haven: Yale University Press, 1989.

Warner, Emily Smith. *The Happy Warrior.* Garden City, NY: Doubleday, 1956.

Watkins, T. H. *Righteous Pilgrim: The Life and Times of Harold L. Ickes, 1874–1952.* New York: Henry Holt, 1990.

Watson, Edward B. *New York Then and Now.* New York: Dover, 1976.

Wells, Anna Mary. *Miss Marks and Miss Woolley.* Boston: Houghton Mifflin, 1978.

White, E. B. *This Is New York.* New York: New York Bound, 1949.

White, Graham, J. *Harold Ickes of the New Deal.* Cambridge: Harvard University Press, 1985.

Whitehill, Walter Muir, and Lawrence W. Kennedy. *Boston: A Topographical History.* Cambridge: Harvard University Press, 2000.

Who's Who in New York, 1924 and 1929 editions.

Williams, Selma. *Red-Listed: Haunted by the Washington Witch Hunt.* Reading, MA: Addison-Wesley, 1993.

Wilson, Charles (later Baron Moran). *Churchill, Taken from the Diaries of Lord Moran.* Boston: Houghton Mifflin, 1966.

Witte, Edwin. *The Development of the Social Security Act.* Madison: University of Wisconsin Press, 1962.

Woloch, Nancy. *Women and the American Experience.* New York: Knopf, 1984.

Zimmerman, Julian H. *The FHA Story in Summary.* Washington, D.C.: Federal Housing Administration, 1959.

Zucker, Bat-Ami. "Frances Perkins and the German-Jewish Refugees, 1933–1940." *American Jewish History* 89 (2001): 35–59.

ARCHIVES AND HISTORICAL SOURCES

Boston Globe archives

Boston Public Library

Bowdoin College

British National Archives, London, United Kingdom

Bryn Mawr College archives and alumni records

Martin P. Catherwood Library, Kheel Center Archives, School of Industrial and Labor Relations, Cornell University

Chicago Historical Society

Churchill Archives Centre, Cambridge College, United Kingdom

Columbia University Oral History Research Office Collection

Columbia University Rare Books and Manuscript Library

Connecticut College

Franklin Delano Roosevelt Presidential Library, Hyde Park, New York

George Washington University

Georgetown University Special Collections

Hagley Museum and Library

Harry S. Truman Presidential Library and Museum, Independence, Missouri

Harvard University Law School Library
Harvard University Business School, Baker Library, Bloomberg Center
Herbert Hoover Presidential Library and Museum, West Branch, Iowa
Illinois Institute of Technology archives
Lake Forest College archives
Library of Congress
Macalester College
Martin Luther King Library, Washingtoniana room
Massachusetts Historical Society
Maternity Center Association archives
Mount Holyoke College Archives and Special Collections
National Archives, Washington, D.C.
National Fire Protection Archives
New York Public Library
New York State Archives, Albany, New York
New York Times historical archives
New York University, Tamiment Library and Robert F. Wagner Labor Archives
Schlesinger Library, Radcliffe Institute, Harvard University
Skidompha Library, Damariscotta, Maine
Slater Mill, Pawtucket, Rhode Island
Syracuse University
U.S. Department of Labor library and archives
University of Chicago library
University of Pennsylvania archives, Wharton school records and history
Vassar College Archives and Special Collections
Washington Post historical archives, newspaper morgue
Worcester public library
Yale University, Beineke Library

ORAL HISTORIES

Abrams, Charles
Albright, Horace
Alexander, Will W.
Altmeyer, Arthur
Appleby, Paul
Armstrong, Barbara
Arnold, Elizabeth Cohen
Baldwin, Roger
Barghusen, Meta
Barkin, Solomon
Bell, Daniel
Bernays, Edward
Bernhard, Lois
Bernstein, Bernice
Binkerd, Robert S.
Bowles, Chester
Brophy, John
Brown, J. Douglas
Bruere, Henry
Bryant, Patricia

Burns, Eveline M.
Cahill, Holger
Calvert, Gregory
Carey, James B.
Carmody, John
Chapman, Oscar L.
Ching, Cyrus
Clague, Ewan
Cohen, Wilbur
Connelly, Matthew J.
Corbin, Hazel
Corry, Maureen
Curran, Joseph
Davis, Chester
Davis, William H.
Dawson, Donald
Dickerman, Marion
Dodson, James
Dorr, Goldwaite Higginson
Dowling, Eddie

Edelman, John
Emerson, Thomas I.
Engle, Lavinia
Falk, Isidore
Flemming, Arthur
Flynn, Edward
Folsom, Marion
Frankfurter, Estelle
Frankfurter, Felix
Frey, John P.
Garrison, Lloyd K.
Gladieux, Bernard L.
Glaser, Herbert R.
Goldstein, Jonah
Haber, William
Hamilton, Carl
Harriman, Daisy
Harrington, Fred
Hart, Kitty Carlisle
Herzog, Paul M.
Hohaus, Richard
Howard, Ernest
Jackson, Robert H.
Keiler, Frank M.
Kelley, Nicholas
Kennedy, Elsie P.
Kerr, Florence
Keyserling, Leon
Landis, James
Lane, Chester
Lasker, Mary
Lathrop, John H.
Lenroot, Katharine
Leuchtenberg, William
Levy, Philip
Lorwin, Lewis
Lubin, Isador
Madden, J. Warren
Merriam, Ida
Meyer, Eugene
Miller, Morton D.
Moley, Raymond

Mulliner, Maurine
O'Brien, James Cuff
Perkins, Frances
Peterson, Esther
Pick, Walter R.
Poletti, Charles
Polier, Justine Wise
Reilly, Gerard D.
Richards, Bernard
Rosenman, Samuel
Rosenthal, Morris
Saposs, David J.
Shiskin, Boris Basil
Smith, Blackwell
Smith, Edwin S.
Smith, Howard
Spivack, Edith
Steelman, John
Stone, M. Hedley
Strauss, Anna Lord
Thorne, Florence
Tolley, Howard E.
Van Arkel, Gerhard
Van Schaick, George
Van Waters, Miriam
Vorse, Mary Heaton
Wagner, Robert
Wallace, Henry A.
Wallstein, Leonard
Warner, Emily Smith
Weinstock, Anna
Wheeler, Burton
Wickard, Claude
Wickenden, Elizabeth
Wickens, Aryness Joy
Wilson, Milburn Lincoln
Witt, Nathan
Wolf, Benedict
Wolman, Leo
Wyzanski, Charles
Zerbe, Jerome

AUTHOR INTERVIEWS

Aaron, Benjamin
Backes, Ruth
Barnes, Katrina
Beam, Alex
Bernard, Elaine
Black, Allida

Blum, Roslyn
Breiseth, Christopher
Bryant, Patricia
Caro, Robert
Carpenter, Liz
Carnahan, Alison Bruere

Coggeshall, John
Coggeshall, Kate
Coggeshall, Susanna
Coggeshall, Tomlin
Cook, Blanche Wiesen
Corry, Maureen
Cox, Archibald
Dallas, Harry
Dalton, Kathleen
Dawson, Donald
Didisheim, Paul
Dubovsky, Melvin
Dunlop, John
Eliot, Lois
Elsey, George M.
Galbraith, John Kenneth
Grant, Casey
Grimberg, Salomon
Gunther, Jane
Harrington, Fred
Hart, Kitty Carlisle
Haynes, John Earl
Heckler, Ken
Hochberg, Severin
Kaiser, Phillip
Lazorchick, Daniel
Lehman, Stuart
Lopez, Nancy
Lubin, Carol Riegelman

MacLaury, Judson
Martin, George
Montgomery, David
Mortimer, David
Mortimer, Kathleen
Mother Virginia
Neufeld, Maurice
O'Day, Daniel
O'Rear, Les
Parry, Sally E.
Plowden, David
Poole, Peter
Reich, Robert
Rideout, Louise
Robboy, Anita
Robeson-Miller, Stephen
Rumsey, Mary
Russatto, Ellen
Schlesinger, Arthur M. Jr.
Shulsky, Abe
Stark, Arthur
Stuart, Sarah Payne
Valliere, Annie
Ware, Susan
Weiss, Murray
Wentzel, Volkmar Kurt
Wolfowitz, Paul
Wyzanski, Charles M.

INDEX

Meet with Interesting People
Enjoy Stimulating Conversation
Discover Wonderful Books

VINTAGE BOOKS / ANCHOR BOOKS ⊕
Reading Group Center
THE READING GROUP SOURCE FOR BOOK LOVERS

Visit ReadingGroupCenter.com where you'll find great reading choices—award winners, bestsellers, beloved classics, and many more—and extensive resources for reading groups such as:

Author Chats
Exciting contests offer reading groups the chance to win one-on-one phone conversations with Vintage and Anchor Books authors.

Behind the Book Features
Specially designed pages which can include photographs, videos, original essays, notes from the author and editor, and book-related information.

Extensive Discussion Guides
Guides for over 450 titles as well as non–title specific discussion questions by category for fiction, nonfiction, memoir, poetry, and mystery.

Reading Planner
Plan ahead by browsing upcoming titles, finding author event schedules, and more.

Personal Advice and Ideas
Reading groups nationwide share ideas, suggestions, helpful tips, and anecdotal information. Participate in the discussion and share your group's experiences.

Special for Spanish-language reading groups
www.grupodelectura.com
A dedicated Spanish-language content area complete with recommended titles from Vintage Español.

A selection of some favorite reading group titles from our list

Atonement by Ian McEwan
Balzac and the Little Chinese Seamstress by Dai Sijie
The Blind Assassin by Margaret Atwood
The Devil in the White City by Erik Larson
Empire Falls by Richard Russo
The English Patient by Michael Ondaatje
A Heartbreaking Work of Staggering Genius by Dave Eggers
The House of Sand and Fog by Andre Dubus III
A Lesson Before Dying by Ernest J. Gaines

Lolita by Vladimir Nabokov
Memoirs of a Geisha by Arthur Golden
Midnight in the Garden of Good and Evil by John Berendt
Midwives by Chris Bohjalian
Push by Sapphire
The Reader by Bernhard Schlink
Snow by Orhan Pamuk
An Unquiet Mind by Kay Redfield Jamison
Waiting by Ha Jin
A Year in Provence by Peter Mayle